CHURCH AND STATE IN YUGOSLAVIA
SINCE 1945

SOVIET AND EAST EUROPEAN STUDIES

Books in the series

A. Boltho *Foreign Trade Criteria in Socialist Economies*
Sheila Fitzpatrick *The Commissariat of Enlightenment*
Donald Male *Russian Peasant Organisation before Collectivisation*
P. Wiles, ed. *The Prediction of Communist Economic Performance*
Vladimir V. Kusin *The Intellectual Origins of the Prague Spring*
Galia Golan *The Czechoslovak Reform Movement*
Naum Jasny *Soviet Economists of the Twenties*
Asha L. Datar *India's Economic Relations with the USSR and Eastern Europe, 1953–1969*
T. M. Podolski *Socialist Banking and Monetary Control*
Rudolf Bićanić *Economic Policy in Socialist Yugoslavia*
S. Galai *Liberation in Russia*
Richard B. Day *Leon Trotsky and the Politics of Economic Isolation*
G. Hosking *The Russian Constitutional Experiment: Government and Duma 1907–14*
A. Teichova *An Economic Background to Munich*
J. Ciechanowski *The Warsaw Rising of 1944*
Edward A. Hewett *Foreign Trade Prices in the Council for Mutual Economic Assistance*
Daniel F. Calhoun *The United Front: the TUC and the Russians 1923–28*
Galia Golan *Yom Kippur and After: the Soviet Union and the Middle East Crisis*
Maureen Perrie *The Agrarian Policy of the Russian Socialist-Revolutionary Party from its Origins through the Revolution of 1905–1907*
Gabriel Gorodetsky *The Precarious Truce: Anglo-Soviet Relations 1924–27*
Paul Vyšný *Neo-Slavism and the Czechs 1898–1914*
James Riordan *Sport in Soviet Society: Development of Sport and Physical Education in Russia and the USSR*
Gregory Walker *Soviet Book Publishing Policy*
Felicity Ann O'Dell *Socialisation through Children's Literature: the Soviet Example*
Stella Alexander *Church and State in Yugoslavia since 1945*
Sheila Fitzpatrick *Education and Social Mobility in the Soviet Union 1921–1934*
T. H. Rigby *Lenin's Government: Sovnarkom 1917–1922*

Church and State in Yugoslavia since 1945

STELLA ALEXANDER

CAMBRIDGE UNIVERSITY PRESS

CAMBRIDGE

LONDON · NEW YORK · MELBOURNE

Published by the Syndics of the Cambridge University Press
The Pitt Building, Trumpington Street, Cambridge CB2 1RP
Bentley House, 200 Euston Road, London NW1 2DB
32 East 57th Street, New York, NY 10022, USA
296 Beaconsfield Parade, Middle Park, Melbourne 3206, Australia

© Cambridge University Press 1979

First published 1979

Printed in Great Britain at the
University Press, Cambridge

Library of Congress Cataloguing in Publication Data
Alexander, Stella.
Church and state in Yugoslavia since 1945.
(Soviet and East European studies)
Bibliography: p.
Includes index.
1. Church and state in Yugoslavia. 2. Yugoslavia –
Church history. 3. Communism and Christianity –
Yugoslavia. I. Title. II. Series.
BR966.3.A4   261.7'09497   77-88668
ISBN 0 521 21942 6

This book is dedicated to my
Yugoslav friends, Catholic, Orthodox and Marxist,
with friendship, admiration and gratitude

...[the historian] gains his knowledge through evidence which, at the very best, is incomplete; which is always contradictory; which raises as many questions as it solves; which breaks off tormentingly just where he needs it most, or, yet more tormentingly, becomes ambiguous and dark. He can never establish the truth; he can only grope towards it... The greatest scholar can never reach more than some kind of partial and personal version of truth as it once was. All the efforts of historical scholarship are ultimately reduced to a mere matter of human opinion. In the preface to his *Civilization of the Renaissance in Italy* Jacob Burckhardt has somewhat discouragingly said: 'In the wide ocean upon which we venture, the possible ways and directions are many and the same studies which have served for this work might easily in other hands not only receive a wholly different treatment but lead also to essentially different conclusions'... but... in Burckhardt's mind this defeatist view was closely linked with another implicit assumption: that neither the uncertainty nor the personal nature of his own judgments exonerates the historian from applying the utmost of his critical faculties and scholarly abilities to establishing the truth, or the fact, according to his own lights. To do anything else is intellectual treason.

C. V. Wedgwood, *Historical Essays* (1960), p. 101.

Contents

List of maps ix
Preface xi
Sources xv
Pronunciation xviii
Terminology xviii
Abbreviations and glossary xx

Prologue   1

1 Wartime: the fateful events   7

The background – Serbia – Croatia – Slovenia – The
Partisans

The Catholic Church

2 The immediate postwar years   53

Croatia – Trieste – Slovenia and Istria

3 The trial of Archbishop Stepinac   95

4 The struggle between the church and the state,
1946–1953   121

The struggle defined – Priests' associations I – Persecution
of the bishops and clergy – Daily difficulties facing the
church – Priests' associations II: rupture with the Vatican
– Abortive negotiations between the bishops and the
government – Stepinac's last days and death

The Serbian Orthodox Church

5 Liberation and its sequel   151

Liberation – Rebuilding the church – Confrontation with
the state: religious instruction and marriage – The
patriarchate – The new constitution of the church –
Harassment of the clergy and Bishop Varnava's trial

6   The struggle to hold the church together   178

The Macedonian dioceses I – Priests' associations I – The
patriarchate – Social insurance – The Law on the Legal
Status of Religious Communities – Priests' associations II
– The Macedonian dioceses II

The legislative framework

7   The constitution and the laws   209

The constitutional position – The Law on Agrarian
Reform – The Laws on Nationalisation and Expropriation –
The Criminal Code – The Basic Law on the Legal Status
of Religious Communities

The Catholic Church

8   The change: why and how it took place   226

Causes of the change – How the change took place –
Renewal of church and state contacts with the Vatican –
Attacks and blandishments – The preliminaries to
negotiations – The Second Vatican Council – The
protocol

The Serbian and Macedonian Orthodox Churches

9   Schisms and accommodations   249

The patriarchate I, 1950–4 – The trial of Metropolitan
Arsenije – The priests' associations – The patriarchate II,
1955–7 – The Macedonian dioceses, 1958 – The patriarchate
III, 1958–9 – The autonomous Macedonian Church, 1959 –
The patriarchate IV, 1960–4 – The Pan-Orthodox
Conference and the Second Vatican Council, 1961–5 –
The life of the church – The schism in North America,
1962–3 – The Macedonian Orthodox Church, 1962–8

Epilogue   289

Appendixes

I   U.S. dollar–dinar exchange rates   295

II Statistical tables   297

    1   Size of religious communities   297
    2   Comparative statistics in 1959   298
    3   Comparative statistics in 1973   299
    4   Changes between 1944 and 1973 in four Catholic
        dioceses   300
    5   Distribution of priests within Serbian Orthodox dioceses 302

6   Land expropriated under the Law on Agrarian Reform   303
7   Breakdown of land expropriations in Croatia   304

III   The British and Foreign Bible Society in Yugoslavia   305

IV   The religious press   308

V   Protocol of discussions between the representatives
    of the SFRY and the representatives of the Holy See   313

    Bibliography   316

    Index   323

Maps

1   Religious distribution of the population   xxii
2   Boundaries of Yugoslavia after the Axis attack in 1941   8
3   Catholic dioceses and sees, 1974   54
4   Serbian and Macedonian Orthodox dioceses and sees,
    c. 1970   152

Preface

When it was suggested to me in 1969 that it might be worth making a study of church–state relations in Yugoslavia since the war, a subject which had only been touched on in larger studies of Yugoslavia as a whole and in a handful of articles, the extent of the field to be covered was not at first clear. There were very few secondary sources, and almost no guidelines. It was not until I arrived in Yugoslavia, which I already knew well, that I discovered what an enormous task I had undertaken.

After spending the winter of 1969 reading all the background material which was available in the Bodleian Library, at St Antony's College, Oxford, and the British Museum, and going through the large and well-indexed collection of cuttings in the Press Library at the Royal Institute of International Affairs at Chatham House, I went to Yugoslavia, where I spent six months in the spring and autumn of 1970 in Zagreb and Ljubljana, as well as visiting a number of coastal towns, including Rijeka, Zadar, Šibenik and Split, and making a preliminary visit to Sarajevo and Skopje. I worked in the university libraries in Zagreb and Ljubljana and in the archdiocesan library in Zagreb, and visited the bishopric of Maribor. As the field of my research became clearer to me I decided to concentrate on the relations between the state and the Roman Catholic Church, the Serbian and Macedonian Orthodox Churches, and the Moslem religious community, leaving aside the small Protestant churches and the remnant of the Jewish community, which comprise only a minute proportion of the inhabitants in Yugoslavia.

As my research proceeded it became obvious that it was touching on matters of great delicacy and political sensitivity. The rising tide of nationalist feelings in various republics of Yugoslavia, and the historical links between nationalism and religion were not the only sensitive areas; any complete account of the subject must also describe the background of the war years, the terrible fratricidal struggle between the Serbs and the Croats in which the churches were deeply involved, and the immediate postwar years of conflict and persecution.

The government archives of this period are still closed and the ecclesiastical authorities in consequence felt unable to show me unpublished material concerning their dealings with the authorities; but a great deal could be learned or inferred by reading the official press, journals of the priests' associations, diocesan gazettes and the gazettes of the Serbian and Macedonian Orthodox Churches. This was fleshed out by numerous conversations with men and women who had lived through these events, Marxists and Partisans, Catholics and Orthodox, both inside and outside Yugoslavia; without their help this would indeed have been a dry chronicle. It also became clear that I was examining material which, although it was available, had apparently never been extensively examined by Western scholars, and that one of the purposes of my study should be to provide, particularly in the critical apparatus and the bibliography, signposts for further research. It is for this reason also, as well as for its intrinsic interest, that I have included a great deal of detail. On the other hand I am well aware that some parts of this study are thin, and that there are a number of gaps; this is because in the spring of 1972, after I had virtually concluded research for the Catholic and Orthodox sections of this work, permission to continue my research was withdrawn and I left Yugoslavia.

This study as it now stands, therefore, deals only with the Catholic and Orthodox Churches; the major part of what I had originally intended has been covered, but the picture is still incomplete without an account of the role of the Moslems, which is important in the history of the republic of Bosnia and Hercegovina, and touches on the Albanian minority. I was also unable to cover the Macedonian Orthodox Church as fully as I would have wished. The manuscript has been read and criticised by Yugoslav Catholic and Orthodox scholars, who have saved me numerous errors of fact; my greatest regret, however, is that I have been unable to discuss the completed work with Marxist scholars, with some of whom I had had illuminating conversations.

I have been helped by so many Yugoslavs, communist and Christian, official and non-official, inside and outside Yugoslavia, that it would be invidious to single out individuals. Their patience and good will were boundless; I was particularly grateful for the fairness, and the assumption that I was making an honest attempt to discover the facts and understand their historical and cultural setting, which I encountered almost everywhere.

I must record my gratitude to Professor Phyllis Auty, formerly
Reader at the School of Slavonic and East European Studies
of the University of London and now Professor and head of
the Department of History, Simon Fraser University, British
Columbia, and Dr Richard Kindersley of St Antony's College,
Oxford, for advice and for reading the manuscript at several
stages; to Dr Ivo Lapenna of the London School of Economics
for reading chapter 7; to Stephen Clissold and Elizabeth Barker
for reading the prologue and parts of chapters 1 and 2; to Max
Alexander for help with the maps; to the staff of the Cambridge
University Press, especially for painstaking and stimulating
sub-editing; to Messrs Collins for permission to use the quotation
from C. V. Wedgwood's *Historical Essays*; to the World Council
of Churches for allowing me to consult their archives. I should
like to thank the Principal and Fellows of St Hilda's College,
Oxford, who kindly invited me to become a member of their
Senior Common Room during the early stages of the work;
Chatham House and the Institute of International Politics and
Economics of Belgrade; and finally the Trustees of the Joseph
Rowntree Charitable Trust, who gave me a grant to cover the
expenses of travel and research assistance, and the Friends
(Quaker) Peace and International Relations Committee, who
administered the grant and gave me their support and
encouragement.

For any errors of fact, and for all opinions and interpretations,
the responsibility is of course mine alone.

Sources

The official Yugoslav archives of the period are still secret, although both the Yugoslav government and the Vatican have made selected documents available to some writers. The patriarchate of the Serbian Orthodox Church published the minutes of the Synod in its official gazette until 1947; after this only occasional decisions are recorded. The sources consulted are thus:

(1) The official Yugoslav press; official Yugoslav government publications, including the official gazette; the official gazette of the Zagreb archdiocese and occasionally other dioceses; copies of pastoral letters to the clergy and faithful issued by Catholic dioceses, mainly Zagreb, and copies of similar letters to the clergy with instructions or information, seen at the Zagreb archdiocese (reference to circulars by number only indicates this source); the official gazette of the patriarchate of the Serbian Orthodox Church and official publications of the Serbian Orthodox Church; the official gazette of the Macedonian Orthodox Church; the Orthodox and Catholic prewar, wartime and postwar religious press; the official journals of various priests' associations; *L'Osservatore Romano*; wartime Partisan pamphlets and other publications.

(2) The Yugoslav historians Dr Branko Petranović and Dr A. Lisac have used some documents from the archives which are not generally accessible. Carlo Falconi, an Italian, has had access to the wartime correspondence between the government of the NDH and its representatives at the Vatican.

(3) Soon after Archbishop Stepinac's trial and sentence the American hierarchy commissioned Dr Richard Pattee, a Canadian scholar, to write a book on the subject, and an extensive selection of documents from the Vatican was made available to him; later the same documents were used by the Rev. T. Dragoun, a Croatian Catholic priest living in Paris. Pattee gives

the full text of numerous documents and Dragoun gives a smaller selection. Some of these have been checked against the Croatian originals when these were available (e.g. the pastoral letters of March and September 1945), and the writer has been assured by an authoritative source in Rome that the documents are authentic. It is safe to assume that this is so.

In 1974, when this study was almost completed, *Memoari Patriarha Srpskog Gavrila* [Memoirs of the Serbian Patriarch Gavrilo] was published in Paris, with an introduction by his former secretary, Mitar Djaković, who was also responsible for the publication of the book. Mr Djaković does not explain what happened to the manuscript during the war and after Gavrilo's death, and why it is being published only now, twenty-four years later. A large part of the book consists of a verbatim record of lengthy conversations between the patriarch and various prewar and wartime personalities, royal and political; there is also an account of his arrest, ill-treatment and summary trial by the Gestapo. But there are many gaps in the narrative and no guarantee that the manuscript has not been tampered with. This source has therefore been used with caution, although the writer has been assured by the Rev. M. Nikolić, the Serbian Orthodox parish priest in London, who came to London in 1944 after being released from a concentration camp in France, that the account of happenings in London is accurate. These memoirs and those of the prewar prime minister of Yugoslavia Dr Milan Stojadinović – *Ni rat, ni pakt* – have been consulted for the background to the abortive effort to conclude a concordat between Yugoslavia and the Vatican between the First and Second World Wars.

(4) A number of Western newspapers had well-informed correspondents in Yugoslavia during this period. The despatches written by M. S. Handler of the *New York Times* and the correspondent of the (U.S.) Religious News Service (a Yugoslav Orthodox Serb) were consistently sober and realistic and based on reliable sources. These two were outstanding among a number of other excellent correspondents. C. L. Sulzberger of the *New York Times* had interviews with Tito and access to many of the Yugoslav leaders. Subsequent checking of many of these reports against Yugoslav sources confirms their general reliability. The Press Library of Chatham House has provided clippings on this period from the *New York Times*, *Le Monde*, the *Christian Science Monitor* (Joseph Harrison), *The Times*, the *Manchester Guardian* and the *Glasgow Herald* (Alexander Werth wrote for the last two); a number of émigré publications were also consulted.

(5) Many secondary sources have been consulted; the majority of these are British or American. Among books by Yugoslavs are three by Dr Djoko Slijepčević, a historian now living in Germany, who is an authority on the Serbian Orthodox Church and has written two useful books on the Macedonian Orthodox Church. He presents the case against the Macedonian Church, but gives many sources and references. In 1974 a new biography of Archbishop Stepinac by the Rev. Aleksa Benigar, a Franciscan, was published by ZIRAL, a Croatian publishing house in Rome. Benigar had access to a number of sources not available to the present writer: the diary kept by the Rev. Josip Vraneković, parish priest of Krašić, during the years when Stepinac was living in forced residence in his parish house and gave him a full account of the events of his life (the present writer was shown Vraneković's account of Stepinac's last days, death and funeral); the archives of the archbishopric in Zagreb; and statements made to him by the Rev. V. Cecelja, one of the military vicars under the NDH, Canon D. Hren and Canon N. Kolarek. Benigar is an admirer of Stepinac but his book is comprehensive and scholarly and will be an indispensable source until all the documents, including Stepinac's diary and the full court record of his trial, are available.

(6) The writer has had numerous long conversations with Yugoslav Marxists, some in official positions, and with Catholics and Orthodox both in Yugoslavia and abroad, many of them participants in the events described. Footnotes in the form 'Catholic source', 'Orthodox source' etc. indicate that the information comes from a reliable and often first-hand source and has whenever possible been checked, and that moreover it fits into the general picture. Portions of the manuscript have been read by several of these persons, to whom the writer's grateful thanks are extended.

Archbishop Stepinac's diary was hidden by him, and discovered by the authorities in 1950. Extracts from it have appeared from time to time in articles in various Yugoslav information publications, and Carlo Falconi was allowed to examine it briefly, but the four volumes have not yet been made generally available to scholars, and the extracts are given out of context. For these reasons none of the extracts has been quoted.

Pronunciation

The principal Slav languages spoken in Yugoslavia are Serbian, Croatian (also known jointly as Serbo-Croat), Slovene and Macedonian. They are spelled phonetically. The Latin alphabet is used in the western part of Yugoslavia, the Cyrillic in the eastern part. The Cyrillic alphabet has letters corresponding to all the sounds in the language; diacritical marks are used with the Latin alphabet.

c   like *ts* in 'fats'
č   like *ch* in 'peach'
ć   a softer sound like *t* in 'future'
dj like *g* in 'ginger'
dž similar to *dj* but harder, as in 'jury'
ž   like *s* in 'pleasure'
š   like *sh* in 'shadow'
j   like *y* in 'yet'; also used after *i* in combination, e.g., Jugoslavija
r   both a consonant and a vowel

Terminology

The Macedonian forms Skopje and Bitola (instead of the Serbian forms Skoplje and Bitolj) have been used throughout, although the Serbian forms were in official use before 1945. The Macedonian forms of the names of councils and bodies set up by the Macedonian clergy have also been used, even when the source of the quotation was Serbian.

The term 'auxiliary bishop' has been used to translate *vikarni-biskup* applying to Catholics, and 'vicar-bishop' for *vikarni-episkop* applying to the Orthodox. There is a slight distinction between the two; in the Catholic Church an auxiliary is a full bishop and a member of the Bishops' Conference, while in the Serbian Orthodox Church he is an assistant bishop, with no diocese of his own, who does not sit in the Bishops' Sabor

(Assembly). The Serbian Orthodox Church has two vicar-bishops who are appointed as assistants to the patriarch.

After consulting some Serbian Orthodox friends, one of whom is a priest, the writer has decided to use 'the Rev.' for all Orthodox clergy except bishops, in order to avoid the complexities of the many ranks within the Orthodox Church. She hopes that purists will forgive her.

Abbreviations and glossary

ASNOM	Antifašističko Sobranie na Narodnoto Oslobodu-vanje na Makedonija: Anti-fascist Council for the National Liberation of Macedonia
ASNOS	Antifašistička Skupština Narodnog Oslobodjenja Serbije: Anti-fascist Council for the National Libera-tion of Serbia
AVNOJ	Antifašističko Vijeće Narodnog Oslobodjenja Jugo-slavije: Anti-fascist Council for the National Libera-tion of Yugoslavia
CMD	Ciril–Metodsko Društvo Duhovnikov LRS: Cyril and Methodius Association of [Catholic] Priests of the PRS
FNRJ	Federativna Narodna Republika Jugoslavija (= SFRY)
HSS	Hrvatska Seljačka Stranka: Croatian Peasant Party
KNO	Kotarski Narodni Odbor: District People's Committee
LCY	League of Communists of Yugoslavia (= SKJ)
LRS	Ljudska Republika Slovenija: People's Republic of Slovenia
NDH	Nezavisna Država Hrvatska: Independent State of Croatia
NOB	Narodno-Oslobodilačka Borba: National Liberation Struggle
NRH	Narodna Republika Hrvatska: People's Republic of Croatia
OF	Osvobodilna Fronta: Liberation Front
ONO	Okružni Narodni Odbor: Regional People's Committee
OZNA	Odeljenje za Zaštitu Naroda: Department for the Protection of the People
PRS	People's Republic of Slovenia (= LRS)
SFRY	Socialist Federative Republic of Yugoslavia (= FNRJ)

SKJ	Savez Komunista Jugoslavije (= LCY)
SNOO	Slovenski Narodno-Osvobodilni Odbor: Slovene National Liberation Committee, 16.ix.41 to 19.ii.44
SNOS	Slovenski Narodno-Osvobodilni Svet: Slovene National Liberation Council, 19.ii.44 onwards
UDBA	Uprava Državne Bezbednosti: Department of State Security; see also OZNA
WCC	World Council of Churches
ZAVNOH	Zemaljsko Antifašističko Vijeće Narodnog Oslo-bodjenja Hrvatske: Territorial Anti-fascist Council for the National Liberation of Croatia
hajduk	Outlaw who fought against the Turks
sin.	Minute of the Synod of the Serbian Orthodox Church (followed by the number of the minute)
Sv.	Sveti: Saint
Synod	Date of meeting of the Synod

Map 1. Religious distribution of the population. (This is only approximate and follows ethnic distribution. There are small numbers of Catholics in the Vojvodina, Serbia, Kosovo-Metohija and Macedonia.)

Prologue

The subject of this study, the relations between the churches and the state in postwar Yugoslavia, is more than a straightforward account of the struggle between atheist Marxism and religious belief, a communist government and religious institutions and communities. Marxist ideology and communist practice are only the latest factors in the complex history of the South Slav lands, and take their place in a long train of events stretching back for centuries. The area is peopled by many different nationalities and races; it has been part of the Roman and Byzantine Empires and was later ruled by the Habsburgs and the Ottoman Turks; its inhabitants are Roman Catholic, Orthodox and Moslem by religion and have tended to identify their religion with their nationality. Foreign rule and oppression have fostered an intractable nationalism which pervades every sphere of life, political, social and religious; Marxism, Catholicism, Orthodoxy and Islam have all been coloured by this, and even the internationalism which is implicit in both communism and Catholicism has not been strong enough to transmute these feelings.

Those who are acquainted with the history of the Balkans, especially with its ecclesiastical history, may find new facts in these pages, but few surprises; the events of the last thirty years spring directly out of the history of the country. For those who come fresh to the subject, this prologue is a brief sketch of the Catholic and Orthodox communities as they were when the new state was established and an outline of the relevant political developments between the two wars, much compressed and necessarily over-simplified. Differences of political tradition, economic development, nationality, language, alphabet and religion divide the country variously between east and west, and north and south, and every generalisation about Yugoslavia is riddled with exceptions.

The inhabitants of Serbia and Montenegro are Orthodox, with an Albanian Moslem minority in southern Serbia. The inhabitants of Croatia–Slavonia, Dalmatia and Slovenia are Catholics, with pockets of Orthodox Serbs living along the old Austrian military frontier in Croatia. The Vojvodina, formerly part of Hungary, had a mixed population of Hungarians, Germans[1] and several different Slav groups, the majority being Serbs; it had been a centre of Serbian cultural development in the nineteenth century. Bosnia–Hercegovina had been governed for centuries by the Turks but was taken under Austro–Hungarian protection in 1878 and finally annexed in 1908. Under the Turks, many of its Slav inhabitants had become Moslems; the majority of the rest were Orthodox Serbs, and the others Catholic Croats. The territory known historically as Macedonia was divided in 1912 between Serbia, Greece and Bulgaria, the largest part going to Serbia. The population is mixed but most are Orthodox Slavs and Moslem Albanians. A special problem was created by the mixed Italian and Slav populations of the Julian region around Trieste and in Istria. These became part of Italy in 1919 and the national and linguistic aspirations of the Slavs were systematically suppressed; after the Second World War the greatest part of this territory was joined to Yugoslavia.

The relations between these national and religious communities were – and still are – further complicated by many anomalous small groups. There are small numbers of Catholic Serbs, particularly on the Montenegrin coast (although Catholic they celebrate the *slava*, a uniquely Serbian Orthodox custom), and Greek Catholic (Uniate) parishes are widely scattered. Groups of Orthodox Serbs and Montenegrins were settled in the Vojvodina after the First and Second World Wars, and small groups of Croat and Slovene Catholics live in the Vojvodina, southern Serbia and Macedonia; there is an Albanian Catholic minority in southern Serbia. There are also a number of very small Protestant groups, mostly in the Vojvodina and Slavonia; and a sizeable Jewish community (today only a tiny remnant) was centred in Bosnia.

In 1919 Slovenia, Croatia–Slavonia, Bosnia–Hercegovina and the Vojvodina, all former Austro–Hungarian territories, were united with the Kingdoms of Serbia and Montenegro to form the Kingdom of the Serbs, Croats and Slovenes, later renamed Yugoslavia.

From the beginning the new state suffered from the conflict between the Serbs' desire that it should be an extension of the former Kingdom of Serbia, and the Croats' view that it should be a union of equal South Slav peoples. The country was ruled by a Serbian dynasty and effectively there was Serbian hegemony

---

[1] The Germans fled or were expelled after the Second World War.

over the whole country; the Croats resented this predominance and agitated for a federal state with considerable local autonomy. The tension between the two overshadowed every aspect of Yugoslav political life between 1919 and 1941.

King Alexander's policy of centralisation, which culminated in the 1929 dictatorship, provoked intense Croat resistance and gave offence as well to many Serbs. Croat émigrés, led by Ante Pavelić, established centres of subversion in Italy and Hungary, modelled on the Italian Fascist movement; they called themselves *ustaše* (from *ustanak*, a rising or rebellion) and their aim was to establish an independent Catholic Croatia, a bastion against the Orthodox east. They were militantly Catholic, anti-Serb and anti-Semitic.

The division of Macedonia in 1912 between Serbia, Greece and Bulgaria created a ferment of violent discontent. The Bulgarian-based Internal Macedonian Revolutionary Organisation (IMRO) made contact with the ustaše, both were supported by the Italian and Hungarian governments, and in 1934 one of their agents assassinated King Alexander during a state visit to France. The country was profoundly shocked, but the differences between the Serbs and Croats, and the discontents of the Macedonians, went too deep to be permanently healed by the tragedy.

This was the political framework within which the Catholic and Orthodox Churches lived after 1919.

The patriarchate of the Serbian Orthodox Church was established in 1919 as soon as the new state came into being, uniting six ecclesiastical organisations with different origins and histories.[2] In the eyes of the church the patriarchate was not new but renewed, the direct successor of the medieval church founded by St Sava, and the spiritual embodiment of the Serbian people; but its several parts had existed independently for centuries and their cohesion had to be fostered. Moreover, for the first time the Serbian Orthodox Church, which had been the state church of Serbia, found itself only one among a number of theoretically equal religious communities. This was a new experience and created a feeling of insecurity and a heightened sensitivity to anything which appeared to touch on its status.

Roman Catholics in the new state were in the overwhelming majority in Croatia–Slavonia, Slovenia and Dalmatia but they were a minority in the whole country; this also was a new and

---

[2] The metropolitanate of Serbia, the patriarchate of Karlovci (Vojvodina), the metropolitanate of Bosnia–Hercegovina, the metropolitanate of Montenegro, the Macedonian dioceses transferred from the patriarchate of Constantinople and the two Dalmatian dioceses of Zara (Zadar) and Kotor.

anxious experience for people used to living in the Austro–Hungarian Empire. There were, moreover, important political differences between Catholics in Slovenia and Croatia. The Croatian Peasant Party (HSS) was anti-clerical, while in Slovenia the dominant Slovene People's Party was led by prelates, and one of its members, Mgr Korošec, was the first deputy premier of the new state. In the nineteenth century the party had been progressive and had encouraged the formation of peasant cooperatives, but later it became increasingly conservative, while the progressives in the party, who included some of the Catholic clergy, were drawn into the Christian Socialist movement; one later result of this was that when Yugoslavia was attacked and occupied by the Axis in 1941, a small but influential group in the church was prepared to join the underground Slovene Liberation Front which was finally dominated by the communists.

These complex tensions were felt at all levels of society. Dr Rudolf Bičanić in his prewar study of how people lived in the poorest parts of Dalmatia and Hercegovina[3] describes their primitive conditions and the absence of any cushion against drought and hunger; the economic crisis of the 1930s brought the destitution of the peasants in this area of mixed Serb and Croat population to its lowest levels. Their bitterness expressed itself in religious and national hatred between the Serbs and Croats, Orthodox and Catholics; when finally war and invasion came and the conflict exploded, both sides fought with primitive savagery.

Yet efforts had been made to avoid this conflict. During the Corfu negotiations leading to the foundation of Yugoslavia, the Croats had insisted that all religions should be equal in the eyes of the state, and the Serbs, who would have liked Orthodoxy to be the state religion, gave way. Both the Catholics and the Orthodox were consciously Slav and this might have provided a bond between them. Both had long resisted the denationalising influence of their hierarchical superiors, the Vatican with its Italianising tendencies and, until the end of the nineteenth century, the Greek Phanariots; both had fought for the right to use their own liturgical language and this had even at one time formed an element of sympathy between the two otherwise deeply divided churches – a phenomenon which was noted by nineteenth-century travellers from the West.[4] But in the end it

---

[3] *Kako živi narod: život u pasivnim krajevima* [How the People Live: Life in the Passive Regions], Zagreb, 1936.
[4] G. M. Muir-Mackenzie and A. P. Irby, *Travels in the Slavonic Provinces of Turkey*, 4th edn (London, 1877), pp. 14–15.

was not strong enough to overcome the antagonism and mistrust.

The Holy See, which had had some misgivings, recognised the new state and in 1919 diplomatic relations were established. At that time a number of concordats regulating the relations between the Vatican and the various regions now forming a part of the new state were in force;[5] and in 1922 negotiations for a single new concordat to replace them were undertaken. These negotiations lapsed but were resumed in 1935 and an agreement between the Vatican and the Yugoslav government was signed.

This coincided with a time of mounting tension between Serbs and Croats and exacerbated feelings among the Serbs. The Serbian Orthodox bishops were alarmed by the terms of the concordat, which seemed to offer the Catholic Church greater privileges than the Serbian Orthodox Church had, while the opposition Serbian political parties seized upon it as a weapon against the government of the regent, Prince Paul, and Dr Milan Stojadinović, the premier. Although the government hastened to assure the Orthodox Church that the privileges offered to the Catholics would also be extended to other churches, and a clause to ensure this was added to the text of the concordat, the Orthodox Church, forced along by public opinion among the laity, joined forces with the Serbian opposition parties in an unbridled campaign against the ratification of the concordat, fed by alarmist rumours, anonymous pamphlets and tendentious articles, all designed to show that the most basic rights of the Serbian Orthodox Church were in imminent danger. The partriarchate announced that Serbian Orthodox members of the government who voted in favour of the concordat would be excommunicated. The concordat was finally submitted to the Skupština (Parliament) and passed by a comfortable majority on July 23, 1937. A demonstration of protest headed by bishops and priests set out from the cathedral the next day and was roughly dispersed by the police. On the same day Patriarch Varnava, whose health had been deteriorating under the strain, died. The threat of excommunication was carried out and Stojadinović found himself with a serious crisis on his hands. In the face of this he decided not to proceed and the concordat was never sent to the Senate for ratification. Relations between the government and the Serbian Orthodox Church were strained for some time

---

[5] Croatia and Slavonia by the Austro–Hungarian concordat, 19.viii.1855; Slovenia and Dalmatia by the law of 1874; Vojvodina by a special law; Bosnia–Hercegovina by a convention of 8.vii.1881; Montenegro by the concordat of 18.viii.1886; Serbia by the concordat of 24.vi.1914 (Spinka).

after this and there was a sharp tussle lasting for several months before a successor to Patriarch Varnava could be agreed upon, a tussle which went on also between factions within the hierarchy. In the end Metropolitan Gavrilo of Montenegro, who had been an opponent of the concordat, was elected patriarch in June 1937, and, as will be seen, served the church with great courage.

The Serbian Orthodox Church's anxiety about its status was certainly one of the reasons it allowed itself to be swept into a political battle between two Serbian factions. The conflict over the concordat was a chance too good to be missed to reassert the leading position of the church. But the affair only added to the tensions between the Serbs and Croats which were already menacing the existence of the country. The Catholic Church refrained on the whole from meeting agitation with counter-agitation; but among Croat extremists feelings of revenge smouldered, especially against the Orthodox bishops who had been known to lead the opposition to the concordat, and eventually found expression in 1941 in the brutal murder of Bishop Platon of Banja Luka and the ill-treatment of Metropolitan Dositej of Zagreb before he was expelled and took refuge in Belgrade.

After the assassination of King Alexander the government of the regent, Prince Paul, introduced some relaxation of the former centralism; in 1939 an agreement (the Sporazum) was signed and an autonomous Banovina of Croatia with Zagreb as its capital was established. But the reforms came too late and matters had reached a grave crisis immediately before the outbreak of the war.

I

Wartime: the fateful events

The background

Yugoslavia had been sorely hit by the great depression of the early 1930s, and its economic position had only begun to improve after favourable trading agreements with Germany had been signed in 1934 and 1936. These, however, tied the Yugoslav economy closely to Germany. In 1937 relations with Italy, which had been very strained, took an unexpected turn for the better; late in 1936 Mussolini referred to 'the astonishing improvement of atmosphere' between the two countries, and in March 1937 a treaty of friendship was signed in Belgrade by Count Ciano. Earlier that year a treaty of friendship had also been signed with Bulgaria. This improvement in her relations with two of her most troublesome neighbours, and her economic links with Germany, all moved Yugoslavia away from her policy of friendship with France and loosened the bonds of the Little Entente (Yugoslavia, Romania and Czechoslovakia). After much pressure from Germany the government signed the Tripartite Pact on March 25, 1941, receiving at the same time assurances from von Ribbentrop that the German government would respect Yugoslavia's sovereignty and territorial integrity, and would not ask for Yugoslav military assistance or the passage of Axis troops through Yugoslav territory.

It was an unpopular step. Patriarch Gavrilo Dožić of the Serbian Orthodox Church protested vigorously to the regent, Prince Paul, and urged him to appeal to the people to rally to the crown and to form a government of all parties. He warned the prime minister, Dragiša Cvetković , and other members of the government, with all the authority of the church, against an action which would betray the interests of the Serbian people and their church. On the day the pact was signed he broadcast an emotional appeal over the Belgrade radio calling on all Serbs to remain true to the ideals and traditions of their church and their nation.[1] The appeal went out also over the radio station in Ljubljana, but not from Zagreb.

[1] *MPG*, pp. 273ff, 399.

7

Map 2. Boundaries of Yugoslavia after the Axis attack in 1941.

Prince Paul's regency was overthrown by a *coup d'état* on March 27, 1941, and King Peter's majority proclaimed. The move was greeted with wild enthusiasm by important sections of the population: the Army, particularly the younger officers; the students and many members of the staff of Belgrade University; the Serbian political parties, especially those among them who had felt that the concessions made to the Croats in 1939 were endangering the interests of the country; and the Serbian Orthodox Church. The Communist Party, still an illegal organisation, also welcomed it. A new government was set up under General Dušan Simović, who had been associated with the leaders of the *coup* and had had previous knowledge of it. Maček, the leader of the Croatian Peasant Party, rebuffed German attempts to enlist his cooperation with the promise of an independent Croat State, and joined the new government as vice-premier.

Hitler was enraged by the Belgrade *coup d'état*, which, he believed, endangered his time-table for the invasion of the Soviet Union. The following day he ordered an overwhelming attack on Yugoslavia designed to crush all resistance, frighten the Turks into neutrality and soften up the Greeks for the attack which he was planning in order to bolster up the unsuccessful Italian invasion. During a heavy aerial bombardment on April 6 many thousands of people were killed in Belgrade; this was followed by a massive invasion of Axis forces which broke down all remaining resistance. The king and his government escaped into exile and on April 17 an armistice was signed and the remnants of the Yugoslav army surrendered unconditionally.

Yugoslavia was parcelled out among the Axis powers and ceased overnight to be a state. The Germans annexed the northern part of Slovenia, occupied the Banat (a part of the Vojvodina) which in practice was administered by the local German minority, the Volksdeutsch, and occupied Serbia south of the Danube, setting up a puppet government under General Nedić, a Serb. The Italians took over the southern part of Slovenia, including Ljubljana, and a portion of the Adriatic coast, and set up two provinces, Dalmatia and Ljubljana; they joined the plain of Kosovo and the western part of Macedonia to Albania (already a puppet Italian state) and installed a governor in Montenegro. The Hungarians annexed two small districts, Prekmurje in Slovenia and Medjumurje in Croatia, and Bačka and Baranja in the Vojvodina, and the Bulgarians annexed the rest of Macedonia. The Independent State of Croatia (Nezavisna Država Hrvatska, referred to as NDH) including Croatia–

Slavonia, parts of Dalmatia, and Bosnia–Hercegovina was established, as the Germans and Italians had promised.[2] It was divided laterally into German and Italian zones of occupation and became in fact, if not formally, a German–Italian protectorate. Germany acquired a large source of forced labour in Serbia and also enlisted many Croatians to work in Germany.

On top of this numbing shock to the life of the country, large numbers of people were expelled from their homes by the occupiers; they included many priests and teachers from the German-occupied part of Slovenia, and Serbian colonists from the Vojvodina and Macedonia, some of whom had been there for centuries and others of whom had acquired their holdings during the land reform after the First World War. All made their way to the rump state of Serbia.

Serbia

The Serbian Patriarch Gavrilo Dožić, then a man of sixty, was in Belgrade during the German air attack on April 6. The patriarchate, standing near the fortress of Kalemegdan which overlooks the confluence of the Danube and the Sava, was badly damaged. The patriarch left during the afternoon and took refuge in the monastery of Rakovica on the outskirts of the city. From there he moved south with the government towards Užice, and then went on to the monastery of Ostrog in Montenegro hoping that the government and army would retreat to the mountains and make a stand there.[3] But after the rout of the army, the king and his government decided that they must leave the country; they moved south, stopping at Ostrog, and finally flew from Nikšić to Greece. Gavrilo writes that he agreed with this decision, but in spite of strong pressure, refused to accompany them; at its meeting on March 29 the Sabor had decided that if war broke out all the bishops would remain in their dioceses.[4] The patriarch took leave of the king on April 14 and gave him his blessing.

German troops entered the monastery of Ostrog on the

---

[2] Pavelić, the Ustaša leader, wanted the Sandjak of Novi Pazar as well, but Ciano, the Italian foreign minister, refused (Ciano, *Diaries*, p. 364). There are differing estimates of the composition of the population of the NDH. The figures given by the Yugoslav government after the war were 5m Croats, 1.9m Serbs, 750,000 Moslems (Slijepčević, p. 673, quoting *Tajni dokumenti*, p. 86). The Serbian Orthodox Church gives 2,403,998 Orthodox Serbs divided into eight dioceses (*Gl.*, 1.iv.46, p. 53). These were Zahumlje–Hercegovina, Dabar–Bosnia, Zvornik–Tuzla, Banja Luka, Dalmatia, Gornjikarlovac, Pakrac and Zagreb; in addition there was the portion of the Belgrade–Karlovci diocese lying north of the Sava, in all nine dioceses.

[3] *MPG*, pp. 441–2, 449.   [4] Ibid. pp. 453–4.

morning of April 23, arrested the patriarch and his nephew, a young man who was his constant attendant and acted as his *chef de cabinet*, and took them to Sarajevo;[5] there he was immediately tried by a drumhead German military court for supporting the uprising of March 27 and encouraging resistance to the German demands. During the arrest and trial he was brutally ill-treated and his nephew Dušan was badly beaten up.[6] From Sarajevo he was taken back to Belgrade where he was kept in prison in very bad conditions until the end of May; then because of his deteriorating health he was transferred to the monastery of Rakovica where he was kept under close guard.[7] He was to spend altogether four years in prisons and concentration camps in Yugoslavia and in Germany[8] resisting all German efforts to make him collaborate with them.

Metropolitan Josif of Skopje was put under house arrest and isolated from his clergy as soon as the Bulgarian invaders had annexed Macedonia.[9] On May 4 he and Bishop Vikentije Prodanov of Zletovo–Strumica (who was also administrator of the diocese of Ohrid) were expelled to Serbia[10] together with Orthodox priests who were not born in Macedonia, or had married Serbian wives, or who were otherwise suspected of being loyal to Serbia.[11]

Metropolitan Josif and Bishop Vikentije arrived in Belgrade on May 5 and were joined almost immediately by Metropolitan Dositej Vasić of Zagreb, who had been severely beaten and went straight into a sanitorium.[12] On May 15 Bishop Nikolaj Jovanović and Bishop Nektarije Krulj arrived, having been expelled from Mostar and Tuzla by the ustaše, and on the same day an official of the ecclesiastical court in Banja Luka, who had managed to escape, brought the first news of the murder of Bishop Platon of Banja Luka. Bishop Vladimir of Mukačev–Prjašev, a Serbian Orthodox diocese in Czechoslovakia, was also expelled by the Germans and made his way to Belgrade.[13] Bishop Nikolaj Velimirović of Žiča, a noted preacher and one of the leaders of the movement of spiritual revival of the Serbian Orthodox Church, was interned at the monastery of Ljubostinja on the Western Morava river[14] and Bishop Serafim of Raška–Prizren was interned by the Albanians in Tirana, where he died in January 1945.[15]

5 Ibid. pp. 15, 464–9.   6 Ibid. pp. 470–91.
7 Ibid. p. 514; Slijepčević, p. 663.   8 *MPG*, p. 15.
9 *SPC*, p. 212.   10 Ibid. p. 213.
11 Slijepčević, p. 667.   12 *SPC*, p. 226.
13 Ibid. p. 226.   14 Ibid. p. 227.
15 Ibid. p. 226. Bishop Valerian of Srem was seriously ill in Split when the war broke out; he died there on June 10, 1941 (ibid. p. 189); the diocese of Pakrac was vacant. Both bishoprics remained vacant until after the war.

Metropolitan Josif, a forceful personality and a natural leader, who had fought with the Komitadji against the Turks in the Balkan Wars, assumed the leadership of the church in the absence of the patriarch, although he was not a member of the Synod.[16] The Germans had taken over the patriarchate building on April 23 with all its contents, records and cash, and makeshift offices had been improvised in an adjoining building which had housed the church's museum.[17] Josif at once began the herculean task of creating some sort of order in the administration of the brutally crippled church but it was not until the end of May that he succeeded in getting permission to visit the patriarch in prison to tell him what was happening and to get the patriarch's written assent to his assumption of power.[18] He was accompanied by two German officers, one of whom peremptorily ordered the patriarch to give Josif the assent he requested. The patriarch told Josif that he approved everything he had done and advised him to carry on as he was doing, acting always in the interests of the church, but he said that he could not give Josif the authority he asked for, since it would be against the constitution of the church. According to Gavrilo's account, Josif was downcast and the officer tried to insist, but Gavrilo stood his ground. The verbal support he gave Josif seems, however, to have satisfied the Synod, and Josif continued to lead it until the end of the war. The other members of the Synod were Bishop Emilijan Piperković of Timok in eastern Serbia and Bishop Jovan Ilić of Niš in Serbia, both of whom could travel between their dioceses and Belgrade; Bishop Nektarije Krulj of Zvornik–Tuzla in Bosnia, who had been expelled from his diocese and was living in Belgrade; and Bishop Irinej Ćirić of Bačka in the Vojvodina, who was not allowed by the Hungarians to leave Novi Sad; the others whenever possible went to him for the meetings of the Synod.[19]

The nine dioceses of the territory of the newly created NDH were the principal casualties; during the course of a few months the structure of the church there was almost totally destroyed and three of the bishops were murdered.

A month after the annexation of Macedonia the Bulgarian Orthodox Church took over the three dioceses of Skopje,

---

[16] The Synod is the standing committee of the Holy Sabor (Assembly) of Serbian Orthodox bishops, and consists of the patriarch and four bishops who serve for a year at a time; during their term of service they live in Belgrade. The constitution of the Serbian Orthodox Church provides that in the event of the death or incapacity of the patriarch, he shall be succeeded by the oldest bishop on the Synod.

[17] *SPC*, p. 225.   [18] *MPG*, pp. 510ff.

[19] *SPC*, p. 228.

Zletovo–Strumica and Ohrid–Bitola, bringing with them 280 priests and other personnel to replace the expelled Serbian clergy.[20] The diocese of the Montenegrin Littoral (Crnogorsko-primorje) was divided by the Italian occupation; Boka Kotorska (the Bay of Kotor) and the coastal strip were annexed by Italy, while the highlands were treated as occupied territory and an Italian governor installed. A rising against the occupation in July 1941 was severely repressed; there were many arrests and imprisonments, and churches and monasteries were damaged.[21] The Italians controlled the administration of church life very strictly; all proclamations and pastoral letters had to be issued in both Serbian and Italian, and names in parish registers given in both forms. An additional problem was created by Serbs from Hercegovina and Dalmatia (taken over by the Ustaša), and from Kosovo and Metohija (annexed by the Italians to Albania), who had taken refuge in Montenegro, often accompanied by their priests.[22] In the Vojvodina, where the Hungarians carried out a number of violent, seemingly purposeless killings of Serbs following mass round-ups, seven priests lost their lives;[23] but after this the church was left in comparative peace.

The Germans at first administered Serbia directly, but in August 1941 they set up a puppet government in Belgrade under General Nedić, a former cabinet minister and chief of staff; he was never fully trusted by the Germans and never had more than limited authority. But the Serbs at least did not have to contend in this 'inner Serbia' with domestic enemies as well as foreign occupiers, and into this comparative sanctuary tens of thousands of refugees, mainly from the NDH, crowded during the summer and autumn of 1941. Some of them had been rounded up and expelled by the NDH authorities as part of the policy of 'Croatising' the country, but the majority had fled in terror.

The church immediately took *ad hoc* measures to deal with the crisis. Bishop Vikentije was appointed to administer the diocese of Žiča in place of the interned Bishop Nikolaj Velimirović.[24] Bishop Nektarije became administrator of four dioceses in the territory of the NDH[25] and in March 1942 directors were appointed for each diocese to be responsible for the refugee priests and faithful.[26] During the summer of 1941 three trans-

---

[20] Ibid. p. 213. [21] Ibid. p. 217.

[22] Ibid.

[23] At Cugara a thousand Serbs were killed on January 5, 1942, and their bodies thrown into the frozen Tisza. Similar incidents took place at Novi Sad, and at Morašin and other villages (ibid. p. 207).

[24] Ibid. p. 227. [25] *Gl.*, 1941, p. 182, quoted in *SPC*, p. 234.

[26] Sin. 2959/37/42, quoted in *SPC*, p. 234.

ports of priests from the NDH arrived at Arandjelovac, south-west of Belgrade, where they were met by Metropolitan Josif and members of his staff; diocesan lists were drawn up. They were assigned to empty parishes or sent to help in other parishes, and some were found administrative jobs in the patriarchate.[27] Josif succeeded in visiting the patriarch during the month of May to discuss the circumstances of the church; one pressing problem was solved when Dušan Letica, the minister of finance in the Nedić government, ordered that the salaries of all the clergy, including those who had taken refuge in Serbia, be paid by the government.[28]

The first civilian transports from Croatia arrived on August 1, crammed with exhausted and hungry people; they were met by the priests who had arrived earlier, many of whom found groups of their own parishioners who had managed to remain together.[29] The government set up a special Commissariat for Refugees:[30] every Serbian household was ordered to receive at least one refugee family[31] and the church appealed to Serbs to take their brothers into their own homes; the response was warm, especially in the villages.[32]

Meanwhile the Synod had managed to obtain permission to visit the patriarch at Rakovica on July 7,[33] and the next day it met officially for the first time since the fall of Yugoslavia.[34] Its first action was to issue a message to the people to bring them what comfort and reassurance they could. The German authorities, it said, had agreed that the unity of the church should be preserved as far as possible under its own constitution; the bishops had pledged themselves to observe the laws of the occupiers and to cooperate in maintaining order and peace and obedience.[35] This message was used after the war to accuse the church of collaboration, but in the chaos of that time it must have seemed the only possible way to protect the people and save them from total destruction. The Orthodox Church was drawing on the experience of centuries of oppression under the Turks, when it survived by compromise and seeming compliance; in everything that happened it never lost sight of its two overriding

---

[27] SPC, p. 230.
[28] Ibid. p 227.
[29] Ibid. p. 230.
[30] Ibid.
[31] Lisac, p. 130.
[32] SPC, p. 230. The Serbian refugees also brought disaffection and resistance. Lisac (pp. 134–5) cites a German report which complained that it was very unwise to send city-dwellers into Serbian mountain villages where they would foment unrest, instead of to the cities where they could be supervised.
[33] Slijepčević, p. 665; MPG, p. 533.
[34] SPC, p. 227.
[35] Sin. 585/3/41: Gl., 1.iii.42.

priorities, the preservation of the unity of the Serbian people and of the Serbian Orthodox Church. The Synod issued two further messages on August 4 and September 26;[36] it exhorted the clergy to gather their flocks around them and make their own lives an example to the faithful. The third message spoke of the persecution of the Serbs outside Serbia and the fratricidal strife which was taking place: 'If this goes on', the message concluded, 'God only knows what the state of the church and our people will be.[37]

The Synod also appealed to the German military authorities in Serbia, begging them to take measures to stop the persecution of the Serbs in the NDH and in the Hungarian- and Albanian-occupied areas,[38] and they enquired urgently about the fate of Bishop Petar Simonjić of Dabar–Bosnia (Sarajevo) and Bishop Sava Trljajić of Gornjikarlovac in Croatia, asking General Dankelmann, the German military commander, to intervene for their release; a second request was sent on September 10, 1941. No answer was received until the following April when the patriarchate was told that the Ustaša authorities could find no trace of them.[39] Both had, in fact, been done to death together with thousands of other Serbs.[40]

A semblance of church life was gradually resumed; services were held, contributions received and accounts published. Metropolitan Josif made heartfelt appeals to Serbian national feelings; in his Easter message in 1942 he exhorted them not to

---

[36] Sin. 1356/61/41: *Gl.* 1.iii.42.

[37] Sin. 1950/229 (26.ix.41): *Gl.* 1.iii.42.

[38] 9.vii.41: *SPC*, p. 228. Two appeals were made, one on July 9 to General Schröder and one in August to his successor, General Dankelmann. Copies of these were brought to London via Istanbul and Cairo in October 1941 by Dr Miloš Sekulić. The second appeal contained a detailed list by counties and localities of Serbs who had been murdered, and of damage to churches and monasteries. It was estimated that 180,000 Serbs had been killed up to August 1941. Copies of these appeals were given to the British government and the Church of England and later they were published in the United States in the *American Srbobran* (on 4.x.41 and 23 and 27–30.x.42 and 2 and 4–6.xi.42). Croatian ministers in the Yugoslav government protested at the reckless anti-Croat use made of the memoranda and pointed out a number of inconsistencies. The writer is indebted for this information to Dr Jozo Tomasevich whose *War and Revolution in Yugoslavia 1941–45*, vol. 1: *The Chetniks* (p. 266) appeared after the present study was completed.

[39] *SPC*, p. 226.

[40] These messages were smuggled out and were one of the first solid pieces of evidence to reach the West of what had happened in the NDH, although rumours had been filtering through to the Vatican. The Croats in the émigré government-in-exile at first refused to believe the news, but Šubašić, the foreign minister, referred to it in a speech in Pittsburgh (16.xi.41) and it was published in the *American Srbobran* of Pittsburgh (14.x.41) (Fotitch, p. 125, and *Times*, 3.xi.41).

forget that 'we are all Serbs, parts of one body, united by one faith, Orthodoxy, by one language, by blood, by our celebrated past, that we are descendants of the celebrated saints, St Sava, St Simeon, St Prince Lazar and the two heroes Miloš and Marko...and it is our obligation to preserve through the ages our motto "Only harmony saves the Serbs".[41]

The Synod was particularly concerned about the training of future priests. All five of the church's seminaries (Sremski Karlovci near Novi Sad, Bitola in Macedonia, Prizren in southern Serbia, Cetinje in Montenegro and Vršac in the Vojvodina) were outside inner Serbia and had been closed down. All the property of the patriarchate in Sremski Karlovci, under Ustaša rule, was confiscated and the contents removed to Zagreb. The buildings of the seminary at Cetinje were taken over by the Italians, but a part was returned in the autumn of 1941[42] and in October an attempt was made to restart the sixth class. In July 1942 the seminary of St Sava was reopened temporarily in Belgrade to hold examinations for pupils of all the other seminaries, and in 1943 examinations were held at Niš for pupils who had continued to study at home, but the training of new priests virtually ceased during the war.

Heavy pressure was brought on the clergy and the bishops to declare themselves for the occupying forces. General Nedić summoned the hierarchy on October 20, 1941 and told them that the occupation authorities were gravely dissatisfied with the attitude of the church, which was 'two-faced'. Josif answered that there was nothing two-faced about their behaviour; they had their own attitude, based on the gospel, and could not lend themselves to any political combinations or pressures. Their duty was to teach the people and for this they had their own methods, based on the apostles and St Sava: the church was the mother of the Serbian Orthodox people and would never say: 'That son is worthless, let him be killed!' The Germans had no right to ask the Serbian Orthodox Church more than they demanded from the Roman Catholic and Protestant churches.[43] Jonić, one of Nedić's ministers, tried to insist that priests 'everywhere and on every occasion' should speak in support of the regime, and some minor officials even attempted to dictate the subjects of sermons and censor them.[44] In December 1942 the German commanding general complained sharply to Nedić that he could no longer tolerate priests spreading Anglo-Saxon propaganda and monasteries becoming hiding-places, and he asked for a change before

[41] Gl., i.iv.42.   [42] SPC, p. 222.
[43] Sin. 1060/237/1947: SPC, pp. 232–3.   [44] SPC, p. 232.

he was forced to take stricter measures.[45] News began to come out of the arrests of many priests in the Ibar, Morava, Studenica, Kosovo and Užice districts of Serbia; many perished in German reprisal actions, and several were shot in Kragujevac on October 21, 1941, when 7,000 Serbs were killed in retaliation for the death of 70 Germans.[46]

Although the patriarchate building had been returned in October 1941, Gestapo supervision continued. The minutes of each meeting of the Synod had to be deposited with the Gestapo, so that decisions which the bishops wished to keep secret were not recorded; a censor was installed in the building to examine all letters going in and out.[47]

During his imprisonment at Rakovica, Gavrilo was allowed to receive visitors on a number of occasions, in the presence of a German officer, accompanied by an interpreter. In spite of these restraints he seems to have managed to exchange a considerable amount of information with his visitors, and to have been well informed about what was going on. Milan Aćimović, the commissar for the interior under the Germans, visited him on June 22, 1941, and, according to the patriarch's memoirs, gave him a graphic account of the early Ustaša brutalities against the Serbian population of the NDH, the long-drawn-out butchery of many priests, and the hideous tortures inflicted on Bishop Platon of Banja Luka.[48] The four bishops composing the Synod, after much difficulty, visited him on July 7,[49] and General Nedić, the head of the puppet Serbian government, saw him on several occasions, the last time in August 1944, just before his deportation to Dachau. Gavrilo noted that Nedić had been severely affected by the events of the occupation and was as much a prisoner as the patriarch and Bishop Nikolaj and all the Serbian people. They had known each other well before the war, and Gavrilo was convinced that he had accepted the German offer to head the puppet government only to spare the Serbian people a worse fate.[50]

At the end of December 1942 the patriarch had been moved to the monastery of Vojlovica, near Pančevo,[51] presumably to isolate him more effectively from Belgrade; there he was joined

[45] Ibid. p. 233.   [46] Ibid. p. 228.
[47] Ibid. pp. 233ff.
[48] MPG, pp. 520ff. The accounts given in SPC and Spomenica omit the details concerning Bishop Platon, perhaps in deference to the policy of the postwar Yugoslav authorities of playing down details of atrocities in an effort to heal the bitterness between Serbs and Croats. Emigré Croat accounts give equally gruesome details of the murder of Croatian priests by Serbian Četniks (see I. Omrčanin, Martyrologe croate, Paris, n.d.).
[49] MPG, pp. 533ff.   [50] Ibid. pp. 540ff.   [51] SPC, p. 227.

by Bishop Nikolaj Velimirović of Žiča, who had been imprisoned in the monastery of Ljubostinja.[52] Finally in August 1944, shortly before the liberation of Belgrade, they were transported, ill and exhausted, by goods wagon and motor-van to Dachau and then moved from one concentration camp to another until they were set free by the U.S. Army on May 8, 1945.[53]

Both men were outstanding leaders in the church, and became symbols of patriotism and steadfast courage. The support, or at least the acquiescence of either, would have greatly weakened Serb resistance and helped the Germans, but neither gave way an inch. Gavrilo's behaviour and his attitude eventually made it possible for him to return to Yugoslavia after the war, where the new government saw that his great prestige would be useful to them.[54]

The position of the church became more difficult as resistance sprang up within the country. There was an early, unsuccessful effort to establish cooperation between Mihailović's Četniks, owing allegiance to the king and the government-in-exile, and the communist-led Partisans. After that in spite of strong Allied pressure, the two movements fought each other relentlessly, each determined to be in control at the end of the war. Small numbers of priests were engaged with both sides, but the majority tried to keep out of the conflict and waited to see how the war would develop.[55]

In 1944 the tide of war turned in Serbia; the Partisans who had earlier been driven out fought their way back and by September the Germans had begun to withdraw; Mihailović's Četniks were disintegrating. Tito concluded an agreement with the Russians to enter Yugoslavia for joint action with the Partisan troops and on October 20 the Partisans and units of the Red Army entered Belgrade. The war continued for nearly seven months, but a victorious Yugoslav government was installed in its own capital.

Six months earlier the Easter message from the Synod had spoken of the sacrifice of Golgotha which led to the Resurrection and prayed 'that every Serbian home and family be morally and spiritually renewed and born again, be in itself a small Church of God like God's Church in which our fatherland and government have always firmly rested'.[36]

---

[52] Ibid.   [53] Ibid. p. 476; *MPG* p. 563.
[54] Bishop Velimirović's position was different. He stood out among all the bishops as a spiritual leader and preacher and his prestige was even greater than the patriarch's. But he was compromised by his close personal friendship with Ljotić, the Serbian fascist leader, who was fervently religious and sang in the cathedral choir; Velimirović did not support him politically but their friendship was well known (Orthodox source).
[55] Slijepčević, p. 670.   [56] *Gl.*, 1.iv.44.

Croatia

The defeat of Yugoslavia was looked upon by most Croats as a release from the prison of the Serbian-dominated state. The Germans had established connections with Dr Ante Pavelić, the Ustaša leader, who was living in exile in Italy and enjoyed Mussolini's support; when Maček, whom they would have preferred, rebuffed their overtures and joined the Simović government, the Germans turned to him. On April 10, the Independent State of Croatia (NDH) was proclaimed in Zagreb by Slavko Kvaternik, the commander of the underground Ustaša forces, in the name of Pavelić, who arrived five days later.

The Catholic Church, headed by Dr Aloysius (Alojzije) Stepinac, the Archbishop of Zagreb, welcomed the new state without any apparent reserve. Dr Stepinac called on Kvaternik on April 12, immediately after the proclamation of the NDH, and on April 16 was received by Pavelić,[57] the Poglavnik (Leader), who had arrived from Italy the previous day.[58] Both these visits took place before the signing of the act of surrender by a representative of the Yugoslav government on April 17; this was a detail which Stepinac, in the confusion of the time, and with the Kingdom of Yugoslavia breaking up before his eyes, could not have taken into account. He had, nevertheless, taken an oath of allegiance to the monarchy when he was consecreted, and at the time of his trial after the war, this point was brought against him. He was, at the very least, not showing the caution which the Holy See always exercises towards changes in jurisdiction brought about by war. The Catholic bishops were not able to meet until the end of June, but although by then tension had already set in, they paid an official visit to Pavelić, led by Stepinac, and cordial speeches were exchanged.[59]

As a young man Stepinac had supported the idea of Yugoslav unity, and in 1916, taken prisoner-of-war in Italy, he had volunteered to fight for the Allies in the Yugoslav Legion on the Salonika front. His career was unusual. He came from a peasant family in Krašić, a village in the mountains south-west of Zagreb. He had a late vocation and had even at one time contemplated marriage, but had renounced this and was sent by his bishop to study in Rome, where he spent seven years and was ordained priest in 1930 at the age of thirty-two. He returned to Zagreb as master of ceremonies to Archbishop Bauer, and three and a half years later, in 1934, when he was still only thirty-six, was named archbishop coadjutor with right of succession. His service on the

[57] *Katolički List*, 16.iv.41.   [58] Auty, *Tito*, p. 167.
[59] *Katolički Tjednik* (Zagreb weekly), 6.vii.41.

Salonika front stood him in good stead; no other likely candidate was acceptable to King Alexander, and although there was no formal need for a royal assent, names of future bishops were customarily submitted to Belgrade for approval. When Archbishop Bauer died in 1937, Stepinac, aged thirty-nine, only seven years a priest, and with no experience of a parish, became archbishop of one of the largest dioceses in Europe.[60] But his attitude towards Yugoslav union was changing. At the 1938 election he had vigorously denied a statement broadcast by the government-controlled radio that he was voting for the Serbian-dominated government and made it clear that he supported the Peasant Party led by Maček,[61] and in 1940 he had taken the occasion of a sermon, preached in front of the regent, Prince Paul, in St Mark's Church in Zagreb to express plainly his feelings about Serbian domination. (He referred obliquely to this in a sermon during the war when he was criticising the NDH.)[62]

The visits to Kvaternik and Pavelić could be interpreted simply as formal gestures from the chief representative of the church to the leaders of the state, but the tone of the circular which he issued to the clergy on April 28[63] welcoming the creation of the 'young Croat state' was rapturous, and showed that he had fallen entirely under the spell of the Croat myth: 'The times are such that it is no longer the tongue which speaks but the blood through its mysterious union with the earth, in which we have glimpsed the light of God, and with the people from which we sprang...it is easy to discern the hand of God at work.' It was a serious lapse of judgment, considering the quarter from which independence was being offered to Croatia. He was bitterly disillusioned when he found that the new leaders had agreed to Italy's annexation of the Dalmation coast; it was a disillusionment which was shared by the majority of the Croats.[64]

Publicly he gave the Ustaša leaders the benefit of the doubt and the circular contains the passage: 'Knowing the men who today govern the destinies of the Croatian people, we are deeply convinced that our work will go forward with full understanding and help. We are convinced and expect that the church in the resurrected state of Croatia will be able to proclaim in complete freedom the uncontestable principles of eternal truth and justice'; and he sounded a warning note to the government when

[60] *Šematizam*, pp. 46–7; Benigar, *passim*; Catholic sources.
[61] Benigar, p. 211.
[62] Sermon, 25.x.43: Pattee, doc. xv, p. 279.
[63] *Katolički List*, 29.iv.41.
[64] *Hrvatska Revija*, March 1966: Ivan Meštrović wrote that Stepinac wept over this; Benigar, p. 363.

he used the phrase: 'Verbum Dei non est alligatum' ('the word of God is not bound' – 2 Timothy 2.9). But behind the scenes tensions had already set in. Pavelić set off for Italy almost immediately to invite the Duke of Spoleto, a cousin of the King of Italy, to accept the 'crown of Zvonimir', a medieval Croatian king. He was accompanied by a delegation which should have included the archbishop. But Pavelić was unwilling to invite Stepinac; and Stepinac on his side was equally determined not to go. He instructed his elderly and aristocratic auxiliary, Bishop Count Salis-Seewis, to go in his stead, and Salis-Seewis, who was uneasy about the whole idea, grumbled, but obeyed. A few months before his death in 1967 he told the story in an interview. Although he was already a very old man his faculties were unimpaired and his reminiscences were clear and lively:

The relations between Pavelić and Stepinac from the beginning were tense and Stepinac didn't go with Pavelić on the delegation. So they looked for someone else and Archbishop Stepinac invited me. I told him I didn't like the idea of being mixed up in this business – I didn't like anything about it. I knew that the people from the Peasant Party were against it; those people were already in sympathy with the English and French. So it wasn't a good thing for me to get mixed up with the question of the 'young king'. The archbishop answered, 'That's the way it is!' (*Kaj je, je*)...at that moment we couldn't all withdraw and someone had to go, as a matter of form. So I had to go...[65]

The Duke of Spoleto accepted and assumed the style of Tomislav II, but was too prudent to travel to Zagreb, and spent the rest of the war in Italy.

On the evening of April 18, 1941, after his offer of the crown of Croatia had been accepted, the Poglavnik was received in private audience by Pope Pius XII.[66] Pavelić was eager for official recognition of the NDH by the Vatican but never managed to achieve more than a form of *de facto* recognition. On June 13, 1941, Mgr Ramiro Marcone, Abbot of Monte Cassino, and not a member of the Vatican diplomatic service, was appointed apostolic visitor; he remained in Zagreb until the end of the war,

[65] *Glas Koncila*, 16.viii.67.
[66] *Katolički List*, 23.v.41. There was some anxiety about this at the Vatican. The Italian government pressed very hard for Pavelić's suite to be received with him but the Vatican was careful not to be manoeuvred into a form of recognition and insisted that this was a private and personal audience. Pavelić's suite were eventually allowed to attend a public audience the following day as ordinary members of the faithful. Neither Pavelić nor the Duke of Spoleto, who also had a private audience of the pope, were received by the secretary of state, which might have implied recognition, and the latter circulated nuncios and apostolic delegates to explain the strictly private nature of the pope's reception of the two men (Vatican Docs., pp. 498, 500, 502, 504).

able to journey freely between Zagreb and Rome, leading an active social and diplomatic life and travelling around the country.[67]

The assault on the Serbian Orthodox Church. The new government at once showed that it intended to cleanse the state of all Serbian elements. A series of decrees was issued: on April 25 the use of the Cyrillic script was forbidden;[68] all kindergartens and primary and secondary schools run by the Orthodox Church were closed;[69] the special 10 per cent tax paid by the Orthodox to the patriarchate, which was one of its chief sources of revenue, was abolished and Serbs were ordered to wear coloured armbands;[70] the use of the term 'Serbian Orthodox religion' was forbidden and the term 'Greek Oriental religion' substituted.[71]

Mile Budak, the minister of education, said on June 22 at Gospić that one-third of the Serbs in the NDH would be expelled, one-third killed and one-third converted to Catholicism.[72] In contrast to the implacable hatred for Serbs and the Serbian Orthodox Church, the Moslems of Bosnia–Hercegovina, who were assumed to be Croat by origin, were treated as brothers and allies. Although Budak was to say only a month later, 'our whole work is based on our fidelity to the church and the Catholic faith, for history teaches us that if we had not been Catholic, we should soon have ceased to exist,'[73] he proclaimed in the same speech at Gospić that the NDH was to be a nation of two religions, Catholic and Moslem. Three minarets were added to the large circular art gallery built on one of Zagreb's central squares to house Ivan Meštrović's sculptures, and it was turned over to the Moslem religious community for a mosque.

An agreement for the deportation of Serbs in Croatia was signed between the NDH and the German authorities in Serbia on June 4, 1941, and an organisation, the Državno Ravnateljstvo za Ponovu (State Directorate for Renewal) was set up on June 24

---

[67] Falconi, pp. 324, 343; Benigar, pp. 372ff.
[68] *Narodne Novine* (official NDH newspaper), 25.iv.41. This and references in nn. 69–71 quoted in *SPC*, pp. 183–4.
[69] Ibid. 21.vi.41.
[70] *Narodne Novine*, 25.vi.41; Slijepčević, p. 674, adds 'Jews', citing *Tajni dokumenti*, p. 90.
[71] Ibid. 19.vii.41; *Hrvatski Narod* (official NDH newspaper), 21.vii.41.
[72] *Hrvatski Narod*, 26.vi.41, and *SPC*, p. 124; also in Basta, p. 91; *Magnum Crimen* also quotes (p. 605) but gives no source.
[73] Budak was one of the leading Croat writers of the day. The *Enciclopedia Cattolica* says of him: 'above all other contemporary prose writers enters into the perspective of eternal light by his elemental creative force, by the richness of his language and his contemplation of existence' (vol. VII, p. 612b, 1951).

to organise and oversee the operation; camps to serve as assembly points were established at Slavonska Požega, Bjelovar and Caprag near Sisak.[74] Arrests of Serbs began in July; they took place at night, as rapidly and as quietly as possible. Families were given thirty minutes to prepare themselves for the journey to the camps.[75] The reasonably humane orders issued to regulate the deportations were disregarded from the start. By the middle of July the camps were overflowing, food was insufficient, arrangements for sending the deportees on into Serbia were breaking down and there was growing danger of epidemics. Through a combination of bureaucracy, inefficiency and brutality, the operation, which brought a catastrophic upheaval in the lives of tens of thousands of people, rapidly degenerated into chaos, which the German command in Serbia finally put an end to by refusing to accept any more transports.[76] They were beginning to find that the methods of the ustaše were driving people into the resistance; the S.S. themselves were shocked by the behaviour of the Ustaša units:

The atrocities perpetrated by the Ustaša units against the Orthodox in Croatian territory must be regarded as the most important reason for the blazing up of guerrilla activities. The Ustaša units have carried out their atrocities not only against male Orthodox of military age, but in particular in the most bestial fashion against unarmed old men, women and children... because of these atrocities innumerable Orthodox have fled to rump Serbia and their reports have roused the Serbian population to great indignation.[77]

The leaders of the Catholic Church themselves, in particular Archbishop Stepinac of Zagreb and Bishop Mišić of Mostar, were beginning to realise that the ustaše were driving people into the Partisans, and doing great harm to the church.

An estimated 15,250 Serbs passed through these camps before the operation was suspended in the autumn.[78] But the refugees continued to stream out; after the war the Serbian Orthodox Church estimated that by 1943 there were 300,000 Serbian refugees from the NDH alone in Serbia.[79] Among the deported were 334 Serbian Orthodox priests (out of a total of 577 in the territory of the NDH) together with 259 wives and 467 children. Most of these had been arrested during the night of July 10/11 and sent to the assembly camps. Although they were legally

[74] SPC, p. 194
[75] Circular of Državno Ravnateljstvo za Ponovu, 2.vii.41: Lisac, pp. 128–9.
[76] Lisac, p. 145.
[77] Akten, doc. 277; Security Police Report of 17.ii.42: Causes of the insurgent movements and guerilla activities.
[78] Lisac, pp. 137, 145
[79] Sin. 1060/237/1947: SPC, p. 195.

entitled to 50 kg of luggage each, many were stripped of their possessions in the camps.[80]

The bishops were dealt with separately. Bishop Irinej Djordjević of Dalmatia was arrested and imprisoned by the Italians and later interned in Italy. He was freed in 1944 and after a brief stay in Rome went to the United States and later to England where he died.[81] Bishop Nektarije Krulj of Zvornik–Tuzla in Bosnia and Bishop Nikolaj Jovanović of Zahumlje–Hercegovina (Mostar) were expelled from their dioceses and went to Serbia;[82] Metropolitan Dositej Vasić of Zagreb was arrested and imprisoned immediately after the proclamation of the NDH, severely beaten and eventually expelled to Serbia. He died in January 1945 from the long-term effects of his ill-treatment.[83] Metropolitan Petar Simonjić of Dabar–Bosnia left Sarajevo briefly for the monastery of Sv. Trojica near Plevlja, but on April 21 he returned to Sarajevo and refused to obey the order to leave. He was arrested on May 12 and on May 15 was transferred to Zagreb prison, shaved, deprived of his ring and cloak and then transferred to a concentration camp – either Gospić or Jasenovac – where he died shortly afterwards.[84] Bishop Sava Trljajić of Gornjikarlovac (in western Croatia) and nine of his clergy were declared hostages when the ustaše took over from the Italians on May 21, 1941. On June 8 he was ordered to leave but refused, declaring that he was bound by canon law to remain in his diocese. Together with three of his priests and thirteen other Serbs he was imprisoned on June 17 and two days later taken to the concentration camp at Gospić where he remained until mid-August. He was then taken together with two thousand other Serbs from the camp to a ravine in the Velebit mountains where they were all killed.[85] On April 10, the day on which the NDH was proclaimed, Bishop Platon Jovanović of Banja Luka was ordered to leave his see within five days. He answered in a dignified letter refusing to break his oath as bishop, but adding that if he was removed by force he must, according to canon law, ask his two neighbouring fellow bishops to take over his duties. On May 4 two police agents came to his residence and ordered him to leave Banja Luka immediately. He appealed to the Roman Catholic Bishop Garić to intervene so that he could at least have two or three days to prepare. Bishop Garić promised to do so and assured him that he would be quite safe. That night,

[80] *SPC*, p. 195.   [81] Ibid. p. 189.
[82] Ibid.   [83] Ibid. p. 186.
[84] Ibid. p. 188, quoting sin. 1060/237/1947.
[85] Ibid. p. 189, quoting sin. 1060/237/1947.

however, six men, led by the bodyguard of the local Ustaša chief, a man notorious for his savagery, burst into the house and forced Bishop Platon to come with them. Together with one of his priests he was driven to a place several kilometres outside the city on the banks of the river Vrbanja, where they were both murdered and thrown into the river. A few days later their bodies were found, washed ashore, and buried.[86]

Only a tiny handful of priests managed to remain.[87] Aside from the human losses there was widespread pillaging and deliberate destruction of churches; one authority estimates a quarter of all churches and monasteries were completely destroyed.[88] It was a fearful toll.

The killings, conversions and deportations continued all summer and into the autumn, when the frenzy at last began to die down. An attempt to complete the de-Serbianisation of the remaining Orthodox and separate them from the influence of the Serbian Orthodox Church vows was made the following spring when Pavelić decreed the establishment of a Croatian Orthodox Church. Bishop Hermogen of the Russian Orthodox Church Abroad (which had established its see at Sremski Karlovci after the Russian revolution) was persuaded to become its head. As soon as the Holy Synod of the Serbian Orthodox Church heard the news they pronounced the new church uncanonical and informed the metropolitan of the Russian Church Abroad; the occupation authorities refused to allow them to inform their sister churches in Greece and Romania and at Constantinople or to publish their decision in *Glasnik*. In August 1944 Pavelić nominated Spiridon Mifka, another émigré Russian priest, a married man who had been suspended from priestly duties in 1936 for his unworthy life, to be bishop of Sarajevo, and he was consecrated by Hermogen and a Romanian bishop. A very few Serbian Orthodox priests who had remained in the NDH and were still at liberty cooperated with the new church in an effort

---

[86] Ibid. p. 187, quoting sin. 1060/237/1947, and *Spomenica*, pp. 24–5. See also n. 48 above. Bishop Platon and Metropolitan Dositej had been two of the most outspoken opponents of the concordat with the Vatican.

[87] There are various estimates of the number of priests who were killed, deported to Serbia or managed to escape. *SPC* (pp. 195–6) gives a total of 577 Serbian Orthodox priests and monks; of these 217 were killed (including 3 bishops), 334 were deported with their families, 18 managed to escape, 5 died natural deaths and 3 were imprisoned. The total agrees with the figures given by Lisac, but *SPC* (p. 193 n. 53) rejects his statement that all priests who were not deported managed to escape. *Glasnik* (1.iv.46) gives 170 priests killed and 3 bishops, and a total of 499 priests who either fled or were deported; Slijepčević (p. 687) gives 171 priests (including bishops) killed.

[88] Slijepčević, p. 687.

to protect their parishioners; these were later forgiven and taken back into the church, but Hermogen and Spiridon eventually paid dearly for their adventure.[89]

The Catholic Church and the NDH. In the meantime the Catholic Church was anticipating a great spate of conversions and was getting ready to welcome the converts with open arms. But from the beginning the state took the initiative in this matter and kept it during the dreadful events of the spring and summer of 1941 in the face of the church's ineffectual attempts to exercise some mollifying influence. On May 15 the NDH authorities passed a new law[90] which cancelled the previous complicated procedure, inherited from the Austrians, for converting from one faith to another. All that was necessary was to make a written application to the proper authorities and request a certificate stating that the convert had fulfilled the requirements of the faith to which he wished to change. Many Catholics had become Orthodox before the war as the result of various pressures: because of mixed marriages, or to gain advancement.[91] Articles appeared in the government press, based on the theory of the Rev. Dr Krunoslav Draganović, that under Turkish domination many Catholics had passed to Orthodoxy,[92] and that conversion to Catholicism was simply a return to the faith of their fathers.

On the same day that the new law appeared the Zagreb archbishopric issued circular 4104/41 to the clergy setting out the principles for conversion to the Catholic faith, and emphasising that the convert must come of his own free will.[93] Great understanding was to be shown to Catholics who had gone over to Orthodoxy under pressure and now wished to return. On June 11 a further circular set out precise and complicated rules, based on canon law, for accepting converts and validating mixed marriages.[94] But the government on its side was determined to eliminate the Serbian Orthodox intelligentsia, who would be

---

[89] *SPC*, pp. 202ff.

[90] Zakonska odredba o prijelazu od jedne vjere na drugu [Legal regulations for converting from one religion to another], 15.v.41; Slijepčević, p. 678.

[91] In mixed marriages the Catholic spouse was considered by the Serbian Orthodox Church to have become Orthodox and was received without further formalities. In spite of the strict Catholic rules about marriage, many Catholic women became Orthodox in this way, and some Catholic men, who found their careers thus enhanced. In other cases Hungarian law – never recognised by the Catholic Church – that in mixed marriages girls followed the mother and boys the father, was followed. It was a very sore point with the Catholic Church.

[92] 'Massenübertritte von Katoliken zur 'Orthodoxie' im kroatischen Sprachgebiet zur Zeit der Türkenherrschaft (Rome, 1937; offprint from *Orientalia Christiana*), quoted in *SPC*, p. 197.

[93] Pattee, doc. L., and *Katolički List*, 15.v.41.   [94] Pattee, doc. LI.

difficult to control, and to allow only peasants and the uneducated to convert to Catholicism; they even insisted that converts must accept the Latin rite and not the Uniate, in order to break their ties with Orthodoxy as completely as possible. The Rev. Radoslav Glavaš, a Franciscan who was head of the Religious Section of the ministry of justice and religious affairs, wrote to the bishops on July 14 informing them about the rules which the government had made for receiving Orthodox into the Catholic Church: no Orthodox could be received into the Greek rite of the Catholic Church (the Uniates, of whom there is a considerable group in Yugoslavia); in general no teachers, priests, merchants, rich artisans and peasants or intelligentsia should be received into the church; individuals who had close links with the Catholic Church (i.e. spouses of Croat Catholics) might be received with permission from the ministry; the lower and poorer sections of the Orthodox population might be received after instruction.[95]

This was a direct challenge to the church's authority in a spiritual matter. It was answered, in a letter signed by Auxiliary Bishop Lach, on July 16 avoiding a confrontation but making it clear that the terms of order were unacceptable.[96] It would be against the spirit and teachings of the church to refuse to receive anyone who had asked to become a Catholic, and the church had always considered the Greek rite equal to the Latin one. The government ignored this letter and issued a circular[97] on July 30 proclaiming the rules which had been set out in its communication to the bishops. In order to speed conversions the state began to enlist parish priests, without the permission of their bishops, to carry out this work.

What the 'work' entailed in reality began to seep out slowly, carried most often by word of mouth. Throughout the territory of the NDH, along the old military frontier, in Lika and particularly in Bosnia–Hercegovina, where there was a large Serbian population, many living in predominantly Serbian village communities, there took place a wholesale slaughter of Serbs, some of whom had refused or were not given the choice of conversion, some even after they had submitted to mass conversion. This had already begun by the end of April. By the summer Stepinac was receiving reports from other bishops[98] of terrible atrocities.

The evidence that a number of priests, particularly in Bosnia–

[95] Unnumbered mimeograph copy of letter.
[96] 9259/41, 16.vii.41.   [97] No. 48468: *Katolički List*, 8.viii.41.
[98] Notably Bishop Mišić of Mostar (Pattee, doc. LII, p. 388).

Hercegovina, were implicated in these comes not only from communist but also from Vatican, Italian and British sources. Many depositions by eye-witnesses, most of whom had themselves suffered, were made after the war and published in *Dokumenti*. Cardinal Tisserant, in a conversation with Dr Rušinović, the NDH representative in Rome, accused the Franciscans, especially in Bosnia–Hercegovina, of behaving abominably and referred to Father Šimić of Knin, who had taken part in attacks on the Serbian population;[99] the newspaper *Resto del Carlino* of Bologna published on September 18 1941, an enquiry by Corrado Zoli of the Italian Geographical Society, quoting eye-witness accounts.[100] The writer Evelyn Waugh, an ardent Catholic, who was a captain in the 37th Military Mission, mentions in a report written later that 'a ruffian in Ustaša uniform bearing the name of Majstorović, who was practising great cruelties on the prisoners at the notorious Jasenovac concentration camp, was identified as the former friar, Father Filipović. At the same time another priest, Father Brkljačić, was serving as an Ustaša officer. Father Bojanović took office as Prefect of Gospić where he is credibly reported to have taken a hand in the massacre of Orthodox peasants.'[101] In an interview with the Soviet writer Ilya Ehrenburg on October 25, 1945, Father Martinčić, provincial of the Franciscans in Croatia, said that Majstorović had been expelled from the Order in May 1942 for having 'taken part in a punitive expedition' against a Serbian village, and had later left the priesthood and the church; two other former Franciscans, Medić and Prejić, against whom serious accusations had also been made, had disobeyed the orders of their superiors to leave their posts as Ustaša military chaplains and left the Order. Martinčić, who was concerned to clear the bishops and the heads of religious orders of responsibility for the crimes of the priests, added that nearly all the priests known for their Ustaša membership and activities were in the army (as military chaplains) and therefore outside the jurisdiction of their regular superiors.[102] Ciano, the Italian foreign minister, recorded that Pavelić had told him at the end of 1941: 'The Catholic clergy...maintains a very favourable attitude in its lower ranks and less so in the higher grades of the hierarchy. Some of the bishops are openly hostile.'[103]

[99] Falconi, p. 382.   [100] Ibid. p. 299.
[101] F.O. 371/48910, Captain Evelyn Waugh to Brigadier Maclean, 30.iii.45; quoted Rhodes, p. 329. Waugh was reporting events which he had learned second-hand.
[102] Pattee, doc. XLVIII, report to the presidency of the Bishops' Conference on the interview with Ehrenburg.
[103] Ciano, *Diplomatic Papers*, p. 472.

Many of these priests had joined the Ustaša movement before the war. In the report quoted above Captain Evelyn Waugh wrote:

For some time the Croat Franciscans had caused misgivings in Rome for their independence and narrow patriotism. They were mainly recruited from the least cultured part of the population and there is abundant evidence that several wholly unworthy men were attracted to the Franciscan Order by the security and comparative ease which it offered. Many of these youths were sent to Italy for training. Their novitiate was in the neighbourhood of Pavelić's H.Q. at Siena where Ustaša agents made contact with them and imbued them with Pavelić's ideas. They in turn, on returning to their country, passed on his ideas to the pupils in their schools. Sarajevo is credibly described as having been a centre of Franciscan Ustašism.[104]

The Franciscan friary and school at Široki Brijeg in Hercegovina in particular had produced a number of leading ustaše, including Artuković and Djumandžić, ministers in the Ustaša government, Glavaš, the head of the Religious Section, and several other high functionaries.[105]

Estimates of the number who perished during this period vary greatly and there is as yet no generally accepted figure. Official Serbian Orthodox sources give 750,000.[106] A report of the German security police dated February 17, 1942, says: 'The number of Orthodox who have been butchered and tortured to death by the most sadistic methods must number an estimated 300,000 persons'[107] – a contemporary estimate made before the killings had ceased. One of the most reliable historians of the period estimates a minimum of 350,000 and thinks this may be too low.[108] Dr Edvard Kardelj, in a speech to the Federal Assembly on December 10, 1952, referred to 'Several hundred thousand killed, 128 Serbian Orthodox priests killed, 25,000 Jews killed, 299 Serbian Orthodox churches burnt'.[109] The slaughter was often carried out with sadistic cruelty;[110] the victims were hacked to death, buried alive after being forced to dig their own graves, hideously tortured and mutilated before being despatched; and in the village of Glina, which became a symbol of Serb suffering, all the male Serbian inhabitants, together with their priest, were locked inside the church and slaughtered. The Serbs retaliated with equal brutality particularly against Moslems; Dedijer's war

[104] Rhodes, p. 328. [105] *Dokumenti*, p. 307.
[106] SPC, p. 201.
[107] *Akten*, doc. 277: Security Police Report, 17.ii.42.
[108] Tomasevich, p. 367.
[109] *Borba*, 19.xii.52.
[110] See *Dokumenti*, pp. 124ff, and *MPG*, p. 521.

diary contains many references to this and information even seeped abroad.[111]

In addition somewhere between 200,000 and 300,000 Orthodox were forcibly converted or asked to be received into the Catholic Church to escape the slaughter.[112] This figure is again tentative and the true numbers will probably never be known. The German security police report of February 17, 1942, quotes a memorandum from the Orthodox Church giving the figure of 10,000 forcibly converted up to that date.[113] The report contains the passage 'It is the case that Serbs living in Croatia who have joined the Catholic Church may live unharmed', showing that reports of the slaughter of some of the converted had not yet reached them. The conversions were at their height from May to September 1941 and then began to tail off, but continued sporadically until 1943.

It is difficult to unravel the attitude of the bishops, particularly of Stepinac, to these events, but it is necessary to try in view of the accusations which were brought against the church and the hierarchy after the war. In principle they welcomed the prospect of thousands of converts; they believed that the Catholic Church, with the pope at its head, was the only true church, and that the Orthodox were schismatics, 'separated ones' who must be brought freely to see the error of their ways and return to their true mother.[114] But these lofty theological concepts had become deeply coloured over the centuries by national and cultural differences between the Croats and the Serbs. Croats were Catholics and Serbs Orthodox; nationality was identified with religion and Serbs who lived in Croatia were not Croatian in any sense which Croats understood.[115] The Croats felt themselves to be European, heirs in part of a great Catholic empire, while the Serbs belonged to the Byzantine East with its ecclesiastical quarrels and schisms. The Croats were used to belonging to a majority religion and had never felt quite comfortable inside

---

[111] Eight hundred Croats were reported killed by Serbs in Krnjeuša (*Tydningen* of Stockholm, 29.viii.41, quoted in *Review of the Foreign Press*, ser. B, July 1941 – June 1942); Roberts, p. 68, quoting Živko Topalović; Maček, p. 231: the inhabitants of two villages in Hercegovina massacred by Četniks in the middle of April 1941; Dedijer, *With Tito*, pp. 56, 58, 61, 63, 64, 65.

[112] Tomasevich, p. 79.   [113] *Akten*, doc. 277.

[114] The diocesan printing press in Djakovo published leaflets addressed to the 'Greek-Eastern' faithful inviting them all to come as soon as possible to the bishopric for conversion to Catholicism (*Gl.*, 1.iv.46).

[115] This was one of the cardinal reproaches made by the communists against the church. To describe Croatia as a Catholic country was an insult to its Serbian and Moslem inhabitants, who equally were citizens – cf. Bakarić's speech to Zagreb students, 25.iv.46 (*Vjesnik*, 30.iv.46).

Yugoslavia where they were in a minority; the Serbs too who had been in an overwhelming Orthodox majority in former Serbia felt uneasy beside a large Catholic minority.[116] The Croats had defended the Catholic West against the Turks and earned the title of 'antemurale Christianitatis'.[117] The Franciscans, devoted and zealous, had laboured for five hundred years in the wild mountains of Bosnia and the arid *karst* of Hercegovina; they had secured for themselves the right to serve as parish priests (and frequently as bishops) in these regions and defended this right jealously against the diocesan clergy; their provincial was as powerful as the bishop and always ready to assert his independence from episcopal control.[118] Suddenly the power of Belgrade was removed, and the bishops saw within their grasp the intoxicating prospect of a huge influx of converts to be led gently back into the fold, a precious gift for the Holy See.[119] Catholicism would become indisputably the majority religion and the Croats the national majority[120] and the victory in the centuries-old struggle for predominance would be won.

The enthusiasm of the bishops at this prospect is understandable, but their public silence in the face of the consequences is more difficult to accept. Their moral confusion provoked a protest from a former member of the Yugoslav government, G. Grisogono, who had remained in Yugoslavia, and who wrote to Stepinac in July 1942:

The inhuman and anti-Christian attitude of the many Croat Catholic priests has dismayed not only some of their brothers but the majority of Croat intellectuals to whom I belong. I have been struck by the absence of all public manifestation of Christian and human sympathy from the Croat hierarchy to the victims of an indescribable regime of massacre and illegality against Orthodox fellow countrymen. I have asked myself with anguish why Croatian Catholic circles have not disavowed publicly in the name of the Catholic Church the forced conversion of the Orthodox and the confiscation of their goods?'[121]

---

[116] Spinka, p. 244.
[117] Cardinal Tisserant was scornful of this claim: 'The Serbs gave the West and Catholicism as much as the Croats, perhaps even more. The Croats were called "antemurale Christianitatis" because they were Catholics' (conversation with Dr Rušinović: Falconi, p. 388; Slijepčević, p. 685, quoting *Tajni dokumenti*, p. 118).   [118] A situation which still persists today.
[119] This phrase was used actually by Rušinović, the NDH unofficial representative in Rome. In a letter to Prince Lobkowicz, (q.v.42), who succeeded him, referring to the establishment of the Croatian Orthodox Church as a step towards a Uniate Church and the disappearance of schism in Croatia: 'this would be the most precious gift which the Croatians could offer to the Holy See' (Slijepčević, p. 684, quoting *Tajni dokumenti*, p. 118).
[120] Since Serbs converted to Catholicism would be counted as Croats.
[121] *Le Monde*, 27.v.53.

A group of Slovenes expelled from Slovenia to Serbia wrote to Archbishop Ujčić in Belgrade protesting, asking that their protest be transmitted to the Holy See and begging the Vatican to forbid any further conversions in present circumstances; instead the Catholic bishops should take the Serbian Orthodox and their priests under their protection, 'with an apostolic courage to meet any sacrifice'.[122] Stepinac, who was so fired by the realisation of Croat independence and who had burnt his boats as far as the former Kingdom of Yugoslavia was concerned, may well have found it hard to accept at first the extent of Ustaša misdeeds, although he was quick to defend the prerogatives of the church against encroachments. He and some of the other bishops watched with dismay the heaven-sent opportunity being thrown away by the brutal methods of men over whom they had no control. Bishop Mišić of Mostar had already issued a circular[123] to all his priests instructing them to tell their congregations from the pulpit that those who murdered or misappropriated the possessions of others would not be granted absolution. Two months later he wrote to Stepinac:

This can serve neither the holy Catholic cause nor the Croatian cause...we might have emerged into a majority in Bosnia–Hercegovina and instead of coveting favours from others be able to dispense them ourselves...In the interests of Croatia and the church I say to His Excellency that we must do all in our power to prevent these disastrous consequences.[124]

Bishop Mišić wrote again on November 7:

At one time it seemed that a large number of schismatics would be converted to the Catholic Church. However (the Ustaša officials)...have abused their positions...with the result that a reign of terror has come to pass...Men are captured like animals, they are slaughtered, murdered, living men are thrown off cliffs. The under-prefect in Mostar, Bajić, a Moslem, has said – it would be better if he kept silent instead of saying such things – that at Ljubinje, in a single day, 700 schismatics were thrown into their graves. From Mostar and from Čapljina a train took six carloads of mothers, young girls, and children...to Šurmanci ...they were led up the mountains and the mothers together with their children were thrown alive off the precipices...In the town of Mostar itself they have been bound by the hundreds, taken in wagons outside the town and then shot down like animals.[125]

Mišić goes on to say that a deputation of Serbs waited on Mussolini in Rome to beg for his protection, with the result that

[122] *Tajni dokumenti*, pp. 98–9.
[123] *SVNZ*, 6.xi.45; date of circular: 30.vi.41.
[124] No. 968/41, 18.viii.41, quoted by Stepinac in a letter to Pavelić, 30.xi.41 (Pattee, doc. LII, p. 389).   [125] 1253/41, quoted by Stepinac as above.

the Italians reoccupied Hercegovina, the Serbian Orthodox priests came out of hiding and the schismatic churches came to life again under Italian protection.[126] The cooperation between the Italian Army and the Četniks was a source of considerable irritation to the church; Stepinac discussed it during his visit to the Vatican in 1942.[127] Mišić adds: 'If the Lord had given to the authorities more understanding to handle the conversions to Catholicism with skill and intelligence...and at a more appropriate time, the number of Catholics would have grown by at least 500,000 to 600,000 and thus in Bosnia–Hercegovina we would have moved from the present number of 700,000 to 1,300,000.'[128]

Archbishop Šarić of Sarajevo, a strong supporter of the ustaše,[129] from whose facile pen flowed many adulatory verses dedicated to the Poglavnik (and to the Emperor Franz Joseph, the Emperor Charles and Maček among others as well), was concerned at the high excise stamp demanded on certificates of conversion, the deliberate delaying tactics of Moslem officials and the attitude of the Evangelical Church which saw no reason why it too should not receive converts from Orthodoxy.[130] Stepinac was concerned to show Pavelić that it was both unwise and uncanonical to forbid converts from Orthodoxy to join Greek Catholic parishes where they would feel more at home than in the Latin rite.

The bishops met in conference again on November 17 and 18, 1941, for the last time until March 1945. Communications were already very difficult and a number of bishops were unable to be present. After the conference Stepinac sent a long letter to Pavelić. He began by giving the decisions of the Bishops' Conference concerning conversions: these lay exclusively within the province of the bishops, no one but the bishops had the right to appoint 'missionaries' to take charge of the conversions; the bishops could only recognise conversions as valid if they had been carried out according to these dogmatic and canonical principles, and the civil authority had no right to annul valid conversions; to be valid, conversions must be carried out without constraint

126 The Italian Army had orders to prevent massacres on religious pretexts; the slowing-down of the massacres after 1942 was due partly to their presence and partly to the growing activity of Serbian Četnik bands on the territory of the NDH (Falconi, pp. 292–3).

127 Ibid. p. 320.

128 Pattee, doc. LII.

129 Falconi alleges that he became a member in 1934. He visited groups of ustaše in South America before the war, and after the murder of King Alexander in 1934 (Dokumenti, pp. 27–8).

130 Pattee, loc. cit. Falconi, p. 286, quotes the letter of the Evangelical Bishop Popp to the Croatian government on this subject.

of any kind. A Committee of Three, Archbishop Stepinac, Bishop Burić of Senj and Bishop Šimrak of Križevci, was appointed to oversee the conversions and would work in agreement with the minister of justice and religion where civil regulations were concerned.

This further effort to assert control over the conversions was as ineffectual as the previous ones; the committee appears to have done no work at all.[131]

The letter continued with very grave charges about events in the country. He was already seriously concerned about reports which had been reaching him, but he could not bring himself to believe that the leaders of the NDH approved of such behaviour. He concluded his letter to Pavelić:

No one can deny that these terrible acts of violence and cruelty have been taking place, for you yourself, Poglavnik, have publicly condemned those which the ustaše have committed and you have ordered executions because of their crimes. The Croat nation has been proud of its thousand-year-old culture and the Christian tradition. That is why we wait for it to show in practice, now that it has achieved its freedom, a greater nobility and humanity than that displayed by its former rulers...All men are the children of God and Christ died for all...we are sure, Poglavnik, that you hold the same position and that you will do all in your power to restrain the violence of certain individuals...If the contrary were true, all work for the conversion of schismatics would be illusory.[132]

These, however, were all private protests. From 1942 onwards Stepinac denounced the injustices and false ideology of the NDH in public sermons in increasingly precise terms.[133] At the end of May 1942 he said:

Our true relations with our neighbour demand that we see in him a man...a child of God...our brother, whom we must love...it would

[131] Pattee, doc. C, p. 235: speech for the defence of Archbishop Stepinac by Dr N. Katičić.
[132] Pattee, doc. LII, p. 395. An article written at the end of 1945 in the official gazette of the Zagreb archdiocese (SVNZ, 19.xi.45) states that this letter aroused great hostility to Stepinac in government circles, but it had an effect and some officials in Hercegovina were replaced. The article alleges that the NDH had decided at this time to arrest Stepinac, but later changed its mind. Cavalli (p. 326) states that it had asked the Vatican on at least three occasions to have Stepinac removed. He gives Masucci, the secretary of Marcone, Vatican representative in Croatia, as the source of this story.
[133] It is worth noting that Stepinac never took an oath of allegiance either to the NDH or to Pavelić personally, unlike some of the other bishops (evidence of Canon Nicholas Kolarek submitted at Stepinac's trial: Pattee, doc. XLVI, p. 357). In his speech in his own defence at his trial in 1946 Stepinac referred to this: 'I was not an ustaša, nor did I take their oath as did some of the officials of this court whom I see here' (Pattee, doc. D, p. 239; see also ch. 3).

be an absurdity to speak of a new order in the world if the human personality is not valued in that order.[134]

On the feast of St Peter, June 29, 1942, he preached in the cathedral on the pope's unique authority:

It is right that we should at this time remember our brothers, separated for centuries from Peter, the visible head of the Church of Christ, to whom these brothers return to the faith of their forebears. God is our witness that we are against any forcible conversion to the Catholic Church. If they have been converted sincerely...they are today equal members of the Catholic Church which today loves them each with no difference. Let it be said quite clearly that the church will do all in its power to defend these children...If they unhappily are unsuccessful, it is not the fault of the church, but of irresponsible elements who...against the laws of God and man take revenge on innocent people.[135]

On March 14, 1943, concerning the application of racial laws to mixed Jewish and Gentile marriages, he said:

This past week...we have witnessed the tears of those who are in danger of the destruction of their families...We, as representatives of the church, could not and should not keep silent without betraying our mission...No one gives to human authority the right to violate the sanctity of the family or of a marriage.[136]

On October 25, 1943:

all nations and all races have their origin in God. Only one race really exists and that is the divine race...the Catholic Church has always condemned and condemns today as well, every injustice and every violence committed in the name of the theories of class, race or nationality.[137]

And on October 31, 1943, at the end of a procession of penance in Zagreb he said:

The Catholic Church knows nothing of races born to rule and races doomed to slavery. The Catholic Church knows races and nations only as creatures of God...for it the Negro of Central Africa is as much as man as a European. For it the king in a royal palace is, as a man, exactly the same as the poorest pauper or gypsy in his tent.

And later in the same sermon:

[134] In October 1943 he wrote to the military vicar forbidding military chaplains to administer the Ustaša oath if a dagger and revolver were lying beside the crucifix (Pattee, doc. XLIX).
[135] Sermon seen by the writer in Zagreb archbishopric.
[136] Sermon preached in the cathedral on the anniversary of the coronation of Pope Pius XII (Pattee, doc. XIV, p. 274).
[137] Sermon preached at the Feast of Christ the King (Pattee, doc. XV, p. 278).

the system of shooting hundreds of hostages for a crime, when the person guilty of the crime cannot be found, is a pagan system which only results in evil.[138]

He warned the government that their measures were driving people into the forest to join the Partisan bands. The Ustaša leaders were furious. Makanec, the minister for public instruction, in an article in *Nova Hrvatska*[139] referred to 'that high ecclesiastical dignitary who has recently, in his sermons, passed beyond the limits of his vocation and begun to meddle in affairs in which he is not competent'. The sermons were mimeographed and widely circulated clandestinely; the Partisans made use of them in their propaganda and the BBC used them on several occasions in its news broadcasts in Serbo-Croat.[140]

By 1942 evidence also accumulates to show that Stepinac was intervening wherever he could, and when he heard in time, in individual cases of persecution. From the beginning, when the racial laws against Jews were passed, he protested against the application of the laws to Jews converted to Catholicism, or to the Jewish spouse in a mixed marriage: he pleads for Jews 'with Aryan characteristics'.[141] The tone of the letters, mild and conciliatory at the beginning, sharpens as time goes on. He writes at length to Pavelić on March 6, 1943, pointing out that the happiness and prosperity of the state depends on its respect for the natural law of God.[142] He had already protested to Artuković, minister of the interior, on May 22, 1941, against forcing Jews to wear special insignia, saying that if this is enforced against converted Jews he will be obliged to tell them not to wear the yellow badge in church.[143] He intervened repeatedly for Serbs, both on his own initiative and on the request of Archbishop Ujčić of Belgrade[144] and in 1942 he succeeded in removing 7,000 children, some belonging to Partisan families, from camps and putting them into private families where they were cared for until the end of the war.[145] Slovenes who had been expelled and were in camp at Banja Luka appealed to him for help, and he sent them money through Caritas. He was particularly incensed at the arrest of Slovene priests expelled from the German-occupied

[138] Pattee, doc. xvi, p. 285.   [139] 6.xi.43: Pattee, doc. xvii.
[140] In four broadcasts on July 7, 1943: Pattee, doc. xviii.
[141] Pattee, doc. xxv. On the other hand he welcomed the suppression of the 'Old Catholics' and made no protest when the NDH announced in February 1945 that all marriages contracted after April 10, 1941, before an Old Catholic priest were invalid (*Katolički List*, 8.ii.45).
[142] Pattee, doc. xxx, p. 311.   [143] Ibid. doc. xxvi.
[144] *SVNZ*, 19.xi.45, 3.xii.45.   [145] Ibid.

portions of Slovenia; after vainly trying to discover the fate of seven of them, in particular the Rev. Franc Rihar, whose sister had been searching for him, and discovering that they had probably all been executed at Jasenovac, he wrote to Pavelić in great anger: 'This is a disgraceful incident and a crime that cries out to heaven for vengeance. Jasenovac camp itself is a shameful stain on the honour of the NDH.'[146]

Because of conditions in the country the bishops were not able to meet again in conference after November 1941, although a number of them managed to travel to Rome. Stepinac himself made three journeys to Rome during the war, in 1941, in April 1942 and at the end of May 1943; Bishop Srebrnić of Krk at the beginning of June 1943 and Bishop Burić of Senj some time in June 1943,[147] and it must be supposed that the Vatican was well informed about what was going on in Croatia. Stepinac's actions and pronouncements took on special importance, as he was assumed to speak for the whole church.[148]

The religious press during this period was fervently Ustaša in tone. *Katolički List* [The Catholic Gazette], from which many quotations have been taken, was a semi-official organ of the Zagreb diocese; it published official circulars, messages and pastoral letters. The editor was appointed by the archbishop but in practice had considerable editorial freedom, although Stepinac was later accused by the communists of being solely responsible for what went into the paper. *Katolički List* (26. vi. 41) welcomed the attack on the Soviet Union, carried adulatory articles about Pavelić and attacked communism. It was under severe Ustaša censorship; material was removed, altered and also inserted.[149] Many dioceses had as well their own official gazette whose editorials, of course, reflected the official attitudes of the hierarchy, and the religious orders also had their own press.

In 1943 Italy collapsed and withdrew from the war and the NDH found itself at once under German occupation. The chances of the NDH being recognised officially by the Vatican,

---

[146] Pattee, doc. xxxv, 24.ii.43. Further instances are given in chs. 2 and 3.

[147] Falconi, p. 412.

[148] During his trial Dr Politeo, his defence counsel, tried to show how little real power he had, but a series of articles appearing at the end of 1945 in the official gazette of the archbishopric, which were a considered defence of the church's behaviour during the war, took a different line: 'even communication by letter was difficult. Individual bishops were unable for long periods to write to each other...this explains the lack of documentary material from the further regions. This is the reason...that the Catholic episcopacy spoke publicly only through the mouth of the president of the Episcopal Conference, the Archbishop of Zagreb' (*SVNZ*, 6.xi.45).

[149] Catholic source.

which had been canvassed so energetically since its formation by its representatives, Dr Rušinović and Prince Lobkowicz, disappeared as it became obvious that the Axis powers were losing the war.[150]

Stepinac continued to maintain formal relations with the NDH, to sing the Te Deum in the cathedral on the anniversary of the founding of the state[151] and to lead the diplomatic corps when they brought New Year greetings to the Poglavnik.[152] The fighting between Yugoslavs continued alongside the struggle against the Germans; in November 1943 at Jajce the Partisans proclaimed themselves the government of Yugoslavia and were recognised as an Allied Army by the Allied powers at Teheran. Conditions in the countryside were dangerous, as villages fell to first one side and then the other. Two circulars[153] which Stepinac sent to his clergy in the spring and autumn of 1944 reflect the mounting chaos. He exhorts them once more to stay out of politics, and to cultivate friendship and understanding with their parishioners; if serious enmity existed it would be better for the priest to ask to be moved. They should collect tithes and church taxes with consideration – any priest who tried to extract more than his due would be severely punished. He reminded them that relations between the church and the civil authorities were in the exclusive competence of the Holy See: they should stick to pastoral work, stay in their parishes and if necessary store away vestments, holy vessels and precious objects in a safe place.

The last two months before the defeat of Germany were filled with comings and goings among representatives of all the groups opposing the Partisans; they were united principally by their fervent belief that the Western Allies would never allow a

---

[150] Falconi, pp. 333ff. The nearest that the Vatican had come to recognising the legality of the NDH was the appointments of the bishops of Mostar and Križevci, in contravention of its usual practice of appointing apostolic administrators, not bishops, in territories under disputed rule (the action taken after the war in the divided dioceses on the Italian border). The assent of the NDH was not sought, much to Pavelić's anger (Falconi, p. 415). The Vatican had managed to evade the open attempts of the NDH to manoeuvre it into *de facto* recognition, although Mgr Marcone, its representative to the Croatian episcopate, who had the rank of apostolic visitor (not delegate), obviously enjoyed the special attentions heaped on him. His name and that of his secretary Masucci were included in the diplomatic list of the foreign ministry of the NDH and they were invited to official receptions as members of the diplomatic corps, where Marcone was given the official precedence usually accorded to representatives of the Holy See. Prof. Milan Bartoš, 'My Answer to the Vatican Paper Osservatore Romano', *Review of International Affairs*, 1.viii.52, and Falconi, pp. 327–8.

[151] *Katolički List*, 13.iv.44.   [152] Ibid. 8.ii.45.

[153] 3508/44 and 6920/44.

communist take-over of at any rate the western part of Yugoslavia. Stepinac, as head of the Catholic Church, was asked by Pavelić to head a provisional government[154] but refused.[155] Zagreb was full of refugees and of rumours about the behaviour of the advancing Partisan forces. The leaders of the NDH, seeing the defeat of the Axis grow nearer, tried to arrange a simultaneous denunciation of Partisan atrocities by the heads of all the religious communities; a memorandum from Dr Pavao Canki of the ministry of justice and religious affairs, dated March 13, proposing this and giving lists of the persons to be invited to Zagreb for this purpose was published by the Yugoslav authorities after the war.[156] Two Catholic bishops from the Dalmatian coast refused, because of the difficulties of travel and the approach of the Easter festivities,[157] and no statements were issued by the Moslems, the Croatian Orthodox Church or the Evangelical Church, but five bishops, members of the Working Committee of the Bishops' Conference,[158] met and issued a pastoral letter on March 24, 1945. It rejected the accusation that the church was guilty of misdeeds: the Croatian people at the

---

[154] Pattee, doc B, p. 218.

[155] Stepinac always made it a firm rule to have as little to do with politics as possible, and to forbid his clergy to play any active part in political life. He had issued circulars to this effect in 1935 and 1938, and on February 8, 1942, he wrote to Pavelić asking him to relieve from their duties several of his diocesan clergy who were members of the Sabor (Pattee, doc. IV). He persisted in this attitude after the war, and one of his circulars (5027/45, 6.vi.45) to his clergy on this subject was interpreted by the authorities as an unfriendly refusal to cooperate with the new government (Petranović, p. 282). Some of the reasons he gives to Pavelić in his letter run like a thread through sermons and circulars long before the war and have persisted after Stepinac's death: 'Times have changed completely. The population has become unruly, the scourge of birth control decimates their ranks, the people are weighed down with sin and vices of every sort, and there are so few priests.' The problem of the falling Croatian birth-rate, the '*bijela kuga*' (white plague) which was reputed to be decimating the population like the medieval Black Plague, was one of the twin spectres which haunted the church in Croatia. The other was swearing, which the Croats have developed to a fine pitch of inventiveness. The church used regularly to hold 'weeks against swearing'. In April 1945, when the NDH was crumbling before their eyes, when the victorious Partisan armies were sweeping across the country towards Zagreb, when the bishops had just issued a pastoral letter denouncing the iniquities of the communists, and when on the fourth anniversary of the founding of the NDH this theme had been re-echoed in an apocalyptic sermon (see below), Stepinac preached on the following Sunday a powerful discourse against swearing.

[156] *Dokumenti*, pp. 405–7.

[157] Ibid. p. 399: statement by Dr Glavaš, head of the Religious Section of the ministry of justice and religious affairs, made after his arrest.

[158] Stepinac, Šarić of Sarajevo, Garić of Banja Luka, Šimrak of Križevci and Akšamović of Djakovo.

beginning of the war had been attacked by others, and unfortunately the Croats had retaliated,[159] but the bishops in 1941 had raised their voices against excesses in self-defence:

> If by chance some misguided priest has sinned against the rights of his fellow men we would not shrink from punishing him according to the church's laws...but today we must decisively bear witness before God and the world against the systematic murder and torture of innocent Catholic priests and people, most of whom have led blameless lives, illegially condemned for imaginary crimes by those who hate the Catholic Church. The enemies of the Catholic Church, and followers of materialist communism...have begun in Croatia to persecute the clergy and attack the best of the faithful.

And it went on: 'History is the witness that the Croatian people through all its 1,300 years has never ceased to proclaim through plebiscites that it will never renounce the right to freedom and independence which every other nation desires.' No one had the right to accuse the Croatian bishops because during the Second World War they respected the desire of the Croatian people for their own state.[160]

A week earlier, on March 16, Stepinac had addressed a conference of students on the same theme of Croatia's right to independence and its unwillingness to accept any regime imposed by force.[161]

The fourth anniversary of the NDH fell on April 10 and the church again invited the clergy to celebrate a mass of thanksgiving.[162] The sermon preached on that occasion in Zagreb cathedral (not by Stepinac) sounded an apocalyptic note:

> Four years ago the Croatian people created their state and fulfilled the dreams of centuries...delight seized everyone. The Croatian state was founded by the sacrifice of thousands of the best Croatians and largely by the efforts of the Poglavnik and the Ustaša movement...The attitude of the church towards communism is clear, towards those who deny the church's very right to exist, which raises monuments to Satan and Judas Iscariot; who all over the world have killed so many priests and religious, destroyed great numbers of churches, ruined many innocent lives and holds millions in the worst slavery...this movement is not only the greatest enemy of the church in all centuries but the greatest enemy of human freedom. We pray God to help the Croatian people in today's fateful hours to save our state.[163]

[159] An allusion to the Croat accusation that the Serbs had started the killing.
[160] Katolički List, 29.iii.45.
[161] Ibid.
[162] Circular 2571; Katolički List, 29.iii.45.
[163] Katolički List, 12.iv.45.

Slovenia

During the war Slovenia was divided between the Axis powers and completely occupied by them; there was no nominally independent state corresponding to the NDH. The Germans annexed the northern portion as far as the river Sava and immediately began a process of Germanisation and assimilation. Thousands of Slovenes, in particular the intelligentsia, including priests and teachers, were deported to Serbia and Bosnia; some managed to escape south, to the region under Italian control. Those who remained were liable to conscription in the German army, and many were sent to fight on the eastern front.

The always latent rivalry between Germany and Italy in the former territories of the Habsburg Empire operated to the advantage of the inhabitants of the Ljubljana province, the Italian zone. The occupation there was far easier, and was intended to be a contrast to the harsh rule in the German zone in the north. The Italians, indeed, might have had very little trouble here if it had not been for the resistance of the Liberation Front, which began very early and was met by Italian reprisals. A number of Slovene armed organisations were formed with Italian encouragement, to oppose the Liberation Front. The Partisans called these the Bela Garda (White Guard) by analogy with the Russian White Guards who fought against the Bolshevik revolution, and it is by this name that they are generally known.[164]

The situation in Istria and the Julian region, a part of Italy proper but inhabited by a mixed Italian and Slav population, was different again, because of the Italian oppression of the Croat and Slovene inhabitants. The Catholic hierarchy (the dioceses involved were Pola–Parenzo, Trieste and Gorizia) varied in its sympathies, but the lower clergy in the Slav parishes were solidly nationalist; Italian policy fed Slav nationalism and when, during the war, this became identified with the communist struggle against fascism, the choice of sides was inevitable.

These differing circumstances were reflected in the attitude of priests from these three areas towards the war. The greater part of the clergy of the Ljubljana diocese under Bishop Rožman's leadership tolerated or collaborated with the Italian occupation. Those who joined the Liberation Front or sympathised with it came for the most part from the Christian Socialist movement.

---

[164] The much smaller Plava Garda (Blue Guard) consisted of Slovene groups supporting the Serbian Četniks and the government-in-exile in London. The Bela Garda was regrouped after the fall of Italy under the name Domobran (Home Guard).

The clergy from the Maribor diocese who were expelled to the east[165] or who managed to escape south had far greater sympathy for the resistance and some joined the Liberation Front. Bishop Držečnik[166] of Maribor wrote later that 1945 was the year of liberation also for the church because the clergy could return to Slovenia. Many priests in Istria and the Julian March sympathised actively with the resistance for nationalist and cultural reasons; the lenient policy of the Italians did not extend to these regions, especially as regards toleration of the Croat and Slovene languages.

On April 20, 1941, shortly after the Italians had assumed power in Slovenia, Bishop Rožman of Ljubljana, accompanied by the vicar-general and the dean of the cathedral, called on the Italian High Commissioner Emilio Grazioli to thank him for the peaceful occupation of the country and for the continuing religious freedom of the people. He acknowledged the Italians as the legal government of the country and assured Grazioli of the obedience of the people.[167] A few days earlier Archbishop Margotti of Gorizia wrote to Cardinal Maglione that he had visited Ljubljana where the occupation was proceeding peacefully; he was sure that General Romero would know how to make the Slovenes of Ljubljana love him for his rectitude and his open profession of faith.[168]

The friendly relations which Rožman established with the Italians continued after 1943 with the Germans. He was far less reserved in his public attitude, especially to the latter, than either Archbishop Stepinac or Bishop Tomažič of Maribor. A conservative, both in politics and in the church, he had been close to the Clerical Party and was strongly influenced by Dr Ehrlich of the theological faculty in Ljubljana, a man of strong anti-communist views and founder of the extreme right wing of the student movement. When Ehrlich and two students from the faculty were shot by Partisans in the spring of 1942, Rožman's attitude hardened still further, and he used all his influence to dissuade priests from joining the resistance, threatening them with ecclesiastical penalties, although later he allowed the Rev. Anton Ilc to act as spiritual vicar in the liberated areas. He was an amiable man, but easily influenced and out of his depth

---

[165] Some, on Archbishop Stepinac's intervention, were received in Croatia.
[166] He succeeded Bishop Tomažič in 1949 when he was appointed apostolic administrator. He was appointed bishop in 1960 (CNS).
[167] Official gazette of the Ljubljana diocese (31.vii.41), quoted in Ude.
[168] Vatican Docs., p. 461.

politically. He was convinced that cooperation with Italy would best serve the cause of the church in Slovenia and by 1943 he was too deeply committed against the Liberation Front to withdraw his cooperation from the Germans. One of the strongest accusations brought against him after the war by the communists was that he had cooperated with the occupiers in their 'denationalising' activities.

The Slovene resistance organisation was unique in the Yugoslav Partisan movement because it was from the beginning broadly based and included a Christian group. It consisted of three principal groups, the Communist Party, the Christian Socialist movement and the Sokols (a national and patriotic organisation of gymnastic clubs) operating as the OF (Osvobodilna Fronta–Liberation Front). Until 1943 the appeal of the OF was nationalist and anti-fascist; its association with Tito's Partisan movement was known only to the communist leadership. Early in 1943 the Christian Socialists and the Sokols agreed to dissolve their separate organisations, and in the interests of unity to allow the Communist Party to lead the resistance;[169] it was from this time that the open ascendency of the party over the OF dated. The OF, however, was not overtly anti-religious; the conflict was political and national and the church was only attacked when it sided with the enemy. Early in 1942 it declared its stand:

The OF of the Slovene nation hereby pledges itself legally and morally and everywhere to honour the religious feelings of the Catholics and in consequence the freedom of religious belief and worship. Therefore we desire that, according to the needs of the new life of the nation, the Catholic Church in Slovenia should stand on its own feet and live freely. The Christians and non-Christians of the OF are convinced that this is the way the freedom of religious and church life will be best guaranteed, just as other freedoms are.[170]

Partisan units had chaplains, and priests were appointed to headquarters as *referents* for religion,[171] whose task was to concern themselves with the religious life of believers among the Partisans.[172]

The OF attempted throughout the war to win over the

[169] This agreement was known as the Dolomitska or Pugliska Izjava.
[170] *Sl. Por.*, 14.ii.42, quoted in Kocijančič.
[171] Appointed 12.i.42: Kocijančič.
[172] Major William Jones was particularly struck by the celebration of mass at Partisan units on all great church festivals; some parish priests were prepared to go out to Partisan units for this purpose (p. 72). Dr Joža Vilfan, a leading Slovene communist, told the author in 1970 that one of his responsibilities was to ensure that there were always priests willing to say mass at Christmas and Easter. Jones also noted that there were nuns nursing in Partisan hospitals. (p. 80).

Slovene clergy. Dr Metod Mikuš, Bishop Rožman's archivist, joined the Partisans and wrote several times to the bishop to explain his action and ask him at least to maintain a neutral attitude towards the OF: repeated appeals were addressed to him by the Christian Socialists, and Dr Edgar Leopold, prior of the Carthusians at Pleterje, where many wounded Partisans had been hidden and nursed, joined his appeal to theirs.[173] In 1943 the OF invited Rožman to meet them outside Ljubljana for a discussion. He ignored the appeals and in 1943 suspended Dr Mikuš from his priestly duties.[174] Attempts were also made to reach the Slovene priests who had been expelled from northern Slovenia, and in 1943 Tone Fajfar, a Christian Socialist and leader in the Christian trade unions, made his way to Otočac in the territory of the NDH to invite Slovene priests who had taken refuge there to join them.[175]

Edvard Kocbek, the poet and writer, Dr Mikuš and Fajfar were all delegates to the second meeting of AVNOJ (Antifašističko Vijeće Narodnog Oslobodjenja Jugoslavije – Anti-fascist Council for the National Liberation of Yugoslavia) at Jajce in Bosnia on November 28/29, 1943. Kocbek's speech showed the depth of his emotional commitment to the concept of a new Yugoslavia, where all men would work side by side like brothers to build a new, better land to live in:

On the basis of a spiritual drawing-together, there has been created today in Slovenia a unity which is not a coalition of parties but a true cooperation of living people who are saving mankind. In Slovenia...men who are divided by perhaps the greatest of spiritual differences, communists and Catholics, are working together...Believing firmly in the gospel, we are happy that today we are working with communists to help resolve all the political, social and moral problems of mankind.[176]

The OF's declaration of its attitude towards religion may have been sincerely meant, but the wartime alliance between the Communist Party and the Christian Socialist movement was an uneasy one, although there had already been some cooperation between them before the war. The party was determined to drive

[173] Kocijančič.
[174] In an article which appeared in one of the roughly printed wartime pamphlets issued by the OF, Dr Mikuš wrote about the motives which led him to join the resistance, to share as a priest in the fight for national survival and to be with the Partisans when they needed a priest, and how difficult it had been for him to explain to his comrades that he could no longer say mass or give them the sacraments: to their credit they had not turned against the church (*Slovenskim Duhovnikom*).
[175] Kocijančič.   [176] *PDZA*, p. 202.

the church out of politics everywhere in Yugoslavia. In Slovenia, with its long tradition of clericalism in politics, this determination was particularly strong. Although the Christian Socialist movement was also anti-clericalist, the leadership of the Communist Party must have found it increasingly irksome to work closely with men whom they did not control, and whose first allegiance was to their faith and not to the Communist Party and the Soviet Union. Pressures on individual members of the Christian Socialists to join the Communist Party became very heavy as the war proceeded, and were the more effective since Christian Socialism was a movement, not a party, and joining the Communist Party did not seem to many to be a desertion; it was even possible during the war to become a member of the party in Slovenia without renouncing Christian beliefs. The young rank and file were left little choice when the finger pointed at them; a few of the leading figures, among them Edvard Kocbek, stood firm. But a number of the young leaders, who had joined the OF as Christian Socialists, ended the war in the Communist Party, and have remained there.

Kocbek published his war memoirs, *Tovarišija* [Comradeship], in 1949. In a foreword to the second edition (1967) he wrote that if it happened again he would still come to the same decision; the revolt could not have been made in any other way. The Slovenes, Kocbek wrote, had needed unified leadership made up of the bravest and most intelligent and strongest groups – the communists, the Christian Socialists and the Sokols – to gain their freedom and national independence, and a new social structure. For Christians there had been the additional burden of a special spiritual responsibility, since it was only by a deeply rooted spiritual adjustment that they could get rid of clericalism and demonstrate that this would not mean the end of Christian civilisation. They were faced with a difficult dilemma; on the one hand they were denounced by the Bela Garda, and on the other, 'the Communist Party tried to persuade us to discard Slovene religious interests and to force us to a generalised attitude towards the whole moral and spiritual complex, and a minimising of the authentic Christian standpoint'. He continues:

The Communist Party of Yugoslavia, because the situation in the whole of Yugoslavia was not yet ripe, had to act differently from the way the three organisations together would have wanted, and which they had solemnly promised at the beginning of the war. In spite of all this I tried to do my best to make a bridge between the pitiless judgment of God on the religious community, my hope in the forces of the new Christianity and the realisation of the inexorable laws of history; to have accepted all this half-heartedly would have led to schisms, unfaithfulness to the comrades and a weakening of the liberation struggle. Today we live in a free Slovenia, and at the same time we are realising the negative consequences of forcing men to change, the victory of bureaucracy and institutions over human spontaneity and responsibility...The task of the Partisans, only partly fulfilled, is changing to a new task; they must rise above themselves and help to build a new Yugoslavia.

The first Commission for Religious Affairs of the new Yugoslavia was set up on Slovene territory by the SNOS (Slovenski Narodno-Osvobodilni Svet – Slovene National Liberation Council) on February 19, 1944.[177] It was not at that time an organ of the party or government (and did not become so until 1952), but was an informal, *ad hoc* body, the majority of whose members were Catholics.[178] Boris Kidrič, who had pressed urgently for its establishment, said: 'Its establishment and work should guarantee freedom of worship and full participation in religious freedom, and settle all questions between the Slovene peoples's authorities and the church.'[179]

The tasks of the commission were set out in a brief constitution.[180] Its foundation was followed by a number of meetings[181] at which the lines of cooperation between the church and the state were further hammered out; the church would be accepted if it joined in the national struggle for freedom but it must remain outside politics.[182]

Dr Lojze Ude, the first president of the commission, spoke at length in September 1944 at Črnomelj to a group of clergy and party activists from the Bela Krajina.[183] After explaining the reasons for the establishment of the commission and reading

---

[177] Ude.
[178] They included Dr Lojze Ude, the president, the Rev. Dr S. Cajnkar (vice-president until 1945), Dr Metod Mikuš, the Rev. Jože Lampret and the Rev. August Cernetič, Viktor Smole, a Catholic layman, and Cene Logar, a communist; Bishop Rožman allowed the Rev. Anton Ilc, spiritual vicar in the liberated territories, to cooperate with the commission (Kocijančič).
[179] *Sl. Por.*, 1.v.44, quoted in Kocijančič.
[180] The constitution contained the following provisions:
Art 1. The Commission for Religious Affairs is established by the SNOS; it will consist of a president and eight members, both clergy and lay nominated by the Praesidium.
Art. 2. The duties of the commission are (1) to ensure freedom of worship; (2) to carry out research into all aspects of public and private life concerning the relationship between the church and the Slovene people in Slovenia; (3) to collaborate mutually to establish a relationship and to resolve any misunderstandings, and to assist the people's authorities in drawing up concrete directives (Ude).
[181] On April 13 and 20, Aug. 31, Sept. 8 and 13 (Kocijančič).
[182] Kocijančič.
[183] Reprinted in Ude, *Slovenski zbornik* (1945).

them its constitution he went on to make a number of other important points. The party did not want to encourage the establishment of a national Slovene Catholic, or any other Christian, Church in opposition to the Catholic Church, even though this was desired by elements within the church itself; but reform within the church was essential after what had taken place during the war. The church must cease to be identified with a political party, and religion must cease to be identified with nationality. Some priests, said Ude, would even deny that a non-Catholic could be a good Slovene: 'this', he said, 'is a complete de-Christianising of Catholicism'. Dr Ude's assurance about a 'national church' was necessary; the Vatican and the Orthodox patriarchate in Constantinople had always been wary of the tendency among nationally conscious Slavs, under Austrian and Turkish rule, to reject the liturgical language of their ecclesiastical superiors and to draw closer together by means of the ancient Slavonic language; the struggle on both sides went back for centuries. In Slovenia the reformist and socialist tendencies of the Slovene priests who joined the OF seemed to carry equally serious threats of schism; the church in Slovenia was the only one in postwar Yugoslavia to have recourse to the excommunication of priests.[184]

Dr Ude also made one of the early statements of a theme which continues to run through the speeches of all the communist leaders; the party was not atheist in the bourgeois, eighteenth-century, rationalist sense, attacking God and religious belief by direct forcible methods, but in a Marxist, humanist sense, believing that the need for religion would disappear when man's economic and social problems had been solved. The party would use anti-religious propaganda only in 'special historical circumstances to attain its political and social goals', but propaganda must never be translated into political pressure and persecution. Ude, a Catholic who was fighting with the Partisans, must, at this time, have been convinced by those assurances.

In view of the behaviour of the Partisans towards the church after they assumed power, it would be easy to accuse them of deliberately and cynically deceiving their non-Communist fellow Partisans, especially the Christian Socialists. It would probably be more accurate to recognise that two powerful and contradictory impulses were at work within the party, one deeply nationalist, socialist (in the Marxist sense), idealist and generous, the other

---

[184] Discussed in ch. 4. Much of the thinking of these priests, especially moderates such as Dr S. Cajnkar, anticipated the social and theological thinking of the Second Vatican Council.

conspiratorial, and strictly trained in recognised conspiratorial methods, ruthless against a ruthless foe, but also, carried forward by its own internal logic, increasingly ruthless against any opposition, or suspicion of opposition, and not prepared to tolerate any resistance to the occupiers which did not come under communist control – not to speak of the usual private vendettas which are a feature of this sort of warfare.

Later the idealism and generosity seemed to have been drowned in the lust for revenge and power, and in the need to make certain that the victory which they had won at such a cost against both their foreign and their domestic enemies would not be snatched from them. But the best proof that the basic line of the party towards religious belief and the church was genuine is that its actions, after the middle 1950s, steadily approximated more closely to the pronouncements of its leaders. Dr Živko Topalović, an important member of the Četnik Central National Committee during the war, later contrasted the attitude of the communists with that of the Četniks: 'The communists, however, took another way, the way of cooperation of all South Slavs, and the way of religious tolerance', indicating that he accepted the genuineness of the communists' statement of tolerance of religious belief.[185] The check to this tendency after 1971 which the churches, in common with other sections of Yugoslav society, are experiencing in the twilight of the Tito era is still unresolved; but the fact that a tolerant coexistence is possible was amply demonstrated in the immediately preceding years.

The Partisans

The Partisans directed their appeal to all the peoples of Yugoslavia, regardless of nationality or religion, to support them in their fight to free Yugoslavia from the invader. The resolutions which were passed at the first meeting of AVNOJ at Bihać in November 1942 and the second meeting at Jajce in November 1943 when the new Democratic Federated Yugoslavia (Demokratska Federativna Jugoslavija) was proclaimed underline this. 'The unity of the peoples of Yugoslavia in the war for liberation includes the broadest masses of all the people of Yugoslavia, all true and sincere patriots without any difference of nationality, faith or party–political affiliation...'[186]

Moše Pijade, the party's elder statesman and ideologue, began his speech 'Brothers of all nationalities and faiths' and the

[185] Tomasevich, p. 87, quoting *Pokreti narodnog otpora u Jugoslaviji 1941–45* (Paris, 1958).
[186] Resolution 4, first meeting of AVNOJ: *PDZA*, p. 56.

meeting sent out an appeal to each separate part of the country, including one addressed directly to the Moslems.[187] The appeal to the Slovenes referred to the cooperation in Slovenia of communists, Christian Socialists, peasants, etc.

Both Catholic and Serbian Orthodox priests joined the Partisans and some of them took an active, and even a leading, part in the liberation movement; the communists on their side encouraged non-communists to occupy positions of leadership while always themselves remaining in overall control. Some of the Orthodox priests, the Rev. Ilija Ćuk and others, came from the Serbian population in the NDH, from Kordun, the Lika and along the Adriatic coast; a few like the famous 'Pop' Zečević[188] left the Četniks and went over to the Partisans, frustrated by Mihailović's passive policy towards the Germans; and some, like the universally respected Rev. Milan Smiljanić,[189] belonged to the progressive group of clergy who were restive under the discipline and traditional attitudes of the hierarchy. In Macedonia the nationalist Macedonian clergy left behind after the expulsion of the bishops were quickly disillusioned by the Bulgarian occupation and by 1943 had made contact with the Partisans, who supported and encouraged them. There was no reason for the bishops to discipline any of these, since they were all resisting the occupiers; it would be true in general to say that local circumstances decided whether a man joined one movement or the others.

Many Catholic priests of Slav origin along the Adriatic coast and in Istria turned naturally to a movement which resisted Italian domination, and in Slovenia priests and laymen who belonged to the Christian Socialist movement cooperated with the Liberation Front, which the communsits controlled. Some bishops suspended, or threatened to suspend, priests who joined

---

[187] '...a sincere and fraternal cooperation of Serbs, Croats and Moslems is necessary if Bosnia–Hercegovina is to go forward as a united community in our fraternal community without regard to difference in faith or party' (*PDZA*, p. 68).

[188] The Rev. Vlada Zečević joined Mihailović at the beginning of the war as commander of a unit, but went over to the Partisans because they were fighting the Germans more actively, taking his detachment with him. He became a member of the Supreme Command and was appointed commissioner for internal affairs and after the war minister of communications. By this time he had left the priesthood and joined the Communist Party.

[189] Smiljanić was the principal Orthodox chaplain with the Partisans and later became minister for agriculture and vice-president of the republican government of Serbia. He remained a priest and later took a prominent part in the Union of Associations of Orthodox Priests (see ch. 6), of which he became chairman.

the Partisans, but others turned a blind eye. There were Serbian Orthodox priests and Catholic laymen among the delegates to Bihać: Zečević, who at that time was a *referent* for religious matters at Partisan headquarters in Serbia and a member of the Executive Committee of AVNOJ, the Rev. Jevstatije Karamitijević, *referent* for the IIIrd Sandjak Brigade and delegate from the Sandjak, the Rev. Blažo Marković, a judge in the ecclesiastical court at Cetinje, and the Rev. Jagoš Simonović from Kolašin, religious *referent* for the IVth Montenegrin Brigade; Tone Fajfar and Edvard Kocbek the writer, both Christian Socialists, were delegates from Slovenia.[190] Two Orthodox priests, the Rev. Jovo Miodragović from Žagrović and the Rev. Ilija Ćuk from Zrmanja in the Lika, and a number of Catholic priests. Mgr Svetozar Rittig of St Mark's Church, Zagreb, who was a member of the Executive Committee, the Rev. Andjelko Buratović from Krk, the Rev. Dr Franjo Didović from Djakovo, the Rev. Ferdo Šenk from Kršan and the Rev. Srećko Stifanić, were members of ZAVNOH (Zemaljsko Antifašističko Vijeće Narodnog Oslobodjenja Hrvatske – Territorial Anti-fascist Council for the National Liberation of Croatia).[191]

The priests wore Partisan uniform, with a cross superimposed onto the red star on their caps. Aside from their priestly duties among the troops, the Orthodox priests reopened churches which had been closed by the ustaše, rehung the bells, celebrated communion and baptised children; in Glamoč in Western Bosnia Zečević baptised more than a hundred children during one day.[192]

At Bihać a programme for teachers in the primary schools which had been set up in liberated territory was drawn up; it included lessons in religion, which were to be given 'in a spirit of mutual religious toleration, religious discipline and deep respect for the religious convictions of others'. Religion must not divide man from man.[193]

When AVNOJ met for the second time at Jajce in 1943 the group of Christians was joined by Dr Metod Mikuš and the Rev. Jože Lampret, both from Slovenia, and Mgr Rittig from St Mark's Church in Zagreb. Zečević was appointed commissioner (poverenik) for internal affairs and Edvard Kocbek commissioner for education in the new government.

The constitutional basis for relations between the state and the churches was laid down in the statutes of the second meeting of AVNOJ. Article 8 stated that all citizens have equal rights

---

[190] *PDZA*. See also *National Liberation Movement of Yugoslavia*.
[191] *Putovi revolucije*, pp. 196ff.   [192] Dedijer, *Tito Speaks*, p. 186.
[193] *PDZA*.

without regard to nationality, race or religious faith, and that any limitation of these rights on the basis of racial, national or religious affiliation, or any incitement to national, racial or religious intolerance, contempt or hatred was punishable at law.

Article 10 guaranteed freedom of religious belief and freedom of conscience to all citizens; Article 11 stated that freedom of speech, the press, association and assembly 'in the framework of the National Liberation Movement' was to be enjoyed by all citizens, but it excluded from the enjoyment of these rights anyone who had in any way served the enemies of the people. This was the declaration on which the church based any hopes it may have had of establishing a workable relationship with the Partisans after liberation; there was room for misunderstanding and different interpretations, especially of the last sentence of Article 11.

An attempt was made at this time to persuade the Vatican to send a representative to liberated territory, on the same basis as Abbot Marcone had been sent to the NDH, i.e. to the church and not to the government. Djilas, one of the leaders of the communists, recently returned from a visit to the USSR, was full of enthusiasm about the patriotic fervour of the Russian Orthodox Church and the new relationship which had developed between the Soviet government and the church during the war. Kocbek, devout Catholic and devoted Partisan that he was, was fired by this account and suggested that an approach might be made to the Vatican. Eventually, in June 1944, Kocbek travelled to Italy, bearing a letter from Tito and empowered to negotiate with the Vatican a friendly arrangement for the separation of church and state which had been decreed at Jajce. He fell ill on the way and did not reach Rome until August, when he had two conversations at the Secretariat of State with Mgr Tardini's deputy. The advance, however, was rebuffed and nothing came of the initiative.[194]

Already before the end of the war there were contacts between some of the bishops and Partisan forces who were fighting their way across the country. The most important of these meetings took place during the extraordinary session of ZAVNOH[195] in Split in April 1945 when Bishop Pušić of Hvar, Bishop Mileta of Šibenik and Vicar-General Fulgosi, representing Bishop Boni-fačić of Split, met the Partisan leaders. Bishop Mileta welcomed the success of the liberation forces, although 'some of his ideas about the role of the Catholic Church in recent happenings were

[194] Interview with Edvard Kocbek, 1971.   [195] Petranović, p. 277.

basically incorrect'.[196] Dr Bakarić, the leading Croat communist, who was then secretary of the Executive Council, suggested some basic formulas for regulating relationships with the Catholic clergy, but emphasised that criminals from among the ranks of the clergy were responsible for many misdeeds. In May Bishop Mileta and the Franciscan provincial each handed a declaration to the president of the government of Bosnia and Hercegovina, Rodoljub Čolaković, concerning the responsibility of the Bosnian Franciscans during the war; there had been some bad elements but the majority had behaved patriotically and tried to help individuals and families. [197]

Archbishop Manzoni of Zadar went to Šibenik as soon as it was liberated to thank 'the Croatian people's authorities' and pledge them his loyalty.[198]

Large parts of Yugoslavia had been liberated by 1944 and were being administered by the Partisans. Villages and small towns changed hands frequently, and individuals equally found their allegiances uncertain. Many priests faced this dilemma and some paid for it with their lives. By 1945 the greater part of the countryside was in the hands of the Partisans and only the cities and bigger towns remained under German control. As the defeat of the Germans became more certain, Yugoslavs who had collaborated with the occupying powers or opposed the Partisan forces looked desperately to the West to help them to salvage their particular interests: the Croats hoped to keep their independent state in some form; the Serbs looked to a restored monarchy, and the Slovenes[199] (by now in touch with General Damjanović, the representative of Mihailović, the Serbian Četnik leader) had hopes of acquiring the Slovene regions of Austrian Carinthia and the Italian Julian region, and were prepared to form part of a restored Yugoslav monarchy. All sorts of local interests and influences entered into the pattern of tensions and expectations. The inhabitants of the Julian region and Istria were determined not to be subjected again to Italian rule; the Dalmatian coast, freed in 1944 by the Partisans, was equally determined that the Italians should never return; and far to the east, at the other end of the country, the Macedonians for the first time in their history grasped at the promise of independent statehood within a Yugoslav federation, their tongue for the first time recognised as a language in its own right.

[196] Ibid. p. 277.   [197] Ibid.
[198] Speech by Mgr Ritting at the founding of the Bosnia and Hercegovina priests' association (*Dobri Pastir*, Feb.–March 1950).
[199] The groups supporting the government in London; see n. 164 above.

2

The Catholic Church
The immediate postwar years

As the war moved rapidly to its end, the main Partisan armies swept west and north through the country, driving the Ustaša forces before them; the government of the NDH prepared to flee. The meetings and negotiations between the Ustaša leaders, the Slovene groups who opposed the Partisans and the representatives of the Serbian Četniks had all been linked to the conviction that the Anglo-American alliance with the Soviet Union was only a temporary expedient until the defeat of Germany, and that the Western Allies would not abandon them to communist rule; all hoped that something could be saved from the ruin. After 1943 Italian democratic groups had continually pressed the Allies for an assurance that they would occupy the Istrian peninsula and the Julian region around Trieste as far north as Monfalcone before the Yugoslav Partisans got there; and the Allies assured them that they intended to do so. The Anti-fascist Councils of Croatia and Slovenia, on the other hand, had declared shortly after the fall of Italy that the territories inhabited by Slovenes and Croats would be incorporated into the territories under Yugoslav jurisdiction and this decision was later approved by AVNOJ. The Partisans were aware of the Allied intentions concerning the Julian region and were determined to thwart them.[1]

The Partisans raced northward, by-passing German forces and taking enormous military risks, to reach Istria and Trieste before the Allies. They reached the centre of the city on May 1 and immediately began to set up an administration; the Allied troops arrived the following day. The port had been designed as a main supply base for the Western Allies, and Field-Marshal Alexander

---

[1] The Partisan High Command was already suspicious of the intentions of the Western Allies. S. Vukmanović-Tempo in his memoirs, *Revolucija koja teče* [Revolution on the Move] (Belgrade, 1971), writes that Bulgarian communists returning from the Soviet Union brought news of the Stalin–Churchill agreement to divide the Balkans into two spheres of influence. Bulgaria was to be in the Soviet sphere, Yugoslavia divided between the Soviet Union and Britain – the so-called '50–50 agreement'.

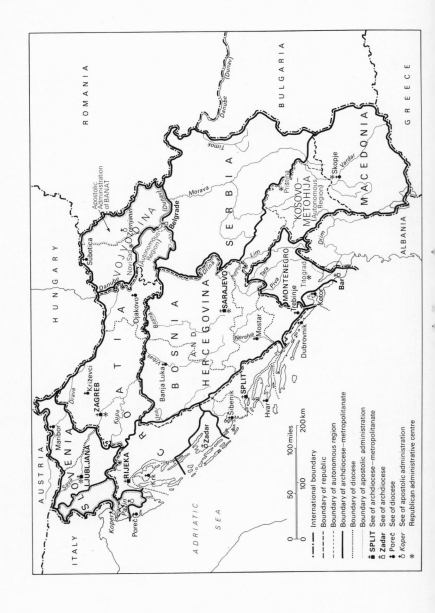

could not concede it to the Yugoslavs. He was unwilling, however, to use force against the Partisans and preferred to negotiate; the following month an agreement to divide the Julian region into two zones was signed.

Archbishop Stepinac remained unshakable in Zagreb but Bishop Rožman of Ljubljana and a number of his clergy joined the Slovene Domobrans and the remnants of Četnik and other forces in their retreat across the frontier; Rožman was convinced that he would be back in a fortnight with the Anglo-American forces. Archbishop Šarić of Sarajevo fled north with the Ustaša forces, picking up the ailing Bishop Garić of Banja Luka on the way. None of the three had sought permission from the Vatican to leave his diocese and none was subsequently ever received by the pope.[2]

In Croatia General von Löhr informed Pavelić on May 6 that the Germans had signed a surrender, and relinquished his command to Pavelić. The next day Pavelić ordered an accelerated withdrawal to Austria and then himself fled to safety, eventually reaching Argentina. The NDH forces accompanied by thousands of civilian refugees moved north and reached the Austrian border where they hoped to find refuge and to surrender to the British forces. But they were turned back, since the Allies had agreed that all enemy troops would surrender to the forces of the countries against which they had fought. They gave themselves up to the Partisans on May 15, 1945. In the same way the retreating Slovene forces, who had at first been put into prisoner-of-war camps in Italy, were returned to Yugoslavia. During the course of the next few weeks the great majority of these returned prisoners were killed by the Partisan forces, who were determined to thwart any plans of their domestic enemies to continue the struggle against communism with the aid of the Western Allies.[3] Many priests, both military chaplains and others, were among the Ustaša and other Croatian forces fleeing from Croatia;[4] an unknown number of these were killed and others escaped. The situation concerning the Slovene Domobrans who were returned is obscure but it appears that there may have been a small number of military chaplains and theological students

---

[2] Catholic sources contemporary to the events. Rožman was allowed to remain in Austria; later he was reported to be living in a monastery in Menzingen near Zug, and Šarić in Gioysiez near Fribourg (*Sl. Por.*, 12.v.48, quoting *Voix Ouvrière* of Geneva, 10.v.48).

[3] Tomasevich, p. 376 n. 134, 136. Later documents show that there was no fighting between Zagreb and the Austrian border.

[4] Petranović estimates 500 (p. 272). An official of the Association of Catholic Priests of Croatia, in conversation with the writer in 1970, estimated 400.

among those who perished. Bishop Rožman and his entourage were allowed to remain in Austria and eventually found refuge in Swiss monasteries.[5] Not all the Ustaša forces fled, however. There were numerous groups, most of them having very little connection with each other, who went 'into the woods'; the old *hajduk* phrase which had been adopted by the Partisans now acquired a different meaning. In the following months others, who had made good their escape, filtered back across the frontiers and either joined the groups in the woods or were hidden by sympathisers.[6]

These groups called themselves *križari* (crusaders), which had been the name of one of the prewar sections of Catholic Action; aside from the name it is difficult to prove any direct connection between the organisations, although the authorities believed, or alleged, that it was the same organisation resurrected to go into underground opposition to the new government.[7]

Croatia

The Partisans entered Zagreb on May 8, 1945. They took over a city – and a state – without a government. A few days earlier at a meeting of the cathedral chapter, Archbishop Stepinac had told his clergy that they were free to follow their own conscience and to leave the country if they wished; for his part he intended to stay. If there had been any waverers this decision stiffened their resolution and very few priests from the Zagreb diocese left.[8]

On May 17 Archbishop Stepinac was taken into protective custody and lodged in a villa in the city.[9] Zagreb was full of

[5] The writer was reliably informed in the spring of 1970 that there were no priests among the forces returned to Slovenia; however, in 1970 the Zgodovinski Odsek Zveze DSPB Tabor (History Section of the Federation DSPB] in Cleveland, Ohio, published *Matica Mrtvih*, a list of 'Slovenes killed by the crimes of the Liberation Front' 1941–5, containing the names of fourteen priests and eight theological students; the majority of the priests were killed with the returned forces.

[6] In Yugoslavia as a whole about 11,800 of the domestic forces which had fought against the Partisans remained in the country; they consisted of about 790 small groups; among them were 2,370 ustaše (Petranović, p. 276, quoting A. Ranković, *Izabrani govori i članci* [Collected Speeches and Articles], p. 267). A year later Bakarić estimated that no more than twenty small groups remained in Croatia, altogether about 150 men (*Vjesnik*, 29.viii.46, speech to Fifth Session of the Sabor).

[7] The prewar Križari was a youth section of Catholic Action; it was founded by Dr Ivan Merc, as the Orlovi (Eagles) and carried on by Dr Ivan Protulipac. The latter was assassinated in Trieste on January 31, 1946, by unknown people who presumably believed that he was a member of the postwar organisation.

[8] Catholic source.

[9] Not imprisoned, as various Western papers reported (Petranović, p. 278,

trigger-happy Serbian and Montenegrin Partisans, convinced that Stepinac was personally responsible for the outrages of the ustaše, and this detention may have been at least partly for his own protection. A fortnight later Tito, who had arrived in the city, intimated that he would like to meet representatives of the higher clergy. On June 2 a delegation headed by the vicar-general, Bishop Salis-Seewis, called first on Dr Bakarić, and then, accompanied by him, on Marshal Tito.[10] Bishop Salis opened the interview by referring to Archbishop Stepinac's absence, which obliged Salis to take his place. He affirmed the willingness of the Catholic Church, as guardian of God's laws, to cooperate loyally with the government where it was in accord with the laws of God and the church, particularly in view of the declaration of the government that it would respect freedom of religion and conscience[11] (which, it was assumed, included the right of the church to form its own organisations and to carry out religious education).[12] He concluded by asking God's blessing on the marshal's work.

The tone of the marshal's answer was amicable, and he phrased his criticisms courteously. He welcomed the opportunity to talk with the clergy and to explain his thought about the relationship between the church and the state, the church and the people. But, speaking as a Croat,[13] he had to say that he was not satisfied with the behaviour of one part of the Catholic clergy in the difficult historical times which had cost such sacrifices. The

confirmed to author by a Catholic source in 1970). Circular 3799/45 issued on 18.v.45 informed the clergy and faithful that Stepinac had been 'deprived of his freedom' on May 17. The clergy were ordered to say collect no. 32 for him at every mass and the faithful were asked to pray for him.

[10] *Vjesnik*, 3.vi.45; *SVNZ*, 5.x.45. The other members of the delegation were Bishop Lach, Canon Lončar (who had been sentenced to death by the Ustaša for his outspoken criticism of its pressure on the church), Canon Borić, Canon Professor Bakšić, Professor Dr Živković, Canon Dr Nikola Kolarek, Fathers Grimm and Belić and the Dominican and Franciscan provincials. Mgr Svetozar Rittig, who had joined the Partisans in 1943, was also present.

[11] AVNOJ declaration, 29.xi.43.

[12] The archbishop had based his action during the NDH period on the 1831 Bull of Gregory XVI *Sollicitudo ecclesiarum*; see ch. 3, n. 53.

[13] There is a fascinating discrepancy at this point between the reports of Tito's words which appeared in *Vjesnik* (3.vi.45) and in *SVNZ* (5.x.45), which are oherwise identical. The former reports Tito as saying 'I, as a Croat...' and the latter as 'I, as a Croat and Catholic...' It is hard to believe that a seasoned communist and Partisan leader would have used these words but just as difficult to believe that the official journal of the archbishopric would have risked trouble by inventing them. One is left speculating whether they slipped out, half by mistake, as the marshal attempted to soften the force of his criticism; a few words later he added: 'I am speaking openly as I think...excuse my frankness.'

bishops must be well aware that many of the younger priests were turning away from their elders, particularly the followers of the great Strossmayer, those who believed in the idea of Yugoslavia.[14] The leaders of the government, he continued, had believed all during the war that the question of religion and the relation of the church to the government should not be resolved by decree, a method which would only harm the community in general and in any case could not succeed. It was with this thought in mind that he had asked the bishops to consult with him so that they could together find a satisfactory solution to the question.

Then follows a passage which gave rise to the conviction that the government wanted the church to separate from Rome and form a schismatic, national Catholic Church.

'I would say for myself', said the marshal, 'that our church should be more national, that it should be more adapted to the nation; perhaps you are surprised that I approach the subject of nationality with such emphasis. Too much blood has flowed, I have seen too much suffering of the people, and I would like the Catholic clergy in Croatia to be more deeply linked in its national feeling with the people than it now is.'

The word used by Tito was *nacionalna* (*nacija, nacionalnost*) meaning specifically 'national', with a connotation here of independence from Rome, and not the more characteristically Slav *narodna* (*narod, narodnost*) which can mean either 'nation' or 'people'.

He would not take it upon himself to condemn Rome, but

'I am critical of it because it has always inclined more to Italy than to our people. I would like to see the Catholic Church...be more independent...this is the basic question which we would like to see resolved, and all other questions are secondary and can easily be solved.'

He went on to the heart of the matter, with a burning conviction which shines through the printed words:

'we want to create a great community of South Slavs and in this community there would be both Orthodox and Catholic, who must be

[14] Bishop of Djakovo (1815–1905), founder of the Yugoslav Academy of Sciences and Arts (in Zagreb) and an exponent of the idea of the unity of the South Slavs. As apostolic administrator of the Catholics in Serbia he lost no opportunity of fostering good relations between the Catholic and Orthodox Churches ('Religion which sows dissension between brothers is not religion but superstition') and abstained until the last moment from voting in favour of papal infallibility at the First Vatican Council, knowing the offence this would give to the Orthodox. He and the Serbian Metropolitan Mihajlo met in Belgrade in 1868 and embraced as a token that religion must not separate sons of the same nation, a gesture which was enthusiastically welcomed by Serbian students (Mousset, pp. 247ff). This is an early example of the communist leaders' frequent approving references to him.

closely linked with all the other Slavs. The Orthodox are nearer to this than the Catholics, and the question of relations between the Orthodox Church and the Catholic Church must also be included in the great idea of the drawing together and close cooperation of the Slav people, who have suffered so much in their history from divisions, the culmination of which was this war, when the attempt was made to destroy Slav nationality. This is fundamental.'[15]

A long discussion followed. Bishop Salis defended the record of the Vatican towards Croatia during the war; the NDH was never recognised *de jure* by the Vatican, and the papal delegate Marcone was accredited to the Croatian episcopate, not to the government; furthermore it had refused to allow any changes in the episcopal jurisdiction over the Medjumurje (annexed to Hungary) and Dalmatia (annexed to Italy). The bishops were bound to the Holy See in matters of dogma and discipline, but in national and social activities they were completely free, and felt no need to demand any greater freedom than they already had. He defended Stepinac's record during the war; the priests who had welcomed the ustaše had been misled by their desire for an independent Croat state and many of them had turned away from the ustaše when they saw the acts of violence and murders. He warned Tito that the concentration camps, 'full of innocent people', were causing great unrest which could only harm the state. Armed Partisans were going around Zagreb preventing nuns from praying with children, turning the nuns' quarters into dormitories and removing crucifixes. Tito promised to look into the excesses at once and repeated that nothing in the sphere of religion must be done by decree;[16] he only asked that no one should interfere with the work of consolidating the state. At Salis-Seewis's suggestion one of the bishops was appointed to maintain contact with the authorities.[17]

The next day, June 3, Stepinac was released from custody and returned to the palace.[18] On June 4 he called on Dr Bakarić during the morning and visited Tito in the afternoon, accompanied by Bakarić.[19] That same morning Tito had received Mgr

---

[15] *Vjesnik*, 3.vi.45.
[16] This assurance was not kept. There was no consultation or agreement about the expropriation of church property, the closing of schools, taxation or many other matters. The government did, however, ask all the religious communities to comment on the 1953 Law on the Status of Religious Communities. The Catholic bishops refused to do so, although some of the associations of Catholic priests (in Slovenia and Bosnia and Hercegovina) did.
[17] Petranović, p. 277.
[18] Catholic source; Benigar, p. 505.
[19] *Vjesnik*, 6.vi.45.

Marcone, and had a 'short, cordial talk'.[20] The conversation between Tito and Stepinac covered the same ground as the talks with the delegation, but Stepinac was insistent that only the Vatican could make any final decisions; individual bishops could only give their opinions. A concordat between the Vatican and the government would be the ideal solution but a *modus vivendi* such as was reached in prewar Czechoslovakia was also possible. In any case it was important that regular diplomatic relations, which were in a confused state following the transfer of power from the London government-in-exile to the government set up by the Partisans, should be resumed. At the end, he urged Tito, with some courage, though also with a certain lack of imagination, to meet 'frankly and courageously with the representatives of the Croatian Peasant Party and with the *honest* adherents of the Ustaša movement'. He begged that lives should be spared, for the loss of life had already been so heavy that another catastrophe would finish with the extermination of the Slavs of southern Europe.[21]

There is no record of further conversations, but it is believed that when the archbishop returned to the palace he was convinced that the government wanted an independent, national Catholic Church, with himself as the head.[22] Perhaps there was some cautious probing, which he magnified as a result of the nervous strain he was under during the difficult conversations which followed on more than two weeks of isolation, or perhaps there was a genuine misunderstanding; on the face of it, it is not likely that men like Dr Bakarić, who had known the Catholic Church from their boyhood, could have seriously entertained such a possibility. A few days later Stepinac saw Edvard Kocbek, now a minister in the government, to try to draw up a basis for a joint approach to relations between the church and the state.[23] Kocbek advised Stepinac to prepare a report on his conversation with Tito for Dr Edvard Kardelj, the Slovene communist leader, who was then the vice-president of the government. The contents of this report, according to Petranović, are not known but it is believed that Stepinac wrote

[20] Marcone remained in Zagreb until after it was liberated, although his functions had ceased; he continued to be much in evidence even after the collapse of Italy (Falconi, p. 326).

[21] Pattee, doc. LXV. Stepinac was charmed by Tito: 'after Maček the most attractive statesman I have met' (Catholic source to whom Stepinac made this statement).

[22] Catholic source.

[23] Petranović, p. 279, quoting here and below from the stenographic record of the Stepinac trial in the Croatian State Archives.

that although difficulties still existed they were not insurmountable. Later, Stepinac visited Bakarić again, but they did not succeed in reaching a basis from which an agreement could have been negotiated.[24] During his conversation with Dr Bakarić on June 4, the archbishop told him that some archives belonging to the NDH had been deposited at the palace for safe-keeping during the bombardment, together with a few items of private property belonging to officials. This was confirmed on June 6 by Stepinac's secretary, the Rev. Ivan Šalić, in a letter to the Commission for Religious Affairs. Mgr Rittig, the president of the commission, answered the same day, with instructions for handing over both the archives and the personal belongings.[25] This incident was to feature among the accusations at Stepinac's trial.

A number of trials by military courts took place in June and July; the biggest of these, on June 29, was a prototype of all the immediate postwar trials – swift, ruthless, with few legal trimmings, and identifying precisely the objects of the authorities' vengeance: those who had 'bloodied their hands',[26] the criminals who had taken part in the slaughter and run the concentration camps; those who had 'put the knife into the hands of such men as Majstorović' etc.[27] by their ideology and their propaganda; those who had founded and run the Croatian Orthodox Church, an artificial creation which had nothing to do with religion but promised the Serbs living in Croatia a quiet life and weakened their resolution to fight; leaders of the German minority and the Moslem collaborators, and those who had helped ustaše to escape after the war. Majstorović, a former Franciscan, Spiridon Mifka, the Orthodox priest who had been consecrated bishop of Sarajevo in the Croatian Orthodox Church, and the Rev. Ivo Guberina[28] were sentenced to be hanged, and Ismet Muftić, mufti of Zagreb, whose name was coupled with Guberina's and who was accused of having incited ustaše and Moslems to slaughter Serbs, was sentenced to be shot. Bishop Hermogen Maksimov,

[24] Petranović, p. 279.
[25] Pattee, doc. LXII.
[26] Tito in conversation with the bishops.
[27] From the indictment of the Rev. Ivo Guberina and others (*Narodni List*, 30.vi.41).
[28] Guberina had become an ustaša in 1940 (*Dokumenti*, p. 30); he had joined Pavelić in Italy in 1940 and returned to Yugoslavia with him in 1941. He was one of the leading ideologues of the Ustaša movement. After his return to Yugoslavia he became an Ustaša captain and archivist to the Ustaša movement (ibid. p. 223). In June 1943 he was suspended from priestly duties by Stepinac because his conduct and his actions had scandalised the faithful (Pattee, doc. XLIV).

the émigré Russian priest who had been persuaded to head the puppet Croatian Orthodox Church, together with priests and others who had collaborated with him, were also sentenced to be shot. A number of priests and nuns were sentenced to various terms of imprisonment.[29] Other priests were condemned at similar trials at Karlovac and Križevci. In a letter to Bakarić, Stepinac described the procedure at the trials; the accused were not told the charges until they appeared in the courtroom, and were not allowed to call witnesses for cross-examination; the public was excluded and the names of the judges were not known.[30] These were not show trials; they were deadly serious, ruthless retribution meted out in the flush of victory after a bloody, merciless war, by men who were convinced that they had every right to do so. They were different in kind and in intention from the later show trials which were staged like morality plays to instruct and to point a political lesson. It seems clear also that many priests were killed, especially during the closing weeks of the war or shortly after, either in skirmishes with the Partisans or summarily without trial.[31]

It was during this period that Bishop Carević of Dubrovnik disappeared and Bishop Šimrak of Križevci was arrested. L'Osservatore Romano later asserted that a body in bishop's attire had been found at the bottom of a well, but it was never positively identified.[32] Šimrak, who was already a sick man, died shortly after his release from prison; he was a Uniate and bishop of the Greek Catholic diocese and was believed to have supported enthusiastically the mass conversions of the Serbian Orthodox and to have played a leading part in the drafting of the text of the pastoral letter of March 1945.

On a more everyday level great changes took place almost at once. Religious instruction in secondary schools was stopped immediately; in primary schools it was allowed to continue on a voluntary basis (although there were constant difficulties and in many places it was virtually non-existent). The religious press

[29] *Narodni List*, 30.vi.45.
[30] Letter to Bakarić, 21.viii.45; Pattee, doc. LXVI, p. 426.
[31] The facts are obscure and disputed. An émigré Croat Catholic view can be found in I. Omrčanin, *Martyrologe croate: prêtres et religieux assassinés en haine de la Foi de 1940 à 1951* (Paris: Nouvelles Editions Latines [n.d. but probably 1962]), which includes in addition names of priests alleged to have been killed by the Četniks.
[32] 17.iii.54. Carević had been relieved of his duties as bishop because of financial irregularities in his diocese and was living in the Zagorje near Zagreb. The writer has been told by a Catholic source, who was at that time living nearby, that Carević was known locally to have been killed in the village of Strmac by Partisans, who made no secret of it.

was suppressed by denying it newsprint or confiscating its presses. The agrarian reform, which had been announced in the AVNOJ programme and legislated for by the Law on Agrarian Reform, had started before the end of the war. It bore hard on the church, which had managed to preserve most of its lands during the agrarian reforms following the First World War. Many schools and buildings belonging to the church had been requisitioned to house the advancing forces.[33]

The archbishop, who must have felt that the worst fears which had been expressed in the March pastoral letter[34] were coming true, tried to steady the nerves and keep up the courage of his clergy. In a circular[35] early in July he exhorted them to firm faith in God, to encourage their congregations in family prayers, devotional reading and attendance at mass. The following April detailed instructions were sent to the clergy about catechism classes for secondary school boys and girls 'who have been left without any kind of instruction in schools'.[36] The religious upringing of children was his main concern and remained the chief preoccupation of the bishops for many years; they return to it again and again in circulars and pastoral letters. He reminded priests that it was still allowed to teach catechism at primary schools and asked them to inform him if anyone tried to interfere; he irritated the authorities by reminding the faithful that they must not read or buy books and pamphlets which spoke against God, the holy faith and the Catholic Church.[37] He urged priests to preach the gospel and avoid secular matters; if possible they should write out their sermons and keep carefully to the text.

At the beginning of July Stepinac ordered the closing-down of all religious associations, including Catholic Action, with the exception of Caritas.[38] The archbishopric had been asked for lists of members of all religious organisations, and rather than compromise individuals, he dissolved the organisations.

A few days later Stepinac attacked the new legislation on marriage in a circular[39] he directed to be read in church without comment, for which he took sole responsibility.

Under the new law marriage was a civil state contracted before the civil authorities; those who wished could subsequently go through a religious service. Matrimonial disputes were brought

---

[33] See ch. 7 for discussion of the agrarian reform.
[34] See pp. 39f.   [35] No. 5027/45.
[36] 2984/46, 16.iv.46.
[37] In a later message (35/BK, *SVNZ*, 27.viii.46) the bishops complained of the great danger to schoolchildren forced to read prohibited books.
[38] Circular 4949/45, 1.vii.45.   [39] No. 4851/45, 5.vii.45.

under the jurisdiction of the civil courts. The circular laid down the Catholic doctrine on marriage uncompromisingly: Catholics can only be married validly in a Catholic church by a Catholic priest; jurisdiction in matrimonial disputes lies with the Catholic matrimonial courts; a consummated Christian marriage is indissoluble during the lifetime of the partners. Any marriage contracted by Catholics outside the church, 'that is, even before the civil authorities, is invalid. It is not only before the church but before God, simply concubinage, a sinful union, in spite of the fact that the civil authorities may on their side accept its validity.' The church's right to judge the marital disputes of its faithful had always been acknowledged in Yugoslavia; if the civil authorities assumed jurisdiction over Catholic marriages, even with the consent of the parties,

they transgress greatly against the right which the church did not assume for itself but was given by its heavenly founder Jesus Christ; any faithful who have recourse to the people's courts show themselves to be unfaithful and disobedient children of the church. Any subsequent civil marriage during the lifetime of the other partner is a grave sin before God and not a marriage but a concubinage.

Although the immediate postwar trials had begun and believers in the city were in a ferment of fear and uncertainty, the authorities decided to sanction the annual votive pilgrimage (on July 8) to the shrine of Marija Bistrica, and the individual parish processions which were traditionally held on the following Monday. The archbishopric sent a circular to the clergy to urge their flocks to take part, especially the children.[40] The response of the faithful was overwhelming. Between 40,000 and 50,000[41] people were in the long column trudging the thirty kilometres to the shrine in the summer heat, including many families of those who had fled, or been killed, or been arrested and disappeared. The authorities were startled and somewhat shaken, although later Bakarić made a virtue of their tolerance in issuing passes to everyone who asked for one.[42]

In the meantime the archbishop's palace was besieged by the relatives of those who had been arrested or had disappeared, or who had never returned from the army of the NDH. Many were penniless; all were desperate and begged the archbishop for help. He had faced Pavelić and the Ustaša government and interceded

[40] No. 3094/45, 26.v.45.
[41] Petranović, p. 283; other (Catholic) estimates put the figure at 100,000.
[42] *Slobodni Dom* (official communist weekly, Zagreb), 29.vii.45: speech to Fourth Session of Croatian Sabor.

for their victims, and now he could not refrain from doing the same for those who were accused of collaborating with the ustaše. Towards the end of July, Stepinac wrote a very long letter to Bakarić.[43] It emanated from the presidency of the Bishops' Conference and was signed by the Archbishop of Zagreb as president.

The tone of the letter was vigorous and uncompromising, more so even than his letter of November 20, 1941, to Pavelić, and covers the whole field of the complaints which the bishops made about the behaviour of the authorities to the church and clergy since they had assumed power less than three months earlier. He reminded Bakarić that Tito had promised the delegation of clergy on June 2 that the cases of imprisoned priests would be dealt with without delay and that those who had no blood on their hands would be quickly freed; instead he received news of new arrests every day. Some priests and seminarians had been released but the Zagreb seminarians were immediately called up for military service; numerous priests had been condemned to death by courts martial in Zagreb, Križevci and Karlovac; he protested against the death sentence on Dr Kerubin Šegvić[44] and two nuns and several priests who were innocent of murder. He and his priests were attacked in the press, while their own was muzzled and they had no right of reply. He complained about the restrictions on religious instruction in the schools, and the confiscation of schools and seminaries.[45] Condemned men were not allowed to receive the final sacraments; they were not given Christian burial and their relatives were not told where they had been buried; deaths were not properly registered so that estates could not be settled. People were held for weeks in grossly overcrowded prisons before being charged and their relatives were not told where they were. He asked the authorities to establish a bureau to give information to the relatives of arrested persons. He pleaded for the soldiers and officers who had fought for the NDH in good faith to redress the injustices suffered by the Croatian people before the war, and in conclusion said that he sincerely wanted collaboration between the church and the state, and to work for the benefit of the Croatian people. On July

---

[43] 64/BK, 21.vii.45: Pattee, doc. LXVI, pp. 426ff. In the English translation it runs to over 6,000 words.

[44] The Rev. Kerubin Šegvić was sent to Rome by the NDH authorities in 1941 to attempt to secure recognition from the Holy See. He originated the theory that Croats are of Gothic origin.

[45] The majority of these had been requisitioned as the Partisan forces advanced, or after they had arrived in the big cities, as living-quarters; many of these were returned by the second half of 1946.

26 Bakarić thanked the archbishop briefly for having sent him his sincere opinion: 'I find that on certain subjects you are badly informed, on other subjects that I do not share your point of view, on still others I am of the opinion that you are absolutely correct.' As soon as his health permitted they could discuss these matters and come to a satisfactory solution.[46]

Bakarić referred to several of these points in a speech on July 28.[47] He acknowledged that there had been irregularities and he did not defend them. In spite of criticism from party members for allowing the procession to Marija Bistrica the authorities would continue to sanction religious processions. But excesses had taken place and he warned the organisers that legal measures could be taken against them.[48] Tito, he said, had been quite clear; the government did not want to concern itself with church dogma or interfere with its internal organisation. The biggest issue was religious education; the government believed that it must not be compulsory and that there must be real freedom either to believe or not to believe, which had not been the case for many years in Yugoslavia.

Stepinac answered him on August 2.[49] He accepted – and this is important – Bakarić's statement that Tito had not intended to suggest an independent, national church, and that the government would not interfere with the internal affairs of the Catholic Church.[50] But he vigorously denied that the pilgrimage to Marija

[46] Pattee, p. 442.

[47] *Slobodni Dom*, 29.vii.45: speech to Fourth Session of Sabor.

[48] During these years there was a rash of visions and miraculous apparitions in both the Catholic and the Orthodox areas of the country. Holy statues spoke and icons materialised, causing unrest and disturbance. The manifestations were disturbing and were severely condemned by the authorities. Bakarić remarked tartly that he had had a Catholic upbringing himself and knew very well what the church thought about such things; but instead of scotching the rumours and urging the people to get on with rebuilding the country, they seemed to be inspiring them (speech to the Fifth Session of the Sabor, *Vjesnik*, 29.viii.46).

A few weeks earlier in a speech at Split Tito had referred to the apparitions of saints: 'Where were those saints when babies were sucking the breasts of their murdered mothers? Where were those saints when our people needed saving?...Let the priests stay in their churches...we have nothing against people praying, against priests doing their job, but we won't have them bringing politics into church' (Tito, vol. II, pp. 267ff).

[49] 67/BK: Pattee, doc. LXVI, p. 443.

[50] This assurance was kept; no attempt was ever made to impose political appointments within the church or to interfere in questions of dogma. In the Sept./Oct. 1969 issue of *Svesci* (Zagreb) Dr V. Bajsić, vice-dean of the theological faculty in Zagreb, wrote: 'There was persecution but never commissars.' (The nearest the government ever got to internal interference was the setting-up of the bitterly disputed priests' associations, discussed in ch. 4.)

Bistrica had been politically motivated and was packed with ustaše. The lists of imprisoned men which were being drawn up at the palace quite openly were not intended for 'the English' but so that enquiries could be made about them. He reminded Bakarić that for four years he had not turned away people from among the Partisan ranks who asked him to intervene for them.[51]

This was followed by a fusillade of letters from the palace. Stepinac wrote at length to Bakarić on religious education in schools,[52] and sent a memo to Tito on confiscations of property.[53] He followed these up by telegrams to Tito and to the presidency of the Assembly in Belgrade protesting forcefully against the proposed Law on Agrarian Reform which was before the Assembly.[54]. The tone of these communications was vigorous and there was no yielding on any of the rights which the church considered were hers. Whatever the recipients of the letters may have thought, or said in their public utterances, their replies continued to be equable and to express the hope that agreement could be reached. Tito wrote to Stepinac on September 1 saying that it had been quite impossible to exempt church lands from the Law on Agrarian Reform but that the maximum holding had been raised from five to ten hectares.[55]

In Slovenia an informal Commission for Religious Affairs had already been set up in 1944 in liberated territory. A decree of August 21, 1945, set up federal and republican Commissions for Religious Affairs, to study all questions touching on the external life of religious communities and their relations with each other

---

[51] The connections between the archbishop's palace and the Partisans have been spoken about very little by either side. Stepinac's two secretaries, Šalić and Lacković, undoubtedly had Ustaša sympathies; they belonged to the generation of young Croats who were growing up at the time of King Alexander's dictatorship in 1929. Many of the politically conscious young men of this generation turned to extremism, becoming either Ustaša or communist. The writer has been informed that Prebendary Mikulček, the estates manager (ekonom) at the archbishopric, was the channel through which the Partisans received copies of some of the archbishop's wartime sermons, in particular the two delivered on the Feast of Christ the King in 1942 and 1943, and distributed clandestinely; he often travelled, certainly with the archbishop's knowledge, to liberated territory, to buy food and obtain passes from the Partisans. Stepinac's brother was killed by the Germans for Partisan activity, and his mother regularly supplied food to Partisans (Catholic source). When Meštrović saw him in Rome in 1943 and warned him that his life was in danger he answered that he expected to be killed either by the ustaše or the communists (article by Ivan Meštrović, Hrvatska Revija, March 1960, p. 23).

[52] Pattee, doc. LXVII.   [53] Ibid. doc. LXVIII.

[54] Ibid. p. 465. The Law on Agrarian Reform was passed in August 1945 and is discussed in ch. 7.

[55] Pattee, doc. LXVIII, p. 466.

and with the people's authorities, and to prepare material for the legal regulation of relations between church and state.[56]

The Croatian Commission for Religious Affairs was set up on August 21, 1945,[57] with Mgr Svetozar Rittig as its first president. Rittig had been parish priest of St Mark's Church in Zagreb[58] before the war; as a young man he had been Bishop Strossmayer's secretary, and he belonged to the small but important group of Croats who had always supported the union of all the South Slavs. He left Zagreb in 1941 and lived at Selce on the Dalmatian coast near Rijeka until the collapse of Italy, when the Germans occupied the territory. He then, at the age of sixty, joined the Partisans and returned to Zagreb with them at the end of the war, becoming a deputy and a minister in the Croatian government. The basis of his cooperation with the Partisans was political and social rather than ideological. He believed in the union of the South Slavs and was much concerned about social justice, but he was not a fellow-travelling 'patriotic priest'. At the solemn high mass and Te Deum which he celebrated in July on the Feast of SS. Cyril and Methodius, at which members of the Croatian government and representatives from the archbishopric were both present, he spoke of the dream of Illyrian regeneration and the prophecy of Strossmayer and Rački (the great protagonists of the union of the South Slavs) which were now fulfilled.[59] There was never any question of his loyalty to the church, nor was he ever threatened with ecclesiastical sanctions. He and Dr Emilio Pallua, secretary of the commission and also a devoted Catholic, were convinced that the Communist Party was the only force which could hold the separate national elements in Yugoslavia together in a federal union. Rittig saw his task as the interpretation of the church and the authorities to each other; his influence with the government lay in his powers of explanation and persuasion. His statement in 1948,[60] which brought him a certain notoriety, that the church in Yugoslavia was not persecuted was technically accurate; at that time a case could still be made for the government's assertion that they were prosecuting individuals for crimes, not persecuting an institution. It was his tribute to the fact that the government never interfered with the internal structure of the church, or (with the

[56] Petranović, p. 284.
[57] An informal group had been in existence since the spring of 1944.
[58] The seat of the government of Croatia is in Radić Square in the old city and St Mark's Church standing in the middle of the square was always associated with it.
[59] *Vjesnik*, 9.vii.45; *Magnum Crimen*, pp. 1087–8.
[60] *Glasgow Herald*, 18.vi.48.

exception of certain minor matters)[61] tried to control appointments. He was dismayed when the pastoral letter of September 1945[62] appeared; he realised that the church was turning its back on any possibility of reconciliation.

There can be no doubt that at this time the government was more concerned to reach a settlement than the Catholic Church. The latter believed that the communist regime would not last and that the best way of hastening its fall was to press it as hard as possible.[63] The government on the other hand had its hands full of problems and difficulties; behind its proffered olive branch there were other considerations of internal balances of power. It hoped, among other things, that a settlement with the Catholic Church would strengthen its hand against the Orthodox Church, which, although it had no outside power to support it, was a deeply rooted and ineradicable part of the whole being of the Serbian nation. It would have suited the government very well to defer its settlement of accounts with the church, but this would only have been a postponement; the church had no intention of giving it this breathing space. On the other hand the government was also under strong Serbian pressure to punish everyone who had any connection with the Ustaša. On the central and crucial point of religious education neither side was willing to yield, and from their own points of view each was quite right. This was a true question of principle on both sides, and like so many conflicts of principle it was never solved in context. The passage of time and changes in circumstance finally made it seem less relevant. Both sides began to think and to live in a different context.

The situation was moving to a crisis, and towards the end of September it came to a head. The Bishops' Conference met in plenary session from September 17 to 22, and on September 20 issued a pastoral letter addressed to the faithful[64] which was the first of the crucial turning points in the relations between the

---

[61] Immediately after the war the authorities insisted that some priests whose links with the wartime authorities had been too friendly should be removed to other parishes.

[62] See below.

[63] There is a reported conversation between the French consul in Zagreb and Andjelko Fazinić, the Dominican provincial, in 1946; the former thought that the bishops' tactics were mistaken; they should seek temporary accommodations with the government and wait for more favourable times. Fazinić answered that the church's unyielding attitude towards the authorities at the end of the war was the best way to attack them (Petranović, p. 276, quoted from Croatian State Archives, fasc. v, an interrogation without date or origin).

[64] Pattee, doc. LXX.

government and the church; Stepinac's trial and its fateful consequences was the second of these and was closely linked to it. The pastoral letter was accompanied by a second, less-well-known but even more emphatic circular addressed to the clergy,[65] whose contents were obviously known to the government, and was followed on September 22 by a letter to Tito with a list of the demands and protests which had appeared in the pastoral letter.[66] The pastoral letter began by referring to the hope the church had entertained after its first contact with the new authorities that outstanding problems would be settled by mutual agreement, and of its gradual disillusionment. The state of the clergy is starkly described: 243 dead, 169 in prisons and concentration camps, 89 missing – a total of 501. In addition 19 theological students, 2 lay brothers and 4 nuns had been killed or executed; it describes the summary justice meted out to the accused and their deaths without the sacraments. The letter acknowledges that an insignificant number of priests had sinned against Christian justice and deserved to answer for their crimes, but the charges against the majority of the Catholic clergy in Yugoslavia were lies. Those in prison were kept in inhuman conditions. The Catholic press was virtually suppressed. Seminaries for the most part had been confiscated or were occupied by the army, a grave blow for the future of the Church; religious education ceased to be a compulsory school subject in the primary schools and was abolished in the secondary schools. The church's various private secondary schools and the institutions for the care of small children had been taken over by the state, and commissars installed to supervise the teaching. Young people were exposed to moral dangers by the organisation of all-night dances, unsupervised and under the influence of alcohol; they were prevented from attending mass and forced to take part in meetings and organised activities. In some places they were taught the theory of man's descent from the apes and the church's teaching on man's origin was ridiculed. Civil marriage had been introduced, and there was a rapid increase in divorces, an attack on family life. The charitable work of Caritas was under government supervision; the church's possessions, obtained lawfully and honestly and the only means of supporting the central offices of the church and its seminaries, had been confiscated without compensation. Catholic nuns were constantly harassed in their educational and charitable work.

The bishops condemned all ideologies and social systems not based on Christian revelation but on the shallow foundations of

[65] Sept. 21; see n. 68 below.   [66] Pattee, doc. LXIX.

materialist, atheist philosophy and rejoiced in the awakening religious spirit shown among the faithful by the lively devotion to the Mother of God and the great number of pilgrimages to her shrines. They did not wish to provoke a conflict with the new government; their thoughts were always directed to peace and an orderly social and public life which would be best attained by respecting the Christian faith and its morality.

In conclusion they repeated their demands to the government: complete freedom for the Catholic press, complete freedom for Catholic schools, complete freedom of religious instruction in every class of the primary and secondary schools, complete freedom for Catholic organisations and Catholic charitable works, full freedom for inalienable personal rights, full respect for Christian marriage, the return of every confiscated institution. Only so could conditions return to normal and lasting internal peace be attained in the country. The circular was signed by Archbishop Stepinac and seventeen other bishops and vicars-general, all those present at the meeting.[67] The circular to the clergy which went out the next day was much longer and showed that the church's claims were as far-reaching as the party's and quite as absolute.[68] It attacked the whole basis of the

---

[67] The only absentees were the bishops of the divided dioceses on the Italo-Yugoslav frontier. The other signatories were: Archbishop Dobrečić of Bar, Archbishop Ujčić of Belgrade, Bishop Mileta of Šibenik, Bishop Bonifačić of Split, Bishop Srebrnić of Krk, Bishop Pušić of Hvar, Bishop Tomažič of Maribor, Bishop Burić of Senj, Bishop Čekada of Skopje, Bishop Čule of Mostar, Bishop Akšamović of Djakovo, Bishop Budanović of Subotica, Vicar-General Buljan of Sarajevo, Vicar-General Ivaniš of Banja Luka, Vicar-General Vovk of Ljubljana, Vicar-General Jerić of Prekmurje and pro-Vicar Vidošević of Križevci. A PS. ascribes the exclusive responsibility for the circular to the bishops signing it.

[68] Circular addressed to the clergy by the archbishops and bishops of Yugoslavia, 21.ix.45, unnumbered. The principal points of this very long circular are as follows – headings as in circular:

Relations between church and state. The separation of church and state, which both proceed from God, is rejected; it is actively harmful to exclude the church from public life. But if the state persists in separation the church must insist on real freedom for itself, including the right to run its own schools and freedom to carry out religious duties. The state must respect church law and not ask Catholics to act contrary to it (i.e. young people forced to take part in processions on Sunday instead of going to mass, or attend lectures where 'somebody or other explains that there is no God').

Respect for man's dignity. The church respects the dignity and convictions of all men and although it proclaims that there is no salvation outside the church, although it would welcome all mankind to its bosom, it would never compel anyone. Materialism has no conception of the spiritual values of Christianity; it can never lead to love, to mercy, to justice, but only to terrible despotism.

Christian upbringing. It is the duty of Christians to use their legal rights to seek the religious upbringing of children in the name of freedom; it is not a favour

government's reforms and rejected the separation of church and state; it rejected lay education and demanded religious education as a sacred right; it demanded not only the restoration of the religious press but the right to criticise 'constructively and courteously' as a control against excesses; it repeated the arguments against the secularisation of marriage contained in the circular on Christian marriage; it utterly rejected the right of the state to expropriate property arbitrarily and stated baldly that giving assistance to its arbitrary alienation is a sin which the Codex punishes with excommunication (Canon 2334), although it added that the Holy See is always most understanding when asked to cede church property for the general good; it said that the church respects the dignity and convictions of all men, and although it

but a holy right. So-called lay education excludes religion, which is the most important part of education.

The Catholic press. The church asks for full rights to publish newspapers, journals and reviews. The right to criticise, if it is done constructively and courteously, is not a danger to the state but a control against excesses. Competition means life and development, monopoly means stagnation and monopoly of the press petrifaction.

The question of marriage. This section repeats the arguments in the circular on Christian marriage (see pp. 63–4 above).

Private property. The church's mission is supernatural but this does not hinder temporal prosperity. Natural law gives man the right to own private property (Leo XVIII, *Rerum novarum*) and this right is inalienable. It is not wrong to own great possessions but only to misuse them. St Thomas taught that great possessions can be good in themselves, for they give to a man the possibility of exercising the virtues of liberality and munificence. The encyclical *Quadragesimo anno* teaches that the first social duty of an owner is to pay his workmen a living wage so that they can live a life of human dignity.

Private property belongs not only to physical individuals but also to moral persons. The highest moral person is without doubt the Catholic Church. 'The church has by natural law, freely and unimpeded by government, the right to acquire, own and manage property for the objects which are peculiar to the church...To deprive the church, against its will, of its property is a transgression of natural law. *To give assistance to the arbitrary alienation of church property is a sin which the Codex punishes (Canon 2334) by excommunication* [emphasis added]. The church is a perfect and independent society; the state therefore has no right, without a previous agreement with the Holy See arbitrarily to dispose of its property...Whenever the general good has required that the church should cede any of its possessions the Holy See has showed itself always full of understanding, but the church cannot accept arbitrary action. What is more, this kind of arbitrary expropriation of church goods has never been accompanied by blessings and prosperity. Joseph II confiscated much property from the church but enriched neither the state nor the people but only the emperor's commissioners who were in charge of the confiscations.' (Other examples are given.)

Charitable works. 'The poor ye have always with you' even in the best-regulated society. The clergy are urged to give of their surplus to the poor.

The circular closes with an expression of fatherly love and is signed by the full conference of bishops.

proclaims that there is no salvation outside the church, it would never compel anyone to enter its fold; the church is against persecution for any reason.

This was a massive frontal attack, an all-out defiance of the government. It unleashed a storm of fury. The bishops had chosen the most difficult possible time for the government. The provisional government set up with the representatives of the London government was disintegrating; the deputy prime minister, Milan Grol, resigned in August and was followed in October by Šubašić, the foreign minister and former prime minister of the London government, and most of their colleagues, destroying the last pretence that the government represented all sections of opinion. The first crucial postwar elections to choose the Constituent Assembly were about to be held, and a great propaganda campaign for unity and support for the new authorities was in progress. The pastoral letter showed decisively that the church was not prepared to cooperate except on terms quite unacceptable to the government; it assumed that its premises were axiomatic, and spoke in the tones of one accustomed to being obeyed.

Tito was deeply angered. After a month's delay during which the storm was gathering he issued a statement which appeared in the front pages of all newspapers.[69] Why had the bishops never issued a pastoral letter against the terrible killing of Serbs in Croatia? Why were they spreading racial hatred at a time when everyone ought to be helping to heal the wounds of the war? Why was it that so many Ustaša leaders had been educated in the seminaries of Bosnia and Hercegovina? 'Hasn't enough blood been shed during these last five years?' If the bishops said now that they were ready to sacrifice themselves they must have been silent under the ustaše not from terror but because they supported them. When he had promised not to interfere with the church's internal affairs, he had expected the bishops to give a lead in expiating the shame which the ustaše had brought to the Croatian people. He denied that the church in Yugoslavia was persecuted; only guilty individuals were being punished. He warned the bishops that laws existed against chauvinism and against the aggravation of the consequences of the great struggle for freedom.

The pastoral letter had been issued to be read in the churches, but in many places this was not done, or only in part. Pressures were certainly brought, but there must have been some priests, especially those who had cooperated with the Partisans, who were

[69] *Vjesnik*, 25.x.45.

disturbed by its tone.[70] There is also some doubt whether all the bishops wished to challenge the government so openly.[71] Archbishop Dobrečić of Bar, Primate of Serbia, refused to allow it to be read or published in his diocese.[72] In territories with a mixed population, in Dubrovnik and its surroundings, and in many parishes in Bosnia and Hercegovina, priests refused to read the letter;[73] the Serbian population would have found it an intolerable affront. Boris Kidrič dismissed the protests against the agrarian reform: 'It is too much to expect that in today's circumstances I should even try to answer this question. Our peasants have for centuries fought for the land – that is all that needs to be said.' The church in Slovenia was at last free of the political ties of the past, he added, and did not receive political instructions from the OF. The Catholic masses in Slovenia were a part of the OF; they shared the new power and the new freedom.[74] (This was a boast which the Slovene authorities could make with more justice than those in any other part of the country.)

When the elections for the Constituent Assembly took place on November 11, 1945, the government received a predictably overwhelming mandate. There was some evidence to indicate that the clergy discouraged their flocks, particularly women, from voting, and Bishop Akšamović had written to Mgr Rittig before the election to say that he thought that members of the HSS (Croatian Peasant Party) would abstain,[75] but this does not appear to have affected the results appreciably. Mgr Rittig was a candidate for Djakovo and became a member of the Croatian government.

From now on attacks against Stepinac in the press became frequent and more violent. He was constantly attacked at public meetings, the walls of the houses where the cathedral clergy lived were covered with the hammer and sickle, slogans and offensive graffiti, nuns and priests were insulted in the street.[76]

---

[70] For example Dr Metod Mikuš regretted that the pastoral letter did not condemn fascism and said nothing about the liberation of the country (Sl. Por., 7.x.45, quoted in Vjesnik, 18.x.45).

[71] Tito referred to this in his statement: 'I don't want to condemn all of those who signed it because some did so under pressure and don't agree with its contents.' Dr Josip Rittig, a brother of Mgr Rittig, told Branko Petranović that some of the bishops were unhappy about the pastoral letter (Petranović, p. 298) and the writer was told in 1970 by an informed Catholic source that a few bishops had been doubtful about the wisdom of publishing the letter openly.

[72] Petranović, p. 295.　　　　　　　　　　　　　[73] Vjesnik, 25.x.45.

[74] Kidrič, reprinted from Sl. Por., 7.x.45.

[75] Petranović, p. 301, citing letter 1.x.45 (no source).　　　[76] Pattee, doc. LXXI.

On All Saints' Day, just before Stepinac left for the cathedral, he was informed by two men 'sent from the authorities' that the people would rise up in arms if he attacked the authorities in church. To his repeated question 'Who are these people?' they answered, 'That is our business.'[77]

On November 4 as the archbishop arrived at Zaprešić to open a new parish, he was attacked by a mob, including men in uniform, who threw stones and eggs and beat up the new administrator of the parish who expostulated with them.[78] Stepinac managed to get back into the car, which drove off. He brought back two sizable stones which had been hurled at him, weighing 700 and 800 grams respectively, as he informed Bakarić on November 10 in an angry letter, denying the allegation in the government's communiqué of November 6 that he had provoked the trouble.[79]

In communicating the circumstances of this attack to the clergy the archbishop wrote that in future he would be unable to undertake any duties which would take him outside the palace. He added: 'I must warn you not to allow a single word to escape you, either when preaching or in the confessional, which could be interpreted as having a political character.'[80]

Shortly after this occurrence the official gazette of the Zagreb archdiocese published a series of seven articles, which were a detailed defence of the archbishop and an attempt to refute all the charges against him.[81] These represent the church's considered defence of its official actions during the war, and have been drawn on extensively by those who have written in the archbishop's defence.[82] They begin with a detailed list of the occasions when Stepinac and the other bishops intervened in defence of individuals or groups – and there were indeed very many such occasions and all sorts and classes of people were helped, the most notable being the rescue of 7,000 children from Serbian and Partisan families, who were cared for until the end of the war and after by Catholic families, and whom Stepinac scrupulously refused to allow to be baptised into the Catholic Church – emphasising how much courage this required in the circumstances of the time. On several occasions he wrote to Pavelić in very strong language:

---

[77] Circular to clergy, dated 7.xi.45, concerning happenings at Zaprešić on 4.xi.45.
[78] Ibid.
[79] Pattee, doc. LXXI.
[80] Ibid. doc. LXXI, p. 481.
[81] SVNZ, 6.xi.45, 19.xi.45, 3.xii.45, 31.xii.45, 15.i.46, 4.ii.46, 20.ii.46.
[82] Cf. Pattee, O'Brien, Dragoun.

This [the execution of a priest for having refused to celebrate mass and sing a Te Deum when the NDH was founded] is a shameful blot and a crime, which cries to heaven for vengeance, just as the whole of Jasenovac is a shameful blot. . . as for me, as priest and bishop, I cry with Christ on the Cross: Father forgive them, for they know not what they do. The whole public, especially the families of those who have been killed, want satisfaction, compensation and the bringing of the criminals to justice. They are the greatest misfortune of Croatia.

He told Pavelić plainly, too, what he thought of the shooting of hostages, and he publicly preached in defence of Jews, gypsies, Serbs and other persecuted minorities. He supported the request of the Jewish religious organisation in Zagreb to continue its work among Jews who were still at liberty, which draws forth the comment from the gazette:

This document is clear evidence of how broad-minded and unprejudiced the actions of the archbishop were. When one remembers the times in which the document was written, the circumstances in which we lived, the meaning of this gesture of the archbishop leaps out at one. It is clear proof of great toleration which at that time went to the uttermost limit of the possible.[83]

Later, however, Stepinac spoke out with far greater force against the communists. Either he feared them less than he feared the ustaše – that is the logical inference from a passage like this – or, what is more likely, he had no mental reservations about the situation of the church under the communists and, being a courageous man, said what he thought.

The last article is devoted to the 'forced conversions' and it is here that the unease of the writers is most evident. They were on delicate ground and they chose their words and arguments carefully. The article sets out the complicated theological problem involved; reiterates the opposition of the church to any compulsion, an opposition which was repeatedly expressed by the bishops during the war; and says frankly: 'The movement for conversion to Catholicism in the NDH during the war had a more political than religious significance.'

The church was in a difficult situation, as individuals and groups were imploring the church to admit them to save their

[83] His interventions with the authorities also showed a certain capacity for accommodation and a willingness to accept the implications of anti-Semitism. In a letter to Artuković, minister of the interior (Pattee, doc. xxvi), he suggested that Jews should not be forced to wear special insignia (i.e. the yellow star) but might be required to buy them so as to defray the cost to the ministry. On the other hand, he hid a Jewish rabbi in the palace (writer's interview with the Rev. S. Lacković, formerly Stepinac's secretary, June 1973, in the USA), an action which certainly called for courage.

lives. 'The church acted according to canon law; it did not close its doors to anyone, but it used no force or persuasion.' Referring to the circular issued to the clergy at that time,[84] the bishops wrote that 'by emphasising the necessity of guarding the dignity of the church it was proclaimed that the church refused to become a blind weapon of the regime in carrying out its policy towards the Serbs. It would have degraded the church if the Orthodox had been received into the church simply out of terror with no regard for the laws of the church.' The church was, in fact, more merciful and more sensible than this passage implies; a circular issued on March 2, 1942, authorised conversions for 'secondary motives', and there were many instances of Orthodox being received into the Catholic Church in a purely formal sense, in an effort to protect them.

It is clear from the articles that the principle of conversion was accepted without hesitation or reservation, but under the bishops' control. The article referred to a passage in the bishops' letter to Pavelić: 'Conversions are carried out by people who often behave as though there were no church authorities. Naturally they make mistake after mistake.'[85]

The 'mistakes' were the ferocious and amply documented slaughter of the Serbian Orthodox population, which was known to the bishops when they wrote the letter, and to the writers of the 1946 articles. The article concludes:

The memorandum to Pavelić...made once and for all impossible the arbitrary and uncanonical interfering of the civil authorities and political people in the delicate matter of people's consciences. It condemned strongly the circumstances of the persecution of the Serbs just when they had converted, so that the Catholic Church cannot be condemned as the persecutor and murderer of the Orthodox converts. The bishops in this memorandum put a decisive end to any action of those religious who did not have a legal canonical mission. Because of this their behaviour was proclaimed non-valid. In a word the bishops clearly and decidedly spoke on the question of converts. Consequently the bishops refused to accept responsibility for the injustices which happened during the conversions to Catholicism. By the demand that Serbs should be given in reality the most basic right to life and possessions, the bishops took a decided and courageous step for the protection of Serbs which will stand the test of history.

These articles were intended to provide the basis for a legal defence of the bishops' actions;[86] but read after the event it must be admitted that they give a disagreeable impression of self-righteousness and self-justification.

[84] 15.iv.41.   [85] 20.xi.41; also Pattee, doc. LII.
[86] Catholic source.

The circulars to the clergy of the archdiocese of Zagreb at this period (1945–6) give a glimpse into the circumstances of the everyday life of the church and the parish clergy, which somehow continued to function, although many parishes were without priests. All wartime conversions were annulled by a regulation of the Territorial Anti-fascist Council of Croatia (ZAVNOH) even before the end of the war.[87] A circular informs priests that any converts wishing to return to their former faith should notify the parish office in writing; this request must be noted in the parish's register of converts and a notification sent to the authorities of the church to which the convert wishes to return.[88]

A large number of churches and parish buildings were damaged during the war. The government had promised compensation but repairs were urgent. Bishop Salis thanked the priests and parishioners of some parishes who had begun repairs themselves without waiting for outside help, and urged others to do likewise.[89] The government had kept its undertaking not to shut down the church's charitable work and the archbishopric was notified in a communication from the Commission for Religious Affairs that the work of Caritas might continue.[90] The archbishop asks the faithful to give as much as they can, especially food for poor families.

On May 9, 1946, the government took over all the official registers of births, marriages and deaths which had formerly been kept by the churches. After that date copies of the parish registers were no longer to be sent to the state but to the archbishopric.[91] The clergy were also warned that they would receive a notification from the general secretariat of the government of an order[92] forbidding the issuing of personal documents to persons living abroad who asked for them privately, by-passing diplomatic and military offices.[93] They were again warned not to mention politics in church.[94] The church's income had suddenly been reduced to almost nothing and there were acute difficulties in dealing with taxation, compulsory deliveries of agricultural produce and the support needed for seminaries. How stark that poverty could be is shown in a brief circular to the Zagreb diocesan clergy, requesting priests who did not own a cassock, and did not have the means to buy one, to inform the archbishopric.[95]

[87] 25.viii.44, quoted in Circular 6060/45, 28.ix.45.
[88] Ibid.   [89] 7135/45, 5.x.45.
[90] 21.ix.45, quoted in Circular 8042, 27.x.45. *SVNZ*, 6.xi.45.
[91] 6728/46, 5.xi.46.   [92] No. 520, 12.x.46.
[93] 6711/46, 8.vi.46.   [94] 5857/46, 30.ix.46.
[95] 1343/51, 27.ii.51.

Among the ustaše who escaped at the end of the war and later infiltrated back into Yugoslavia was Colonel Erih Lisak, director of public order and security and state secretary in the ministry of the interior of the NDH. He secretly visited the archbishop's palace; after he was caught and the investigation against him was under way the Rev. Ivan Šalić, one of the archbishop's secretaries,[96] and two catechists, Crnković and Šimecki, were arrested in December 1945. Two searches of the archbishop's palace were carried out by OZNA (Odeljenje za Zaštitu Naroda – Department for the Protection of the People) during which it was alleged that medical supplies for the ustaše groups in the woods were discovered, and also boxes containing the complete speeches of Pavelić. Evidence was also uncovered that a flag for the *križari* (crusaders) which had been specially made by nuns was secretly blessed at a service in the archbishop's private chapel in the palace and then taken to the woods. At about this time the chancellor, Canon Dr Borić, had found an unknown young man in the cathedral, exhausted and semi-conscious, and had fed him and given him overnight shelter. The man was Grema, a secondary-school student who had shot the Partisan Captain Globnička in the street and taken refuge in the cathedral.[97] Bakarić reported these facts at a press conference on December 15, 1945,[98] as evidence of the close connection between the higher clergy and the ustaše. He hinted that Lisak's visit to the palace was not unconnected with the contents of the September pastoral letter but he insisted that the arrests were not part of a campaign against the letter but the 'consequences of concrete events'. There had been no change in the government's attitude to the church; it was the higher clergy who bore the entire responsibility for the unsatisfactory relations between church and state, and it depended on the church's energy and sincerity whether those relations would develop well.

Stepinac hit back the next day in a vigorous circular[99] to the clergy. He denied that he had known about the blessing of the flag,[100] the bound volume of Pavelić's speeches or the medical supplies for groups in the forest. Many people came to the palace,

---

[96] Lacković, the other, had left Yugoslavia in July 1945 on a mission to Rome; when he asked the Yugoslav representative in Rome for an extension to his three-week valid passport, it was confiscated and he was refused permission to return (interview with the Rev. S. Lacković, June 1973, in the USA).

[97] Borić was condemned to five years' imprisonment for this act of compassion and served his sentence in Lepoglava prison, where he was one of the two companions whom Stepinac was allowed to have with him.

[98] *Narodni List* and *Vjesnik*, 16.xii.45.

[99] 8976/45.

[100] At his subsequent trial Stepinac denied that Šalić, his secretary, had told him about this, but stated that he had learned about it later from Šimecki.

and he could not be expected to know if someone gave a false name.[101] He rejected scornfully the suggestion that Lisak's visit had anything to do with the September pastoral letter.[102] He defended Canon Borić, who had performed a simple act of Christian charity. His conscience was clear and at rest before God, before the Holy See, before the Catholics of the country and before the Croatian people. The church still wished to see an agreement with the state and had handed in its demands but so far had not received any reply; in any case it was the Holy See which must have the last word as far as the church was concerned.

Each side washed its hands of responsibility for the state of relations between them and put all the onus on the other.

Stepinac must have realised by now that the net was closing around him, but the vigour of his pronouncements did not abate and he continued to exhort his clergy to stand fast, while not giving unnecessary cause for attacks on the church. In the middle of January a mob protesting against black-marketeers turned into a demonstration against Stepinac, calling for his arrest and trial;[103] a week later the palace was again raided by police and archives and church records were seized.[104] The news which came out of Yugoslavia was difficult to confirm or deny; the Catholic press abroad, headed by *L'Osservatore Romano*, made the most of it. The Yugoslav authorities vigorously denied that the church was persecuted and said that only priests who had been criminals had been tried and sentenced. They accused the Vatican of timing the reports to coincide with the Paris peace conference.[105]

It was possible until about 1946 or 1947 for both sides to make a valid case; it depended on the definition of war crimes, and how one viewed the church's claim that its privileges, power and possessions belonged to it by divine right. After this time, as we shall see, the harrying of the clergy, particularly the higher clergy, became a matter of policy, often carried to excess especially by local authorities, to try to break down the rigid stand of the clergy against the authorities; trials became show trials, and, after the 1948 break with the Cominform until 1951 or 1952, they were intended to prove that the Yugoslavs were as good, or even better communists than the rest of the communist world. All the evidence taken together, the foreign press reports, the

101 Lisak had called himself Petrović.
102 The incident of Lisak's visit is treated at length in ch. 3.
103 *Daily Telegraph*, 18.i.46.
104 *Times*, 24.i.46.   105 *NYT*, 26.vii.46.

items appearing in the Yugoslav press and the memories, twenty years later, of people who lived through that time, both Marxist and Catholic, leaves no doubt that the immediate retribution on the clergy was extremely harsh. In the months after the end of the war, it was too swift to give time for appeals or second thoughts; and later the trials, the accusations and the harrying became an object lesson designed to prove that the Catholic Church in Yugoslavia had collaborated with the Axis powers during the war and, since 1945, was in alliance through the Vatican with Italy, a hostile foreign power, which had territorial claims on Yugoslavia.

Trieste

Before going on to the situation in Slovenia it is necessary to turn aside from what was happening to the church to describe the background of political events centring around Trieste and the Julian region, which had such a profound effect on the relations between the Yugoslav authorities and the Catholic Church.

After the Partisans had been forced to withdraw, protesting vigorously, from Trieste, the Belgrade agreement was negotiated between the Anglo-Americans and the Yugoslavs and signed on June 9, 1945, dividing the disputed territories of Trieste and the Julian region into Zones A and B.[106] Zone A included Trieste and its hinterland to the north-west, together with Pola (Pula), and was administered by the Allied military government; Zone B included the rest of the Julian region and was administered by the Yugoslav military administration.

The history of the next eight years in this region is basically the struggle between Italy and Yugoslavia for the territory of these two zones, with the Western Allies at first holding the ring but later veering increasingly towards support of Italy, until the expulsion of Yugoslavia from the Cominform and the transformation in the balance of power in south-east Europe reversed this trend.

Yugoslavia's foreign policy and its propaganda both external and internal were focussed with great intensity on this struggle, which was one of the principal facets of the complex and dangerous external relationships which the new state, ravaged by war and civil strife, had to deal with. Its relations with the Catholic Church during this period were one aspect of this struggle.

The Yugoslav authorities were unwilling to cooperate with

106 Zone A. 361,000 inhabitants, of whom 25 per cent were Slovene; Zone B: much larger area and smaller population (65,000), of whom over 50 per cent were Slovene and Croat (*Italian Genocide Policy against the Slovenes and Croats*, p. 163).

non-communists in Zone A, and the Allied military government therefore set up an administration which was largely Italian, based on the Italian legal system and employing minor civil servants who had been members of the Fascist Party. The Yugoslavs protested, and in retaliation introduced into Zone B the new Yugoslav system of government based on National Liberation Committees and People's Courts. The revolution which took place in this zone was nationalist as much as it was communist; Italians were ousted from the leading positions which they had held and Yugoslavs took over, a change which had the support of virtually the whole Slav population. The Law on Agrarian Reform, carried out during the course of 1946, dispossessed Italian landlords and gave land to their Croat and Slovene tenants, and the decree voiding the compulsory sales at auction of Croat farms in Istria for non-payment of taxes and bank loans, which had taken place after the First World War, returned much land to its original owners.[107]

The Yugoslavs, supported at this time by the Italian Communist Party, inundated the Council of Foreign Ministers who were negotiating the peace treaty with Italy[108] with letters, memoranda and telegrams, signed by all sections of the population, including groups of priests, demanding the incorporation of the whole territory under dispute into Yugoslavia. The growing rift between the great powers was reflected in the Soviet support of Yugoslavia's claims and the Western Allies' support of Italy. Yugoslavs were genuinely indignant to find that a former enemy, and one, moreover, under whose occupation they had suffered, was favoured over a wartime ally which had made spectacular sacrifices for the common victory. They accused the Western powers of imperialism and abetting Italian expansion, and from their own point of view, it is difficult to blame them. The Allies on the other hand, watching the Soviet grip tighten over central and eastern Europe and seeing Yugoslavia's support for the Soviet Union, were reluctant to cede any further footholds to a communist government, particularly an important strategic port such as Trieste.

The Italian peace treaty of 1947 redrew the zonal boundaries, putting the major part of Istria including Pula into the Yugoslav-administered Zone B; great friction developed between the two zones, a faithful reflection of the growing tension between East and West. In practice Yugoslavia administered Zone B as a part of its own territory and Zone A came increasingly under Italian

---

[107] B. Novak, pp. 237–8: 3,393 tenants received an average of 3 hectares each.
[108] From Sept. 1945 to Feb. 1947.

influence; Italian control over education grew and the Slovene language was relegated to a secondary status which provoked further Yugoslav protests and aroused indignation among all Slovenes, not least the nationally conscious clergy. During this period various Slovene Catholic groups which had found refuge in Zone A were active; a weekly *Slovenski Primorec* [The Coastal Slovene] was published in Gorizia by a group of Catholics, and later *Nedelja* [Sunday], a religious weekly, appeared in Trieste. A Catholic cultural organisation was formed in 1946 in Gorizia and in 1947 Catholics from Gorizia and liberals from Trieste united to form the Slovenska Demokratska Zveza (Slovene Democratic Alliance) which published the weekly *Demokracija*. The Yugoslav authorities treated these groups as enemies and banned their publications. The Rev. Jozef Kragelj, a priest at Livek near Kobarid, was tried in 1949 for distributing *Slovenski Primorec* and *Demokracija*.[109]

Yugoslavia's expulsion from the Cominform in 1948 changed the situation dramatically. It was almost a year before the effects of this began to be felt in the relations between East and West, but when Britain and America finally accepted the reality and permanence of the break, they began to act on the changed strategic situation. Now aid poured into Yugoslavia from the West, while to the east the Soviet Union and its satellites set up a total blockade.

One consequence of the changed situation was that Yugoslavia and Italy, prodded and helped by Britain and the United States, moved slowly towards direct negotiations over the disputed territory. Both the approach to the negotiations and the negotiations themselves which began in 1951 were difficult and long-drawn-out and while they were proceeding each zone became increasingly incorporated into its patron state. Zone B was in practice administered as a part of Yugoslavia; the Law on Workers' Self-Management was introduced into the zone in 1951 and social welfare provisions were greatly increased and extended. Italian influence continued to grow in Zone A until in 1953 Britain and France withdrew their troops and handed the zone over to the Italians; at the same time an unlikely community of interest developed between the Catholic Church, under its strongly anti-communist and pro-Italian bishop Mgr Santin, and the local pro-Moscow Communist Party under its

---

[109] *Sl. Por.*, 8.vii.49. Kragelj was accused of various other crimes, including giving information to foreign intelligence services, and sentenced to death. He was, however, reprieved and finally released in 1960 (Marxist source, confirmed by a Catholic source).

Italian leader Vidali; they became the leaders of anti-Yugoslav feeling in Trieste.

The noisy propaganda which accompanied the negotiations faithfully reflected their state of progress or deadlock. Bishop Santin, for example, issued a detailed list of religious persecutions in Zone B and cabled to Archbishop Spellman of New York appealing for protection from 'raging, pitiless religious persecution',[110] giving Spellman a weapon to bring pressure on the American government to stop sending aid to Yugoslavia; the Yugoslavs accused the Vatican of collaborating with Italian expansionism. They had already opened Zone B to American and British military and civilian personnel to prove that Italian accusations about the situation there were unfounded.[111]

By the time the final agreement was reached in 1954 both sides had realised that permanent partition was the only solution. A memorandum of understanding, usually known as the London Agreement, gave Zone B to Yugoslavia and Zone A (with slight frontier adjustments in favour of Yugoslavia) and the city of Trieste to Italy, and created a free port in Trieste. There were to be no reprisals, the rights of minorities were carefully guarded and those who wished could transfer from one country to the other. Neither government formally renounced its territorial claims, but the great powers, including the Soviet Union (which after Stalin's death had entered into a new phase in its foreign policy and accepted the agreement), considered the question closed. It has stood the test of time. Both the Yugoslav and the Italian governments lived up to the spirit of the London Agreement and ceased giving support to dissident groups and provocative acts. One of the consequences of the new situation was the beginning of a change in the position of the Catholic Church.

Slovenia and Istria

The Partisans had liberated large portions of Slovenia before the end of the war, and had set up local National Liberation Committees to administer them. The situation was confused as the war drew to an end; many German commanders refused to surrender to Partisan units, and some took hostages to protect themselves. The Partisans did not enter Ljubljana until May 9, 1945, ten days after reaching their prime objective, Trieste.

The church authorites in Ljubljana immediately made contact with the leaders of the OF. Dr M. Miklavčič of the theological faculty, who had supported the OF during the war, made the

[110] B. Novak, p. 379.   [111] Ibid. p. 376.

first approach and immediately afterwards a delegation led by Dr Vovk, the vicar-general, called on Boris Kidrič, the head of the Slovene government.[112]

A requiem for the dead was celebrated in the cathedral, attended by representatives of the government,[113] the army and all sections of the population.[114]

Dr Vovk followed this first encounter with the authorities with a second visit on July 11. The meeting between the communist leaders and the Zagreb clergy had taken place at the beginning of June at Marshal Tito's invitation. In Ljubljana the initiative came from the church, and the communist leaders found the attitude of their visitors more acceptable.[115] The delegation presented a memorandum welcoming the new Slovene government, and referring particularly to its concern for ordinary men and women, for the victims of the war and for the education of the people; they declared their support for the political unity of the whole of Slovene ethnic territory. They condemned the wartime collaboration of the clergy and laity but tried to explain why it had happened; they hoped the government would allow the religious education of children, the religious celebration of marriage, the religious press, the training of priests and the security of church property necessary for the work of the church.[116]

There were a number of reasons why Dr Vovk's approach to the new authorities should have differed from that of the Zagreb delegation. Bishop Rožman had fled and there was the chance of a fresh start. In Slovenia there was a sharp difference between the clergy who had collaborated or tolerated the occupation (for the most part from the diocese of Ljubljana) and those who had collaborated or sympathised with the resistance (the clergy from the German-occupied zones and from the Julian region). The Croatian clergy had at least had the semblance of an independent state to claim their allegiance. In Slovenia, moreover, there was a real and largely spontaneous movement among the clergy who had fought with the OF to take part in the socialist reconstruction of Slovenia, a movement which found expression when the Commission for Religious Affairs was set up in February 1944 and

[112] Writer's interview with Dr Maks Miklavčič, July 1970. After Bishop Rožman's flight Dr Vovk had been elected by the chapter to act in his place; he was consecrated in October 1946 and appointed auxiliary bishop. Other members of the delegation were Vicar-General Dr Nadrah and Edvard Kocbek, by now a vice-president of the federal government.
[113] Including Kocbek and Dr Marjan Brecelj, who had belonged to the Christian Socialists but was now a member of the Communist Party.
[114] *Sl. Por.*, 15.v.45.   [115] Petranović, p. 280.
[116] *Vjesnik*, 16.vii.45, quoted by Petranović, p. 280.

in the meetings of priests which began shortly after the end of the war[117] and led to the founding of the priests' association.[118]

The July visit was not followed by the improvement in relations which both sides may have hoped for.[119] Both Dr Vovk and Bishop Tomažič of Maribor signed the bishops' pastoral letter of September 1945, and Boris Kidrič's reaction was very sharp.[120] There were no further contacts after this between the bishops and the government, although Catholic intellectuals and members of the theological faculty continued to meet government and party leaders informally and Dr Miklavčič frequently served as an intermediary between Dr Vovk and the authorities.[121] Dr Slapšak, one of Bishop Rožman's secretaries, was arrested before the end of the year and preparations were begun for the trial of Bishop Rožman *in absentia*, together with the leading German and Slovene personalities who had ruled Slovenia during the war. The first attempt at forming a Slovene priests' association fell into the hands of extremists who made no attempt to reconcile their brother priests or to moderate their language. A further complication was the division of the three border dioceses (Pola–Parenzo, Trieste and Gorizia) between Yugoslavia and Italy. The sees were all in Zone A, apostolic administrators being appointed for the portions of the dioceses lying in Zone B. Bishop Margotti of Gorizia, who was Italian, and Bishop Santin of Trieste, who was born in Istria but had strong Italian and fascist sympathies, were constantly attacked in the Yugoslav press.[122]

Nevertheless there were a few hopeful indications. Some of the seminaries which had been requisitioned for housing were returned;[123] three new religious publications appeared. *Oznanilo* [Church Notices], a semi-official organ of the diocese of Ljubljana, *Verski List* [Religious Gazette] in the diocese of Maribor, and *Gore Srca* [Lift Up Your Hearts], a fortnightly.[124] The first Croatian seminary in Istria had been opened in Pazin on December 11, 1945, by Bishop Santin of Trieste.[125] The lower clergy of Istria had always been largely Slav, and the relations between them and the new authorities were from the beginning easier than in Zagreb. In particular the Istrian clergy genuinely

---

[117] The first took place on Sept. 27, 1945 (*Bilten*, 4.xi.48).
[118] Discussed in ch. 4.   [119] Petranović, p. 281.
[120] *Sl. Por.*, 7.x.45.   [121] Interview with Dr Miklavčič, July 1970.
[122] See e.g. *Sl. Por.*, 8.v.52, and *Borba*, 26.viii.52.
[123] Interview with Boris Kidrič, *Sl. Por.*, 7.x.45.
[124] The last was edited from the seminary in Pazin; the first number (1.iv.46) was published in Trieste, but on July 1 it moved to Rijeka and eventually to Zagreb.
[125] *Gore Srca*, 1.iv.46.

welcomed the agrarian reform which had already begun in the liberated areas in 1944; parish land holdings were as exiguous as those of the peasants and almost none had the legal maximum of 10 hectares allowed by the Law on Agrarian Reform. The clergy did not stand to gain by it, but they did not lose, and they saw land being distributed to their landless parishioners. The majority also supported Yugoslavia's claim to Istria.[126] Elsewhere pilgrimages had been resumed and some churches were already repaired.[127] Nevertheless, 67 (out of 285) of the parishes in the diocese of Ljubljana were without a priest;[128] the incumbents had fled, or perished, or were in prison.[129] Over all hung the shadow of the long struggle for Trieste and the Julian region.

Kidrič expressed the attitude of the authorities in the same interview[130] in which he attacked the pastoral letter: 'the Catholic Church is not only composed of upper clergy and priests but also the broad masses of the Slovene Catholic peoples, who are a part of the OF and share in the freedom and rights it has brought to the country'. There is no doubt that some priests in Slovenia and Istria agreed with him and were hopeful for the future.

In August 1946 Bishop Rožman was put on trial *in absentia*, accused of treason to the people and the state; the other accused in the trial were Rupnik, president of the wartime civil government of Ljubljana and a former Yugoslav army general, Rösener, the German S.S. general in command in Slovenia, Dr Hacin, the Ljubljana wartime police chief, Dr Krek, a former minister who had spent the war years in England and was also tried *in absentia*, and others.[131] This was not only a trial of war criminals – with whom the government associated Rožman – but also a show trial designed to prove the criminal collaboration of the accused with the German army, the 'Anglo-Saxon intelligence' and the 'Royal Army' (i.e. the Serbian Četniks). Rožman was accused of conspiring at the beginning of the war with other Slovene leaders, some of whom were to stay in Ljubljana and collaborate with the occupiers, while Dr Krek and others joined the government-in-exile, but held themselves in readiness to return if the Axis powers were victorious. He was also accused

---

[126] Letter from seven prominent Istrian priests to the Inter-Allied Commission, 21.iii.46; *Sl. Por.* 23.iii.46.

[127] *Oznanilo*, 1.xi.45.   [128] Ibid. 1.xi.45.

[129] Boris Kidrič said in October that there were twenty priests in prison awaiting trial: *Sl. Por.*, 7.x.45.   [130] Ibid.

[131] *Proces proti vojnim zločincem in izdaljcem Rupniku, Röseneru, Rožmanu, Kreku, Vizjaku in Hacinu* [The Trial of the War Criminals and Traitors Rupnik, Rösener, Rožman, Krek, Vizjak and Hacin], Ljubljana, 1946.

of having used his influence to persuade his clergy to collaborate with the occupiers, and of persecuting and threatening with excommunication those who joined the OF. The prosecution laid stress on the 'denationalising' activities of Rožman and his willing cooperation with the occupiers. He was accused of sending a memorandum to Mussolini in May 1941 expressing pleasure at the annexation of Slovenia to the Kingdom of Italy and promising cooperation and loyalty to the Duce; in 1943 he had been present when the newly formed Domobrans (Home Guards) took the oath of allegiance in front of Rösener, the German commanding general. He was sentenced to eighteen years' imprisonment.

His former chancellor, Dr Metod Mikuš, wrote after he had fled: it is 'no excuse that he was weak, indecisive, good-hearted, not well-informed...he had every opportunity to change his mind, and as a Catholic bishop and a Slovene he ought to have done so. The reasons which kept him from doing so are no longer interesting.'[132] Unlike the trial of Archbishop Stepinac, Bishop Rožman's trial had little effect on the subsequent life of the church.

Dr Vovk was consecrated auxiliary bishop in 1946 but was not installed as bishop until 1959, after Rožman's death.[133] He was a courageous, practical man, with considerable pastoral gifts, who guided his diocese tactfully through the next difficult ten years without compromising the essentials of the Catholic faith.[134] A circular to the clergy of the archdiocese in 1952 is a characteristic example of his pastoral style.[135] The relevant portion, an exposition of Canon 1925, section 1 (Christians are bound to profess their faith openly; silence, tergiversation, or behaviour which conveys implicit denial, a contempt of religion or injury to God or scandal to neighbours is forbidden), is written in Latin as an indication that this was meant for the eyes of the clergy only.[136] He reminds the clergy that no believer may learn or teach

[132] *Sl. Por.*, 31.v.45.
[133] *CNS*. The Vatican's unwillingness to deprive Rožman of his title to the see and to confirm Dr Vovk as bishop until after Rožman's death was a source of continuing resentment to the government. The see became an archbishopric on Dec. 22, 1961.
[134] One of his canons said to the writer in 1970: 'he had a peasant's grasp of reality, and he was always honest with the government and the party; they understood this and appreciated it'. When the Catholic secondary school at St Vid was nationalised he refused to lodge a complaint with the federal government in Belgrade as he was not willing to 'complain to outsiders about other Slovenes'.
[135] No. 5/1952, 30.iv.52.
[136] Obviously the church knew that its correspondence was censored. During his imprisonment Canon Dr Lenič was given Latin correspondence intercepted

any atheistic system (e.g. materialism) in schools, or any politico-socio-cultural system of which atheism is an essential part, without at the same time demonstrating the falsity of atheism and recognising only the part of the system which is good, true or merely indifferent in relation to the Catholic religion. No believer may make a promise to any authority to omit any of the essential practices of his religion (prayer, receiving the sacraments, going to mass on Sundays and holy days of obligation, religious instruction and communication with any priest) or decide privately out of fear to omit consistently these practices. But priests are advised to be gentle 'each time' in the confessional to the faithful who are afraid to go to mass, urging them to persevere in private prayer. Parents who are afraid to send their children publicly to religious instruction must be responsible for seeing that they are properly instructed at home. The circular continues: 'Let Christians remember that they are sometimes obliged to undertake even heroic acts of faith and that such acts are possible with the grace of God.'

The tone is very different from the thundering denunciations which issued from the archbishop's palace in Zagreb six years earlier, but the essentials of the faith are there, expressed with a tact and gentleness which make the picture of the life of the faithful which it mirrors more credible than any amount of minatory rumblings from *L'Osservatore Romano*. On the other hand it is understandable that the government refused then and for many years after to allow openly practising believers to teach, especially in primary schools.

The press reported that the bishop had ordered the faithful to observe Sundays and holy days 'even if they had fallen into disuse' and had ordered them to send their children to catechism even if they were non-believers; he was accused of inciting the clergy to use the confessional to teach the faithful to be two-faced and of giving the impression that conditions in Yugoslavia were very bad by speaking of 'the need for heroism', whereas priests were allowed to give religious instruction and to say mass daily.[137]

Dr Vovk was a brave man and a resolute one. Earlier in 1952, on January 20, he had been the victim of a particularly brutal attack and barely escaped serious injury; he had been assaulted in the station at Novo Mesto and petrol was thrown over him and ignited. Nevertheless he continued to visit his diocese and to keep

by the security police to translate (information from a former fellow prisoner).
[137] *Sl. Por.*, 27.v.52.

in touch with his clergy. Shortly before the incident he had sent a circular to the clergy on the religious instruction of children, for which he was fined 10,000 dinars; in March he sent the pope's discourses against abortion to his clergy and was fined 5,000 dinars, since the Yugoslav government had recently authorised abortion in certain circumstances; and his Latin circular cost him 10,000 dinars.[138] The incident at Novo Mesto occurred towards the end of the period when the clergy were in frequent danger of physical assault and harassment, and seems to have shaken the authorities, who sent him an apology,[139] while Kardelj expressed his regrets to the chargé d'affairs at the nunciature[140] and *Borba* (reported by *The Times*) said that the incident was 'uncalled for' and 'not in accordance with our policy of complete tolerance to the Roman Catholic Church'.[141] Dr Vovk's dignified behaviour and refusal to dramatise the incident contributed to the general lowering of tension which set in shortly after this time. His assailant was tried and sentenced to ten days' imprisonment.[142]

During the period from 1946 into the early fifties many priests in Slovenia and Istria were tried both for wartime collaboration and for postwar spying and anti-national activities, and often for a combination of both. In every case the lesson that this all formed part of a central conspiracy involving the Western Allies – 'the imperialists' – the Vatican, the Italians and Moscow, was driven home by the terms of the indictments, the judgments and the press accounts. Doubtless there was truth in many of the accusations, particularly of hiding former ustaše or Bela Gardists and helping them to get out of the country, and of sending information to the Vatican about what was happening in Yugoslavia. If the positions had been reversed the Partisans would have been doing the same thing, even more efficiently. It is the way the facts are marshalled in the reports of each of these trials, and the reiterated similarity of the interpretation put on them, which in the end induce disbelief on the part of the reader.

Dr Stanislav Blatnik, the former superior of the Salesian monastery at Rakovnik, was in Rome; his name appears in several trials as an agent of the Italian intelligence service and the head of a spy-ring to whom priests and religious were sending information. He was later tried *in absentia* and sentenced to five years for spying for the Vatican.[143] A group of Franciscans

[138] *L'O.R.*, 1.iv.54.
[140] *Times*, 28.i.52.
[142] Ibid. 22.ii.52.

[139] *MG*, 31.i.52.
[141] Ibid.
[143] *Daily Telegraph*, i.ix.52.

from Pula, Rovinj and Pazin were tried in Pula on December 19, 1947, shortly after Pula had been returned to Yugoslavia by the 1947 peace treaty, accused of collecting secret military, political and economic information and conveying it to the enemy, collecting slanderous information about the government to be conveyed to international reactionary circles and sending this information through a secret transmitter and other channels.[144] A few days earlier[145] another group of Franciscans went on trial in Ljubljana, accused of organising the escape of ustaše to Italy and Austria, sending information to Dr Blatnik and to ustaše abroad, and of collaborating with Martinčić, the provincial of the Croatian Franciscans,[146] who had come to Ljubljana to organise the escape routes.[147] A week later Canon Dr Stanilas Lenič (formerly secretary to Bishop Rožman), the Rev. J. Šimenc, a Lazarist father, the Rev. M. Cantala and several laymen were tried in Ljubljana, accused of contacts with Dr Blatnik, and through him being linked with the Franciscans Tavcar and Valenčak. Lenič was sentenced to six years, Šimenc to two years and Cantala to five years.[148]

In a speech a few months after this Boris Krajger, a leading Slovene communist, said that thirty-seven priests had been arrested in Slovenia, eighteen from the Maribor diocese, sixteen from Ljubljana and six from the Primorska.[149]

Wartime collaboration with the Slovene Četniks, the small group who supported the royal government-in-exile and had tenuous links with the Serbian Četnik leader Mihailović, was also punished. The Rev. Franc Ramšak and the Rev. Aloyz Tome, together with a number of other priests, were tried in May 1949 for cooperation with the Četniks during the war and contacts after the war with the Bitenc spy-ring.[150] They were accused of being the leaders of the spy-rings which had their headquarters

[144] The accused were Fra Gomiero of Pula, Fra Beninca and Fra Bellato of Rovinj, Fra Kocijančič of Pazin and Fra Mattielo, the superior of the monastery of St Anton in Pula who was accused of allowing the monastery to be used as a headquarters by the group: *Sl. Por.*, 1.xii.47.

[145] On Dec. 18, 1947.

[146] Tried the previous year in Zagreb, together with Archbishop Stepinac; see ch. 3.

[147] The accused were Franc Tovcar, condemned to four years at hard labour; Anton Valenčak, six years; Franc Suhač, three years; Munda Vinko, three years; Jakov Rižner, two years; H. Karla, six months; Joseph Planišek, six months. A nun, Sister Brigitta Dvoršak, was acquitted (*Sl. Por.*, 21.xii.47).

[148] Ibid. 27.xii.47.

[149] Ibid. 19.v.48; speech to Slovene People's Assembly on 17.v.48.

[150] Ramšak was condemned to sixteen years six months, Tome to ten years five months: *Sl. Por.*, 21.v.49.

in the bishop's palace in Ljubljana; Dr Lenič, who had been sentenced the previous year, was named as one of their associates.[151] The *Slovenski Poročevalec* commented:

This trial shows that the anti-national clergy during the war were not only members of the Bela Garda but also supported the Četniks and the occupiers. The imperialist spies had their main support from the anti-national clergy. These spies received help from the bishop's palace where the spy Bitenc had the headquarters of this centre... These actions of the bishop's chancery are entirely in harmony with the well-known politics of the Vatican, that old enemy of any progress and the centre of the clero-fascist reaction, which fought the liberation movement and supported the fascists, and is now completely harnessed to the chariot of the imperialist warmongers.[152]

The same week a group of Jesuits, including the Rev. Ludwig Lederhas, superior of the community in Ljubljana, was tried, and all Jesuit property in Ljubljana was confiscated.[153]

The trials continued until 1953, reflecting the political struggle with the Western Allies and with Italy over Trieste. A group of former Salesian seminarians was tried in Ljubljana in September 1952 for sending information to Dr Blatnik, their former superior, in Rome.[154] The Rev. Jakob Širaj, and Marija Kralj, the prioress of the Marijina Družba (Congregation of Mary), were tried early in 1952, Širaj accused of helping the Bela Garda during the war and informing against Partisans and continuing his contacts with war criminals after the war and giving them the sacraments, and the prioress for giving food and shelter to Bela Gardists after the war.[155] A few months later the Rev. Joze Smolič, the parish priest at Stopice, was sentenced to twenty years' hard labour for collaborating with the Bela Garda, spying for the Italians and informing against Partisans.[156]

At the same time numerous articles appeared in the press, denouncing individual priests by name, either for their wartime activities or lack of cooperation with the new authorities after the war.[157]

---

[151] Ibid. 22.v.49.
[152] Ibid.
[153] The other accused were the Rev. Janez Lavh, the Rev. Aloyz Trontelj (a Lazarist), the Revs. Ivan Prijatelj, Joze Preac, Janko Koncilja and Rudolf Pate (ibid. 4.v.49). The property confiscated included the Church of St Jozef, which was turned into a film studio and has never been returned. The Jesuits now have a house at Dravlje (Marxist source).
[154] *Sl. Por.*, 4.v.49.
[155] Ibid. 19.1.52.
[156] Ibid. 11.v.52.
[157] See Ibid. 23.xii.45, on the Rev. H. Gorican, later arrested and imprisoned; ibid. 31.i.52 on Father Godrič of Vrtojba; ibid. 18.v.52 on Dr Bevk of Semič, as well

It appears to have been the practice at this time, particularly in political trials, to impose drastically long sentences, intended to shock and frighten, and then to release or to amnesty prisoners before they had completed their terms.[158] On the other hand some who refused to give way under interrogation or whose crimes were considered particularly damaging served out their full sentences.

Conditions varied from prison to prison in different parts of the country and at different periods, but all were harsh, especially in the early years after the war when life everywhere in Yugoslavia was harsh and food was scarce. Curiously enough there was more opportunity for religious observances in prison immediately after the war. At Stara Gradiška, mass was regularly said until 1947, sometimes attended by prison warders; in the prison at Ig priests were wakened an hour earlier than other prisoners on Sunday mornings for mass, which lay prisoners were not allowed to attend. Bread and wine were provided by the prison authorities. After the break with the Cominform in 1948 when the Yugoslav leaders were intent on proving that they were more communist than anybody else, prison discipline became stricter;[159] many young ordinands and seminarians, called up for military service in the 1950s and sentenced by courts martial for various disciplinary offences, did their military service and served their prison sentences (usually periods of up to three years) without receiving the sacraments or seeing a confessor. This was a particularly harsh deprivation for the sick and dying.[160]

Prison sentences for more severe offences were nearly always coupled with 'deprivation of civil rights' for a further period of years (and sometimes confiscation of property as well) and this carried serious civil disabilities, particularly when seeking

as numerous articles attacking Bishop Santin of Trieste and Bishop Margotti of Gorizia.

[158] E.g. Šalić, Archbishop Stepinac's secretary, sentenced to twelve years, served six years; Martinčić, the provincial of the Croatian Franciscans, tried at the same time, sentenced to five years, served three years (see ch. 3); Bishop Čule of Mostar, sentenced to eleven years, served seven years; and of course Stepinac himself, although he was a special case. A large number of priests were amnestied in 1953.

[159] It was especially hard between 1948 and 1950 before Alexander Ranković's important speech to the Fourth Plenum of the Communist Party of Yugoslavia in 1951 on the strengthening of legality (see ch. 8).

[160] The information contained in this paragraph was gathered by the writer from conversations with many priests, some living in Yugoslavia and others abroad, who had served prison terms, and should be viewed as a general impression. The writer was struck by the absence of bitterness or resentment, especially among priests who have continued to live and work in Yugoslavia, and the readiness to acknowledge the great changes which have taken place.

employment. One of these disabilities, affecting priests and catechists, concerned religious instruction. Laws and regulations differed in different parts of the country; in Slovenia and Croatia teachers of religion in primary schools[161] had to apply for a licence which was not granted unless a certificate of citizenship, a certificate of the right to vote and a certificate that the holder had not been condemned in a court of law could be produced.[162] Priests who taught catechism without licence were heavily fined and sometimes imprisoned. In Slovenia priests who were suspected of collaborating or sympathising with the occupiers were refused licences, a regulation which was very strictly applied in the early years after the war. Later the need for a licence to teach was used to threaten uncooperative priests[163] and as a means of bringing pressure on priests to join the priests' associations.[164] In Slovenia there was also some interference in the placing of priests immediately after the war; the authorities insisted that priests who had collaborated or shown sympathy with the occupiers, or insufficient sympathy for the OF, should be moved to different parishes; this tendency then became 'bureaucratised' and bore hardly on the church.[165]

[161] Religious instruction was given in primary schools until 1952 to children whose parents requested it. After this different arrangements were made.

[162] Official circular 3838/1950, 16.viii.50: SVNZ, 1950, unnumbered, no month or day.

[163] The parish priest at Vrtobraj was fined for continuing to give instruction although he had been refused a license, for 'bringing pressure on children to come to church, and sowing religious intolerance among them' (Sl. Por., 31.i.52).

[164] In Slovenia for a short period after 1948 when the first priests' association was formed, licences were granted only to members (Catholic source, member of priests' association).

[165] Communist source.

3

The Catholic Church
The trial of Archbishop Stepinac

Note on sources for the trial of Archbishop Stepinac and others

The court record of the trial of Archbishop Stepinac and the others who were tried at the same time is not available for research. Evidence must therefore be sought in published accounts. The official account of the trial, *Sudjenje Lisaku, Stepincu, Šaliću i družini, ustaško–križarskim zločincima i njihovim pomagačima* [The Trial of Lisak, Stepinac, Šalić and their Associates, Ustaša–Crusader Criminals and their Helpers] (referred to as *Sudjenje*), was published by the Yugoslav authorities in Zagreb in 1946. The introduction states that the book contains the essential material from the stenographic record and gives a chronological account of events; that it does not include the entire examination of Lisak but that the portion concerned with his secret arrival in the country, his stay and his conversations in the archbishop's palace is published in full because of their importance in the trial considered as a whole. 'The criterion which the editors of this book have used has been to give the essence of the material concerning each of the accused, which taken altogether gives the essence of the trial.'

Sudjenje, however, omits the speeches of Stepinac's two lawyers, Dr Politeo and Dr Katičić, the archbishop's speech in his own defence, the testimony of the witnesses called by the defence and the attempts – for the most part interrupted by the court – of the defence lawyers to cross-examine prosecution witnesses.

The two principal Zagreb newspapers, *Narodni List* and *Vjesnik*, reported the trial extensively, often supplementing the account in *Sudjenje*. The former gave a shortened version of Dr Politeo's defence of the archbishop, and almost all of Stepinac's own speech. The writer has been informed by contemporaries of the event that the material in *Sudjenje* is accurate as far as it goes, although there is no indication in the text where material has been omitted. Essential documents for the defence are given in *The Case of Cardinal Aloysius Stepinac* by Richard Pattee and *Le dossier du Cardinal Stepinac* by Theodore Dragoun, O.P. In one case an omitted sentence has been supplied from Falconi.

Much of the evidence against the other accused is contained in their own statements made to the interrogators during a stay of many months in prison, and introduced into the trial. Some of this evidence is corroborated by documents produced by the prosecution. Stepinac himself was in prison about ten days between his arrest and the beginning of his trial; there has never been any suggestion that pressure was brought on him, and his demeanour and behaviour in court would not support such an allegation.

The following account includes the main points of the accusation against the principal defendants and a summary of the principal points of the evidence, summaries of Stepinac's statement in his own defence, and of the speeches of his two lawyers. The complete story is long and very complex, and some of the secondary episodes have been omitted; but the main story is here.

On September 9, 1946, in Zagreb, the trial was opened of a heterogeneous group of eighteen men, including a number of priests and friars. The chief defendant was Erih Lisak, the former Ustaša police chief, and among the others were the Rev. Ivan Šalić, one of Archbishop Stepinac's two secretaries, who had been arrested the preceding December, and Fra Modesto Martinčić, the provincial of the Franciscans in Zagreb.[1]

The president of the court was Dr Žarko Vimpulšek, and the public prosecutor Jakov Blažević.[2]

The arrested men were accused under Article 13, clause 2 of the Law concerning Crimes against the People and the State, and under various clauses of Article 3 of the same law. The substance of the accusations is lengthy but the main points necessary for the understanding of the intricate case which was being built up, with all the threads leading to Archbishop Stepinac and the archbishop's palace, were as follows:

Lisak was accused first of various crimes including mass murders, increasing in scope as his position and responsibilities grew from 1941 to 1945: specific examples were given. Under the second part of the indictment he was accused of having collaborated with Pavelić, Moškov (an Ustaša general) and others, in organising terrorist acts from the beginning of May to the middle of October 1945, of organising križari groups at prisoner-of-war camps in Austria to infiltrate back into Yugoslavia, and conspiring with Moškov to return to Yugoslavia to take command

---

[1] The complete list of accused together with dates of birth and the sentences ultimately imposed is as follows: Erih Lisak, 1912, Ustaša colonel, director of public order and security, state secretary for the interior, NDH: death by hanging. Ivan Šalić, 1911, secretary to Dr Stepinac: twelve years. Josip Šimecki, 1910, catechist: fourteen years. Djuro Marić, 1913, priest and captain of Ustaša: five years. Dr Pavao Gulin, 1910, veterinary surgeon: death by shooting. Josip Crnković, 1914, draughtsman: eleven years. Fra Modesto Martinčić, 1897, provincial, Franciscans in Zagreb: five years. Fra Klemen Krešo, 1912, superior, Franciscan monastery, Zagreb, during the war: three years. Fra Mamerto Margetić, 1916, Franciscan: thirteen years. Fra Tiburcije (Franjo Pavlek), 1887: one year. Fratri Kvirin (Mirko Kolednjak), 1903, Valerije (Josip Vodović), 1911: six months each. Fratri Pio (Stjepan Svasta), 1918, Leopold (Ivan Ivanković), 1922, Mladen (Josep Majnarić), 1921: not guilty.

[2] Sudjenje, pp. 1–3.

of the *križari* groups there, keeping in touch through the archbishop's palace in Zagreb; of illegally returning to Yugoslavia on September 15, 1945, and arranging through various intermediaries to visit the archbishop's palace where he met Stepinac, Šalić and Masucci, the secretary of Marcone, the papal delegate in Zagreb.[3]

Šalić, Archbishop Stepinac's secretary, was accused of having admitted Lisak to the palace on September 19 and taking him to Stepinac, who left a session of the Bishops' Conference to see him; he received Lisak again on September 21, and gave him a good deal of information about conditions in the country; he arranged that Lisak should see Masucci that same evening and then allowed him to stay over night in the palace; he remained in touch with Lisak until the latter's arrest on October 2; he received another of the accused, Dr Gulin, who had brought letters from Moškov to Stepinac, and through Gulin sent information to General Moškov about the Bishops' Conference and the pastoral letter issued by the bishops in September 1945; he put Crnković and some students in touch with Moškov in the woods; he arranged for and took part in the blessing of a flag for a group of *križari* in the archbishop's private chapel on October 21, and organised the collection of medical supplies for the *križari*.[4]

Šimecki was accused of officiating at the service to bless the *križari* flag; of helping to collect material for the *križari* and duplicating leaflets for them;[5] Crnković was accused of ordering the making of the flag by the Sisters of Mercy;[6] Dr Gulin, the veterinary surgeon who had been an organiser of the Slovene Legion of Četniks in Slovenia during the war, and had fled from Slovenia to Croatia in 1942, was accused of carrying messages between Moškov in the woods and the archbishop's palace, and of helping Moškov and others escape back into Austria on October 2.[7] Martinčić, the Franciscan provincial at Zagreb, was accused of receiving a large number of boxes of gold and silver treasure from Glavaš, chief of the Department of Religious Affairs of the NDH, also a Franciscan, and allowing them to be hidden in his monastery, knowing that the treasure had been pillaged from the victims of the ustaše and included jewellery, gold teeth, etc. The treasure was concealed by the other accused friars, who were bound to complete secrecy under pain of mortal sin. Margetić was accused of sheltering Franciscans after the

[3] Ibid. pp. 7–10.   [4] Ibid. pp. 10–13.
[5] Ibid. pp. 13–14.   [6] Ibid. pp. 17–18.
[7] Ibid. pp. 15–16.

liberation, including many from other provinces, who were ustaše attempting to leave the country illegally at the end of January 1946, to join enemy organisations.[8]

A massive dossier of documents, statements made by the accused, and a long procession of witnesses were produced in evidence by the prosecution. The accused sat in a long row on benches facing the court. Lisak was called first. As a leading ustaša he must have known that he had no chance of escaping death. He was curt and straightforward and made no attempt to justify himself; there was even an occasional gleam of grim levity in his answers. He pleaded not guilty because he considered that he had been doing his simple duty as an ustaša. Šalić and Martinčić were led by the presiding judge and the public prosecutor through their evidence; both were verbose and eager to talk, to excuse themselves and to shift the blame. (Martinčić certainly, and probably Šalić as well, in common with a good many others, were convinced that no one would dare to touch the Archbishop of Zagreb, and that it was quite safe to put the blame onto his shoulders.) Šalić referred to himself as an employee (činovnik) and as an unimportant man (mali čovjek). Martinčić, pressed by the president to explain why he had acquiesced in the hiding of the Ustaša treasure in the Franciscan monastery, exclaimed: 'It would have been better if I had asked your advice...but I was mad with fear...and I floundered around from left to right instead of taking advice from some clever man.'

The evidence unfolded an involved story. Lisak had fled to Austria with the retreating armies and returned secretly to Yugoslavia, crossing the border on September 15, 1945. He arranged through an intermediary to be received at the archbishop's palace, and was told to present himself and give the name Petrović.[9] In the meantime Bishop Lach told Šalić, on the morning of September 19 or 21 (he could not remember exactly), towards the end of the sessions of the Bishops' Conference, that at seven that evening, a certain Petrović would present himself at the door of the palace; Šalić was to admit him and inform the archbishop.[10] When Lisak rang, the door was opened by a priest whom at first he did not recognise in the dark, but who beckoned him to enter; they went upstairs to the secretariat and there he recognised Šalić. The latter looked at him, puzzled, and said: 'Mr Petrović, you look exactly like somebody.' Lisak, who was wearing a coat and glasses, smiled and

[8] Ibid. pp. 18–21.   [9] Lisak's evidence, ibid. p. 39.
[10] Šalić's evidence, ibid. p. 58.

said 'Maybe.' Šalić looked more closely and exclaimed: 'I know you.' Lisak smiled still more broadly. Šalić said: 'Please say the first and last letters of your name.' Lisak answered: 'Certainly – L and k', and Šalić said: 'L...and k...Lisak!' Lisak answered: 'That's right!'[11] Šalić went to the room where the session of the Bishops' Conference had just risen; half the bishops had already left but Stepinac was in conversation with several of the others. Šalić went up to him and said that a certain Petrović, whom he had been ordered to admit, had arrived, but that he had recognised him as Lisak. Stepinac seemed astonished.[12] He went into the secretariat and there Lisak, who was standing in the shadows and who saw that Stepinac did not recognise him, presented himself: 'Colonel Lisak, state secretary.'[13] Stepinac took him into a neighbouring room and they talked there for fifteen or twenty minutes. Lisak, who had already stated that he had returned to Yugoslavia for the purpose of organising armed resistance to the new authorities, refused to admit that he had spoken to Stepinac about these plans; he asserted that he had told him only about the Ustaša fugitives, including Pavelić, who had escaped safely to Austria; he had told Stepinac that his (Lisak's) presence in Yugoslavia did not mean that there would be terrorist action: enough blood had already been shed. There was scornful laughter in the court at this, and the president said it was difficult to believe that he had run the considerable risk of going to the palace just to let Stepinac know that Pavelić was alive and well. But Lisak stuck to his testimony; he was the only one of the defendants both intelligent enough to realise where the evidence was leading and courageous enough to refuse to incriminate the archbishop. He admitted only that he had asked Stepinac to help him while he was in Zagreb, as much as the archbishop was able. Stepinac, who had listened to him without comment, told him to return the next day; Šalić would give him an answer. But the next day Šalić was not there.[14] He had taken fright; he admitted frankly that he had felt 'This all smells like prison.' He went out at 6.30 p.m. leaving a message that he was not at home. Lisak returned at the same time the following day, when Šalić received him and told him immediately that his visits to the palace were liable to get them all into trouble.[15] Lisak was aware of Šalić's unease, but nevertheless insisted on seeing Masucci, secretary to Marcone, the apostolic visitor, and to Šalić's considerable discomfiture[16] waited several hours until Masucci

[11] Ibid. p. 58.
[13] Lisak's evidence, ibid. p. 40.
[15] Šalić's evidence, ibid. pp. 58–9.
[12] Ibid.
[14] Ibid. pp. 42–3.
[16] Ibid. p. 60.

returned from the city. They talked at length about conditions in Italy. Lisak, whose main interest appears to have been to preserve an independent Croat state, hoped that the Western Allies would come to their help now that Germany and Italy, their first supporters, had been defeated. It was very late before they finished talking, and Lisak decided it would be safer to sleep at the palace. Šalić, again most unwilling,[17] showed him to a room and the next morning the two men continued their conversation. Šalić told him about the pastoral letter (of September 20, 1945) and showed him extracts from it.[18]

The court then questioned Šalić about the letters which had been sent by General Moškov through Dr Gulin, and about the blessing of the križari flag in the private chapel of the palace. On September 17, Gulin, whom Šalić knew only by name, had brought a letter from Moškov addressed to Lacković, Stepinac's other secretary, who was in Italy. He took it to the archbishop, who opened it, glanced at it and then told him to throw it away and to try to find out who Gulin was. A day or two later Gulin reappeared with a second letter from Moškov, this time a direct appeal to the archbishop to lead and defend the Croatian people. Stepinac again told him to destroy the letter and warned him to be careful about receiving visits and letters from Ustaša sources.[19]

A few weeks later, on October 21, as Šalić was walking up and down the balcony reading, Šimecki approached him and asked if the archbishop would bless a flag. Startled, Šalić replied that neither the archbishop, nor much less he himself, would have anything to do with it. Šimecki then said that he would bless the flag himself. Without informing the archbishop Šalić allowed Šimecki and his companions to use the private chapel and vestments; afterwards he invited them for a glass of plum brandy.[20]

By now Šalić was being harried by questions from the judge and bullied by the public prosecutor; the president had to ask him to speak a little louder and more slowly so as to be understood. The public prosecutor pounded away at the fact that all the threads from the illegal Ustaša underground led to the palace and to the person of the archbishop. Lisak had not looked for some Ustaša centre but had gone straight to the palace; he had been there during the sessions of the Bishops' Conference and Šalić had spoken to him about the pastoral letter, a confidential matter; on Stepinac's instructions Šalić had received

[17] Ibid. p. 63.   [18] Lisak's evidence, ibid. pp. 43–4.
[19] Šalić's evidence, ibid. pp. 65–70.   [20] Ibid. pp. 70–2.

the archives of the NDH foreign ministry for safe-keeping. Stepinac had visited Dr Maček, the leader of the Croatian Peasant Party (who had been under house arrest and who left the country with the NDH forces).[21] There had been a visit from Brašić, a representative of the Četnik leader Mihailović, and contacts with the British consul, Harrison, to whom Šalić gave a copy of the circular concerning events at Zaprešić.[22] At the same time the public prosecutor drew from him the admission that he had been well treated in prison, whereas he had always thought that prison was a terrible place where one was beaten up; perhaps it was a good thing that this had happened and that 'we and they' had got to know and understand each other much better.[23]

Martinčić, the Franciscan provincial, said that he had been unwilling to have the Ustaša treasure hidden in the monastery in Zagreb; it had been done without his knowledge by the door-keeper, Margetić, who in his turn had been persuaded by Glavaš, the Franciscan who had been head of the Department of Religious Affairs of the NDH. The boxes were walled up in the graveyard chapel, but so clumsily that when Martinčić was shown the place, he made them dig a pit by the confessional for the deaf and rebury the treasure there.[24] Both Martinčić and Šalić tried to shift blame onto Stepinac: if only he had given a lead to the clergy their attitude would have been different, but they had been influenced by his attitude shown in his pastoral letters and circulars. Martinčić and Dr Gulin, in his evidence, both said that they had heard rumours of disagreements among the bishops over the contents of the pastoral letter. Gulin's evidence confirmed Šalić's account of the delivery of the two letters from Moškov[25] and Margetić's evidence about the burying of the treasure added nothing new.

The public prosecutor then read depositions by witnesses whose villages had been attacked by bands of *križari*, who had killed men who refused to join them; and a number of witnesses were called, most of them from villages with a Serbian population

[21] According to Maček, General Moškov called on him on May 4, 1945, and urged him to leave the country to avoid being killed by the communists; he left on May 6. Maček speculates whether Moškov wanted to save him from the communists, or from the Ustaša who might have killed him to keep him from collaborating with the communists (Maček, p. 258).
[22] See above, p. 75. The president: 'Didn't you understand that this was a direct invitation to foreign intervention?'
[23] Šalić's testimony, *Sudjenje*, p. 79.
[24] Martinčić's testimony, ibid. pp. 170ff.
[25] Gulin's testimony, ibid. pp. 143ff.

which had been subjected to forcible conversion, each with a terrible and heart-rending tale to tell.

At this point the public prosecutor rose. He stated that the evidence the court had heard made it clear that Dr Alojizije Stepinac was directly involved and a prime mover in the matter before the court, and should be brought to trial with the other accused. He had therefore ordered the arrest of Dr Stepinac and asked for an adjournment so that the indictment against him could be prepared.

On the same day, September 18, Archbishop Stepinac was arrested.

Ten days later, on September 28, the trial was resumed. The archbishop had joined the accused, sitting between Lisak and his secretary Šalić; together with the others they occupied the whole first row facing the judges, Lisak in an open-necked shirt, Stepinac and Šalić wearing cassocks, the long line of friars in their brown habits. The next row was filled with uniformed guards.[26] Stepinac refused to be defended, but the court appointed two well-known lawyers, Dr Ivo Politeo and Dr N. Katičić, to act for him.[27] The Vatican did not react publicly at the time of Stepinac's arrest, but Mgr Patrick Hurley, the chargé d'affaires at the Nunciature, returned immediately to Belgrade from Rome, and was present during the whole trial.[28] The Western press was well represented and the trial fully reported. It was widely assumed that the principal reason for Stepinac's arrest was the pastoral letter of September 1945 and its unmistakable defiance of the new government.[29]

The public prosecutor opened the case against Stepinac with a lengthy statement followed by the specific clauses of the accusation, each of which was enlarged upon and illustrated, and concluded with a commentary which ranged very widely over the background of the case. The accusation was as follows (summary):

[26] *Sudjenje*, photo facing p. 40.

[27] Dr Politeo was president of the Zagreb Chamber of Advocates and one of the most highly regarded lawyers in the city; he had defended Tito at his trial in 1928 and was later – in 1954 – to defend Dr Vladimir Dedijer, the minister of information who fell into disgrace at the time of the Djilas affair. When he died in the 1950s, his requiem mass was celebrated in the cathedral by Archbishop Šeper, Stepinac's successor, and the pallbearers included a number of prominent communist lawyers (Catholic source).

[28] It was noted that as Stepinac entered and left the court each day Mgr Hurley rose and bowed deeply to him (O'Brien, facing p. 60).

[29] *NYT*, 20.ix.46, which also noted the preliminary arrangements in Zagreb for a big show trial.

1. (a) The accused Stepinac, in his capacity as Croatian metropolitan, had called on 'Field-Marshal' Kvaternik on April 12, 1941, and on the criminal Pavelić on April 16, 1941, while the Yugoslav armies were still fighting the German and Italian forces; he had issued a circular to his clergy on April 18, inviting them to cooperate with the new government, and on April 26, 1941, at the conclusion of a meeting of the Bishops' Conference he had led the other bishops to a formal audience with Pavelić, and promised their loyal support.

(b) He had exercised supreme control over the Catholic press during the war, as president of the Bishops' Conference and president of Catholic Action, and supported its fascist line; many examples were cited.

(c) The various organisations grouped together as Catholic Action of which he was president, in particular the Veliko Križarsko Bratstvo (Great Crusader Brotherhood) and Veliko Križarsko Sestrinstvo (Great Crusader Sisterhood) and Domagoj, became the heart and centre of ustašism.

(d) He had turned traditional church festivals and processions into political demonstrations for Pavelić; he had celebrated mass every year on April 10, the anniversary of the founding of the NDH, and had said mass for the opening of the NDH Sabor (parliament).

2. When the Ustaša had threatened death to Serbs if they did not convert to Catholicism, he received into the Catholic Church tens of thousands of Serbs who had knives at their throats, thus countenancing these crimes and instigating the Ustaša to further crimes, digging an unbridgeable gulf between Serbs and Croats and weakening their unity in the struggle against the occupier and lowering the national dignity. A long list of statements by Serbs followed.

3. In 1942 he was appointed military vicar and chose as his deputies Vučetić and Cecelja, two priests who were well known for their Ustaša sympathies; he had sent a Christmas message of encouragement to the Croats working in Germany.

4. During 1944 and 1945 before the fall of Hitler, Germany and its satellites he had entered into close relations with Maček, the Peasant Party leader, Pavelić and others, with the object of inviting armed intervention from the outside to preserve the NDH.

(a) and (b) gave extracts from his anti-communist speeches in 1944 to the Domagoj and in 1945 to students.

(c) In March 1945 the NDH government had called a Bishops' Conference for the purpose of giving support to the NDH as the saviour of the Croatian people; the pastoral letter issued by the Conference on March 24, 1945, under Archbishop Stepinac's presidency had been drafted by Ivo Bogdan, an NDH official, revised to give it an ecclesiastical character by Bishop Šimrak and approved by Pavelić. No other religious community had acceded to Pavelić's request to issue a similar proclamation.

(d) He had received and hidden the archives of the NDH ministry of foreign affairs.

(e) Early in the spring of 1945 he had conspired with Pavelić and Maček to invite a fresh occupation of the country by foreigners in order to overthrow the people's government, already established in a large portion of Yugoslav territory.

5. He had encouraged Ustaša resistance after the liberation of the country and bolstered up the hope of a change of regime; he had received Lisak twice, as well as several other ustaše, received two letters from Moškov, approved and concealed the actions of Šalić, Šimecki, Crnković and Gulin; the Bishops' Conference under his presidency had issued a pastoral letter in September 1945, full of lies about the people's government and encouragement to the *križari* in the woods, just at the time of the first elections after the war. (The accusations were made under various paragraphs of Articles 2, 3 and 4 of the Law concerning Criminal Actions against the People and State.)[30]

The public prosecutor's introductory remarks and the commentary put the accusations in their historical setting. Stepinac, 'in his fanatical hatred of everything that is of the people, progressive and democratic', had begun preparing a fifth column long before the war, but could never have been successful without the help of Maček and the leaders of the HSS (Hrvatska Seljačka Stranka – the Croatian Peasant Party) and the pro-Ustaša portion of the Catholic clergy. Stepinac and a portion of the clergy[31] supported the Ustaša government and approved of the forced conversions of the Serbs which advanced Vatican interests in the Balkans and the cause of Italian imperialism; Stepinac had issued a succession of circulars to the clergy on this subject. He had laid down the general line in the Catholic press of praise and support for Hitler and given his approval to various clero-fascist organisations such as the Veliko Križarsko Bratstvo, a great many of whose members went on to occupy leading positions in the NDH government. Stepinac had supported and taken a direct part in the central organisation which had inspired the resistance of the *križari* groups and attempted to restore the former authorities with the help of the new imperialist leaders, and whose members were that day on trial before the People's Court.

It was clear that this was to be a major political trial, the government's uncompromising answer to the continued defiance of the bishops, to the September pastoral letter, and to the refusal of the Vatican to remove Stepinac from his archbishopric.[32]

---

[30] *Sudjenje*, pp. 195 ff.

[31] It is significant that the communist attacks against the church always speak of 'a part of the clergy' and never the Catholic clergy as a whole; cf. the title of the important collection of documents published by the Yugoslav government in 1946: *Dokumenti...jednog dijela katoličkog klera* [...of a part of the Catholic clergy].

[32] Tito had warned Mgr Hurley, chargé d'affaires at the Nunciature, that he had proof of Stepinac's collaboration with the Germans and the Ustaša, and asked

Stepinac pleaded not guilty and said that he did not wish to defend himself; he confirmed that he had not been subjected to any pressures during his examination in prison and that his statement had been freely signed. After this he refused to answer the president's questions. The president read extracts from *Katolički List*, the semi-official organ of the Zagreb archdiocese, recording Stepinac's visits, as representative of the Catholic Church and Metropolitan of Croatia, to Kvaternik and Pavelić, before the capitulation of Yugoslavia, and accused him of treason. Stepinac refused to answer.[33] The public prosecutor asked him whether he had ordered a mass of thanksgiving when the country was liberated from the Germans and Italians. Stepinac remained silent. As the questioning proceeded he occasionally answered on a point of fact; when the president referred to the proclamation issued by Maček in 1941, calling for support of the NDH, and asked him whether he considered Maček his leader he answered with a decided affirmative. But when the president asked if he was putting the responsibility onto Maček, he drew back sharply and said there was nothing to be responsible for.[34] The court argued that all the organs of the Catholic Church, including Catholic Action and the Catholic press, came under his authority as archbishop, and that he was therefore responsible for their actions. It was not difficult to find pro-Ustaša and pro-fascist material in the Catholic press; the court cited, among others, an article in *Katolički List*[35] published before the German attack on Yugoslavia, praising the setting-up of the independent republic of Slovakia after the occupation and break-up of Czechoslovakia.

In answer to questions, Stepinac replied that the president of the *križari*,[36] Dr Niedzielski, acted on his own responsibility but reported to Stepinac once a year. He refused very decidedly to tell the court whether he had ever reproved the *križari* for their actions; that was 'an internal matter'. The president retorted that there were no 'official secrets' from the court.[37]

The questioning went relentlessly on, with the court, in the face of Stepinac's silence, showing considerable patience. The president made an occasional effective point. Stepinac had

him to urge the Vatican to withdraw him in order to avoid a trial. See n. 78 below.

[33] *Sudjenje*, p. 220, and see above, p. 19.
[34] *Sudjenje*, p. 223.   [35] 30.i.41.
[36] This was a reference to the prewar and wartime organisation, not the groups 'in the woods' after the war.
[37] The text does not record whether the president pressed the matter further (*Sudjenje*, p. 234).

spoken of the Croatians fighting for their freedom; did he really think that they were free under German and Italian occupation? Stepinac denied that he ordered a mass of thanksgiving to be said every April 10 (the anniversary of the founding of the NDH) but refused to answer a similar question about masses on Pavelić's birthday; the president then read his circular ordering the mass in 1942, and the report in *Katolički List* of his celebration of the mass in 1944.[38] The president read the introduction to Stepinac's speech on the occasion of the opening of the Sabor on February 13, 1942:

Poglavnik! The restoration of the Croatian Sabor is evidence of your deep and lively sense of responsibility; it is a heavy burden which you will share with your colleagues. The prayers of the church and of our hearts accompany this restoration; may the Eternal Judge, who governs the fate of the people, with his almighty right hand build the foundations of the Croatian Sabor and engrave on the hearts of your colleagues an equally deep and lively sense of responsibility, so that you, the leader of the NDH, may successfully help in the renewal and raising-up of our beloved homeland on the eternal foundations of the gospel of Christ's teaching.

Eight months after April 1941 did Stepinac still think that the Ustaša government was an honest one? Stepinac was stung to reply that he was describing what he thought the government ought to be[39] but the president retorted that at that time there was no excuse for ignorance; he was not giving advice to a child but greeting a blood-stained criminal. When Stepinac said that he was present only for formal reasons, in the same way that he had been present on various formal occasions after liberation, the public prosecutor, enraged, asked him how he dared to compare the two things.

The court then turned to the forced conversions.[40] By this time Stepinac was answering the court's questions more often than he had done at the beginning. He denied that he knew how many new converts there had been, although he admitted that the number was greater than usual; he denied that there had been any force used by the church: what others did could not be laid at his door. In the statement he had made under examination he had said that there had been fewer Serbs converted to Catholicism under the NDH than Croats converted to Orthodoxy in former Yugoslavia, and that force had certainly been used on the Croats at that time. He answered questions about the way in

[38] Ibid. p. 236. [39] Ibid. pp. 237–8.
[40] Ibid. pp. 242ff.

which the hierarchy had ordered that requests for conversions should be dealt with, and the setting-up of a Committee of Three, consisting of himself, Bishop Burić and Bishop Šimrak, to have a general oversight of the conversions and ensure that they were conducted properly, without compulsion. He was led into contradicting himself, and when the court began to question him about the excesses of individual priests he once more refused to answer. Finally he declared: 'Mr President, I have already said that I don't wish to defend myself and that at the end of the trial I will answer all these questions. If you think I am guilty, then please judge me as you will, but my conscience is clear.'

The president turned to Lisak, sitting beside Stepinac and said: 'Accused Lisak, is your conscience clear with regard to the crimes you have committed?' Lisak answered: 'I did my patriotic duty and my conscience is clear.' The President then said to Stepinac: 'You see, accused Stepinac, Lisak's conscience also is clear. So the idea of a clear conscience is a relative one and not really an argument to use in the courts.' After this Stepinac's answers were much briefer and he repeated several times than when all the documents came to light history would justify him.

When the question of the military vicariate was raised he vigorously defended Cecelja, one of his deputies. He rejected the accusation that his pastoral message to the Croatian workers in Germany had helped the Ustaša. He denied that an NDH official had drafted the March 1945 pastoral letter. The president turned to Martinčić and asked him whether he, as Franciscan provincial, had signed the letter. Martinčić replied that he had refused to, thank God, and that in consequence there had been a little quarrel.[41]

Stepinac agreed that he had received the archives of the NDH foreign ministry, but only to protect them in case of bombardment; he had not accepted responsibility for them, and after the liberation the new authorities had been notified and had removed them.[42] He had called on Maček shortly before the fall of Germany, on his own initiative and not on orders from Pavelić, to urge him to take precautions not to come to any harm. He acknowledged that Pavelić had asked him to head a regency

[41] Ibid. p. 281.
[42] A letter informing the authorities that the archives were in the archbishop's palace was sent on June 6, immediately after Stepinac returned to the palace from his two-week detention and the conversations with Tito; he received a receipt from the secretary of the Commission for Religious Affairs (Pattee, doc. LXII).

council since it was traditional for the Archbishop of Zagreb to assume power in such circumstances, but he had refused; he had however urged Maček to assume the leadership. He denied any knowledge of contacts with the Allied forces.

He acknowledged that he had received Lisak but had not known that 'Petrović' was Lisak until he went into the room and Lisak presented himself.[43] Šalić had been mistaken if he thought he had warned him beforehand, and he was also mistaken about the date, which was September 24 (or thereabouts, but certainly not the 19th); there was no question of Lisak's having had any contact with the Bishops' Conference. He had not wished to see Lisak again and told Šalić to deal with him when he returned. He denied that Šalić had told him that Lisak had spent the night in the palace, or about the blessing of the *križari* flag. Šalić, who had repeated his former testimony, now directly contradicted the archbishop, and for the first time Stepinac answered him, and retorted sharply that he was mistaken. Stepinac added that Šimecki had informed him about the blessing of the flag; he had told Šimecki that he did not want to hear about it and that he (Šimecki) ought not to be meddling in such matters. As for the rest he had received many letters and many people had come to visit him at that time, and he did not remember them all precisely. He recalled glancing at the letters from Moškov and telling Šalić to throw them away. He had tried as far as possible to keep from being involved in political happenings and to care for the welfare of his people.

The archbishop had resumed the cold, self-contained manner which had shown signs of being shaken during the questioning about the forced conversions, when the text of *Sudjenje* gives the impression that he was having to draw on all the reserves of his self-possession and convictions. By now also it was obvious that many of the men around him were mediocre busy-bodies, stuffed with romantic ideas but without much courage or common sense. Stepinac, on the other hand, never lost his dignity and the sense of his position as archbishop and metropolitan, and this was combined, rather unexpectedly, with a strong impression of personal modesty.[44]

The public prosecutor then read lengthy extracts from a document[45] which he alleged was a copy of a report, dated May

---

[43] *Sudjenje*, p. 287.
[44] B. Petranović cites, without giving the source, a letter from Bishop Akšamović to Mgr Rittig (23.xii.45) comparing Stepinac's staff unfavourably with the court of his predecessor Archbishop Bauer (p. 301).
[45] *Sudjenje*, pp. 297ff.

18, 1943, addressed personally to the pope by Stepinac.[46] Stepinac denied writing it.[47]

Among other things the report accused the Serbian Četniks of widespread slaughter of Croation Catholics and terrible atrocities against them; they had behaved far worse against defenceless women and children than the Partisans. It accused the Great Serbs of planning to extend the borders of Serbia to include most of Croatia, reducing Croatia to the regions immediately surrounding Zagreb, 'in effect what can be seen from the towers of Zagreb cathedral', and of planning the forcible conversion of the majority of Catholics to the Orthodox Church. The report concluded with the solemn warning that the destruction of Catholicism in Croatia would bring the waves of Orthodoxy and the Byzantine offensive lapping at the frontiers of Italy; the writer implored the Holy Father not to forget the young Croatian nation, fighting for its life. This, the court commented, was again a direct appeal for foreign intervention.

The public prosecutor then went on to quote from the reports

[46] The document, which has never been satisfactorily explained, was found in the archives of the foreign ministry of the NDH; it was written in Italian and not, as would have been expected, in Latin, and no original has ever come to light. (See Dr Politeo's speech for the defence below.) On the other hand Falconi asserts (p. 312) that a copy of this letter, running to sixteen pages, was enclosed in Stepinac's diary, vol. IV. This diary, which was his official, not his private spiritual, journal, was sometimes written by him and sometimes by members of his immediate staff; copies of letters and other documents were sometimes pasted in. It was hidden and not discovered by the secret police until 1950 and so did not figure in his trial. Very few people, among them Petranović and Falconi, have been allowed to see these volumes, Falconi only very briefly. Extracts from them have appeared from time to time in Yugoslav official propaganda publications.

[47] The denial does not appear in *Sudjenje* but is referred to by Dr Politeo in his speech for the defence (Pattee, pp. 211–12, and Dragoun, p. 141). Falconi (p. 311) suggests that Stepinac *showed* the report to the pope during his visit to Rome in May 1943, but nothing in either Dr Politeo's speech or in *Sudjenje* provides any evidence for this. The exchange between the public prosecutor and Stepinac was reported in *Sudjenje* (pp. 297ff) as follows:
P.P. Accused Stepinac, please tell us how many reports you sent to the pope during the occupation?
STEPINAC. I am not obliged to give this information.
P.P. What?
STEPINAC. I cannot give any information about this.
P.P. You force us to settle your problems ourselves.
STEPINAC. As you please.
P.P. Did you send a report in 1943?
STEPINAC. May I see it, please? (Stepinac examined the document.)
For some time after this exchange he replied to every question: 'I have no comment' or, when questioned about the authenticity of another document: 'I am not interested in whether the document is authentic or not.'

of Dr Nikola Rušinović, the NDH's first unofficial envoy to Rome, and his successor Prince Lobkowicz, both of whom wrote lengthy accounts of their efforts to make the Vatican look favourably on the NDH, and their busy searches for useful contacts in Rome. He then read from the depositions of Alajbegović and Košak, two of Pavelić's ministers, accounts of the efforts which were made during the last days before the fall of Germany to persuade Stepinac, the only personality who enjoyed the confidence of all the diverse groups, to assume the regency. Stepinac still refused to comment.

In the end all the complicated threads of the testimony led to one conclusion only, said the public prosecutor: Stepinac was the leader and centre of all the fascist and anti-national forces; all had turned first of all to Stepinac, and after the liberation and the flight of the ustaše, all the threads of evidence continued to lead to the palace and to Stepinac.

When the archbishop finally rose to make his statement he was brief and direct. The 'accused Stepinac' he said, could not have wielded enough influence to carry out the deeds he had been accused of. It was the Archbishop of Zagreb who was on trial. For seventeen months he had been under house arrest.[48]

He did not spend much time defending himself from the accusations. One could not speak of rebaptism of the Serbs since no one could be baptised twice; it was a question of change of religion, and the judgment of history would clear him in this matter; his conscience was at peace. He had even been obliged to remove one priest from his parish when the Orthodox threatened to kill him for not proceeding fast enough with the conversions, thus endangering their lives. He had been military vicar before the war and remained responsible for the spiritual care of Croatian soldiers. He had not been *persona grata* either to the Germans or the Ustaša nor had he taken the Ustaša oath, as some of the court officials whom he saw before him that day had done.[49] His support of the right of the Croats to their own state was in accordance with the basic principles of the Allies expressed in the Atlantic Charter; he had honoured and respected the will of the Croatian people. He had been accused of being an enemy of the people's authority; he acknowledged

---

[48] Not formally; but he was under such close surveillance that it was virtually impossible for him to receive visitors; after the attack on him at Zaprešić he did not leave the city (Pattee, doc. D, for this and the rest of Stepinac's defence).

[49] The two associate judges and court officials were all professional members of the judiciary, who had served under the Ustaša regime as well as before the war.

their authority, which had been his authority since May 8, 1945, but not before that. To whom should he have given his obedience before that – the government in London, the government in Cairo, the Partisans in the woods, or the NDH in Zagreb? It had been impossible to ignore the fact that the NDH was the authority in Zagreb. There was no proof that he had committed any act of terrorism, and his conscience did not trouble him that people had come to see him and given false names, or that he had received letters which he did not bother to read. Whether the court believed him or not did not matter; the Archbishop of Zagreb knew not only how to suffer but also how to die.

He then turned to the attack. How could the public prosecutor say that there was freedom of conscience in the country? He repeated: 260 to 270 priests had been killed by the National Liberation movement; the people would never forgive them for this. The work of the Catholic seminaries had been made impossible, orphanages had been closed, printing presses destroyed, religious instruction in the schools hampered, the work of Caritas interfered with, church lands seized without prior negotiation and civil marriage made pre-eminent over the religious sacrament. Not one priest or bishop could be certain of his life; he himself, and several other bishops had been assaulted. Children were taught at school that Jesus Christ had never existed: but Jesus Christ is God, and for him, said the archbishop, we are ready to die. The court had expressed its concern for Orthodox Serbs; how could there be Orthodoxy without Christ? They must not think that he wanted conflict; let the present authorities come to an understanding with the Holy See. If that was accomplished the bishops would know their duty.

He concluded with a few words to the Communist Party who in reality was his accuser; they were mistaken if they thought that the church was hostile to them because of its material losses; it was not opposed to social reform, which was in the spirit of papal encyclicals. But if the adherents of communism were allowed to propagate their materialist doctrine, let Catholics also be allowed to propagate their principles.[50]

Many Catholics had died for this right and they would die again in the future. With good will they could reach an understanding, but the initiative must come from the authorities. Neither he nor the hierarchy could enter into this basic argument; this must be

[50] Less than twenty-five years later, in 1969, this was being proposed by some leading Marxist theoreticians; see Zlatko Frid, Esad Ćimić, Zdenko Roter (references given below at end of epilogue).

done by the state and the Holy See. As for himself, he did not
seek mercy; his conscience was at rest.

A further procession of Serbian witnesses then each told his
terrible story of the atrocities accompanying the forced conversions and the public prosecutor summed up the evidence
against each of the accused.

Dr Politeo, the principal advocate for the defence, then rose.
He was in a difficult position, since he had been appointed by
the court, and a head-on clash with the prosecution might have
made world headlines but would have angered the court and
harmed his client. His defence was obstructed in various ways;
fourteen of the witnesses he proposed to call were disqualified,[51]
and when he attempted to cross-examine Martinčić the bench cut
him short.[52] He had had less than a week to prepare his case and
very little time to consult Stepinac. He conducted his case
skilfully.

He accepted the court's assumptions and the historical setting
of the case; he spoke as a loyal Yugoslav citizen and as an
opponent of the former NDH, and from that basis attempted to
show that Stepinac's actions could bear a different interpretation.
He regretted that Stepinac was unable to defend himself in the
press where he had been attacked, and that he had decided not
to defend himself in court; the whole truth could only help him.
He pointed out that the indictment had lumped together
Stepinac's actions with the actions of others, some of which had
taken place outside his diocese. He reminded the court that in
1937 Stepinac had become a member of the Committee for Aid
to Refugees which was set up to help the victims of Hitlerism,
and in 1938 had publicly voted for Maček and the Peasant Party
who at that time were the authentic representatives of the Croat
people. Under the NDH government Stepinac had based his
attitude on the ecclasiastical constitution *Sollicitudo ecclesiarum* of
Gregory XVI promulgated in 1831.[53]

Everyone during the occupation was living under a threat.
Stepinac's calls on Kvaternik and Pavelić had been formal

---

[51] *NYT*, 8.x.46. The public prosecutor had been offensive about them; he
objected in principle to hearing defence witnesses, especially priests who had
been traitors and pro-fascists and who since the war had organised terrorist
groups; the court already knew what to think of the worth of these witnesses
(*Narodni List*, i.x.46).

[52] *Narodni List*, 8.x.46; Pattee, p. 62.

[53] This states that in a revolutionary situation a *de facto* recognition of power by
the church is not *de jure* recognition and is based on the assumption that no
previously held legitimate rights are violated. This was only one of a number
of delicate ironies in Dr Politeo's speech in which could be detected a comment
on the attitude of the Yugoslav authorities.

necessities without which he could not have done anything to help people who needed his protection; he had not ordered a welcoming Te Deum in the cathedral, and his circular to the clergy acclaiming the new state had also included an appeal to the authorities to behave according to God's commandments.

Politeo played down Stepinac's authority; he was Archbishop of Zagreb and responsible only for what went on in his own diocese;[54] even there he exercised power only over the secular priests and not over the monastic orders. Many of the religious publications which had been cited came from other dioceses, or belonged to a religious order; in any case the press had been subjected to a rigorous preventive censorship, and the censors often changed and even inserted material.

His public sermons represented a courageous stand for Christian morality at a time when it was very dangerous to speak out; Politeo quoted from several of the most outspoken. The sermons had been duplicated and circulated clandestinely during the occupation and used in broadcasting from London in 1942 and 1943, to the anger of the NDH government.[55] The lives of thousands of individual Jews, Serbs and others had been saved by his efforts. Mgr Svetozar Rittig (who at the time of the trial was already president of the Croatian Commission for Religious Affairs) had written to Stepinac in December 1943 to thank him for what he had done for the people.[56] Dr Politeo turned to Stepinac's speech at the opening of the Sabor in 1942, which had been quoted by the prosecution, and read further extracts from it, exhortations to the authorities to behave according to the gospels of Christ.[57]

He analysed the alleged report of May 1943, addressed to the pope, with particular attention. He was convinced that it was either a forgery or, more probably, written by the Franciscan Glavaš, head of the NDH Department for Religious Affairs, who hoped to persuade Stepinac to send something of the sort to Rome. The alleged report contained a good deal of detailed information about Bosnia which Stepinac was unlikely to know,

---

[54] This line of defence contradicted the statement in the first of the articles 'On the Recent Past' (*SVNZ*, 6.xi.45) that during the war the Archbishop of Zagreb was the real representative of the Catholic Church in the NDH, and the spokesman of the Catholic episcopacy during a period when travel and communications were very difficult; for this reason the archbishop's name appears on the majority of proclamations, letters, documents, etc.

[55] Pattee, p. 208.

[56] This letter was presented to the court but never read (Pattee, p. 208 and doc. VI).

[57] There is contemporary evidence that Pavelić was infuriated by what he regarded as a piece of governessy interference.

whereas Glavaš had made a special study of Bosnian history. No other copy was ever found; it was written in Italian and not in Latin and did not have the customary address and conclusion; its style was quite unlike the Curial style which was always used in reports of this kind; Stepinac did not send copies of his reports to the NDH foreign ministry; no copy of any other similar report was found in its files.[58]

He then turned to the Bishops' Conference of March 1945. He agreed that the bishops had accepted the help of the NDH government to arrange their travel, but cited a statement made by Dr Pavao Canki, NDH minister of justice and religious affairs, that the request had come from Stepinac.[59] He conceded that Bishop Šimrak might have produced a draft for the pastoral letter drawn up by Ivo Bogdan, one of the Ustaša ideologues, but the bishops had considered several drafts and in the end Šimrak's was not accepted.[60] At the time Zagreb was full of refugees from the liberated areas and was flooded with exaggerated stories of Partisan slaughter of priests; the archbishop had made the mistake of believing this propaganda, but this was a mistake, not a crime.

He had not hidden the NDH archives, but agreed to receive them without accepting responsibility for them, and on June 6 had informed the authorities that they were stored in the palace and handed them over. Stepinac could not be held guilty because others had tried to persuade him to take power in 1945. He had refused because of his constant principle that the church should not take part in politics, because he did not want to take anything from Pavelić, and because he was a democrat and believed that power should come from the people, not from Pavelić. Alajbegović, one of the NDH ministers, had testified that power was offered to Stepinac because he enjoyed the confidence

[58] After the trial L'Osservatore Romano published an authorised statement, on October 10, 1946, denying in rather circuitous language that the document was authentic (O'Brien, p. 78).

[59] Conditions were already so chaotic that only the five bishops forming the working committee were able to come to Zagreb (SVNZ, 6.xi.45).

[60] This statement was confirmed verbally to the author in 1970 by a contemporary of the events. It is obvious, however, even from the defence, that the NDH was closely involved with the Bishops' Conference and that the pastoral letter suited them even if it differed from their original draft; this was confirmed in statements made under examination by Dr Radoslav Glavaš, head of the Religious Section of the ministry of religious affairs and justice, and Dr Nikola Mandić, who became president of the NDH in 1943 (Dokumenti, pp. 398–402). The writer was told by the Rev. S. Lacković, one of Stepinac's two secretaries, who acted as secretary of the Bishops' Conference, that the draft did not come from the NDH, and that Šimrak himself probably drew up the first draft (interview in 1973 in the USA).

of the people: this was so because he was known to be hostile to the NDH. He went to see Maček accompanied by General Moškov because Maček was under house arrest and not free to receive visitors, to see if anything could be done to avert the threatened massacres during the German and NDH retreat.

Dr Politeo then turned to the accusations about Stepinac's postwar activities; he agreed that Stepinac had seen Lisak and other ustaše, and received the letters from Moškov, but these were only a few among the many people and communications which arrived daily at the palace; he received Lisak without knowing who he was (Politeo preferred to believe the archbishop's evidence rather than Šalić's), put Moškov's letters into the wastepaper basket, barely remembered the other persons; this was hardly sufficient basis for accusing him of directing the *križari* groups in the forest.

The defence of the pastoral letter of September 1945 was adroit. The text of the letter stated that it had been published out of concern for the spiritual welfare of the people, for the purpose of re-establishing normal conditions in the country. The abnormal conditions consisted in the points of conflict between the church and the state which remained unsettled (e.g. the suppression of the Catholic press, death sentences on priests and innocent people who could not defend themselves, the treatment of prisoners in concentration camps, the suppression in various ways of Catholic education, obligatory civil marriage, the way in which agrarian reform was carried out, the propagation of a materialistic and atheistic spirit, and several other points). Some of these facts were *true*, e.g. the suppression of the press, civil marriage, etc., and it was a matter of *opinion* whether the objections to the facts were justified or not. But it was not a crime to hold an opinion. Other statements were *false*, e.g. that innocent priests had been killed, the statements on the concentration camps, etc. Speaking for himself Dr Politeo said that he could not prove any of these statements, but the archbishop had stated that he had received information on these matters and therefore he had not simply invented slanders but had accepted false information as the truth. This was a subjective question of opinion and even false opinions were not always blameworthy. As for the death sentences on priests, who could say that the courts were always infallible? The administration of justice in all countries was full of contradictory verdicts, and because of this the appeals procedure had been set up.[61]

---

[61] There was no appeal from the verdicts of the postwar trials for war crimes.

The bishops had stated in the September pastoral letter that they did not want conflict with the new government, but that it was the Holy See which must regulate relations between the state and the church. Dr Politeo urged that the pastoral letter, in spite of its inaccuracies and exaggerations, could not really induce anyone to hostile activity against the state.

As he drew to a conclusion he stated that his defence had been hampered by the refusal of the court to accept some of the documents he had wanted to introduce in evidence, and by Stepinac's refusal to defend himself. Thousands of telegrams demanding the conviction of Stepinac had been appearing in the press; he presented to the court a statement signed by 150 priests refuting the accusations against the archbishop,[62] and reminded them also that many thousands of Croats were praying for the archbishop, convinced of his innocence.[63]

Dr Katičić dealt with the portions of the accusation concerning forced conversions.[64] He interpreted the procedure which the hierarchy had established, and the circulars which the church issued in 1941 and 1942, with detailed regulations for the reception of Orthodox converts into the Catholic Church, as the church's method of delaying and procrastinating in the face of actions which it totally disapproved. He cited complaints from the local ustaše of the unconscionable time it took to get replies from the bishops' consistories, and the fact that when the NDH's agency Državno Ravnateljstvo za Ponovu sent out missionaries, the bishops had issued a circular sharply condemning this practice. By keeping every aspect of the conversions in its own hands the hierarchy hoped to keep control until the situation had cooled off. But when it was obvious that the lives of thousands of Orthodox could only be saved by admitting them swiftly into the Catholic Church, a further circular was issued, on March 2, 1942, saying that 'secondary motives' for conversion should not be an obstacle to being received; thus the 'door was opened' to receive these people. As for the military vicariate, the two Ustaša priests Vučetić and Cecelja had been appointed a month before Stepinac's own appointment and it was impossible for him to get rid of them.

The public prosecutor presented counter-arguments to the points which the defence counsel had made and, after counsel

---

[62] Pattee, doc. v.
[63] During the trial the churches were full of people praying for Stepinac; the police forbade gatherings of more than five in front of the churches (*NYT*, 12.x.46).
[64] Pattee, doc. C, pp. 230ff.

for the remaining defendants had been heard, he rose and made what was, in effect, a clear statement of the purpose of the trial: to unmask before the world a plot by the Western imperialist powers against the new Yugoslavia. The facts which had been revealed, he said, considered as a whole, proved beyond a shadow of doubt that there had been a concerted conspiracy, directed by the imperialist powers, against the new Yugoslavia. The individual actions of the accused were only a part of the truth, but the fundamental, underlying truth which had been demonstrated was that the remnants of the reactionary forces which had fought against the progressive forces of the people through the four years of the war had continued their struggle after the liberation in 1945. On the one hand, he concluded dramatically, there were the efforts of millions of people, who were building roads and railways and helping to put their country on its feet, and on the other people who opened up the graves of dead priests to bury stolen treasure, snatched from the bodies of the victims of fascism.

The verdicts were handed down; all the accused, except three friars, were found guilty. Archbishop Stepinac was condemned to sixteen years' hard labour, Lisak to death by hanging and Gulin to death by shooting, Šalić to twelve years' hard labour and Martinčić to five years.[65]

The sentences provoked widespread indignation in the West, especially among Catholics, mingled with relief that Stepinac had not been condemned to death.[66] For days the pages of *L'Osservatore Romano* were full of messages and protests from all over the world. The Foreign Office in London received 550 petitions signed by 216,600 people relating to Stepinac's imprisonment.[67] The Yugoslav authorites on their side published their version in a number of pamphlets and the Yugoslav ambassador to Washington said at a dinner for the American Committee for Yugoslav Relief that Stepinac had supported a plot, hatched during the war, to set up a new state of Catholic Central Europe, consisting of Croatia, Slovenia, Austria, Hungary, Slovakia and possibly Bavaria, with Otto of Habsburg at its head.[68]

The pope revealed that already at the beginning of 1942 he had informed the Yugoslav legation to the Holy See (accredited by the Yugoslav government-in-exile), who had made enquiries

---

[65] For a complete list of sentences see n. 1 above.
[66] Archbishop Spellman of New York had already predicted his execution (*NYT*, 7.x.46).
[67] *Times*, 30.xi.46.
[68] *NYT*, 25.x.46.

when reports of the forcible conversions of Orthodox began to seep out, that the Catholic Church could not accept anyone who did not come of his own free will, and that the sudden conversion of a large number of 'dissidents' (Orthodox) had given rise to concern among the Croatian bishops, who had informed the state authorities that 'the return of the dissidents should allow for complete liberty on their part'.[69]

On October 14 *L'Osservatore Romano* published a decree of the Sacred Congregation of the Council excommunicating all those who had taken part physically or morally in the trial.[70] A few days later Bishop Margotti of Gorizia (one of the dioceses divided by the temporary frontier between Italy and Yugoslavia; apostolic administrators were appointed for the Yugoslav parts) announced the excommunication of the staffs of a number of Italian and Slovene newspapers who had conducted an anti-Vatican campaign during the Stepinac trial.[71] Mgr Nicolo Moscatello, counsellor of the Yugoslav legation to the Holy See for many years, resigned in protest at the sentence on Stepinac.[72]

A number of other trials about this time served to buttress the accusations against Stepinac. In Varaždin a group which included several priests was sentenced for helping ustaše to escape illegally. Among them was the Rev. Gazivoda, who stated at his trial that the attitude shown in Archbishop Stepinac's circulars, pastoral letters and instructions had influenced his actions. Leading articles in the press campaign which was mounted against Stepinac even before his arrest spoke of him as the leader of all the priests who were then on trial.[73] Early in October the Vicar-General of Prekmurje (Slovenia), Ivan Jerič, and a group of others, were tried before a military court in Maribor, accused of contacts with émigré groups in Austria.[74]

Speaking at a gathering of students on September 25, 1946,[75] and again at a meeting of the First Congress of the Croatian People's Front in the middle of October,[76] Dr Bakarić insisted that the government was not trying to destroy the church, or to persecute it, or to create new enemies for itself; but church and state must be separated, all religious communities must be equal,

[69] Memorandum from the Vatican secretariat of state to the Yugoslav legation, 25.i.43, quoted by the pope in his address to the Sacred Roman Rota, 5.x.46 (O'Brien, p. 76).
[70] O'Brien, pp. 78–9.
[71] *NYT*, 25.x.46.
[72] Ibid. 27.x.46.
[73] *Vjesnik*, 16.ix.46.
[74] Ibid. 9.x.46.
[75] Ibid. 30.ix.46.
[76] Ibid. 15.x.46.

and religious belief, or lack of it, the private concern of the individual. He quoted Stjepan Radić, the prewar Croat Peasant Party leader, speaking about an earlier bishop: 'If [he] had written about a religious problem...it would be for the pope to judge if the bishop's belief is right or wrong, but when he writes about political matters and wants to be the political leader of the Croatian people, then our duty is to come to a conclusion about it and if necessary, condemn it.'[77]

The action of the government in bringing Stepinac to trial was understandable. It was convinced that it had prevented an invasion by the Western Allies in the weeks following the end of the war by an unmistakable demonstration of its determination to hold onto its victory and not to yield territory which it considered to be Yugoslav. Its precarious hold on power had been menaced in the months that followed by the Ustaša bands in the woods; and in its view the Catholic Church was the only institution which could have formed a solid basis for opposition to gather around. Archbishop Stepinac was the outstanding personality in the church; his position and his personal integrity put him in a different sphere from the rest of the hierarchy. Bishop Rožman of Ljubljana and Bishop Garić of Banja Luka and Archbishop Šarić of Sarajevo had already discredited themselves by flight; if Stepinac could not be induced to leave he also must be discredited.

Nevertheless the archbishop's trial and condemnation had consequences which were more far-reaching than the government had perhaps foreseen. There were signs that his introduction into the trial had been hastily prepared, even though the intention had been there for some time,[78] but once embarked on this path the government could not draw back. Stepinac, who had been told by the Vatican that he could decide his own course of action and that it would not press him to leave Yugoslavia,[79] believed that a bishop's place was with his people and in any case had no intention of making things easier for the government by removing himself; he never courted martyrdom but was quite prepared to accept it. The ambiguities and divided loyalties of

---

[77] There are numerous references during this period in the speeches of the communist leaders to the Radić brothers and to Bishop Strossmayer, names which brought an echo from all Croatian hearts.

[78] In an election speech early in November Tito declared that the Vatican had had several months' warning of the arrest of Stepinac and that he had urged Mgr Hurley, the nuncio, to ask the Vatican to remove him, since Yugoslavia was not prepared to tolerate citizens who served the interests of others (*NYT*, 2.xi.46).

[79] Catholic source.

the period of the NDH were over; here was an issue on which he could take an unequivocal stand.

The trial thus became the symbolic act which determined the nature of the relations between the Catholic Church and the state and between the Vatican and Yugoslavia for the next fifteen years; if it had not taken place it is possible that diplomatic relations would not have been severed and that an accord between the two would have been reached earlier. The government felt that its efforts to reach a *modus vivendi* with the church had been spurned, and was confirmed in its conviction that the Vatican supported the expansionist aims of Italy directed against Yugoslavia; and the Catholic Church, wounded and deeply shaken by the consequences of its complaisant attitude to the NDH, was offered a symbol and a rallying point whose bearing and firmness had a profound effect on the subsequent behaviour of the church.[80] His uncompromising attitude, which. hardened as the years went by – he was allowed to receive a number of visitors including foreign journalists in his native village of Krašić, near Zagreb – made it impossible for the church to change its policy during his lifetime. He continued to be an embarrassment to the government; in 1949 and again in 1950 Tito offered to release him on condition he left Yugoslavia.[81] The decision of the Vatican in 1952 to make Stepinac a cardinal gave the Yugoslav government the opportunity to sever diplomatic relations with the Vatican, a course which it appears already to have decided was inevitable.

The trial thus set the stage for a dogged and sometime savage battle of wills between the two sides.

This struggle forms the theme of the next chapter.

[80] The government was well aware of the danger of creating a martyr, and Stepinac was treated both in prison and in his subsequent forced residence with considerable leniency in comparison with other bishops and priests, and in comparison with the Orthodox bishops. He was isolated from other prisoners but had two priests as companions, a cell to himself, and an adjoining cell where a small chapel was installed. See ch. 4 for his interview in *Vjesnik* on his release from prison.

[81] In interviews with C. L. Sulzberger of the *NYT:* Armstrong, p. 124.

4

The Catholic Church
The struggle between the church and the
state, 1946–1953

The struggle defined

An attempt has been made in the preceding chapters to show how profoundly religion and nationalism were identified in Yugoslavia, how each of these concepts had been affected, and in their more extreme forms distorted, by the other, and how the communists were determined to change this by enforcing a fundamental separation of church and state. This determination stemmed not only from their Marxist conception of the role of religion in the alienation of man, but in their understanding of the way in which religion fed on nationalist feelings, and was used to perpetuate the conflicts between South Slavs, especially the most dangerous of all, those between Croats and Serbs. They were also determined to break the political power of the Catholic and Orthodox Churches; both had played an important role in prewar Yugoslavia, either directly, through party politics, or indirectly, through their strong influence over the faithful, and in the case of the Catholic Church, through its ties with the Vatican. The church was to be virtually restricted to the performance of religious rites for the faithful; its place in the new Yugoslavia was to be peripheral and eventually, as the goal of socialism was approached, vestigial.

The social transformation was only one aspect of the enormous revolutionary task which the Yugoslav communists had undertaken; they were trying at the same time to change the Yugoslav economy from a largely peasant to a predominantly industrial one, and to reorient their foreign policy after the break with the Cominform and the economic blockade imposed by the Eastern bloc.[1] This task was attacked at every level.

The agrarian reform, and the nationalisation and expropria-

---

[1] It was during this period that Yugoslavia developed friendly relations with Turkey, Greece and Italy, all members of NATO, and received massive economic and later military aid from the West.

tion of church possessions,[2] radically changed the economic basis of the Catholic Church and reduced it to poverty. The nationalisation of its primary and secondary schools, leaving only seminaries and the two theological faculties for the training of priests, and in 1952 the final abolition of optional religious instruction in primary schools and the separation of the theological faculties from the universities removed the last traces of church influence from the educational system. Education was now controlled entirely by the state. The 1953 Law on the Status of Religious Communities gave legal embodiment to the provisions of the 1946 constitution dealing with the separation of the churches from the state.

The trials of war criminals and collaborationists, among them some priests, were part of the aftermath of the war, which in one form or another took place in every Allied country; but the later trials for 'anti-national activities' were linked to the political struggle over the frontiers with Italy and were used as a means of propaganda and instruction. At the same time there were many trials for infringements of the new laws, and countless 'administrative' – i.e. extra-legal – actions against the clergy and believers. All of this drove home the lesson that the old order was finished and that the church must change its ways and learn to assume its proper place in the new society.

At the same time the government initiated and encouraged organisations through which the churches could cooperate with the state, the priests' associations; these were vigorously resisted by the church. Religious education and the priests' associations were two of the main points of the conflict with the government over the next few years; the question of the church's support for Yugoslavia's position in the frontier dispute with Italy was the third.

Dr Bakarić put the government's position in an interview[3] at the beginning of 1947 shortly after the Stepinac trial. There had been a marked improvement, he said, in relations between the government and the church, after the moral defeat of a 'hostile centre', and, although they had not yet achieved all they hoped for, 'in the foreseeable future we shall have a church whose activities will be in full accordance with the basic trends of the

---

[2] The Catholic Church was not particularly wealthy in land; only Zagreb, Djakovo and the Vojvodina had extensive estates. The parishes in areas such as the old military frontier, Lika, the Dalmatian coast and Bosnia and Hercegovina as a rule owned less than the permitted maximum. Buildings of various sorts and building lots in towns were a much more important source of revenue and future expansion (Catholic source).

[3] *Vjesnik*, 29.i.47.

people'. He criticised the activities of the Nunciature, which interfered with the decisions of the hierarchy instead of letting them develop their own relations with the government, and he appealed to the traditions of Bishop Strossmayer and the national pride of the Croatian clergy, who were much better able to deal with everyday problems of Croatian life than any outsiders.

Whatever the leaders of the new government might have wished for privately as Marxists and atheists, they knew that the elimination of the churches would be, in practical terms, impossible. They did not intend to destroy the churches but to force them to change, to identify themselves with the new Yugoslavia rather than with Serbs, or Croats and Slovenes; they expected them to help, or at the very least, not to hinder the building of the new state. The distinction between destroying and changing, however, was not always clear to the middle and lower bureaucracy of the party and the state, or at the grass-roots level of former Partisans. It is true that the Catholic Church was not only defending the faith but fighting for its powers, its privileges and possessions; nevertheless many things were done which gave the Vatican and Western Catholics reason to believe that the church was also fighting for its life.

Bakarić was well aware of this. Later in the same interview he acknowledged that there had been 'errors', some of which had broken the good will of priests who were trying to work with the people, and had even created doubts about the basic line of the People's Front and the authorities;[4] these were the mistakes of inexperience, and warnings had gone out. What was now needed was a decisive conciliatory move from the church: he suggested that it might begin by stopping attacks on atheists, who according to the church were responsible for war and all the evils of society. But the trial and imprisonment of Stepinac had made such a gesture from the church impossible; his behaviour at his trial and subsequently during his imprisonment was one of the major factors in stiffening the will to resist of the clergy, and prevented many of them, particularly in Croatia, from joining the priests' associations.

[4] Bakarić was not the only leader who admitted to excesses; at various times Tito, Kardelj and Boris Krajger, and in Serbia Ranković and Djilas, all made similar admissions.

Priests' associations I

Viewed in retrospect, it is clear that the government was looking for some way of controlling the clergy, particularly the lower clergy. It would have preferred to negotiate with the bishops, but these, despite occasional murmurs, were loyal to their obedience to the Vatican. The Vatican consistently refused to allow the bishops to negotiate any agreement, not only because this was juridically the province of the Vatican, but because it felt, probably with reason, that it was in a much stronger position to delay until it could obtain satisfactory terms. The idea of professional organisations of priests, a sort of clerical trade union, through which questions of social welfare, subventions and so forth could be negotiated, looked respectable enough, and there were precedents for them. But the bishops, both Catholic and Orthodox, were from the beginning opposed to associations which would usurp a part of their authority, and which they were certain would be manipulated by the secret police. In fact the origins of the priests' associations were varied, and depended on local and historical circumstances.

The first Catholic priests' association[5] was the Istrian, founded in 1948 with Dr Božo Milanović as president; he was dean of the newly opened seminary at Pazin and widely respected. The atmosphere in the diocese was relaxed; representatives of the army and government were present at a solemn mass for the Feast of the Immaculate Conception at Pazin, the see.[6] The great majority of Istrian priests joined it, and Bishop Nežić approved its rules.[7] In the same year the first abortive association of Slovene priests was formed, and in 1949 the Ciril–Metodsko Društvo (CMD – the Association of Cyril and Methodius) of Slovene priests was founded with a membership of 135 priests.[8] This was followed in January 1950 by Dobri Pastir (the Good Shepherd), the association of Catholic priests of Bosnia and Hercegovina.[9] The Istrian and Slovene associations were largely spontaneous and sprang from the clergy themselves, although in both these regions the links between the Liberation Front and the clergy who cooperated with them were so close that it would be difficult to disentangle the motives. The authorities encouraged them from the start, although the benevolent attitude of

[5] There is mention of an Association of Serbian Priests in Croatia founded in March 1945 by the Rev. Milan Mačura (*Vjesnik*, 5.iii.45).
[6] *Oznanilo*, 12.i.47.
[7] Ibid.   [8] *SRCY.*
[9] *Dobri Pastir* (journal of the association), Feb.–March 1950, and *SRCY.*

the bishops towards the Istrian Priests' Association did not necessarily commend it to the authorities.[10]

It was not until November 1953, nearly four years after the creation of Dobri Pastir and after a good deal of officially inspired encouragement and meetings held all over Croatia, that an Association of Catholic Priests in Croatia was founded with the venerable Mgr Rittig as its honorary president.[11] The Association of Catholic Priests in the Vojvodina, the Association of Catholic Priests in Serbia and the Association of Catholic Priests in Montenegro were all founded at about this time. These were set up in direct opposition to the known wishes of the bishops, who had on April 26, 1950, pronounced membership of the associations 'inexpedient' (non expedit).[12]

After 1953, when the government realised that it would have to negotiate with the bishops if it wanted to reach a modus vivendi with the Catholic Church, the professional aspects of the priests' associations were increasingly emphasised. The Slovene CMD signed an agreement with the Council for Public Health of the Republic of Slovenia in February 1952 for health insurance for its members[13] and in November 1953 negotiated outstanding questions concerning social insurance and land taxes;[14] the Croatian association signed an agreement for the social insurance of its members as soon as it was founded.[15] These benefits were only available to members of the associations, a fact which was used as an additional lever to persuade priests to join. In addition the associations paid the insurance contributions of their members and gave a small monthly grant to priests in need, a method of indirect government subvention. To counterbalance this, the church shortly afterwards set up diocesan insurance funds on a more modest basis, to insure priests against illness and provide retirement pensions.[16]

[10] Catholic source.
[11] NYT, 21.ii.53; Vjesnik, 16.viii.53; RNS, 15.xi.53; Spomen knjiga osnivačke skupštine staleškog društva katoličkih svećenika NRH [Booklet Commemorating the Founding Congress of the Professional Association of Catholic Priests of the NRH], Zagreb, 1953. See ch. 8.
[12] 'In conventu Episcoporum habito Zagrebiae die 26 Aprilis 1950, enuntiatum est: NON EXPEDIT nomen dare associationi sacerdotum, in cujus statutio nec mentio fit autoritatis Episcoporum qui a Spiritu Sancto positi sunt regere Ecclesiam Dei. Sacerdotes memores sint exhortationis Pii X "Haerent animo" de die 4 Augusti 1908 qui statuit, illas tantum conjunctiones sacerdotum licere, "quam episcopalis auctoritas firmet et moderetur"' (unnumbered circular to clergy).
[13] Sl. Por., 20.ii.52.
[14] Ibid. 27.xi.53.   [15] RNS, 15.xi.53.
[16] SVNZ, no. 3, 1954; no. 3, 1955.

Pressure was brought both on the clergy, to force them to join the associations, and on bishops who disciplined their clergy for joining or warned them against doing so; this was held to be an unconstitutional attempt to prevent Yugoslav citizens from joining legal organisations. Official permission to give religious instruction (in schools before 1952 and subsequently in other places) was at first given only to members of the priests' associations; priests in prison or awaiting trial or serving sentences were offered remissions or easing of their conditions if they would join, and they were constantly pressed to sign resolutions in favour of the associations.[17]

At the end of 1952, Kardelj told the Federal Assembly that nearly all the Istrian priests had joined their association, 80 per cent of the priests in Bosnia and Hercegovina belonged to Dobri Pastir and 60 per cent of the Slovene priests to the CMD.[18]

Among the associations of Catholic priests Dobri Pastir and the Ciril–Metodsko Društvo were the most important, Dobri Pastir because it was founded by the Franciscans, who were largely independent of the control of the bishops of Sarajevo and Mostar, and the CMD because it sprang out of the Christian Socialist movement and had genuine roots among the clergy. Both came into existence before the bishops had declared the associations to be inexpedient.

Dobri Pastir was founded at a meeting held in Sarajevo on January 25, 1950; it was attended by representatives of a number of other Catholic associations, by a leading representative of the Association of Orthodox Priests in Serbia and by a representative of the Commission for Religious Affairs of Bosnia and Hercegovina; the head of the Moslem religious community sent greetings. The provincials of Hercegovina and Dalmatia welcomed the gathering.[19]

---

[17] A curious incident occurred early in 1953 after the bishops had forbidden (*non licet*) the priests' associations, which illustrates the strength of the government's feelings on this question. The Slovene bishops wanted to except the CMD from the decision and were authorised by the Bishops' Conference to ask the Vatican's permission. But the government at once warned the bishops that this would be illegal, since they would be asking a foreign power to decide on an internal Yugoslav matter. Its determination to keep the Vatican from interfering in Yugoslavia's internal affairs overrode the obvious advantages of breaking down some of the opposition to the priests' associations; it maintained that the constitution guaranteed the right of every Yugoslav citizen to belong to any legal Yugoslav organisation of his choice (Catholic and communist sources).

[18] Speech on foreign policy to the Federal Assembly, 18.xii.52 (*Borba*, 19.xii.52).

[19] *Dobri Pastir*, Feb.–March 1950.

An Organising Committee had been set up in August 1949, headed by Fra Bono Ostojić, a parish priest who was also a member of the republic Commission for Religious Affairs; its other members were Dr Karlo Karin, professor of theology, Dr Ratislav Drljić, director of the Franciscan seminary, and two other parish priests. They had consulted the republican authorities, the bishops and the Franciscan provincials, and received help and advice from the Istrian Priests' Association.[20] Ostojić, who was elected president of the association, said that it would do its best to work in harmony with the laws of the church and appealed to the delegates to avoid attacks on the hierarchy and other church dignitaries.[21] The themes running through all the speeches were the need for the South Slavs, but especially the two great Christian confessions, the Serbian Orthodox and the Roman Catholics, to live together in brotherly accord, and the need for social justice. There appeared to be a real desire that the association should be a unifying factor between the churches which had been divided by such terrible strife, and a bridge between the church and the authorities.

One hundred and sixty-seven priests had already joined before the official establishment of the association, the great majority of them Franciscans,[22] and it grew rapidly.

The Slovene priests' association The founding of the Slovene priests' association is unusually well documented and is worth describing. Meetings of priests who had fought with the Liberation front began almost immediately after the war; the first was held in the early autumn of 1945 at Oplotnica, near Konjica.[23] The first Organising Committee was established on October 22, 1947, by priests from the Primorska, and out of this grew the Organising Committee of Priests Members of the OF, which met on October 26, 1948, at Maribor, and started a weekly journal, *Bilten*.[24] Close links were established with the Commission for Religious Affairs.[25] A resolution was passed at this meeting attacking 'some high functionaries of the Catholic Church and the Vatican, who had given moral support to the capitalist imperialist powers' and appealing to canon law (Canon 141) against priests who had collaborated with the occupiers and 'foreign spies'.[26] This was the first time that members of the

[20] Ibid.
[21] Ibid.
[22] Ibid.
[23] *Bilten*, 4.xi.48.
[24] Ibid.
[25] Kocijančič.
[26] *Bilten*, 4.xi.48. Among the signatories of the resolution were several priests who later became professors at the theological faculty.

Catholic Church had publicly denounced the crimes of the Ustaša and Bela Garda by name and without excuses, and called for support for the government in the name of Christian social justice. Later they accused the hierarchy and the Vatican of punishing priests who had fought with the Liberation Front for establishing priests' associations, and remaining silent about the crimes of other priests.[27] The language of the resolution and of *Bilten* itself yielded nothing to the party in its vehement denunciation of the Vatican and the hierarchy, and the journal was soon banned by a Vatican decree of April 12, 1949.[28] It was evident that the committee was in the hands of extremists, still flushed with the spirit of the resistance and the Partisan victories.

The brief career of the Organising Committee culminated in a long list of demands, signed by 283 priests, all members of the Liberation Front, sent to Mgr Hurley, chargé d'affaires at the Nunciature. They demanded the dismissal of Bishop Rožman and the appointment of a new bishop who enjoyed the respect of the people and would be instructed to take action against guilty priests; the lifting of the suspension pronounced on the Rev. Jože Lampret, editor of *Bilten*, and the removing of the decree banning *Bilten*; and that Radio Vatican should cease its 'lying broadcasts' against Yugoslavia. According to the lively account which appeared in the paper,[29] a delegation consisting of Lampret, Bajt and three other priests called on Mgr Hurley, who agreed to receive them one by one, an action which the priests interpreted as a refusal to recognise an organisation representing over three hundred priests and a demonstration of Hurley's 'scorn for the lower clergy'. The interviews were disagreeable; according to *Bilten* Hurley questioned them about their political beliefs, asked if they were members of the Communist Party and accused them of acting under pressure from the secret police; he had a sharp exchange with Lampret, who came in last, and terminated the interview with: 'Marchez, c'est la porte!' The five priests hurried home and between July 19 and August 9 held meetings all over Slovenia to protest against Hurley's behaviour and to publicise their demands.[30]

It was clear that if the church and the government in Slovenia were to move towards a *modus vivendi* different methods must be used. Fortunately a number of more moderate priests who had cooperated with the Liberation Front, among them Dr S.

---

[27] Ibid. 5.ii.49.
[29] Ibid.
[28] Ibid. 15.vii.49.
[30] Ibid. 31.viii.49.

Cajnkar and Dr M. Miklavčič, had maintained a certain reserve towards the Organising Committee, and had not signed the resolution or written for *Bilten*. While Bajt and Lampret were holding their protest meetings, a number of Liberation Front priests met on August 3 at Grosuplje and decided to bring the first committee to an end and set up a new group at first called the Stanovsko–Politično Društvo Duhovnikov (Professional–Political Association of Priests). Medvešček, who had signed the resolution, played a leading part in this transformation. Further meetings were held, the group was again renamed[31] and the wise decision taken to submit the rules to the hierarchy for their approval. They were sent to Dr Mihailj Toroš, apostolic administrator of the Slovene portion of the diocese of Gorizia, who, after suggesting some modifications, accepted them.[32] The association, though not approved, was at least for the time being tolerated, and finally it was formally established under the name Ciril–Metodsko Društvo Duhovnikov LRS (Cyril and Methodius Association of the Catholic Priests of the People's Republic of Slovenia – CMD) at a meeting held on September 20 and 21 in Ljubljana.[33] It chose to take the name of the prewar Associations of Cyril and Methodius, founded at the end of the nineteenth century in Slovenia and in Istria to oppose the Germanisation and Italianisation of these areas.[34] At the same time a Zadruga (Cooperative), the Buying and Selling Cooperative of the Slovene Catholic Church in the PRS was set up to demonstrate that the priests practised what they preached.

Although he had played a leading part in the first Organising Committee, Bajt became president of the new Association. Dr Cajnkar was not at first a member of the committee but he later became a vice-president; he assured the Slovene bishops that there was no intention of forming a separate ecclesiastical organisation and that he would use his influence to try to make the CMD an association with which the bishops could collaborate.[35] *Bilten* ceased publication and a new monthly journal, *Nova Pot*, appeared in November 1949; its tone was in striking contrast. The clergy, it said, must accept the conditions in which they lived, and try to reconcile everyday life with the life of the spirit. The leading article set out the concerns of the CMD: to even out the great differences between cities and

---

[31] Društvo Slovenskih Katoličkih Duhovnikov LRS (the Association of Slovene Catholic Priests of the PRS).
[32] *Bilten*, 31.viii.49.   [33] *Nova Pot*, Nov. 1949.
[34] B. Novak, p. 18.
[35] Conversation with Dr Cajnkar in 1970.

villages and try to bring them closer to each other, and to find employment for the unemployed; to look for the common elements which join Catholics to their brothers of different faiths; to support the authorities in their struggle for equality between nations and states, so as to build brotherhood in the world. It welcomed the agricultural reform which had restored to the people the great possessions of the church, which in the past had been a burden and an offence. It greeted with particular joy the presence of Orthodox priests in brotherly comradeship at the founding of the association.

The working papers for the first plenum of the CMD emphasised that the priest must identify himself with the poor, not the rich, in accord with the principles of real religious life. He is a citizen as well as a believer, with duties to the state of which he is an equal citizen; he must seek social justice in the spirit of 2 Corinthians and the Epistle of St James. The program of the CMD was full of anticipations of the Second Vatican Council, a fact which was later made much of.

A delegation from the new association, which included Dr Edgar Leopold, the elderly and respected prior of the Carthusians at Pleterje where many wounded Partisans had been hidden and nursed during the war, and Lampret, who was now secretary of the Commission for Religious Affairs of the Slovene government, paid a call on Tito.[36]

It was a courageous beginning. The hierarchy had not abated its hostility, and on the other side, there were pressures and interference from the secret police to be resisted.[37] But the association grew out of a genuine desire of priests who had been with the Liberation Front to cooperate with the government in its social and national aims; the character of some of its leading members, their known integrity and independence, was a guarantee that this was not a puppet organisation. By 1950 its membership had risen to 478[38] and in 1952 over 500 out of 1,030 Slovene priests had joined.[39]

Lampret was a convinced socialist, believed by many of his fellow priests to be a member of the Communist Party, and he had thrown the first committee uncritically behind the government. It had taken the authorities and the 'patriotic priests' barely a year to learn that this headlong approach would not serve the purpose. The CMD approached its task differently; it tried

[36] *Nova Pot*, Dec. 1949, p. 27.   [37] Catholic and Marxist sources.
[38] *SRCY*.   [39] *NYT*, 3.vii.52.

to be more objective, to keep in touch with both sides. *Nova Pot* explained the actions of the government and the church instead of either attacking or blindly supporting them, and the government welcomed this. The bishops respected men like Cajnkar and Miklavčič, even if they did not approve of their actions.[40] The behaviour of Cajnkar in particular, a scholarly, peace-loving man who had been a member of the Christian Socialist movement since long before the war, was marked by tact, moderation and judgment; he was no fiery leader, but he had the qualities which were needed to maintain a relationship with the government during the next few difficult years without entirely alienating the hierarchy. He had always opposed the clericalism which permeated Slovenian political life for many years before the war, and this earned him the trust of the government. In 1952 he was elected dean of the theological faculty in Ljubljana by his colleagues. By then the Bishops' Conference had declared that membership of the priests' association was forbidden (*non licet*) – a pronouncement which has never been revoked – and in consequence Dr Cajnkar has never received a *nihil obstat* from the Vatican, the formal permission to teach.[41]

On the other hand the extremist positions of Bajt and Lampret were not forgiven by their bishop[42] and they compounded their offences by ignoring their suspension (*suspensio a divinis*) and continuing to administer the sacraments. For this disobedience both were excommunicated in 1950.[43] It was not until the Second Vatican Council that they made their peace with the church and were given absolution.

Persecution of the bishops and clergy

Estimates appeared from time to time in the Western press of the number of priests and religious killed, arrested or missing, the number of empty parishes, and the number of religious schools closed. The *New York Times* published a report claiming that 300 priests were awaiting trial in jail, kept in abominable conditions.[44] At the same period, on the other hand, Auxiliary

---

[40] Cajnkar became editor of *Nova Pot* in February 1950 with the tacit approval of the bishops.

[41] This was true also of the late Dr Miklavčič and one or two others; but they received the *nihil obstat* in 1970 while Dr Cajnkar had still in 1971 not received his (conversation with Dr Cajnkar in 1971).

[42] Bishop Margotti of Gorizia.

[43] *NYT*, 11.xi.50. [44] *NYT*, 14.xi.50.

Bishop Salis stated in a circular[45] that there were 40 priests from the Zagreb diocese – by far the largest in Yugoslavia – in prison, (although he was probably referring to diocesan priests, not religious). Three years later Ranković said that in February 1953 there were 161 priests in prison, and he was referring to priests of all denominations.[46] The Vatican was slowly collecting information,[47] but the diocesan statistics given in the official publication *Annuario Pontificio* remained the same from 1944 to 1952. In that year (and in the case of a few dioceses in immediately subsequent years) new figures were given[48] which show the results of these investigations and form the basis for the allegations of the Vatican about the state of the Catholic Church in Yugoslavia.

The number of diocesan priests in the Zagreb archdiocese had dropped from 826 to 612, and religious from 538 to 359; in the Ljubljana diocese where the reaction against clericalism was strong the number of priests dropped from 614 to 336 and of religious from 326 to 119 (1956 figures); in the Sarajevo diocese the number of priests dropped from 113 to 68 but the number of religious on the other hand increased from 228 to 295; and in the Split archdiocese priests dropped from 173 to 153 and religious from 140 to 51. There was a sharp drop in the number of seminarians, a reflection of the number of Catholic schools and minor seminaries which had been closed. Many convent buildings belonging to women's religious orders were expropriated; Slovenia (47 houses out of 60) and Bosnia and Hercegovina (39 houses out of 42) suffered particularly severely in this respect and although 794 out of 1,310 nuns remained in Slovenia, in Bosnia and Hercegovina there was almost a clean sweep and only 31 nuns (1956) remained of the 605 of 1944. In these two dioceses nuns were also forbidden to wear their habits in public.[49] The picture is one of a religious community very hard hit, but far from totally destroyed (and indeed there has since then been a vigorous renewal in the numbers of priests and religious, both men and women).

Material help was arriving from abroad through Caritas in Germany and the National Catholic Welfare Conference in the

[45] 6053/1950, 19.xii.50.
[46] *Vjesnik*, 22.v.53: speech to the Federal Executive Council presenting the Law on the Status of Religious Communities.
[47] Its sources seem to have been good. A number of priests served terms of imprisonment for unauthorised contacts with the Nunciature (Catholic sources).
[48] See Appendix II, table 4.
[49] Catholic and Marxist sources and personal observation.

USA;[50] this helped to alleviate the church's difficult financial position. The archbishopric, however, had to enforce strict rules about its distribution and insist that all requests, even from heads of religious orders, should be made through the archbishopric.[51]

An illuminating sidelight is thrown by a circular[52] from the archbishopric of Zagreb to the clergy in 1950, reporting on the material help which was being sent to priests in prison. Bishop Salis writes that each priest receives either two 7-kg packages a month, with fat, flour, meat, cheese, sugar and small quantities of jam, walnuts, preserves etc.; or the priests' families received 2,000 dinars to send them food. He thanks each of the clergy for having sent either 1,000 dinars or food: the central diocesan fund made up the rest. The costs for the next year would be higher because of the rising cost of living; American Catholics had sent 1,500 kg of wheat, and the diocesan, and if necessary the parish, funds could be drawn on, but he asks each priest to contribute 2,000 dinars monthly, or 14 kg of food and soap, matches, cigarettes or clothes. The circular ends pointedly: 'Please send as quickly as possible for our need is great. We are confident that this provisioning will be understood, for if you give, perhaps you will be giving to yourselves.'

It is difficult, nevertheless, to appreciate the full impact of the struggle on the church without realising the nature of the pressure under which the bishops and clergy lived until the middle 1950s. As well as the imprisonment of Archbishop Stepinac, and the disappearance of Bishop Carević and the death of Bishop Šimrak, both in the immediate aftermath of the war, Bishop Čule of Mostar was sentenced in July 1948 to eleven and a half years imprisonment for collaboration, of which he served seven,[53] and Mgr Stjepevac of Kotor was sentenced in December 1950 to six years for collaboration.[54] Bishop Srebrnić of Krk was imprisoned for two months in 1945 and Bishop Bäuerlein of Djakovo was under house arrest for three months in the summer of 1953.[55] Bishops touring their dioceses, especially for confirmations, were constantly obstructed and harassed.[56] The harassment, which usually took the form of obstructing the passage of the clergy by jeering, shouting crowds, was often accompanied by beating and stoning which sometimes had serious and even

[50] Catholic source.
[51] 5/51, 9.i.51.
[52] 6053/1950, 18.xii.50.
[53] L'O.R., 1.iv.54; MG, 1.xi.55.
[54] L'O.R., 17.iii.54.
[55] Ibid. 17.iii.54, 1.iv.54.
[56] L'O.R. gives many examples; see also NYT, 18.iii.46, and Narodni List, 6.x.46, describing the demonstrations against Bishop Pušić on the island of Brač.

fatal consequences. These attacks moreover were often reported, favourably, in the official press. Auxiliary Bishop Franić of Split was attacked by mobs in several places during a diocesan visitation;[57] Mgr Ukmar was beaten and his companion the Rev. M. Buletić was killed when visiting Lanišće for confirmations.[58] Ukmar was sentenced to six years for provocation; the two men who killed Buletić were sentenced to five and three months respectively.[59] Bishop Vovk of Ljubljana was brutally attacked and narrowly escaped being killed; Mgr Čelik, the Apostolic Administrator of Banja Luka, and his secretary were assaulted during confirmation visits in June 1953,[60] and Mgr Budanović, the Apostolic Administrator of Bačka (Vojvodina), a man of over eighty, was assaulted during a visit to Sombor for confirmations in September 1953;[61] Čelik was expelled from his diocese and not allowed to return until March 1954.[62] Bishop Držečnik of Maribor was assaulted and expelled from Ptuj in May 1951 and deprived of his right to travel for three weeks because the red star had been removed, without his knowledge, from the Yugoslav tricolour flag which was being carried at the head of a procession which formed to welcome him.[63] Sometimes protests against this sort of violence were effective; Držečnik on this occasion protested to the local authorities, as Archbishop Ujčić had done in June 1949, and they made an effort to restore order.[64]

Bishops were constantly under attack for forbidding their clergy to join the priests' associations. Bishop Pušić of Hvar was fined 40,000 dinars for this,[65] Bishop Bonifačić of Split was attacked in the press and cautioned by the public prosecutor that he was infringing the law[66] and Borba attacked four bishops (Budanović of Subotica, Bukatko of Križevci, Ujčić of Belgrade and Bäuerlein of Djakovo) for persecuting members of the priests' associations.[67] Bishop Nežić of Poreč–Pula and Bishop

[57] Slobodna Dalmacija, 26.vii.53.
[59] Times, 8.xi.47.
[61] Ibid.
[63] NYHT, 30.vi.51.
[64] L'O.R., 1.iv.54. L'O.R. published two long articles, signed F.A., on March 17 and April 1, 1954, on the subject of violence against the Yugoslav bishops. The accounts are frequently confirmed by articles which appeared in the Yugoslav and foreign press: cf. the account of the demonstrations in July 1953 against Bishop Franić, Bishop Bonifačić and Bishop Pušić in L'O.R. and in Borba and Slobodna Dalmacija, 26.vii.53. NYHT, 30.vi.50, quotes Ljudska Pravica on the attack on Bishop Držečnik at Ptuj.
[65] Il Popolo, 12.vi.54; RNS, 11.vi.54.
[66] Slobodna Dalmacija, 14.vii.53.

[58] MG, 28.viii.47; L'O.R., 1.iv.54.
[60] L'O.R., 1.iv.54.
[62] RNS, 24.vi.53, 9.iii.54.

[67] NYT, 28.xi.54.

Pavlišić of Senj were called up for military service in 1953 and assigned to cavalry units as grooms.[68] The pressure against believers and the church went in waves. It increased sharply, for example, towards the end of 1951 and developed to a point of great intensity by the middle of 1952.[69] *The Times* reported that it was particularly strong in Slovenia where the church was accused of interfering in civil affairs and trying to recover its prewar prerogatives; Miha Marinko, the Slovene premier, accused the Vatican of persistent interference in Yugoslavia's internal affairs, and accused the hierarchy of systematically persecuting priests who tried to cooperate with the government.[70] There were strong attacks against Catholic influence on young people. Thirty secondary-school pupils in Maribor were expelled for going to church.[71] A little earlier thirteen students and two priests from the Zagreb seminary were arrested at the end of 1950 and brought to trial in June 1951, accused of sending threatening anonymous letters to local authorities.[72] Several, including Dr Salač, the spiritual director, were sentenced to considerable terms of imprisonment. The seminary was not closed, but the director, Dr (later Cardinal Archbishop) Šeper resigned and spent some time as a parish priest on the outskirts of Zagreb. A year later the director of the Bishop's Seminary at Koper, Dr Marcel Labor, was accused of food hoarding and 'denationalising activities' and sentenced to one year of hard labour, but again the seminary was not closed.[73]

These attacks were not directed against an unimportant minority, remnants of the reactionary past, but against a church to which the majority of the population still adhered, as the communists were somewhat shocked to discover in 1953. The census of that year – the only postwar census which asked about religious affiliation – showed that only 12.4 per cent of the inhabitants of Yugoslavia declared that they had no religious affilitation.[74] Ranković's speech to the Fourth Plenum of the Communist Party in June 1951 revealed the extent of the illegal arrests and unjustifiable prosecutions which had been taking place[75] and continued for some time after.

[68] RNS, 18.xi.53.
[69] *CSM*, 7.i.52; *NYT* 10.ii.52, 20.vi.52. The latter reported that the Central Committee of the Slovene Communist Party had given instructions for an 'all-out and systematic struggle against the Slovene hierarchy and clericalism'.
[70] 10.xii.51.   [71] RNS, 19.v.52.
[72] *NYHT*, 26.xi.50; *Vjesnik* 5 and 8.vi.51; *NYT*, 17.vi.51.
[73] *Sl. Por.*, 7.x.52.
[74] See Appendix II, table 1.   [75] See ch. 8, n. 7.

It was becoming clear that neither the church in Yugoslavia nor the Vatican was responding to violent methods, and that Yugoslavia's reputation in the West, a matter of increasing concern to her, was being seriously harmed. Talks between the government and the bishops (discussed below) had broken down. Radio Vatican had broadcast an order to the clergy not to join the priests' associations[76] to which Ranković had retorted by accusing the Vatican of interfering in Yugoslavia's internal affairs.[77] But the tide had turned and the attacks gradually died down in the second half of 1953. Already forty-three priests had been amnestied at the beginning of the year.[78] There was a last outbreak in the summer, when Bishop Franić, Bishop Čelik and Bishop Budanović were attacked by mobs, but September marked the change. The signal to desist came from the top, when Marshal Tito in a speech at Ruma[79] deplored violence against priests:

excesses have taken place which ought not to happen in a socialist country like ours. We don't agree with them and we condemn such acts because we have far stronger means for the struggle...you can, by your behaviour and showing that you do not believe what they preach, and by ignoring them, see that they do not have a fertile soil for their hostile acts. This is much worse for them than physical attacks...which are an uncultured phenomenon. This is illegal and we demand that the law should be respected in our country.

He went on to say that the best method of fighting religion was to educate young people. The warning was repeated by officials in other parts of the country, and after this the struggle began to move into a different level.

Daily difficulties facing the church

This, however, was still in the future. In 1950 the church's situation was still bad. The government had survived, for the moment, the break with the Cominform, but it was still struggling to maintain itself, and discipline over the whole country was draconian. Archbishop Ujčić was acting president of the Bishops' Conference (and remained so until Stepinac's death) but six dioceses were without bishops and under apostolic administrators[80] and the bishops lacked strong leadership.

[76] 8.iv.53, reported in *Review of International Affairs*, 16.iv.53.
[77] *Vjesnik*, 22.v.53.   [78] *Times*, 9.i.53.
[79] *Vjesnik*, 28.ix.53.
[80] Banja Luka, Dubrovnik, Križevci, Ljubljana, Sarajevo and Zagreb, whose bishops had either died, fled or been imprisoned.

Unofficial contacts between the church and the authorities took place behind the scenes, and Mgr Rittig, the president of the Commission for Religious Affairs of Croatia, was constantly active in his efforts to lower the tension and bring about some sort of settlement. He made it possible for Dr Oberški, vice-dean of the theological faculty in Zagreb, and Dr Marić, a member of the faculty, to travel to Rome late in 1950 to sound out the Vatican about a possible settlement.[81] but nothing came of this initiative.

The government made a conciliatory gesture when it released Archbishop Stepinac from Lepoglava prison on December 5, 1951, and sent him to his native village, Krašić, to live in the parish house. He was guarded and could not leave the village, but access to him was easier. During his imprisonment a number of foreign correspondents had been allowed to visit him, and his answers to their questions showed that his opinions had not changed.[82] On the day of his release he told a Yugoslav correspondent that he had had visits from a number of bishops and priests, as well as eight visits from foreign journalists; he had been adequately treated and allowed to pursue his own studies, had celebrated mass daily in a cell which was arranged as a chapel, and had received all the books he required.[83] The government hoped that this gesture would ease the tension and remove some of the acerbity from their relations with the church, but it continued to attack the Nunciature for going beyond its diplomatic functions and mixing in Yugoslavia's internal affairs.[84]

There were a number of other developments at this time. Religious education, which had been allowed in primary schools for children whose parents asked for it, was discontinued, and priests were given permission to hold catechism classes in churches (which were a place of public access; classes were prohibited in parish houses or private houses). All theological faculties were separated from the universities of which they had previously formed a part.[85] The question of the secrecy of the confessional was clarified and priests were relieved of the legal obligation to report information about crimes which they had received from penitents.

The church was suffering acute financial hardship; one of its

[81] Catholic source. The visit was reported by *CSM*, 16.xi.50, and picked up later by the Cominform, who alleged that Tito had offered to amnesty all priests (*NYT*, 8.iv.51).

[82] *CSM* and *NYT*, 7.iv.51; *NYT*, 8.iv.51 (C. L. Sulzberger).

[83] *Vjesnik*, 6.xii.51.

[84] *Le Monde*, 26.xii.51, quoting *Politika* interview with Bakarić.

[85] To take effect 28.vi.52; *CSM*, 20.ii.52.

principal preoccupations was to find means to educate boys who continued to stream into the seminaries and faculties. Bishop Salis in a circular to deans[86] quoted Don Bosco (founder of the Salesians) who told the faithful: 'Do you know where the salvation of human society lies?. . . right in your pockets.' Money was needed to educate young priests so that the church could be carried on. Fees at the seminary were doubled, from 500 to 1,000 dinars a month,[87] and at the theological faculty raised to 750 dinars a month, 25 per cent of the full cost. Priests were asked to contribute from their own pockets, and to try to raise money from their parishioners. Parents were constantly reminded of their sacred responsibility responsibility for the religious education of their children.[88]

Priests' associations II: rupture with the Vatican

The government now found time to give its attention again to the contest of wills with the hierarchy over the priests' associations. The bishops had pronounced membership of the associations 'inexpedient' in 1950, but their policy was uncoordinated and the decree was applied with varying firmness. Some bishops were unwilling to court trouble with the authorities by threatening ecclesiastical sanctions against priests who joined the associations, while others were strict, sometimes at the request of their own priests, who needed to be able to cite their bishops' orders when pressed to join the associations. The question was becoming acute and the clergy urged their bishops to give them definite guidance. Bishop Salis wrote to the clergy[89] giving a provisional opinion: on the basis of Canons 235 and 336 the bishop has the right to decide whether there are justifiable reasons for the establishment of professional but not strictly ecclesiastical associations for the clergy, and the clergy must obey the directions of the bishop. Accordingly the bishops would consider the question at the forthcoming conference and inform the clergy of their decision. This circular was interpreted by the government as meaning that there was no canonical prohibition of priests' associations and was used extensively in government propaganda at the time.

The bishops then sought guidance from the Vatican; the reply came, transmitted through the Nunciature, that the Vatican hoped that the Yugoslav bishops would oppose 'the heavy threat

---

[86] 221/1951, 7.xi.51.
[88] Circular 4174/1952, 1.ix.52.

[87] Letter no. 228, SVNZ, 10.xi.51.
[89] Circular 4513/1952, 18.ix.52.

represented by the priests' associations'.[90] Accordingly at the end of the meeting of the Bishops' Conference, the bishops issued a declaration forbidding the clergy either to found or become members of a priests' association (*non licet*).[91] The bishops also wrote to Marshal Tito about the position of religion and the church;[92] there was, they said, no complete religious freedom in Yugoslavia, but only a partial freedom of worship; they listed in detail the grievances of the church;[93] they opposed the priests' associations because they had been started by the authorities and did not help to promote good relations between church and state. If associations were to exist, their rules must be in accord with canonical regulations and they must be under the control of the bishops.

They concluded by declaring their loyalty and patriotism; they would urge the clergy and the faithful to show a friendly attitude to everything that was positive in the existing system. But they could not be expected to take part in the political life of the country; their responsibility was social and spiritual. The tone was gentler than previous letters but they had put their fingers on a contradiction in the attitude of the government, which courted the political support of the clergy but reacted angrily against anything which they could interpret as criticism or independent initiative in the political field.

Mgr Oddi, the chargé d'affaires at the Nunciature, had left Belgrade in order not to appear to be bringing pressure on the bishops, and the message from the Vatican was transmitted to Archbishop Ujčić by a secretary at the Nunciature, who allowed the archbishop to take a copy with him. When Ujčić read the letter to the Conference, two of the bishops, Držečnik and Vovk, took notes. Vovk later tried to destroy his notes, but was not entirely successful, and Držečnik hid his.[94] There was indiscreet talk, and the existence of the letter became known. The secret police swooped and their search was successful: photostats of the notes taken by the two bishops appeared in the press.[95] The authorities

---

[90] Letter from Yugoslav government to Vatican, 1.xi.52: *L'O.R.*, 14.i.53.

[91] There is no copy of the text of the *Non licet* in the collection of circulars seen by the writer at the Zagreb archbishopric. It is referred to in the text of the Yugoslav government's letter to the Vatican of Nov. 1, 1952 (*L'O.R.*, 14.i.53) as 'the declaration on the ecclesiastical associations: Non licet' issued by the bishops after receiving instructions from the Vatican.

[92] Pattee, doc. LXXIII, 26.ix.52.

[93] These were quoted at length in the Vatican's note to the Yugoslav government, 15.xii.52 (see n. 105 below).

[94] *Vjesnik*, 6.x.53, an account whose general accuracy has been confirmed to the writer from a Catholic source.

[95] *Vjesnik*, 7.x.53.

were triumphant; at last they had incontrovertible evidence that the Vatican was directing the bishops' actions.

A formal complaint conveyed by Dr Aleš Bebler was addressed to the Vatican on November 1, 1952, stating that the Yugoslav government was aware that a letter had been transmitted to Dr Ujčić expressing the hope that the Yugoslav clergy would oppose the priests' associations. This was a fresh example of the unwarrantable interference of the Vatican, and an attempt to deprive priests who were citizens of Yugoslavia of their fundamental civil rights guaranteed by the constitution. In view of the fact that similar associations in other countries were tolerated by the Holy See, the government assumed that the Vatican wished to exacerbate its relations with the Yugoslav government. On its side, it was willing, as it always had been, to negotiate a satisfactory agreement with the Vatican on the basis of the constitutional separation of church and the state, and the guarantee of freedom of worship, an arrangement which had been satisfactorily concluded with the other churches of Yugoslavia.[96]

In an interview with the writer in 1970, Cardinal Oddi explained the subsequent course of events. The Vatican's answer was delayed for several weeks, as the under-secretary of state, Mgr Tardini, decided to deal himself with the whole range of questions at issue. In the meantime, on November 29, 1952, which happened also to be Yugoslavia's National Day, the Vatican issued a list of new cardinals in which the name of Archbishop Stepinac appeared. Mgr Oddi heard the news in the early afternoon and at once sent a telegram to Stepinac; that evening he went to the presidential reception. A foreign journalist there told Oddi that he intended to visit Stepinac the next day, and Oddi asked him to give Stepinac the news. The journalist left the reception immediately and travelled through the night, arriving at Krašić the next morning in time for mass. He went to Stepinac afterwards and greeted him as 'Eminence'. Stepinac, who had not yet received Oddi's telegram, demurred, but the journalist gave him the message and asked him if he would now go to Rome. Stepinac answered that he would not leave his diocese unless the pope ordered him to do so. This was reported by the journalist and appeared next morning in the world press. Stepinac thus made his own position – which had never changed – clear from the start, but also made it much more difficult for the Vatican to recall him.[97]

The Yugoslav government reacted angrily, apparently to the

[96] L'O.R., 14.i.53, which gives the text of the exchanges; Vjesnik, 3.xi.52.
[97] Interview with Cardinal Oddi, Nov. 1970.

surprise and distress of Pius XII, who, according to Cardinal Oddi, had simply wished to honour a man who he thought deserved it, not to administer a rebuff to Yugoslavia, and had neglected to consult Oddi before including Stepinac's name.[98] It is also possible that the Vatican's action was intended to furnish a pretext for recalling Stepinac to Rome, thus easing the tension; but Stepinac's declaration made this difficult, and the Yugoslav government acted so quickly that it had no time for further manoeuvre. It considered that the Vatican's action, coming so soon after the government's note, to which it had had no answer, was a calculated snub. Tito spoke at Smederevska Palanka on December 18: 'We want to be on good terms with the Vatican, we constantly offer them our hand, but they spit on us...[our citizens] are tired of the past, the sick days when our country was a bargaining counter. The Vatican hates socialism and does everything it can against it.'[99] Kardelj, the foreign minister, speaking later in the federal Executive Council during the debate on the rupture, accused the Vatican of supporting Italy's irredentist policy; the Italian government was just as opposed as the Vatican to Tito's forthcoming visit to Britain. He again repeated the party's thesis that religion was a social phenomenon which could not be eliminated by persecution or directives, even if it had wanted to.[100]

Oddi was summoned to the ministry of foreign affairs on December 16, to be told that since no answer had been received to the Yugoslav government's note, but that instead Stepinac had been made a cardinal, it was obvious that the Vatican did not wish for improved relations; there was no further reason to maintain diplomatic relations, which would cease forthwith. There were indications that the Yugoslav government had had this step in mind for some time. The Yugoslav chargé d'affaires was absent from the Vatican on prolonged leave and one of the secretaries had departed quietly without taking his official congé, leaving the legation with only a caretaker.[101] On the same day, however, the Vatican's long-delayed answer had finally been despatched, one copy through the diplomatic bag and one through the open post. The latter arrived first and was at once taken to the ministry. It was sent back unopened, with a message that it was unable to receive any communications from the Holy See since no diplomatic relations existed.[102]

[98] Ibid. See also *L'O.R.*, 2/3.i.53, for editorial comment on the rupture.
[99] *Vjesnik*, 9.xii.52.   [100] *Borba*, 19.xii.52.
[101] Oddi interview.
[102] Ibid. Dr Bebler has confirmed to the writer that his recollection of the events coincides with Cardinal Oddi's.

The Vatican's answer, which together with the Yugoslav government's original note was published by *L'Osservatore Romano* on January 14, 1953, went at length into all the points at issue.[103] The letter began with a paragraph which referred to the inalienable rights of religion and the Catholic Church which it was the duty of the Holy See to protect; its actions therefore were not unwarrantable interference, since Catholics as well as being citizens of a particular country were also members of the church. (It was precisely this double loyalty, particularly among the bishops, which the Yugoslav government complained about.) It went on to cite examples of persecution and discrimination, quoting from the Yugoslav press, and followed this with a long list of Catholic organisations and institutions which had been closed down or nationalised[104] and the obstacles put in the way of even the restricted religious instruction which was still allowed. It was against this background that the Vatican viewed the priests' associations. These had been started by the authorities, and priests who refused to join were subjected to various disabilities and pressures; police were present at their meetings and political personalities frequently took part; they were often directed by priests who were under ecclesiastical sanction. The bishops were naturally concerned about this state of affairs, which raised the danger of a schism in the church. The note concluded with a list of the church's demands, based on its fundamental rights: full and genuine liberty of worship, the right to Catholic schools and press, charitable and welfare organisations, and the right to maintain the clergy and build new churches. The faithful must be in contact with and dependent on the bishops, who must be able to visit parishes, carry out their ecclesiastical duties, preach Catholic doctrine and issue documents for the instruction and pastoral care of their people. The clergy must not be impeded in the religious instruction of children and there must be seminaries open for the instruction of priests; the important charitable and educational work of the religious orders must not be interfered with.

Although the struggle was ostensibly about the education of the young and the priests' associations (and these were very real disputes), the political nature of the quarrel was generally

[103] No. 414385/52, 1.xi.52, from the ministry of foreign affairs, and 9414/52, 15.xii.52, from the Vatican.

[104] 152 Catholic publications, 24 major publishing houses, 8 seminaries closed; women's orders in Slovenia and Bosnia and Hercegovina dissolved, 200 priests still in prison and 30 killed, the church reduced to poverty by the agrarian reform and now being exorbitantly taxed.

recognised abroad. The question of Trieste and Zones A and B was entering into its last acute phase, and the Yugoslav government was convinced that the Vatican supported Italy in this quarrel and sought every opportunity of poisoning Yugoslavia's relations with the West.[105] Bishop Santin of Trieste was indefatigable in his support of the Italian case and had enlisted the help of Archbishop Spellman of New York, who urged the United States government to cease sending aid to Yugoslavia; the Catholic hierarchy in Britain was conducting a campaign of protest against Tito's forthcoming visit to Britain at Anthony Eden's invitation. It was not difficult to conclude that the Vatican, knowing Yugoslavia's isolation from the Soviet bloc and its growing economic dependence on the West, felt able to be more intransigeant with Yugoslavia than with, for example, Poland, where in spite of the declaration of loyalty by the hierarchy the government intervened far more in the internal life of the church than did the Yugoslav government.[106]

The rupture of diplomatic relations had a number of other, minor, consequences. The Commission for Religious Affairs of Slovenia, which had been an unofficial body including both Catholics and communists, was re-formed and became an official body attached to the Executive Council; all of the members of the new body were communists. Mgr Rittig, who had worked actively for an improvement in church–state relations, became a much less influential figure, although he was elected a member of the Executive Committee of the Croatian Assembly.[107] He was no longer used by the government as a negotiator[108] and on January 1, 1954, he retired.[109]

Abortive negotiations between the bishops and the government

After the rupture the government lost no time in resuming negotiations with the bishops. Marshal Tito invited them to a further meeting with him on January 8;[110] Archbishop Ujčić, Bishop Akšamović, Bishop Salis, Bishop Lach, Bishop Vovk,

---

[105] Among many others Vukmanović-Tempo (vice-chairman of the Federal Assembly) put it bluntly: the Vatican had joined the hostile Italian campaign against Yugoslavia; all who worked against Yugoslavia helped the Soviet Union and all those working against international peace and understanding (*Le Monde*, 2.xii.52).
[106] For further comment on this see *Le Monde*, 19.xii.52, and *NYHT*, 2.i.53, article by Richard Lowenthal.
[107] *Vjesnik*, 7.ii.53.
[108] Catholic source.
[109] *Zagrebačka Panorama*, 1.iii.61 (obituary).
[110] *Vjesnik*, 10.i.53.

Bishop Alaupović of Sarajevo and Bishop Burić of Senj attended,[111] bringing with them a memorandum listing their complaints and demands.[112] No official statement was issued after the meeting but Bishop Akšamović said that he was optimistic.[113] A joint commission of bishops and government representatives, with Boris Krajger[114] in the chair, was set up to discuss the questions at issue between them and try to work out a *modus vivendi*. The government hoped that it would at last succeed in persuading the hierarchy to deal directly with it, not only about the priests' associations but about the proposed new law on the status of religious communities, as both the Orthodox and the Moslems were doing, and as groups of clergy and, unofficially, Bishop Akšamović had already done.[115]

Stepinac, interviewed by the *New York Times*, however, was less sanguine: there could never be an agreement without the Holy See, and while the Holy See was always ready to negotiate with men of good will it would never do so under compulsion.[116]

Both sides must have gone into the commission with mixed feelings. It was important for Tito, on the eve of his visit to London, to quieten the attacks which were being made on him both in Britain and the United States, and to persuade the bishops to deal with him directly. The bishops were in a difficult position. They had no authorisation from the Vatican to negotiate, but it was possible that Tito had new proposals to make, and they wished to put their memorandum before him; they also hoped by joining the commission to forestall the possibility that the government would negotiate a settlement directly with the priests' associations.

The talks broke down at the end of April.[117] It was later revealed by Ranković[118] that Mgr Tardini had written to Archbishop Ujčić on February 16 reminding him in unequivocal terms that: 'the leaders of the church, without the approval of the Holy See, must not in any way promise anything or confirm

---

[111] *NYT* and *Sl. Por.*, 10.i.53.   [112] Catholic source.

[113] *Vjesnik*, 18.8.53.

[114] At that time president of both the federal and Slovene Commissions for Religious Affairs.

[115] Foreign observers reported that an all-out propaganda campaign was launched to establish the idea that a final settlement depended on the success of the commission, and that government circles spoke with great optimism (*NYT*, 11.i.53).

[116] *NYT*, 13.i.53.

[117] *Times* and Tanjug (official Yugoslav news agency), 25.iv.53.

[118] In a speech to the federal Parliament presenting the draft of the new Law on the Status of Religious Communities (*Vjesnik*, 22.v.53).

anything, not even orally, and this includes the draft or concept of any agreement. This is not only against canon law, but harmful to the church and to souls.' A warning to the Croatian clergy not to join priests' associations was also broadcast on April 8 by Radio Vatican.[119]

It is a matter for speculation whether the letter, couched in these uncompromising terms, was intended to strengthen the hands of the bishops, or to warn them, should there be any weakening among them.[120] In any case, when the government representatives asked for comment on the new law, the bishops handed in a statement saying that for formal legal reasons they could not accept such laws as a satisfactory solution to the relations of church and state;[121] they also declared that they were not competent to come to any agreements and could only attend the commission 'for information'.

The government was exasperated by this fresh setback. Boris Krajger, the president of the commission, said in an interview[122] a few days later that the government started from the basis that believers and clergy are citizens, and interested in the successful building of the state: it was the business of the church to find the way to cooperate, and it was the business of the authorities to help them – this was to their mutual advantage. But the bishops had ignored the proposals for a new law on the status of religious communities and spoke in the commission as if they were subjects only of the Vatican with no civil rights, and not equal citizens of the state. The Vatican supported Italy, which still dreamt of extending its power in the Mediterranean, and the bishops were being used as tools. If the Vatican thought that Yugoslavia was in such a difficult position that it would have to bow to pressure, it was making a short-sighted miscalculation. The future of relations between the state and the church depended entirely on the attitude of the church.

Nevertheless a government spokesman had already declared to foreign journalists that the rupture had not been over a matter of principle and that the government was prepared to negotiate directly with the Vatican on church–state relations, if the Vatican would keep out of Yugoslav internal affairs.[123]

---

[119] *Review of International Affairs*, 16.iv.53. This may have been simply a rebroadcast of the original declaration of *non licet*.

[120] A young Catholic historian said emphatically to the writer in 1970: 'Both'.

[121] *Vjesnik*, 25.iv.53.   [122] *Sl. Por.*, 4.v.53.

[123] *NYT*, 1.v.53.

Stepinac's last days and death

Relations between the church and the state were entering into a quieter phase, lasting about ten years, during which the situation developed slowly and away from the public gaze. Retribution for the events of the war was long since past and public oppression was beginning to lighten. The Law on the Legal Status of Religious Communities was passed on April 27, 1953; it codified the constitutional provisions for the separation of church and state and the guarantees of freedom of conscience and religious belief. The first draft had been revised after representations from various religious communities, and several improvements secured;[124] this sowed the seeds of a slow – very slow – but nevertheless growing confidence in the possibility of obtaining justice under the law. In September Tito made his widely reported speech at Ruma. The bishops, meeting for their annual conference in October of that year, found it worth testing the new attitude by sending a memorandum to the government concerning the continuing persecution of the clergy and appealing to Articles 28 and 29 of the constitution guaranteeing personal freedoms. They cited a list of the most glaring instances, going back to 1947, and protested at being called traitors and enemies of the people. The text found its way abroad and was published by the Catholic news agency KIPA.[125]

The continued detention of Stepinac was considered by the church to be an absolute obstacle to any official collaboration with the state.[126] He lived in the parish house of his native village of Krašić, receiving visits from a secretary every week, and other church personages from time to time. Occasional visitors attended mass in the parish church, and stopped afterwards to speak to Stepinac in the sacristy. But he felt himself isolated[127] and he was a sick man. In 1953 his doctors had diagnosed polycythemia, a rare blood disease resulting in an overproduction of red blood cells;[128] he developed thrombosis in his left leg and was told he must be moved to a warmer climate. The authorities let it be known that they would accede to an official request from Stepinac to be moved, as they had no wish to have an ailing martyr on their hands;[129] he proudly and stubbornly refused to ask any

[124] The new law is discussed in detail in ch. 7.
[125] *Il Popolo*, 16.ix.54. The memorandum was dated Oct. 7, 1953.
[126] The Catholics were the only religious community not represented on the Yugoslav National Commission for the Defence of Peace in the World, formed in 1948 after the break with the Cominform.
[127] *Times*, 18.iv.57.   [128] *Il Popolo*, 10.vii.53.
[129] *NYT*, 11.vii.53.

favour of the communist government. Tito was exasperated but declared that he would not order Stepinac to be transferred out of his diocese without a request and then risk being blamed if anything went wrong.[130] In December 1959 he received a summons from the district court at Osijek to give evidence in the case of the Rev. Dr Ćiril Kos and others from the theological seminary at Djakovo who were accused of chauvinism and open opposition to the government and sentenced to several years' imprisonment. The letter he wrote refusing to obey the summons was angry and bitter, and uncharacteristically self-pitying.[131] By this time he was suffering from inflammation of both lungs and an enlarged prostate; the constant presence of police guards who followed him everywhere outside the house had been for a long time an unbearable irritation and finally drove him to give up his daily walks. Early in February 1960 he was taken seriously ill with an embolism of the pulmonary arteries and three days later, on Wednesday, February 10, he died.

Archbishop Coadjutor Šeper immediately started to negotiate with the authorities about the funeral.[132] The authorities were faced with a dilemma; if the funeral was held privately in Krašić the Catholic population would be offended, but if they allowed it to take place in Zagreb in the cathedral they feared the effect of the demonstrations this might provoke.[133] The immediate decision was that the funeral should be private, and the security police in Krašić instructed the parish priest to begin preparations. An autopsy was ordered (presumably in order to protect the government from any imputation of responsibility) and the archbishop's body was removed to Zagreb and returned to Krašić the same evening after being embalmed. It was laid out in the parish church, dressed in the violet bishop's attire which had been prepared for his death by the Discalced Carmelites of Brezovica whose house he had founded; on his head was the mitre given to him by the parishioners of Krašić for his last jubilee. The church and parish house were surrounded by police and plainclothesmen, the road leading to the village were blocked and no one was allowed to enter or leave. A tomb was prepared for him in front of the altar and all Thursday night and Friday the parishioners filed past the bier. A bus was waiting in Zagreb for

[130] Interview with United Press (news agency), 7.ii.53. Tito, *Govori*, vol. VIII, p. 152; *Sl. Por.*, 11.vii.53.
[131] Benigar, pp. 828ff; *Hrvatska Revija*, March 1960, p. 137. Wording differs from Benigar; probably translated into Croatian from Italian translation of Croat original.
[132] RNS, 10.ii.60.   [133] Ibid.

the bishops who had arrived from all over the country for the funeral.

At this point there was a change of plans. Whether, as has been suggested to the writer, Pope John XXIII made a personal intervention with Tito through the good offices of the French embassy, which had charge of Vatican interests, whether Archbishop Šeper was able to give sufficient assurance that there would be no trouble, or whether the gesture (which must have been decided in the highest Yugoslav quarters) was a spontaneous one, is not known for certain. But on Friday the astonished (and very put-out) parish priest at Krašić was told by the journalists who had arrived from Zagreb that the funeral was to take place on Saturday in Zagreb cathedral with all the honours due to a cardinal and archbishop. The archbishopric issued a circular ordering that black hangings should be put up in all the Zagreb churches and their bells tolled twice daily until the funeral, as is customary for the dead. Although there had been no public announcement the cathedral was full and most of the bishops were present. The open coffin was placed on a bier surrounded by wreaths. All night long the procession of faithful filed past. On the morning of the 13th the cathedral filled early and the crowd overflowed onto the forecourt and square outside; members of the consular corps were in the congregation. A further note of distress was added when it was learnt that Cardinal Koenig of Vienna, who was travelling by car to attend the funeral, had been seriously injured in a car crash and taken to the hospital in Varaždin.

The solemn requiem was conducted by Archbishop Coadjutor Šeper and Stepinac's body was buried behind the higher altar. The tomb at once became a shrine where candles burn perpetually and a few faithful can usually be found at prayer.[134]

Pope John, like his predecessor Pius XII, had ignored both Bishop Rožman of Ljubljana and Archbishop Šarić of Sarajevo, who had fled from their dioceses without permission at the end of the war; but he did Stepinac the unusual honour of celebrating a special papal requiem mass in St Peter's and wound up his funeral oration (in which he acknowledged the gesture of the Yugoslav government and thanked them for it) by putting Yugoslavia under the special heavenly protection of the defunct cardinal.[135]

But Tito's gesture also had its effect. Ten years after the event

---

[134] Sources: *SVNZ*, 1960, no. 1, and an account of Stepinac's last illness and death written shortly after the event by the Rev. Josip Vraneković, parish priest of Krašić (shown privately to the writer), together with verbal eye-witness accounts; also RNS.

[135] *L'O.R.*, 18.ii.60.

this writer was told by a Catholic prelate in Yugoslavia that the permission given for Stepinac's funeral to be held in the cathedral had made a profound impression on him at the time and wakened a first hope of better times to come, and that he now recognised it as one of the crucial turning points in the relations between the Yugoslav government and the church. For the Orthodox Serbs it was a puzzling and unwelcome 'posthumous amnesty'.

Stepinac's first and deepest loyalty was to the church, centred for him in the Vatican and the person of the pope. He was not primarily interested in politics (his anti-communism faithfully reflected the encyclicals of Pius XI and Pius XII) but he had become disillusioned with South Slav unity as it had worked out in practice; in this he reflected rather than led the opinion of the majority of Croats. When the invasion and break-up of Yugoslavia happened, he welcomed the prospect of Croatian independence, even though it came from the dubious hands of the Ustaša; the tone of his welcome seemed to show that he had closed his eyes to the fact that behind them were the Italian fascists and Nazi Germany. His pastoral letters and circulars, his sermons, the evidence which came out at his trial, and accounts given by people who knew him well reveal many contradictions: a man of moderate intelligence, disciplined but lacking in wider insight, and an unreliable judge of men. Like many of his generation and upbringing he thought that 'Jews, Freemasons and communists' were sworn enemies of the church, but when it came to the point he did what he could to protect and rescue the Jewish victims of Nazi racialism – particularly those who had been baptised. (He had been president before the war of a committee set up in Zagreb to help Jewish refugees.)[136] His outward inflexibility concealed troubled doubts about the best course to pursue; he was courageous, perhaps to a heroic degree, but his outlook was blinkered. His devotion to duty made flight or even withdrawal from his diocese unthinkable; during his imprisonment and the years at Krašić, he refused to ask a single favour from the authorities.

His narrow, intense faith and his political short-sightedness limited his grasp of the apocalyptic events of 1941 to the immediate future of Croatia and the Catholic Church in Croatia, and left him open to the charge of complicity in the terrible crimes of the ustaše; the same blinkered outlook later kept him from seizing the opportunity to establish some kind of *modus vivendi* with the new government.

There was also another side to the man. Nearly everyone who

136 Pattee, doc. B., p. 194.

came into contact with him (with the exception of most of the journalists who interviewed him during his imprisonment, who were chilled by his mask of cold formality) held him in esteem and affection. His personal life was ascetic; the numbers of dinners and receptions at the palace diminished sharply under his rule, and among some of his clergy he was known privately as the 'bolshevik archbishop'.[137] He spent very little on himself and the balance of his emoluments was given at once to the poor. He left no possessions on his death.[138]

The terrible times in which he was fated to play a role called for a moral and spiritual giant, and he did not quite measure up to them. During his trial and the years of imprisonment and growing ill-health his bearing was courageous and undeviating, but the martyrdom which he would have accepted without complaint was denied to him by the Yugoslav authorities, who handled him with considerable care.

Stepinac's dogmatic faith, which made it natural for him (and for most other Croat Catholics of the time) to think of the Orthodox as schismatics, *dissidentes*, to be brought back to the fold of the only true church, was soon to be left behind by a church moving into a new, post-Conciliar age; and happily for Yugoslavia, its rulers were almost simultaneously discarding their Stalinist past and taking the first, hesitating steps on the path to decentralisation, liberalisation and a loosening of the old rigidities.

And yet his inflexibility served a purpose. The Catholic Church in Croatia was traditionalist, authoritarian and even at that time old-fashioned; it had been severely shocked by the blows of the immediate postwar years, the change in its financial circumstances and the growing realisation that the new government had come to stay. An accommodation reached when it was in this condition would have proceeded from weakness and might well have led to further demoralisation. The church needed time to find itself again, to recover from its wounds and begin to reconsider its position. The fifteen years of withdrawal gathering as it could its flock around it, were also a time of slow renewal for the church. Stepinac's uncompromising bearing in prison, his refusal to yield an inch on any side, gave the church the moral backbone it needed to help it to recover. In this respect, perhaps fortunately, he did not outlive his usefulness, and after his death the church emerged able to undertake a self-respecting relationship with the government, without sacrificing its Christian fundamentals.

[137] Ivan Meštrović's reminiscences in *Hrvatska Revija*, Sept. 1956.
[138] Stepinac's testament, ibid., Dec. 1960.

5

The Serbian Orthodox Church
Liberation and its sequel

Liberation

Partisan forces and units of the Red Army entered Belgrade on October 20, 1944. The liberation was greeted by the Serbian Orthodox Church with a paean of rejoicing:

from Avala rises the triumphant scream of the eagle, and the flag of freedom flutters in the air...the capital of Yugoslavia, our own white city, is freed from slavery and alien occupation. Our brothers and sisters from the great, far-flung Slav land of Russia and our own heroes and heroines together chorus songs of joy. The liberators in the ardent brotherhood of war proclaim that nothing is more beautiful than Mother Russia...our countrymen received their brothers and sisters from great, far-away Russia on the frontiers of our beloved country. The capital opened wide its doors, its hearts and its homes to receive our eagerly awaited brothers and sisters, liberators from that great country, Russia...Happy is the country which bears its cross to the end, which is worthy of its Saviour...let brotherly love and equal justice for all abide among us.[1]

The thanks and greetings to the Russians were repeated in the Synod's Christmas message.

As the bitter Serbian winter approached Metropolitan Josif summoned the elders of all the Belgrade churches and organised a house-to-house collection by the clergy for the Partisan and Russian wounded.[2]

The commanding officer of the city of Belgrade, Major-General Djurić, called at the patriarchate on November 5, 1944, accompanied by members of his staff, and had a long talk with Metropolitan Josif and three other bishops.[3] There is no published record of the conversation but it is probable that the resumption of church life and the return of the clergy to the liberated territories was discussed. The Synod was anxious to gather the scattered fragments of the church together and reassert its control. There had already been a demand for an independent Macedonian Church from a group of priests who

[1] *Gl.*, 31.xii.44.   [2] Ibid.
[3] Ibid.

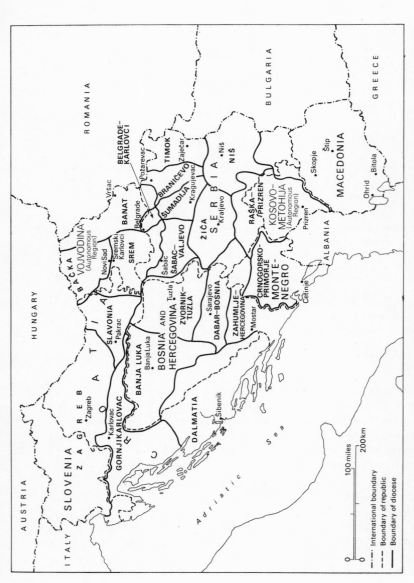

Map 4. Serbian and Macedonian Orthodox dioceses, and sees, c. 1970. No recent map of the Serbian Orthodox dioceses has been published and the boundaries are altered from time to time. It has not been possible to obtain a map giving the boundaries of the Macedonian Orthodox dioceses; the sees of the three

had been in contact with the Partisans during the war; Josif, who had fought for Serbia in the Balkan Wars as a *komitadji*, was impatient to return and restore discipline. But permission to return, as we shall see, was never given to him, and it was not until 1951 that any member of the Serbian hierarchy was allowed to visit Macedonia. He travelled, however, on November 22 to Sremski Karlovci with Vicar-Bishop Arsenije Bradvarović, who remained there to undertake the reorganisation of the diocese; it was one of the treasure-houses of the church and had been thoroughly pillaged by the ustaše.[4]

Two days later a solemn requiem was held in the cathedral in Belgrade for the last victims of the German occupation, prisoners in a camp at Banjica, who had been killed just before the fighting ended. Representatives of the government and army were there, together with a detachment from the Red Army and huge crowds of the families of the victims and ordinary citizens of Belgrade. Fifty priests took part in the service and Vicar-Bishop Valerian preached the sermon.[5]

Rebuilding the church

One of the Synod's first actions was to issue an order, on October 31, 1944, to priests and bishops from the liberated areas to return immediately to their dioceses and parishes; whenever possible parish priests were to take their people with them, while the bishops would re-establish diocesan and parish councils.[6]

The clergy were given precise instructions:

a   Every priest without exception must return to his own parish in keeping with canon law.

b   The bishops would re-establish diocesan and parish councils, confirming in office those who had remained faithful and removing those who had failed in their duties.

c   Priests were to receive back into the church those who had been forcibly converted, and begin to restore damaged and pillaged churches; neighbouring parishes were asked to help those which had been left entirely empty.

d   Priests were to search for children who had lost their families and been put into institutions with the aim of destroying all traces of their Serbian and Orthodox origins; they were to make every effort to trace each child's family, and to care for each child, healing the effects of imprisonment, denationalisation and conversion.[7]

[4]   Ibid.   [5]   Ibid.
[6]   Synod, 15–29.xi.44. *Gl.*, 31.xii.44.
[7]   Searches went on for years. Bishop Arsenije, administrator of the Croatian dioceses, was still looking for Serbian war orphans in 1947 and later (Synod, 6.iii–3.iv.47. *Gl.*, 1.v.47).

e   Children who had been baptised as Catholics were to be
     christened, given new names and entered into the parish
     registers.
f   Couples married by Catholic rites were to be remarried by
     Orthodox rites.
g   Funeral services were to be said over the graves of those who had
     been buried with non-Orthodox rites.
h   All parish registers were to be restored to the churches, and
     priests should try to reconstruct those which had been destroyed.
i   All priests who had joined the Croatian Orthodox Church were
     suspended and would come before ecclasiastical courts.
j   Priests were to try to trace church property, especially libraries
     and other church treasures, and restore the objects to their
     original homes.[8]

The bare recital of the instructions gives a poignant picture.
It was to be a symbolic cleansing of the people from a hated alien
church which had been imposed on them, an exorcism of death
and terror. The authorities supported the Serbian Orthodox
Church in annulling the forced conversions. ZAVNOH at its
session of August 25, 1944, ordered that the names of all those
who had been forcibly converted to the Roman Catholic faith be
erased from the registers. The Zagreb archdiocese notified its
clergy concerning this decision in circular 6060/45 of September
28, 1945.

But they were many obstacles to the return of the clergy.
Before the end of the session the Synod was informed by the
government that priests wanting to return to their parishes or
travel on church business must first get a permit from the
authorities: 'We would point out that the right to travel and the
support of the government cannot be enjoyed by those who in
the course of their duties in Serbia or in the Vojvodina offended
in any way against the interests of the people.'[9] This meant in
practice that none of the bishops and priests who had been
expelled from Macedonia were allowed to return, since the
leadership of the clergy there had passed into the hands of
Macedonian priests who had cooperated with the Partisans
during the war and enjoyed the support of the new Macedonian
authorities, and who were determined to free themselves from
Serbian control.

There was also the reluctance of some priests, who had
established themselves within Serbia during the war, to return
to the ruined parishes and the hardships facing them in Croatia
and Bosnia and Hercegovina. A number had taken secular jobs[10]

[8] Sin. 1526/1944, 29.ix.44. *Gl.*, 31.xii.44.
[9] 18.xi.44. *Gl.*, 31.xii.44.   [10] *Gl.*, 1.v.46.

without permission or were working part-time.[11] The Synod
asked all bishops to provide them with lists of these priests within
their dioceses;[12] further urgent pleas to return were published
from time to time and recalcitrant priests were threatened with
suspension.[13] But it was not always possible to know whether a
priest had merely absented himself or was really missing, and
furthermore a number of priests had been imprisoned by the new
authorities after the war; although the Synod did not publish the
figures, it kept a list of these and in March 1947 minuted that
it had been brought up to date.[14] Bishops were advised not to
fill the posts of priests about whose fate nothing sure was known,
but to divide their work among neighbouring parishes and pay
half their salaries to their families, including the families of
priests in prison.[15]

The surviving bishops divided the responsibility for the
dioceses between them. In June 1945 Bishop Arsenije Bradvarović was appointed administrator of four Croatian dioceses,
Zagreb, Gornjikarlovac, Pakrac (Slavonia) and Dalmatia;[16] the
bishops of the first two had perished, the see of Pakrac was vacant
and Bishop Irinej Djordjević of Dalmatia did not return to
Yugoslavia after his release from internment in Italy. Arsenije
was faced with a catastrophic shortage of priests; in Gornjikarlovac sixty-six had been killed, and in Dalmatia twenty-two;[17] he
asked his fellow bishops to seek out displaced priests in their
dioceses and press them to return to their own parishes.[18] Bishop
Nektarije Krulj of Zvornik–Tuzla visited the four dioceses of
Bosnia and Hercegovina, his own (where thirty-six priests had
been killed), Banja Luka, Dabar–Bosnia (Sarejevo) and Zahumlje–
Hercegovina (Mostar), to gather information about the priests
and people who had been killed, to see for himself the condition
of the church buildings and to bring spiritual consolation to the
survivors.[19]

The clergy and hierarchy of the church, and its administrative
structure, had suffered crippling blows, but only less serious was
the widespread destruction of churches and church buildings.
These were heaviest in the territory of the former NDH. Before
the the war the Serbian patriarchate had over 4,200 churches and
chapels and 220 monasteries (without counting the North
American and Canadian dioceses).[20] Of these, 330 churches, 49

[11] Ibid. 1.vi.46.
[13] E.g. Synod 6.iii–3.iv.47. Gl., 1.v.47.
[15] Ibid.
[17] SPC, p. 231.
[19] Synod 5–29.ix.45. Gl., 1.xi.45.

[12] Synod, 19–30.iii.46. Gl., 1.v.46.
[14] Ibid.
[16] Sin. 912/299/45. Gl., 30.vi.45.
[18] Synod. 6.iii–3.iv.47. Gl., 1.v.47.
[20] SPC, p. 253.

chapels and 17 monasteries were destroyed, and 335 churches, 23 chapels and 17 monasteries were seriously damaged.[21] The diocese of Gornjikarlovac (Croatia) was the worst hit: 175 out of 237 churches and chapels were destroyed and only 14 of the remainder were in a fit state for use.[22] In the others the iconostases had been destroyed and the furnishings of the church plundered. In the Bosnian part of the diocese of Dalmatia 18 churches were destroyed and many others plundered and made unfit for use; in the diocese of Srem 44 churches and monasteries were destroyed,[23] in the diocese of Pakrac (Slavonia) 55 churches out of 78, and 3 monasteries, were destroyed, and 25 parish houses badly damaged.[24]

The disaster was overwhelming, but Metropolitan Josif, with his driving energy, urged the people to begin the first stages of reconstruction themselves. The greater part of this work, especially in the early years, was carried out by the voluntary labour of parishioners and by voluntary contributions.[25]

The financial situation of the church was also desperate. All its usual sources of income had ceased; it was a struggle to survive from day to day.

According to the official history of the fifty years of the Serbian patriarchate, from which many of the foregoing figures have been quoted, the church lost 70,000 hectares of land in the agrarian reform; 1,180 church buildings, valued at 8,000m dinars, the church's printing presses and its insurance fund, were all nationalised; the value of its pension and other funds was drastically reduced by the postwar monetary reform; and a capital sum which had been settled on the church by the prewar government as compensation for past confiscations and damages and which had produced an income of 40m dinars a year, was

[21] Pavlowitch, *ECR*, 2(1), p. 30, quoting *The Serbian Orthodox Church: Its Past and Present*, ed. Patriarchate, Belgrade, 1966.

[22] *SPC*, p. 253.

[23] The monasteries included the beautiful and historic group in the Fruška Gora, the wooded hills lying just south and west of Novi Sad. Some were undamaged and had been taken over by the authorities; in 1946 Krušedol was being used as an orphanage, Vrdnik and Beočin as hospitals. Grgeteg was empty except for a woman and a child who were living in one of the outhouses. Two nuns and a novice had built themselves a shelter in the ruins of Kuveždin, and a neighbouring village priest said the liturgy for them; two monks were still living at Privina Glava and saying the liturgy; a neighbouring Russian priest sometimes said the liturgy at Jazak; but Dipša, which had been a convent before the war, was empty and in ruins (*Gl.*, 1.iv.47).

[24] *SPC*, pp. 253–4.

[25] *SPC*, p. 254. Later, contributions from the Serbian emigrants in the United States and Canada played an important part in the rebuilding of churches (ibid.).

reduced to an income of 60,000 dinars a year.[26] The government subvention which before the war had been fixed (by the Law on the Support of the Church of June 7, 1939, at 68m dinars a year) ceased, and the special tax for the support of the patriarchate, which produced 60m dinars a year, was repealed.[27] It was even for some time forbidden for priests to collect alms.[28]

The government agreed to pay the pensions of church dependants until other arrangements were made, but refused to be responsible for pensions which had been paid wholly out of church funds.[29] The church improvised from day to day. In September 1945 the Synod decided to pay 40 per cent of the pensions due that month to pensioners who were wholly dependent on the church.[30] It turned to the government of Croatia and asked it, because of the peculiarly harsh circumstances, to assist the clergy returning to their parishes out of state funds until the question of federal government assistance was settled.[31] There is no record of whether this request was met, but two months later, at its November session, the Synod authorised lump-sum grants of 3,000 dinars for parish priests and 1,000 dinars for monks doing parochial work, to all clergy from Croatia, Bosnia and Hercegovina, Montenegro (a notoriously poor region) and Macedonia, 'who are in full unity with the Serbian Church'. Clergy from other dioceses would receive the same help if they were in real need.[32] In November 1946 the Synod appealed to other dioceses to send special help to the dioceses of Dalmatia, the Montenegrin Littoral (Crnogorsko-primorje), Gornjikarlovac (Croatia) and Zahumlje–Hercegovina (Mostar) where conditions were particularly bad as a result of the war.[33]

But these were only palliatives to a desperate situation. At its meeting in March 1946 the Synod had before it a brief budget:

Expenditure for 1946	27,523,181 dns.
Income for 1946	2,575,000 dns.
Deficit	24,940,175 dns.

Bishop Jovan Ilić of Niš, a member of the Synod, had visited the

[26] *SPC*, p. 241ff.
[27] Ibid.
[28] Synod, 29.x–30.xi.46: *Gl.*, 1.i.47.
[29] Ministry of Finance 15737: *Gl.*, 31.vi.45.
[30] Synod, 5–29.ix.45. *Gl.*, 1.xi.45.
[31] Ibid.
[32] Working Committee 4320/139/45, 8.ix.45: *Gl.*, 31.xii.45.
[33] Synod 29.x–30.xi.46: *Gl.*, 1.i.47.

ministry of finance to try to negotiate a solution of the situation, and the Synod awaited an answer.[34]

The Serbian Orthodox Church never solved the dilemma of its dependence on outside sources of finance. Later the government paid yearly subventions to the church, partly in the form of social insurance for priests and grants to the priests' associations, but partly also in direct grants to the patriarchate, who accepted them as token compensation for all that had been confiscated. The payments depended on the government's good will and had to be negotiated each year, giving the government a lever which was particularly harsh against a church with married clergy.

Help also now began to arrive from abroad. The first mention is a gift of $750.00 from the American Episcopal Church at the end of 1946, which the Synod decided to share out among the six poorest dioceses for the families of the poorest priests.[35] In 1947 the theological faculty received 20,000 Swiss francs for general relief and $1,250 for food and clothing for students.[36] By 1948 there was a regular flow of help from Inter-Church Aid (of the World Council of Churches) in Geneva in the form of money and of material goods. Blankets, beds and mattresses, cloth, boots and shoes, medicine and food, paper, duplicators and stencils, paraffin wax and beeswax (for candles, from the sale of which a good part of the church's income came), canvas for icons, equipment for schools, help to the theological faculty and the seminaries and to their students, and general funds for the church – all these appear in the accounts of Inter-Church Aid. The two theological seminaries at Rakovica and Prizren were still running shortened courses because there was no money to buy fuel and the seminaries were closed during the three winter months. A grant at the beginning of 1956 enabled the seminaries to buy fuel and extra food, and to instil running water and a bathroom at Rakovica.[37] Funds were sent to resettle priests and their families in the destitute recovered areas; special help was sent for the widows and orphans of the clergy. An imaginative contribution was the provision of short convalescent holidays in sanatoria abroad for priests who had become ill. Money was sent for church repairs; a special contribution was made to the

[34] Sin. 1056/1946, 19–30.iii.46: Gl., 1.v.46.
[35] Gl., 1.i.47.
[36] This figure and all the subsequent ones are taken from the files of the World Council of Churches in Geneva. Inter-Church Aid, which is now a commission of the WCC was founded in 1945, and was the source of the earlier contributions.
[37] RNS, 8.i.56.

expenses of Patriarch Gavrilo's funeral; in 1951 there was a contribution to the expenses of the travel of Vicar-Bishop German and Dr Glumac to the United States, the first direct contact since the war with the North American diocese. There was a contribution in 1952 to the Union of Associations of Orthodox Priests, possibly a tactful gesture. In 1955 two jeeps were sent.

Figures from the WCC files show that large amounts of surplus commodities and money were being channelled through Inter-Church Aid for general Yugoslav relief. The share of the Serbian Orthodox Church in this was substantial:

1953	$1,320,400
1954	$1,379,843
1955	$2,577,157
1956	$6,436,118
1957	$17,210,854
1958	$18,558,933
1959	$9,128,749
1960	$9,339,189
1961	$5,960,042

(In addition, of course, help from Catholic sources, Caritas in Germany and the National Conference for Catholic Welfare (USA), was being sent to the Catholic Church.)

In August 1951 the WCC sent a delegation of eighteen, headed by Dr Robert Tobias of Inter-Church Aid, on a mission of fellowship to the churches in Yugoslavia; this was not an investigation, but was precisely what it called itself. They were welcomed and entertained by Patriarch Vikentije and a special service was held in the cathedral.[38]

Confrontation with the state: religious instruction and marriage

The church was almost immediately faced with two matters which struck at its fundamental beliefs and its position in society: the religious education of children and the institution of civil marriage as the only legally valid form of matrimony. The government decreed that religious instruction might be given to children whose parents asked for it, if the children also were willing.[39] The Synod issued an explanation and clarification of the instructions:

---

[38] *CSM*, 24.viii.51.
[39] Reg. 48, 3.iii.45, Education Department of ASNOS (Antifašistička Skupština Narodnog Oslobodjenja Serbije – Anti-fascist Council for the National Liberation of Serbia): *Gl.*, 30.iv.45.

The teacher must enquire whether pupils want religious instruction but it was not their 'right nor their duty' to try to bring pressure on either parents or children, or to create conflicts at school. It was the duty of the authorities to make provision for religious instruction to be held in schools until suitable places could be found outside. Teachers of religion would for the time being continue to be paid by the state, and the state must send teachers out to villages if the church was unable to do so.[40]

This was a fair interpretation of the regulations, but in practice there were constant difficulties, some created by the authorities, who made all sorts of administrative difficulties, but others real. The law stipulated that religious instruction must be given in schools, and the shortage of space was acute. The period of compulsory education had been increased after the war from four to eight years, and there was a large influx of children into school. Many school buildings had been damaged or destroyed; for years after the war children went to school in three shifts daily. (Even today most schools work in two shifts.)

There was also a secular, radical tradition among teachers in Serbia when went back to the beginning of the century, and which made it easier for them to accept the new government. Some teachers even objected that the authorities were too tolerant of religious instruction in schools, although this independence of mind made some of them object equally to the dogmatic teaching of Marxism.[41] Moreover, all teachers of religion had to be licensed by the local People's Committees, which had wide powers of discretion and habitually refused to license priests with a hostile record.[42]

In 1946 the Synod complained that the policy of the Serbian government was making it impossible to give religious lessons in schools and the protest was repeated in 1947.[43] Metropolitan Josif called on Mitra Mitrović, the minister for education for Serbia, in 1947, and without beating about the bush told her that he knew the difficulties must be coming from the top.[44]

[40] Sin. 569/162/1945, 4.iv.45: Gl., 30.iv.45.
[41] Conversation with Mitra Mitrović, minister of education in the republic of Serbia 1945–54, in 1972.
[42] Synod. 6.iii–3.iv.47. Gl., 1.v.47.
[43] Synod 19–30.iii.46: Gl., 1.v.46; Synod 6.iii–3.iv.47: Gl., 1.v.47.
[44] Conversation with Mitra Mitrović in 1972. The encounter between Josif and the energetic, brilliant young revolutionary went off better than might have been expected. Both came from Užice, the centre of Serbia and the heart of Serbianism, and they understood each other very well, although they were opponents. Mitra Mitrović later called on several occasions at the patriarchate in the course of her duties.

Religious instruction in schools had virtually ceased long before 1952, when it was officially stopped. At that time the church was too weakened, and the shortage of priests and catechists too great, for any effective counter-pressures to be brought. After 1952 religious instruction was allowed in churches and other designated buildings, but the administrative obstacles persisted. Sometimes, especially in villages or small towns, local party officials interfered illegally, or made their opposition clear enough to constitute a threat; if the priest protested he was harassed, usually with the results the authorities desired.[45] It had not been the custom, in any case, for children to be taught religion in church; this had been done in school by catechists. The acute shortage of Orthodox priests, so much greater than in Catholic areas, again made itself felt.[46]

There were great difficulties in reopening religious seminaries and making a start at replenishing the diminished priesthood. The work of training priests had virtually ceased during the war, when all five Orthodox seminaries had been closed, although examinations for seminarians had been held in Belgrade and Niš on two or three occasions. In May 1945 the Synod decided to reopen the seminary at Prizren (in southern Serbia) with one class of forty boys and a shortened syllabus[47] but was told by the government that it was not yet possible.[48] Bishop Damaskin of the Banat also failed to reopen the seminary at Vršac.[49] The Synod returned to the attack in 1946,[50] and finally permission was granted by the Serbian government at the beginning of 1947 to reopen the seminary at Prizren.[51] It opened with only one class of fifty boys, drawn from every diocese, with special preference given to the dioceses which suffered from the greatest shortage of priests. The students were between fifteen and twenty-two years old and had completed eight years of schooling; they were also 'not married, healthy in mind and body with a developed

---

[45] Numerous Orthodox sources.

[46] The weakness of the Serbian Orthodox clergy had only been exacerbated by the events of the war; it went back at least to the nineteenth century (see Mousset, *passim*) and was certainly a factor in the mistrust and fear which poisoned the relations between the two historic Christian confessions in the territory of the South Slavs. The Catholic priesthood was not only more numerous (see Appendix II), it was also better educated. All Catholic priests go to the theological faculty or its equivalent before ordination, while the Orthodox clergy may be ordained after completing a five- to six-year training at the seminary, and only a small proportion go on to the theological faculty.

[47] Sin. 843/239, 16.v.45, and 833/287, 31.v.45: *Gl.*, 30.vi.45.

[48] Synod 5–29.ix.45: *Gl.*, 1.xi.45.   [49] Ibid.

[50] Synod 19–30.iii.46: *Gl.*, 1.v.46.   [51] No. 227, 24.ii.47: *Gl.*, 1.iv.47.

ear and good voice for singing, and had a knowledge of the catechism and the feasts of Our Lord and Our Lady' and must undertake to serve as priests or monks in their own dioceses. Poor students were accepted without payment, while those who could afford it paid between 400 and 600 dinars a month. Because of the shortage of priests, the course was shortened from six years to four.[52]

The seminary of Sv. Sava at Rakovica on the outskirts of Belgrade was not opened until the spring of 1950; there were thirty-five pupils.[53] Because of the cold and the shortage of fuel, it had to be closed from November until the following March.[54] By 1951 the course of study at both seminaries had been increased to five years, but the numbers at Prizren had fallen off and there were only thirty-five students at the opening of the school year 1950–1.[55]

The federal government published the draft of the proposed new law on marriage in the summer of 1945. It made civil marriage obligatory for all couples and the only legally valid form of matrimony, but allowed the celebration of religious marriage rites after the civil ceremony if the couple wished it; divorce proceedings were also put into the hands of the civil courts. The Serbian Orthodox Church was as much opposed to its provisions laicising marriage and divorce as the Catholic Church but phrased its objections less provocatively:

the new law laicises marriage and divorce with no regard for the church and its regulations. The Synod hopes that the federal government did not intend to assume an unfriendly attitude to the church as such, or to affront it, but on the contrary noted its good faith to create marriage laws in the spirit of modern principles as has been done by other states...so that...marriage relations can be regulated in a better way than previously.

After describing the Christian view of marriage and the moral crisis which was one of the worst consequences of the war, it continued:

Religion is even today a very powerful force among the masses in spite of some exceptions among the intelligentsia. The people consider that the marriage relationship is sacred...they will find the laicising of the marriage relationship difficult to accept...Although we believe that only a small proportion of the intelligentsia who have fallen away from the church want civil marriage, and that they should be subordinated to the majority, the Serbian Orthodox Church, believing that marriage is such

[52] Gl., 1.v.47.
[54] Ibid. 1.vi.50.
[53] Ibid., 1.vi.51.
[55] Ibid. 1.vi.51.

a sensitive subject, and respecting individual feelings and freedom, suggests that civil marriage should be instituted for the minority of our people who for any reason wish to have it...[signed by Metropolitan Josif][56]

The new law was passed and came into force the following spring,[57] cancelling all previous laws on marriage.[58] The Synod appealed to the faithful to fulfil their religious duties as fully as their civil ones; it repeated that it did not consider civil marriage and divorce valid for members of the Orthodox Church, and that only men and women whose marriages had been dissolved by the church could validly remarry. Only children born of religious marriages could be considered legitimate; others would be entered in the parish register as 'born of a civil marriage' although they could be legitimised by the subsequent religious marriage of the parents. The church later also forbade parents to appoint as godparents persons who had not had a religious but only a civil marriage, 'because their religious and moral character is not such as the church looks for in godparents'.[59]

The patriarchate

Early in 1945, before the final surrender of the Germans, the Russian Orthodox Church held an election for a new patriarch and invited heads of other Orthodox Churches to be present. The Synod replied that Metropolitan Josif would come in place of the patriarch ('whose whereabouts are unknown') together with Bishop Jovan Ilić of Niš and Bishop Emilijan Piperković of Timok.[60] They left for Moscow on March 23, 1945, with a party of laymen and priests which included the Rev. Jevstatije Karamatijević, who had fought with the Partisans and was to play a leading part in the priests' associations, and accompanied by a doctor of the Soviet military mission. A reception was held before their departure and the head of the Soviet military mission sent his car to take the delegation to the airport. This was the first official postwar contact of the Serbian Orthodox Church with other Orthodox Churches, and it set the pattern of government approval and government assistance for the contacts which were to follow in later years. The communists understood

---

[56] Sin. 1608/379/45, i.ix.45: *Gl.*, 31.xii.45.
[57] *Službeni List* [Official Gazette], 9.iv.46, no. 29.
[58] Before the war marriages had been regulated by a number of different laws in different parts of the country. There had been no civil marriage except in the Vojvodina.
[59] Synod 6.iii–3.iv.47: *Gl.*, 1.v.47.   [60] *Gl.*, 15.ii.45.

how useful the Serbian Orthodox Church could be in fostering good relations with countries where there were other Orthodox Churches.

In the meantime the Synod had been trying unsuccessfully to discover the patriarch's whereabouts; they knew only that he had been taken from Yugoslavia to a German concentration camp. In his memoirs, Gavrilo writes that he, together with Bishop Nikolaj Velimirović and his secretary Mitar Djaković, were liberated on May 8, 1945, by American troops.[61] They had been moved from one concentration camp to another and had spent some time in Dachau, a fact which was later to symbolise Gabrilo's patriotism and devotion to the Serbian Church and people; he was by then a man of sixty-four, exhausted and ill.

After a short convalescence he spent the next few months visiting Rome, London (where on October 24 he baptised the baby Crown Prince Alexander), Paris and again Rome.[62] He saw most of the leading Yugoslav political figures abroad and was deeply disturbed by what he learned – the dissensions of the Yugoslav government-in-exile and the switch in Allied support from the Serbian Četnik leader Draža Mihailović to Tito's communist-led Partisans. The only consolation was a meeting with Maček in Paris when the leader of the Croatian Peasant Party expressed his shame and sorrow for the misdeeds of the ustaše and told him that he still believed that Serbs and Croats could and must work together for a united Yugoslavia.[63] He refused proudly to accept the offer of a comfortable house in Rome and help in resettling Serbian refugees which was conveyed to him from the pope by Dr Miha Krek, a Slovene and former deputy premier of Yugoslavia; how could he, the patriarch of the Serbs and the spiritual leader of a people which was still suffering, he wrote, accept favours from the pope who had not lifted a finger to help them during the war when they were being slaughtered?[64]

Patriarch Gavrilo's memoirs come to an abrupt end at this point and we have no account from him of the circumstances of his return to Yugoslavia. Mitar Djaković, who edited the memoirs, says in his introduction that he returned at the invitation of Metropolitan Josif and all the bishops.[65] Tito told a group of visiting American churchmen in 1947 that he had himself invited the patriarch to return hoping that his presence would curb the

[61] MPG, p. 563.
[63] Ibid., pp. 585ff.
[65] Ibid. p. 16.

[62] Ibid. pp. 563ff passim.
[64] Ibid. pp. 600ff.

activities of some personalities in the Serbian Orthodox Church who opposed the government.[66] It seems certain, therefore, that the Yugoslav authorities established contact with Gavrilo during this period; they must have wanted to conduct their own negotiations and make sure of his attitude before allowing him to come back, which would explain the blank wall they presented to the Synod during this period.

In September 1945 the government informed the Synod that the patriarch and Bishop Nikolaj were in Italy.[67] The Synod at once wrote to the patriarch but had no answer. In March 1946, having made further fruitless enquiries of the government and hearing that Gavrilo was ill, they asked permission for a delegation to visit him.[68] This permission was not granted and the Synod had no further official information about him for eight months.

Private letters however had been passing between Gavrilo and Metropolitan Josif, who urged him to return and told him that nothing but his presence and authority would keep the Serbian Orthodox Church from disintegrating.[69] In the face of Josif's appeals (and perhaps also being satisfied by assurances from the authorities, although this must remain a speculation), Gavrilo's duty must have seemed clear. Bishop Irinej, a sick man exhausted by his long internment, and Bishop Nikolaj were in a different position. It is possible that the three men decided together that Nikolaj and Irinej could be more useful abroad. Both went to the United States where they gave interviews attacking the new Yugoslav government. Irinej returned to England in 1949 and died in Cambridge in 1952,[70] and Nikolaj remained in the United States where he died in 1956.[71] The patriarch returned to Belgrade on November 14, 1946.[72]

The desire of the Yugoslav authorities to have the patriarch back was understandable. His stature as an anti-Nazi and a Serbian patriot was very great, and he believed in the unity of Yugoslavia. If he could be persuaded that it was worth cooperating with the new government for the sake of his people and his church, he would confer great authority on them. Moreover the Yugoslav authorities knew that they would have to put on trial and execute Draža Mihailović when they caught him (which

---

[66] Tito, *Govori*, vol. III, p. 81 (9.viii.47).

[67] Synod 5–29.ix.45: *Gl.*, 1.xi.45.

[68] Synod 19–30.iii.46: *Gl.*, 1.v.46.

[69] Conversation with the Rev. M. Nikolić, Serbian Orthodox parish priest in London, 1973.

[70] *SPC*, p. 512. [71] Ibid. p. 514.

[72] *Gl.*, 1.i.47.

they did in the spring of 1946) and Gavrilo's return would prove that the government was not anti-Serb, as it was already accused of being. Tito was a realist about the patriarch's position; he knew that Gavrilo was not all-powerful, but he also knew that Gavrilo would now carry greater weight than ever in the church. Tito counted on Gavrilo's strong Slav patriotism and his devotion to his church to reinforce his loyalty to Yugoslavia, and his calculation was correct.

The new leaders of Yugoslavia, in fact, wanted an accommodation rather than a confrontation with all the religious communities at this difficult period. At the same time they were determined to punish any priests who had collaborated with their enemies during the war, and were prepared to stigmatise as collaborators any of the clergy who continued to stand against them – Bishop Irinej and Bishop Nikolaj in the United States, Metropolitan Josif, Vicar-Bishop Varnava Nastić and others in Yugoslavia. When Patriarch Gavrilo finally returned he was treated correctly, and his stature as a patriot enabled him to hold his own with vigour during his private discussions with the government. Having accepted the separation of church and state he insisted that the government also should accept all its implications.[73]

The desire for an accommodation with the churches did not inhibit the widespread harassment of the clergy and believers which took place all over Yugoslavia then and for some years after. Parish priests were evicted from their homes,[74] harried and beaten up[75] and imprisoned on flimsy charges.[76] Bishop Irinej Ćirić of Bačka had been beaten up by a mob during an official visit to Odžaci.[77] Individual protests had already been made but the Synod now decided to send a general and formal protest to the government, describing in detail the assault on Bishop Irinej, as an example of the government's failure to ensure the freedoms guaranteed by the constitution.[78]

[73] Conversation with the Rev. M. Nikolić, Serbian Orthodox priest in London, 1973.
[74] The local People's Committee at Srbac evicted two priests at Bosanska Nova (Synod 29.ix–30.x.46: Gl., 1.i.47) and the priest at Kraljević in the Banat (Synod 6.iii–3.iv.47: Gl., 1.v.47).
[75] The priest at Beli Potok near Belgrade (Synod 6.iii–3.iv.47: Gl., 1.v.47) and Simon Kondić, the priest at Bosanska Nova (Synod 29.ix–30.x.46: Gl., 1.i.47).
[76] Dušan Radovanović, priest of the Niš diocese, condemned to a year's imprisonment for urging young people to marry in church (Synod 6.iii–3.iv.47. Gl., 1.v.47).
[77] Synod 29.x–30.xi.46: Gl., 1.i.47. (These examples are culled at random from among many others.)   [78] Ibid.

The ministry of foreign affairs had already complained to the Synod about the activities of Bishop Dionisije of the American–Canadian diocese, and some of his priests. It cited a memorandum which Dionisije had sent on his own responsibility to Geneva, and asked the Synod to prevent any further activity on his part against the new Yugoslavia.[79] The Synod answered that the church authorities could only call bishops to account on matters of faith or canonical discipline; in any case, the American–Canadian diocese, 'which is an organic part of the Serbian Orthodox Church', had a special constitution which made it responsible only to the government of the USA for its independent external activities. It continued with a feline counter-thrust:

the Synod has no information about these priests nor any memorandum sent by them, and still less has it had any part in the memorandum. This is probably the result of the postwar lack of discipline which is apparent also here in Yugoslavia, though in a different form, as e.g. the gatherings in Prokuplje, Vranje, Valjevo, Šabac, Nikšić and Skopje; the declaration made at Prokuplje even appeared in the gazette of the Moscow patriarchate. The Synod hopes that these events among the clergy either abroad or at home will have no untoward consequences, the more so as our clergy during the worst days of the terrible war showed that it knew how to defend itself against the profane and unrestrained political aggression levelled at the Serbian Orthodox Church.[80]

The Synod was referring to the unrest among a part of the clergy and the meetings being held in various parts of the country, which preceded the revival of the prewar priests' associations.

The Synod, at its session in November 1946, went through the form of noting that as Bishop Nikolaj Velimirović, Bishop Irinej of Dalmatia and Bishop Dionisije of America–Canada were in the United States they would be unable to be present at the next conference of bishops on November 15; the Synod informed them that the patriarch had returned and that the next regular meeting of the Sabor (the assembly of bishops) would take place on April 24, 1947.[81] It thus fulfilled the canonical requirements which the government accused them of disregarding.

Strong attacks on the Synod now appeared in two of the leading government newspapers, Borba[82] and Politika.[83] They condemned the Synod for not disciplining Bishop Dionisije and removing him from his see; they accused him of defending

---

[79] Synod 5–29.ix.45: Gl., 1.xi.45. [80] Ibid.
[81] Synod 29.x–30.xi.46: Gl., 1.i.45. [82] 12.x.46.
[83] 13.x.46.

Mihailović and Konstantin Fotitch (the royal Yugoslav government's ambassador in Washington, who had played a leading part
abroad in opposing the new government) and removing from
his parish the Rev. Vojislav Gačinović of Pittsburgh, who had
opposed Dionisije's political attitudes. Moreover, 'two Serbian
Orthodox bishops who had escaped to the United States by way
of Italy had joined Dionisije' (referring to Bishop Irinej and
Bishop Nikolaj Velimirović). They were, the attacks continued,
concerning themselves with politics, not religion, and calling on
Serbs to renounce the Soviet Union and the new Yugoslavia; it
was the canonical duty of the Synod to recall them to their
dioceses.

While the Synod was debating these matters it received the
news that the patriarch was in Karlovy Vary in Czechoslovakia
and had recovered from his illness; permission had been
obtained for his return to Yugoslavia. Then, on November 14,
without warning, a message from the ministry of foreign affairs
arrived at the patriarchate that Patriarch Gavrilo's plane would
be landing at the airfield in ten minutes. The Synod, which was
in session, immediately rose and the bishops hurried out to meet
him; the plane landed precisely at noon. The minute of the Synod
continues: 'The patriarch was asked to resume his duties as
president of the Synod. Metropolitan Josif was asked to remain
a regular member of the Synod.'[84]

Gavrilo's return at once brought a fresh wind into the
deliberations of the Synod. He was determined to try to work
with the new government and not to seek unnecessary quarrels
– there were quite enough unavoidable ones. His presence and
authority strengthened the Synod, and together they determined
to embark on much closer association with the government so
that a whole range of matters could be better dealt with:[85]

a   The new legal position of the church must be examined; Article
    25 of the constitution, which decreed the separation of church
    and state, and the law which nullified all laws passed before April
    6, 1941, and during the occupation, brought many of the church's
    previous rights into doubt and removed many activities from its
    sphere.
b   The government's new Commission for Religious Affairs, set up
    in 1945, was charged with preparing material on the relations
    between church and state, and its organisation was of cardinal
    importance to the church.
c   The financial position of the church after the agrarian reform,
    the Law on the Nationalisation of Buildings, the abolition of the

[84] Synod 29.x–30.xi.46: Gl., 1.i.47.
[85] Ibid.

special tax for the patriarchate, and the difficulties put in the way even of collecting alms in church must be discussed.

d In addition the Synod decided to face the government with a long list of procedural harassments which were making its work increasingly difficult: obstacles were put in the way of religious instruction, buildings which housed church institutions were confiscated, priests brought before the courts were always given the heaviest possible fines and prison sentences, and in particular local People's Committees and other local authorities behaved in ways which denied the basic legal rights of the church guaranteed by the constitution.

e Lastly, they would tackle the government squarely about what the church considered was the government's encouragement of separatist priests in Montenegro and Macedonia who were attacking the unity and integrity of the church.[86]

As a first step the patriarch, accompanied by Metropolitan Josif and Bishop Nektarije of Zvornik–Tuzla, and by the Rev. Milan Smiljanić, who had served with the Partisans and was vice-present of the Presidium of the Serbian Assembly, called on Marshal Tito, the president of the federal government, on December 6 and stayed for about an hour; the conversation according to *Borba* was 'warm and friendly'; Tito returned the call on January 23, 1947. A series of calls to other government officials followed, to the Presidium of the federal government and to the president of the government of Serbia, Dr Blagoje Nešković.[87] On the basis of these calls the Synod wrote to Tito, enclosing two memoranda. The first presented nine points for discussion on ways of bringing to an end the injustices from which the church was suffering, and the second described these injustices and illegalities inflicted by some organs of the people's authorities.[88]

The patriarch's position as a patriot was strong and gave additional force to the representations of the Synod. He spoke on December 11, 1946, at a meeting of the Pan-Slav Congress held in Belgrade, and repeated the praise and thanks to Mother Russia for preserving Slav unity which Metropolitan Josif had voiced when Belgrade was liberated. The Serbian Orthodox Church, he continued, had always been a national church and tried to serve its people in the spirit of Jesus of Nazareth, who for the sake of truth and justice and freedom, and for his love of human beings, had sacrificed his life.

Gavrilo's Christmas message that year reflected the shock he

[86] Ibid.
[87] *Borba*, 7.xii.46; Synod 6.iii–3.iv.7: *Gl.*, 1.v.47.
[88] 321/47, 3.ii.47, Synod 6.iii.–3.iv.47: *Gl.*, 1.v.47. The second memorandum, enclosed with the first, was dated 17.ix.46.

felt when he at last saw for himself the state of the country and the church after the devastation of the war: 'our soul was shaken by the condition of our people and our church...but do not be distressed that some people have little respect for our Christian faith. This has happened before and it happened during the time of our Lord Jesus Christ.'[89]

The new constitution of the church

The Holy Episcopal Sabor, the assembly of bishops which is the highest governing body of the Serbian Orthodox Church, had last met in March 1941. It assembled again in April 1947 and sat for a month, reviewing and confirming the actions of the Synod which had conducted the affairs of the church since it had last met and taking a number of urgent decisions about the administration of the church.[90] Two new dioceses were created, Šumadija, with its see at Kragujevac in central Serbia, and Budimlje–Polimje with its see at Bijelo–Polje in southern Serbia,[91] and six new bishops elected, two of these auxiliaries to the patriarch, to fill the nine empty dioceses. One of the auxiliaries, Vicar-Bishop Varnava Nastić, was sent to Sarajevo as administrator of the diocese of Dabar–Bosnia (Sarajevo) and Zahumlje–Hercegovina (Mostar) under Bishop Nektarije of Tuzla. There was a general reshuffling of bishops, and several of them, including the patriarch, assumed responsibility for two dioceses.

The Sabor also promulgated a new constitution for the church to replace the 1931 constitution. The 1947 constitution was designed for the changed conditions of the church; its provisions accorded with the separation of church and state and unobtrusively attempted to protect the church from the more obvious forms of pressure.

The former oath of allegiance to the king and the promise to uphold the laws of the state as well as of the church[92] were abolished, and a new oath of allegiance to the Holy Orthodox Church swearing to uphold its canons, constitution and regulations was substituted;[93] it was taken by all the bishops, and all members of the patriarch's, bishops' and parish councils. The articles in the 1931 constitution which exempted priests and monks from carrying out certain public duties (i.e. military service) and which exempted the church from postal and

[89] Gl., 1.i.47.   [90] Gl., 1.vi.47.
[91] Budimlje–Polimje was abolished in 1956 and its territory returned to the neighbouring dioceses from which it had been carved.
[92] Art. 44, 1931.   [93] Art. 39, 1947.

telephone charges were abolished. Article 40 defined the church's new financial situation. Under the 1931 constitution the church had received a regular subvention from the government to compensate it for the loss of lands in the agrarian reform carried out after the First World War; there was also a church tax whose proceeds were paid to the patriarchate. In addition the patriarch had received a representation allowance of 35,000 dinars a month, an automobile and means of transportation suitable to his position, and a furnished apartment in the patriarchate.[94] Under the new dispensation the church was supported by the income from church property of all kinds (i.e. the ten hectares left to each parish and monastery under the Agrarian Reform Law, except for historic monasteries, which had a larger maximum), church fees, voluntary contributions and the income from church institutions and foundations, which had for the most part been expropriated or greatly reduced in value by the monetary reform.

A concession to the demands of the Macedonian clergy (a question which is discussed in the next chapter in the context of the Macedonian schism) was made in Article 4 of the new constitution, which allowed, in exceptional circumstances, the use of a language other than Serbian.

Finally, the procedure for electing the patriarch was changed. Elections had formerly been regulated by the law of April 6, 1930.[95] The 1947 constitution provided that the Bishops' Sabor, with a quorum of at least two-thirds, should choose three candidates from among bishops with five or more years' seniority.[96] These names were then sent to a special Elective Sabor consisting of all the bishops and the vicar-bishops of the Serbian Orthodox Church together with a number of other church dignitaries: the archdeacons (*namesnici*) of five republican capitals and two historic sees, the heads of nine historic monasteries, the members of the patriarch's Executive Committee, the vice-presidents of all the diocesan councils, and, an important concession, the president of the Council of Diocesan Priests' Associations.[97] A simple majority of the electors (but including two-thirds of the bishops) would constitute a quorum and the chosen candidate must receive an absolute majority of votes.[98]

In 1967 a number of amendments were made, the most

---

[94] Art. 48, 1931.   [95] Art. 46, 1931.

[96] Art. 43, 1947.

[97] Art. 44(4), 1947. This council did not yet exist; the priests' associations were formed on a republican, not a diocesan, basis. This point was finally conceded to the hierarchy in 1953.

[98] Arts. 47 and 50, 1947.

important of which was an entirely new procedure for the election of the patriarch.[99] In future the patriarch would be elected by bishops and vicar-bishops only, without an Elective Sabor; the usual quorum would elect three candidates by secret ballot and the new patriarch would be chosen by lot from among these three. The change, according to the official history of the Serbian Orthodox Church, 'reaffirmed the episcopacy of the church and was in accord with the separation of the church and state'.[100] The latter phrase indicates the underlying reason for this unusual procedure; it would in future be impossible for any particular bishop to be imposed on the church as patriarch. The most that could be done was to ensure that any bishop to whom the government particularly objected would not be among the top three in the ballot.

Another important change concerned parish councils. Before 1967 they had been elected by the parishioners; now they would be appointed by the bishops; this in fact simply regularised the existing situation.[101]

The official history, commenting on these changes, which it admits do not seem to be progressive, says that they were made to deal with the situation of the church as it really was, needing strong leadership in a society ruled by chaotic ideas which destroy authority.[102] Their real effect, however, was not only to make it more difficult to bring outside pressure on the church, but to strengthen the bishops against internal efforts to reform it.

Harassment of the clergy and Bishop Varnava's trial

The chronicler of these events, looking for sources of information is, faced with the fact that during this period the Orthodox Church aroused less interest in the West than the Catholic Church, and was reported in less detail. Information from Orthodox sources was much sparser, and, although there was some reporting in Anglican and Protestant circles, and both the Archbishop of Canterbury and the Presiding Bishop of the Episcopal Church in the United States deplored the arrests of Orthodox bishops and clergy, there was no world centre of Orthodoxy to match the Vatican with its multifarious sources of information and excellent means of publicity. The Orthodox Church, in lands which had been under Ottoman rule, had for five hundred years used silence, evasion and mystification to defend itself, habits which are not easily lost. Moreover, the

---

[99] Sin. 51/8 of 15.ix.67: *SPC*, p. 246.   [100] *SPC*, pp. 246–7.
[101] Ibid. pp. 247–8.   [102] Ibid. p. 248.

conflict between the communists and the Orthodox Church was of a different nature from the conflict between the communists and the Catholics. International politics, and the support which the communists believed that the Vatican gave to the territorial claims of Italy played a large part in the latter. The political element in the conflict with the Serbian Orthodox Church turned on its claims to embody the historical Serbian people and on its consequent tendency to 'Great Serbianism'. The communists saw that Serbian power within Yugoslavia would have to be cut down if Yugoslavia as a federation of equal nations was to become a reality; the Serbian Orthodox Church saw this as a crippling of the Serbian nation without which the communists could never govern it.

The church was difficult to assail on patriotic grounds. In the everyday knockabout of press polemics (if indeed this Anglo-Saxon concept can be used in the deadly climate of Balkan conflict) Metropolitan Josif was attacked for worming his way into the patriarch's seat during the war; Bishop Irinej Djordjević and Bishop Nikolaj Velimirović were attacked for collaborating with the occupiers (at a time when Irenej was interned in Italy and Nikolaj was with the patriarch in Dachau), which was unconvincing, and for hostile propaganda against the new government from their refuge in the United States, which was true.[103] *Vesnik*, the journal of the Union of Associations of Orthodox Priests in Yugoslavia, which echoed these attacks faithfully at the time that they appeared in the government press, later published a moving tribute to Bishop Irinej three years after his death.[104] Politically the communists attacked individual bishops and priests for Serbian nationalism and chauvinism, for hostile propaganda against the new government and opposition to the priests' associations; there was certainly truth in some of these accusations. Ideologically they wanted to break the hold of religion and the churches over the people everywhere in Yugoslavia, and, particularly in the Orthodox parts, to reduce it to a folklore survival. But they continued to repeat that they did not want to destroy the churches or prohibit religion. The pattern of harassment of priests and bishops which occurred in the Catholic areas was equally widespread in the Orthodox areas, though it was probably less severe, and there was no central event like the trial of Archbishop Stepinac in Zagreb which influenced the course of church–state relations for more than a decade and caused a world-wide sensation.

Metropolitan Josif was arrested, or detained, at least twice; the

[103] *Borba*, 12.x.46.   [104] *Vesnik*, 15.iv.55.

first time in 1945[105] and the second time after Patriarch Gavrilo's death in 1950, when he was released on condition that he went to live in a monastery.[106] Confirmation of this imprisonment appears in an interview which Patriarch Vikentije gave to Tanjug, the official news agency, some time after his election; the reporter referred to the release of Metropolitan Josif, and Patriarch Vikentije thanked the authorities, in terms of great formality, for this 'act of kindness'.[107] Metropolitan Nektarije of Tuzla was beaten up. A number of bishops who were known for their opposition to the priests' associations were attacked by name: Jovan of Niš, Emilijan, Simeon, Arsenije, Makarije, Vasilije, and Nektarije;[108] the position of the clergy continued to be very difficult.

The first full-dress show trial of an Orthodox bishop came in 1946, when Vicar-Bishop Varnava Nastić, who was administrator of the diocese of Dabar–Bosnia under Bishop Nektarije, was arrested in Sarajevo.

Bishop Varnava was born in 1914 at Gary, Indiana, in the United States, to a family of Bosnian Serb emigrants. He returned to Yugoslavia when he was nine, but was always proud of his American origins and his knowledge of English. During the war he had been one of the handful of Orthodox priests who remained in the NDH and survived. Pavelić summoned him to Zagreb in 1942 to press on him the leadership of the puppet Croatian Orthodox Church; he refused,[109] a dangerous thing to do, and for a short time took refuge with the Partisans in Serbia, but quarrelled with them and left.[110] He was a single-minded Christian with a true monastic vocation who sat very light to the more nationalist aspects of Serbian Orthodoxy, and an anti-communist who after the war hoped for a common front of the churches against communism, and was therefore increasingly tolerant of Catholicism. In addition he was by temperament a man of reckless moral courage who spoke the truth as he saw it and had never learned to hold his tongue. He believed that he was on God's side – not that God was on his side. This difference set him apart from some of the other members of the hierarchy (whom in any case he took no pains to conciliate), in particular those who were principally concerned to salvage the terribly damaged structure of the institutional church.

---

[105] *NYT*, 11.ix.45.
[106] RNS, 27.vi.50, and *Le Monde*, 28.vi.50.
[107] *Vesnik*, 1.xii.51.   [108] *Borba*, 3.vii.52.
[109] RNS and *NYT*, 4.vii.51: interview after his release from prison; *Gl.*, Dec. 1964 (obituary).
[110] Orthodox source close to Bishop Varnava.

He was arrested shortly after arriving in Sarajevo in 1947 and put on trial in February 1948, accused of treasonably weakening the military and economic strength of Yugoslavia, of helping terrorist bands, and of hostile propaganda.[111] He admitted that he had belittled the power of the Yugoslav Army to defend the country and had taught English to some of his friends against the day when the Americans would arrive, and that he had said in a sermon that the five-year plan would fail. He had also had links with Čondrić, the Croatian Catholic priest who had approached him after the war to sound him out about a common anti-communist front.[112]

His cross-examination gave him the opportunity of showing his sympathy for the United States, and his attitude, unusual for a Serb, to armed conflict:

PUBLIC PROSECUTOR   What is your attitude towards defending the country?

V.N.   I was not only against offensive, but also against defensive war.

P.P.   Are you for or against the defence of the fatherland?

V.N.   I am against any form of war.

P.P.   What is your attitude to the Yugoslav Army?

V.N.   My attitude towards the army is the same as towards all armies.

P.P.   What did you do against our army? – we are not interested in your philosophical attitudes.

V.N.   I don't live outside my philosophy. I express myself only philosophically.

He acknowledged that he had said that an army is an institution for killing people, but that this had not been meant as an attack on the Yugoslav Army in particular.

P.P.   Our army exists to defend our country and not to kill people. Why didn't you talk like this before the war, and during the occupation?

PRESIDENT OF THE COURT   How did you describe the people's authorities?

V.N.   I have always said that I didn't support the dictatorships, whether it was a dictatorship of a majority over a minority or the other way around. I am against all dictators. If God was a dictator I would be against him. (General laughter).

P.P.   Did you expect a change of authority?

V.N.   I expected a change in the social order, but I didn't go into the question of the form and the way. I did not believe that it would be brought about by internal forces. I expected intervention from foreign forces which would lead to a world conflict, or that a change would come about by pressure from Western forces. I wished for this change.

He described the cooperation of the Četniks with the occupiers

[111] *Oslobodjenje*, no. 418, report dated 28.ii.48.   [112] Ibid.

as 'tactics': 'I cannot call this betrayal although they might have confessed this at their trial.'

P.P. You came here when you were nine years old. Do you feel like a Serb or an American?
V.N. I feel like both. I am an American and I like machinery and mechanisation.

In reply to a question, Varnava said that he was against the separation of the church and the state.

P.P. Did you think that the church and state should work together?
V.N. I refused the kind of cooperation proposed by the Holy Synod.
P.P. Is this your opinion or the opinion of others?
V.N. The patriarch's opinion is different from mine. When I received the decree of the Synod I went to visit Nektarije to see what all this was about. He demanded my agreement but I answered: 'Let him who will sign it', but I didn't.
P.P. Is there anyone else who disagrees with the Holy Synod?
V.N. I know the attitude of Bishop Jovan of Niš and others [he mentioned Metropolitan Josif and Bishop Damaskin] though they signed the decision. Only the Bishop of Karlovci agrees with the patriarch.[113]

(This last was an unkind dig. The Serbian patriarch is always concurrently Bishop of Karlovci.)

It was widely believed that his answers were framed to attract sympathy for the Orthodox Church in the United States, and perhaps also to deflect some of the hostility of the government away from the rest of the hierarchy onto his own head. If so it would have been characteristically reckless and characteristically saintly, a gesture compounded of selflessness and spiritual arrogance. He was sentenced to eleven years' imprisonment and sent to the prison at Sremska Mitrovica, where Tito, Moše Pijade, Djilas and many other communists had been imprisoned before the war. Three years later he was injured in a railway accident; he was being transferred to another prison with a group of other prisoners, all shackled together, among whom was the Roman Catholic Bishop Čule of Mostar. Both bishops were hurt; Varnava suffered a badly broken leg. The Synod was gravely-concerned at the state of his health and determined to seek his release. It was clear that the authorities would never allow him to return to his diocese, and he was an embarrassment to the patriarch's policy of cooperating whenever possible with the government. A formula was finally devised. The bishops' Sabor, during the meeting of May 31 – June 12, 1951, petitioned the

[113] Ibid. 27.ii.48.

patriarch to allow Varnava to resign from his diocese; Varnava joined his petition to the Sabor's and it was granted. At the same time he petitioned the authorities for a pardon, and this also was granted[114] after he had served three years of his eleven-year term. The manoeuvre must have cost him much pain.

He spent the rest of his life in forced residence in various monasteries, first, for a brief period after his release, at Vavedenje in Belgrade, then in the isolated monastery of Gomionica in the mountains near Banja Luka. In 1960 he was transferred to Beočin in the Vojvodina, becoming increasingly isolated from the Synod and the patriarch by his undisguised contempt for their policy, his opposition to the government unabated.[115] When the Synod visited him to ask him to declare himself against Bishop Dionisije of North America, and commiserated with him on his forced residence, he answered briefly: 'I am free; it is you who are in prison.'[116] He died at Beočin on November 12, 1964, a solitary, somewhat eccentric figure, but a man of extraordinary courage and constancy.

A delayed obituary in *Glasnik* gave him his full due: 'both eminent and humble, cultured and simple, courageous and with a child-like innocence...he loved everyone and helped everyone who asked; he divided all his income among the poor and left nothing for himself'.[117] Three bishops officiated at his funeral, which was attended by the patriarch and other bishops. He was not a convenient colleague but his death was properly honoured.

---

[114] *Borba,* 10.vii.51.

[115] The writer has been shown a rough pencilled draft of a telegram which he sent to Marshal Tito on an occasion when telegrams of congratulation were pouring in. It was couched in terms of the greatest insolence. Towards the end of his life he wrote a similar letter to the local police.

[116] Orthodox source.   [117] *Gl.,* Dec. 1964.

6

The Serbian Orthodox Church
The struggle to hold the church together

The political life of Yugoslavia since its foundation in 1919 has been coloured by the tensions between those who thought of the new state as simply an extension of the old Kingdom of Serbia and those for whom it is a union of equal South Slav peoples. The Serbian Orthodox Church, which considers itself to be the religious and national embodiment of the Serbian people, falls into the first category, and has a tendency to be 'Great Serb' in this sense. The conviction, expressed in émigré Serb writings (an example can be found in Slijepčević's *Pitanje Makedonske Pravoslavne Crkve*, p. 25ff), that the communist government of Yugoslavia has weakened and divided the Serbian nation because it would be unable to rule a strong, united Serbia, is tacitly shared by the Serbian Orthodox Church. It ignores the fact that the other Yugoslav nations, particularly the Croats and the Macedonians, found the prewar Serbian hegemony in Yugoslav life intolerable, and that one of the conditions for a united Yugoslavia is a conviction among each of its peoples that they form part of a union of truly equal nations. This was recognised by the Yugoslav Communist Party and set out by Tito in 1942 in an article 'The National Question in Yugoslavia in the Light of the National Liberation Struggle'[1] which was widely reproduced and helped to gain much support for the Partisan cause during the war.

The Serbian Orthodox Church, formed by a union of a number of separate ecclesiastical jurisdictions with differing historical backgrounds, felt itself gravely threatened by the political dispositions after the war. In fact it identified itself so completely with Serbia, as a concept, as a nation and as a state, that the threat to Serbia and the threat to the church seemed to it to be identical. The Catholic Church, on the other hand, reacted specifically to the communist attack on the faith and on the Catholic Church as an institution. In the attitude of both churches there were, of course, political elements as well.

[1] In *Proleter*, no. 16, Dec. 1942.

The Synod and the bishops, in the midst of all their material and financial difficulties, saw that they must apply themselves immediately to opposing the challenges to their authority which began to arise even before the end of the war.

There was first the matter of the Croatian Orthodox Church, that Ustaša wartime creation, to which an official *finis* had to be written.[2] After reviewing its history (which had been pieced together by a commission set up by the Synod at the end of 1941 to collect information about the persecution of Serbs in the NDH)[3] the Synod passed a resolution on March 23, 1946, formally cancelling all the acts of Hermogen and Spiridon Mifka, the two émigré Russian priests who had been consecrated as Metropolitan of Croatia and Bishop of Sarajevo, but allowing priests who had collaborated with them to return to the Serbian Orthodox Church through the rites prescribed for the reception of repentent schismatics. Both Hermogen and Spiridon had been tried and executed by the new government immediately after the end of the war.

The Serbian Orthodox Church had jurisdiction for historical reasons over a number of dioceses outside the frontiers of Yugoslavia, some of which had formed part of the metropolitanate of Karlovci in the former Habsburg monarchy: Mukačev–Prjašev and Czech–Moravia in Czechoslovakia, Temešvar (Timişoara) in Romania and Budim (Buda) in Hungary. The American–Canadian diocese included also all the communities of Serbian emigrants in South America. Difficulties arose soon after the war in the dioceses lying immediately outside the Yugoslav frontiers.

Neither of the two dioceses in Czechoslovakia contained any Serbs, so that no ethnic questions arose when they wished to break away from the Serbian patriarchate. In 1945, at the request of Patriarch Alexei of Moscow,[4] the Mukačev–Prjašev diocese was transferred to the jurisdiction of the patriarchate of Moscow, and in 1948 the Czech–Moravia diocese was also transferred.[5] In 1951 they were granted autocephaly and now form the Czechoslovak Orthodox Church, which remains closely dependent on the Moscow patriarchate.[6]

Trouble started in the Budim diocese soon after the war, and in March 1946 the Synod sent a request to the Russian Orthodox Church not to give assistance to persons who were trying to establish a Hungarian Orthodox Church.[7] After the expulsion

[2] Sin. 1926/56/1946: *Gl.*, 1.iv.46.   [3] Sin. 3008/1941, 17.xii.41: *Gl.*, 1, iv.46.
[4] Synod 5–29.ix.45: *Gl.*, 1.xi.45.   [5] *SPC*, p. 535.
[6] Ware, p. 177.   [7] Synod 5–29.iii.46: *Gl.*, 1.v.46.

of Yugoslavia from the Cominform in 1948 regular communication between Bishop Georgije Zubković and the patriarchate became impossible, although he managed to maintain some links with Belgrade. When Bishop Georgije died in 1951 his successor, Hrizostom Vojinović, was not allowed to travel to his see to take up his duties; nor have the two subsequent incumbents, German Djorić (the present patriarch) and Arsenije Bradvarović. Budim gradually assumed the character of a titular see and provided a convenient shelf to which to transfer Metropolitan Arsenije some time after his release from imprisonment in 1956.

There were similar difficulties in the portions of the Temešvar (Timişoara) diocese within Romania; the Rev. Slobodan Kostić, whom Bishop Irinej of Bačka appointed as his vicar, was not allowed to take up his duties, and the Synod sent the Rev. Stefan Samuilov to investigate. The situation there was not finally resolved until 1969 when by a decree of the Sabor of the Serbian Orthodox Church the parishes lying within the frontiers of Romania were joined to the Romanian diocese of Timişoara.[8] Whatever the reasons for these difficulties, which were partly historical, the Serbian Orthodox Church was convinced that the Russian Orthodox Church – and probably the Soviet government – was behind them.[9]

There was also unrest among the clergy in Montenegro arising partly from separatist tendencies but also directly linked to the beginnings of the agitation for a priests' association, which demanded a more democratic structure inside the church and was strongly supported by the government.

The Metropolitan of the Montenegrin Littoral, Joanike Lipovac, had fled from Cetinje with a group of seventy priests in 1945 as the Partisan forces spread across the country. He had been close to the Montenegrin Četniks, who collaborated with the Italians. It is believed that they were killed somewhere in the Šumadija,[10] probably while fleeing from the Partisans. When the Synod reorganised the administration of the dioceses outside Serbia, Metropolitan Josif became temporary administrator of the diocese until Vicar-Bishop Arsenije was appointed metropolitan in 1947.

A group of Montenegrin priests, led by Petar Kapičić, held a meeting at Nikšić on June 14/15, 1945, and sent a resolution to the Synod, asking that the Orthodox Church in Yugoslavia should be organised so that 'all Orthodox without regard to national origin should have equal standing'.[11] This shaft was

---

[8] *Gl.*, 1.i.47, and *SPC*, pp. 531–2.   [9] See below, pp. 193f.
[10] *SPC*, p. 534.
[11] *Gl.*, 10.x.45, quotedin Slijepčević, Mac. 1959, p. 30.

aimed at Metropolitan Josif, who was still Metropolitan of Skopje, although he had not been allowed to travel there. The group refused to accept Josif as their temporary administrator, 'because of his anti-national activities, and because he had been imposed on them'.[12] The resolution attacked the Synod for not serving the interests of the people and demanded the establishment of a Central Priests' Association which would

immediately put the affairs of the Orthodox Church in our country and the relations between federated Yugoslavia and the Orthodox Church into order, since the present Synod of the Serbian Orthodox Church has not done so. The behaviour of the Synod is not in accord with the interests of the people and the Holy Church which must not be the channel of any Great Serbian chauvinistic ideas. A democratic church rule should be introduced and the law and constitution of the Serbian Orthodox Church changed so that the people and priests have the right to take part directly in the election of all church representatives.[13]

The Synod reacted decisively; it rejected the resolution and called the rebellious priests to order:

one part of our clergy in Montenegro, finding themselves abandoned after the departure of the diocesan bishop and a part of the clergy, and without waiting first to discover the intentions of the Synod, have undertaken certain actions which are in absolute opposition to the accepted and legal regulations of our church, and have taken upon themselves rights and duties which do not appertain to them – their resolution goes beyond permissible bounds. The priests have taken upon themselves to direct the affairs of the Orthodox Church in our country and in the Montenegrin diocese, by-passing the head of the church, the patriarch, and the Synod, who alone are competent in this.[14]

The question of the dioceses in Macedonia was so crucial and has had such a profound effect on the whole life of the Serbian Orthodox Church that it must be treated separately and will form an important part of the rest of this account of the Serbian Orthodox Church and its relations with the government.

The unrest among the clergy in Montenegro and Macedonia was largely nationalist, but this was not the only cause of their restlessness; the leaders, at any rate, of the agitation also wanted greater democracy within the church, and the participation of the laity in its management. The bishops, especially the older and more conservative ones, feared for their authority, but they also saw that they must protect the church from manipulation and infiltration by the authorities under the guise of democratisation. Thus the struggle over the priests' associations and, to a lesser extent, the Macedonian dioceses was waged on more than one front, and the issues were not as clear-cut as they seemed.

[12] Ibid.   [13] Ibid.
[14] Ibid.

The breakaway of a part of the American–Canadian diocese came much later and its causes were different.

The Macedonian dioceses I

The strongest attack on the unity of the Serbian Church came from Macedonia, and was directly connected with the recognition by the Yugoslav communists of the existence of a separate Macedonian nation. The Bulgarian occupation of Macedonia in 1941 was accompanied by intense efforts to Bulgarianise the population. The Bulgarian Orthodox Church assumed jurisdiction over the three dioceses in the territory and the Serbian bishops and many priests were expelled. About eight hundred Bulgarian schools were established and six hundred teachers were trained at special courses held in Bulgaria; all Bulgarian teachers were obliged to spend a year, and Bulgarian priests four months, in Macedonia.[15] A national theatre, a library and the King Boris University in Skopje were founded.[16]

The Bulgarian Communist Party at first attempted to take over control of the Macedonian Communist Party. The Yugoslav Communist Party appealed to the Comintern, which in August 1941 decided that the Macedonian Communist Party should come under the jurisdiction of the Yugoslav party. The latter had by this time accepted the Comintern thesis on the right of self-determination of small nations,[17] even though it recognised the threat to the unity of Yugoslavia, and foresaw the possible emergence of an independent Macedonia formed from territory held by Yugoslavia, Bulgaria and Greece. It at once began to organise resistance in Macedonia and early in 1943 sent Vukmanović-Tempo, a member of the Central Committee, to lead it. The equal status of Macedonia with the other Yugoslav nations was affirmed at the second meeting of AVNOJ in November 1945.[18]

The Bulgarian occupation, which had at first been welcomed by most of the population, became increasingly unpopular.[19] The

---

[15] Barker, p. 79.   [16] Ibid.
[17] See resolution of the Fifth Conference of the Yugoslav Communist Party in 1940, 'The Struggle in National Equality and Freedom', quoted in Apostolski, p. 267.
[18] Barker, p. 94.
[19] 'Insofar as it is possible to generalise, it seems that the Bulgarian occupation of 1941–4 was sufficiently unpleasant to disillusion most of the population of Yugoslav Macedonia about the advantages of belonging to Bulgaria, but it still left a large enough sediment of pro-Bulgarian and anti-Yugoslav feeling to make difficulties for Marshal Tito in the post-war Federal Yugoslavia' (Barker, p. 80).

native-born clergy, who felt themselves to be Macedonian, or at any rate more Bulgarian then Serb, had been allowed to remain when the Serbian clergy (or those who felt themselves more Serb than Bulgar) were expelled by the Bulgarians. There appear to have been early contacts between the priests who had remained behind and the Partisan detachments which began to form shortly after the occupation. It is difficult to say whether the conception of an independent Macedonian church sprang from the clergy themselves or whether it was suggested to them by the Partisans; the former on the whole seems more probable. There is no mention of the church or of the clergy in the manifesto issued by the headquarters of the Army of National Liberation and the Partisan companies of Macedonia in October 1943, nor in the documents issued by the first session of ASNOM (Antifašistiško Sobranie na Narodnoto Osloboduvanje na Makedonija – Anti-fascist Council for the National Liberation of Macedonia), which met on August 2, 1944.[20] The latter, however, included a declaration on the use of Macedonian as the national language of the new republic of Macedonia, and, as we shall see, the use of Macedonian for church affairs, in the liturgy and in sermons became one of the principal demands of the Macedonian clergy.

The first-fruits of the collaboration between the clergy and the Partisans appeared in the autumn of 1943. On October 15 the high command of the National Liberation forces appointed the Rev. Veljo Mančevski to take charge of religious affairs[21] and on November 11 the high command, meeting at Crvena Voda near Ohrid, passed a resolution to form a bureau of religious affairs.[22] At the end of that month a group of priests met at Izdeglavje;[23] they drew up a scheme for the administration of the church in territory controlled by the Partisan forces, divided it into nine deaneries, and appointed nine priests to take charge of these.[24] This was the first joint official action of the group of Macedonian clergy; it is clear that they already intended to demand an independent Macedonian church.

This was followed shortly after the liberation of Belgrade by a letter of Christmas greetings addressed to the Synod and signed by the Rev. Metodije Gogov, the Rev. Nikola Apostolov and the Rev. Kiril Stojanov,[25] who described themselves as representa-

---

[20] Apostolski, pp. 255–61, 284ff. [21] Dimevski, pp. 216.
[22] Ibid. p. 216. [23] Ibid.
[24] Ibid. pp. 216–17.
[25] 3.i.45: *Gl.*, 1.xi.45. Both the Serbian and the Macedonian forms of names appear in documents, the press and Slijepčević, Mac. 1959 and 1969.

tives of the Orthodox Church in Macedonia and members of the Organising Committee for the Founding of an Independent Church in Macedonia and the Restoration of the Historic Archbishopric of Ohrid.[26] According to Slijepčević, Gogov and Apostolov had been known as pro-Bulgarians during their time at the theological faculty in Belgrade.

Metropolitan Josif answered immediately on January 9, warning them sharply to be careful, since by their action they were 'placing themselves on an independent pedestal and on an equal level with the Synod', and advised them to use more calm and tact and reconsider their attitude from the standpoint of the church. He promised to try to meet them either in Belgrade or Skopje. The Synod endorsed his letter on January 21 and advised the Macedonian committee to communicate directly with Josif, their appointed bishop.[27]

The Organising Committee reacted by summoning a Macedonian Church and National Assembly (Crkovno–naroden Sobor) on March 4 and proclaiming the formation of the independent Macedonian Orthodox Church (Samostojna Makedonska Pravoslavna Crkva) and the restoration of the Ohrid archbishopric.[28] The Synod was informed of this decision in a letter of March 8, 1945, and the news appeared simultaneously in the government press.[29] Three hundred delegates from both clergy and laity were present at the meeting, which was opened by the Rev. Kiril Stojanov; a delegation was appointed to visit all the sister Orthodox Churches to explain the assembly's decision.[30]

The Synod at once called all the available bishops into conference.[31] They declared that the Macedonian People's Committee[32] was uncanonical and that there could be no discussion or debate about its proceedings. Metropolitan Josif was appointed to go to Skopje as soon as possible to inform the Macedonian clergy of the Synod's decision and to do everything possible to protect the interests of the Serbian Orthodox Church.

It is difficult to know whether a more tactful reaction from the

[26] Inicijativen Odbor za organiziranje na Samostojna Makedonska Pravoslavna Crkva i obnovuvanje na istoriskata Ohridska Arhiepiskopija (Slijepčević, Mac. 1959, p. 28).
[27] 21.i.45: Gl., 1.xi.45.
[28] Gl., 1.xi.45; Ilevski, pp. 75ff.
[29] Gl., 1.xi.45.
[30] Ibid.
[31] On 12.iii.45 (ibid.). Metropolitan Josif, Bishop Nektarije of Zvornik–Tuzla, Bishop Venjamin of Braničevo, Bishop Simeon of Šabac, Bishop Vladimir of Mukačev–Prjašev and Vicar-Bishop Valerijan were present.
[32] Makedonski Naroden Odbor. This refers to the Organising Committee.

Synod would have persuaded the government to allow Josif to travel to Skopje, and whether in the long run this would have made any difference to the outcome of the long battle which was now launched. At any rate, Josif's request for a permit to travel to Skopje was refused by the ministry of the interior 'for the moment',[33] and the Synod summoned the Macedonian clergy to come to Belgrade instead.

A series of pin-pricks followed. Emanuel Čučkov, the minister for Macedonia, asked the Synod to return the sum of 15m dinars, the Macedonian Church's share of the grant from the federal ministry of finances received by the Serbian Orthodox Church.[34] Metropolitan Josif answered that the money would be used for the Macedonian dioceses when they returned to their mother church from which they had voluntarily departed; any other procedure would be unnatural and illogical.[35]

The Organising Committee wrote a letter to the Synod[36] which was forwarded through the Democratic Federated Macedonian government[37] with several complaints: Glasnik, the official gazette of the Serbian Orthodox Church, was being sent to 'the Serbian Orthodox Church' in the Macedonian dioceses, whereas the name of the church was the Macedonian National Orthodox Church (Makedonska Narodna Pravoslavna Crkva) of Sv. Kliment; an ecclesiastical court had been held at Vranje, sowing dissension by sending Serbian priests into Macedonia;[38] the Macedonian people refused to accept grants of 100,000 dinars to each of the three Macedonian dioceses, paid by the patriarchate, and instead insisted that it should come through the Macedonian Commission for Religious Affairs.[39]

The Synod answered on September 22 with a considered statement of the position:

[The dioceses of Skopje, Zletovo–Strumica (Štip) and Ohrid–Bitola in the territory of the Federated Republic of Macedonia were a part of the Serbian Orthodox Church and the Orthodox population had been under the jurisdiction of the Serbian Orthodox Church] not only since 1920 when these dioceses, canonically and in proper order, were united or, better, returned to the arms of a united Serbian Orthodox Church, as witnessed by the communication of the ecumenical patriarchate of Constantinople, but were in union with the patriarchate of Peć much earlier, from which they were separated by historical forces. [The Synod therefore could not recognise the independent church in Macedonia

---

[33] No. 173, 17.iii.45: Gl., 1.xi.45. [34] No. 822, 18.vii.45: Gl., 1.xi.45.
[35] Gl., 1.xi.45. [36] 23.vii.45: Gl., 1.xi.45.
[37] No. 1428, 25.vii.45: Gl., 1.xi.45.
[38] Vranje is in eastern Macedonia just over the border from Serbia.
[39] Gl., 1.xi.45.

which had been proclaimed without the permission of the canonical hierarchy of these areas; it considered that the proclamation of an independent Macedonian church was arbitrary and uncanonical; and it did not recognise the actions of the self-styled Organising Committee which had unlawfully taken over the management of these dioceses from the lawful hierarchy.]

The Synod called on all the clergy and the 'honest laity' from these dioceses to return to their lawful bishops and follow their advice, and commands, and discuss with them the needs of the church in the spirit of canon law. The statement was signed by Bishop Nektarije,[40] as Metropolitan Josif had been arrested a fortnight earlier; according to the foreign press he had criticised the nationalisation of church property,[41] but his opposition to the demands of the Macedonian clergy may also have been an additional reason.

Before the end of the year the Synod issued a further appeal to the clergy in 'South Serbia and Montenegro' to remain loyal to the church[42] and wrote to the federal government asking it to prevent the uninvited interference of the Montenegrin Commission for Religious Affairs in the province of the official church authorities, and the uncanonical activities of the so-called Organising Committee and the Priests' Association in Macedonia.[43] This was a formal gesture, since the Synod was aware that the Macedonian clergy could not have been acting without the support of the government. A more interesting point which continues to pose itself is to what extent the Macedonian clergy were simply willing fellow travellers, and to what extent they themselves provided the initiative in this complex struggle which is still today not finished. An opinion widely held within the Serbian Orthodox Church but expressed publicly only outside Yugoslavia (e.g. by Slijepčević) is that the Macedonian Orthodox Church is simply a communist creation; to this writer, they do not at any stage give the impression of being merely puppets manipulated by the authorities.

A further request to the authorities in 1947 to allow Metropolitan Josif and Bishop Vikentije to return to their dioceses, 'for this is the only canonical and the best way to bring conditions back to normal in these regions', was not granted.[44]

Nevertheless, nothing further was heard for the moment about the Independent Macedonian Orthodox Church. The Mace-

[40] No. 1279, 22.ix.45: Gl., 1.xi.45.   [41] NYT, 11.ix.45.
[42] Synod 7–26.xii.45: Gl., 1.ii.46.   [43] Ibid.
[44] Gl., 1.v.47.

donian clergy were in practice outside the control of the Synod in Belgrade, but realised that they would have no canonical standing and thus no chance of being recognised by other Orthodox Churches unless they were governed by validly consecrated bishops, whom they could get only through the Serbian Orthodox Church. This became their next principal objective, for which they had to wait until 1959, owing to the skilful procrastination and delay of the Serbian bishops.

The church made a minor concession when its new constitution was adopted in 1947. Article 4 stated that the language of the church was Serbian, but that in exceptional circumstances, the Synod could allow another language to be used for internal purposes, thus providing a constitutional basis for the use of Macedonian. But the three Macedonian dioceses appeared in the list of dioceses of the Serbian Orthodox Church contained in the new constitution of the church (Article 14), and Article 112 (106 in the 1931 constitution), which expressly forbade any change in the administration of a diocese while the see was vacant, was left unchanged.[45] It was a useful constitutional barrier.

Priests' associations I

Associations of priests were not a new thing in the Serbian Orthodox church. The first one was founded in 1889, as a time of conflict between the Serbian government and the bishops. It was the expression of a movement of renewal within the church, chiefly among the lower clergy, aimed at improving their faith and the moral influence of the church among the people, improving the standard of preaching and culture within the church and diminishing superstitious practices, and also raising the material circumstances of the clergy, which, particularly in villages and small towns, were very low. Although a few bishops supported the movement, it was considered by most of them to be in opposition to the hierarchy, and a challenge to the authority of the bishops. During the 1930s there was unrest in the association, as the bishops tried to assert their control over it. The situation was confused by the war, when the clergy were divided in their allegiance; the majority tried to stay clear of the conflict, but some priests joined the Serbian Četniks, and others, many of whom had been active in the priests' association, fought

---

[45] 'During the vacancy of a see, nothing touching on the organisation of the diocese may be undertaken, nor may any important changes in the circumstances of the diocese, which are already under way, be completed while the see is vacant.'

with the Partisans[46] and continued after the war to support the views of the priests' associations, which they identified with the aims of the liberation struggle. The real constitutional links between the prewar and the postwar Serbian Orthodox priests' associations were obscure, but were always insisted upon by these priests. The government found this existing organisation a useful instrument against the hierarchy.

The first recorded wartime meeting of Orthodox priests took place on November 15, 1942, at Srpska Jesenica in Bosnia, when twenty-five priests and theological students 'united themselves with the broad masses of the people to fight with rifle and cross in their hands for freedom and social justice'.[47] Other meetings followed at which priests were urged to found or renew associations of priests. They not only fought, but they opened up churches which had been pillaged and burnt, christened babies, conducted marriage and funeral services and said the liturgy.[48]

After the war the movement pushed forward energetically: priests' associations were set up for most of the new federated republics; in Nikšić for Montenegro in June 1945, in Zagreb for Croatia in August 1947, in Sarajevo for Bosnia and Hercegovina in October 1947, in Belgrade for Serbia in December 1947 and in Skopje for Macedonia in December 1947.[49] This matched the federal structure of the government and indicated a closer affinity to it than to the diocesan structure of the church. It gave grounds for the accusation that the associations were simply instruments of the government; the bishops seized on it as one of the pretexts for not recognising the associations.

The new associations called meetings all over the country to recruit local priests, and at the same time to support the new government. In November 1946 the Rev. Milan Nastasević spoke to a gathering at Kragujevac, the tragic Serbian town where the Germans had killed 7,000 hostages in one day, and urged them to join the People's Front;[50] two days later priests from the district of Mačva passed a resolution declaring that they would take part in the elections for the Serbian Constituent Assembly.[51] The government at that time was using every means of publicity

---

[46] Local circumstances also came into play. In Serbia proper there was very little Partisan activity during the early years of the war. In Bosnia–Hercegovina and the border regions of Croatia, Lika, Kordun and Dalmatia, the Partisans were active. Many priests joined the nearest resistance group.

[47] *UPSJ*, p. 40.

[48] Ibid. p. 41.

[49] Ibid. But see ch. 4, n. 5, for the association in Croatia.

[50] *Borba*, 8.xi.46.   [51] Ibid. 10.xi.46.

and persuasion to ensure a large turnout in this first vital election. These groups were already referring to themselves as priests' associations.

It is difficult to say to what extent the associations were a spontaneous movement of the clergy and how far they were stimulated by the government as a means of controlling the church; certainly at this stage they were completely under government control. They threw themselves with enthusiasm into the rebuilding of the shattered country and were active in the Red Cross, the People's Front and various other social organisations. *Borba* reported in 1952 that 1,700 priests were members of the priests' associations, 80 per cent of the total; 81 were elected to organs of the people's authorities, 201 were working in state agricultural enterprises, 527 were working in the People's Front, 452 were active workers in the Red Cross, 122 in cooperative farms (*zadruga*) and 220 in educational–cultural associations.[52] They were not necessarily puppets, or venal (although the financial advantages of membership were a powerful factor in recruiting ordinary parish priests). Their freedom, however, was as constricted as that of all the other non-communists who cooperated with the communists, and for some years their public pronouncements merely echoed the government line. They became, in fact, the religious arm of the government and fulfilled their task with considerable zeal until 1954, or thereabouts, when their influence began to wane, as the government found it increasingly possible to deal directly with the hierarchy. That, however, still lay in the future.

The bishops, struggling to rebuild the structure of the church and reassert their authority over it, and harassed on every side by the authorities, viewed the resurrected associations with concern. They saw that publicly the associations enjoyed the full support of the authorities, and they were certain that behind the scenes they were being directed by the secret police. Bishop Venjamin of Braničevo informed the Synod in November 1946 that a conference of priests had been held in Kragujevac 'at the request of organs of the government and in their presence', during which a telegram was sent to the authorities and the church.[53] Similar conferences were held at Niš, in the Banat, and at Žiča, where 160 priests and 20 monks were present. They forbade the holding of further conferences without permission.[54] There were signs, however, that the bishops were not in complete agreement among themselves on the matter; a minute

[52] Ibid. 3.vii.52.
[53] Synod 28.x–30.xi.47: *Gl.*, 1.i.47.
[54] Synod 6.iii–3.iv.47: *Gl.*, 1.v.47.

of this session asks bishops to stop harmful gossip among their clergy about differences of opinion in the hierarchy, by explaining the real situation to them.[55]

Contacts between these priests and the patriarchate were nevertheless maintained. The Rev. Milan Smiljanić, a man of considerable calibre and unquestioned devotion to the Orthodox faith, who was vice-president of the Serbian Assembly, called on the patriarch with a group of priests who were all members of the People's Front and were all received in friendly fashion. The patriarch advised them to carry out their parish work faithfully and well; this was the first of their duties. After, if there was still time, they could undertake other work which was in accord with their priestly duties and calling. The priests, according to the Synod minute, were pleasantly surprised by their gracious reception, accepted the patriarch's fatherly advice and promised that they would never in any circumstances cast a shadow on their priestly calling by their behaviour.[56] Nevertheless they continued to set up priests' associations and the bishops to oppose them; when the Serbian association was established in December 1947 the Synod ruled that it was uncanonical and worked against the unity of the church, and they advised priests not to join.[57]

During the course of 1948 conversations continued between the Synod and the priests' associations. A joint commission of representatives of the church and the associations was set up to examine the draft rules of a proposed union of priests' associations.[58] Both sides agreed that a union was desirable; the differences between them centred on two questions of cardinal importance. The bishops wanted associations to be based on dioceses, the priests wanted them based on the territorial boundaries of the federal republics; the bishops wanted membership of the associations confined to active parish priests, the associations wanted all priests to be eligible.[59]

On the first question the associations argued that there were only a small number of members in each diocese, and that in any case the civil administration of the country was on a federal basis; from their point of view, diocesan associations would have broken them up into groups which the bishops would have found it easier to control, which was what the bishops wished. The second question turned on the fact that all the leaders of the priests' associations and many of their members held jobs in

[55] Ibid.   [56] Synod 7–22.iii.47: *Gl.*, 1.iv.47.
[57] *Vesnik*, 1.ix.49.   [58] *UPSJ*, p. 42.
[59] *Vesnik*, 1.ix.49.

various social or political bodies, or in the associations themselves, and did not depend materially or psychologically on the bishops; if they had been forced to return to parish work their strength would have been greatly curtailed. The bishops not only realised this but were desperately concerned at the shortage of clergy for parish work and had issued repeated appeals for priests to return to their parishes.

No agreement was reached, and in May 1948 the Sabor rejected the rules of the associations.[60] The bishops were not strong enough to fight an aggressive battle; their best course was to temporise and delay, which they did over the next few years with patience and skill.[61]

The leaders of the associations went ahead with their plans. A journal, *Vesnik* [Herald], was founded; its first number appeared on March 1, 1949. An assembly of delegates of the associations was called in March 1949 and attended by 245 priests.[62] It met in Belgrade in a large hall; the officers sat on a platform with the Yugoslav and Soviet flags draped above the large bust of Marshal Tito; there were no other icons. The assembly voted on March 3 to set up the Union of Associations of Orthodox Priests in Yugoslavia (Savez Udruženja Pravoslav-nog Sveštenstva Jugoslavije) and the government immediately approved it.[63] Telegrams of greeting were sent to the patriarch and to Marshal Tito.[64] (It is important to notice that the term 'Orthodox' and not 'Serbian Orthodox' was used. This is itself expressed a sharp difference in attitude and confirmed the worst suspicions of the hierarchy.)

The assembly notified the Synod of the founding of the union and sent them a copy of its rules for approval; the Synod replied immediately that the associations were uncanonical. Faced with this the assembly settled down to further discussion and drew up a list of the aims of the union.[65] Its members would devote themselves to the following objectives:

1   To help their parishioners fulfil their duties as law-abiding citizens, teaching them by their example to defend the interests of their country.

---

[60] *UPSJ*, p. 42.
[61] The bishops were never united on this question. Some opposed the priests' associations strenuously, others were prepared to make tactical compromises. During the 1950s and later some bishops were chosen from the general membership of the associations, though never from among the leaders. A good deal of manoeuvring went on within the Sabor.
[62] *SRCY*.
[63] *Vesnik*, 1.ix.49. See also photograph of the assembly.
[64] Ibid.   [65] Ibid.

2 To foster love and harmony among their parishioners, brothers and sons of the same fatherland.

3 To teach mutual forgiveness in the spirit of the gospels.

4 To cooperate with the civil authorities to fight illiteracy and to help with classes for illiterates.

5 To cooperate with cultural and educational institutions.

6 To assist the peoples' authorities by helping people to acquire the necessary knowledge to work well and successfully.

7 To cooperate with the work of the Red Cross and in general with the public-health work of the authorities.

8 To help in the work of cooperatives (*zadruga*) of all kinds.[66]

Other meetings followed quickly and further resolutions were passed; *Vesnik* was full of attacks on the Synod and on individual bishops. Bishop Nikolaj Velimirović of Žiča, Bishop Irinej of Dalmatia and Bishop Dionisije of North America were condemned for their treacherous anti-national and anti-church activities abroad, and the Sabor was urged to remove them from their positions.[67] Bishop Jovan of Niš, Bishop Venjamin of Braničevo and Bishop Vasilije of Banja Luka were attacked by the union's Administrative Committee for opposing the union, representing 70 per cent of the Orthodox clergy,[68] and Metropolitan Josif for refusing to resolve the Macedonian question.[69] A long article appeared in *Vesnik* on May 5 repeating the attacks and summing up the complaints of the union against the church as represented by the hierarchy – its refusal to adapt itself to the new society, shown by the quite inadequate changes in the 1947 constitution, its continuing refusal to remove the treacherous bishops and its appointment of new bishops from the elements in the clergy most hostile to the fruits of the liberation struggle (they singled out Auxiliary Bishop Varnava Nastić and Bishop Vasilije) and its refusal to recognise a union of associations representing the great majority of the clergy.

All this pressure was building up for the yearly Sabor of bishops, which was due to convene on May 11, but before it could meet the situation changed dramatically. Patriarch Gavrilo died suddenly on May 4, 1950.[70]

---

[66] Ibid. *UPSJ* (p. 42), published twenty years later, rephrases these objectives and adds a further one, to represent the interests of the Orthodox clergy in Yugoslavia. By that time this was in fact becoming one of the principal functions of the associations.

[67] *Vesnik*, 1.i.50. The dioceses of Žiča and Dalmatia had been put under administrators, and residential bishops were not appointed until after the deaths of Nikolaj and Irinej.

[68] 22–3.xii.49: *Vesnik*, 1.i.50.   [69] Ibid.

[70] *Gl.*, 7.v.50.

The patriarchate

The patriarchate's links with other Orthodox Churches had been severed during the war, and now they slowly resumed. These links were always at the mercy of political considerations, but, except for the period after 1948 when Yugoslavia was completely isolated from Moscow and the other East European communist countries, the ties with East Europe, Greece and the Middle Eastern countries were considered by the government to be useful adjuncts to Yugoslav foreign policy and were encouraged and supported.

The church had sent a delegation to Moscow in 1945 to be present at the election of the new patriarch, and on July 9, 1948, at the moment of Yugoslavia's expulsion from the Cominform, Gavrilo, accompanied by Metropolitan Josif and Bishop Venjamin of Braničevo, travelled to Moscow at the invitation of Patriarch Alexei for the celebrations of the five hundredth anniversary of the autocephaly of the Moscow patriarchate.[71] This and all the subsequent travels of the patriarch were made possible by government subventions, and of course government permission to travel; the government was always punctiliously and publicly thanked for its assistance.

The leaders of all the autocephalous Orthodox Churches were present and, aside from the festivities, discussions took place about the attitude of the Orthodox Churches to the ecumenical movement, the relations of the Vatican with the Orthodox Churches during the past thirty years, the calendar, and the recognition of the validity of Anglican orders.[72] There had also been persistent rumours of a move by the Russian Orthodox Church, backed by the Soviet government, to assume a hegemony over all the Eastern Orthodox Churches, thus displacing the primacy of Constantinople. Patriarch Alexei took the opportunity to deny that the Russian Orthodox Church had any such ambition. Patriarch Gavrilo in conversation with Patriarch Alexei spoke his mind about the Orthodox Church in Hungary. This diocese had always come under the Serbian Orthodox Church, since its members were all Serbs living in Hungary; but the Russians now intended to send an exarch to Budapest and there had been talk of establishing an independent Hungarian Orthodox Church. Gavrilo protested vigorously against this 'uncanonical meddling by the Russian Orthodox Church' and warned that it would have undesirable consequences; it would

[71] Ibid. 1.viii.48. [72] Ibid.

be a bad precedent and against the interests of Orthodoxy and the Slavs. Patriarch Alexei was soothing but non-committal.[73] Both the Serbs and the Russians realised that they stood on the brink of great political changes which might either bring the Serbian Orthodox Church decisively under the sway of the Moscow patriarchate, or make any further contacts between them impossible for a long time. Gavrilo also, consistently with the attitude which he had adopted from the time of his return to Yugoslavia, gave his blessing to the Soviet Army which had given its blood to liberate the Serbian people.[74]

His public attitude to the government was invariably correct. The Associated Press correspondent interviewed him on August 11, 1949, and asked whether it was possible to be loyal at the same time to the Serbian Orthodox Church and the Communist Party, in a material and spiritual sense. The patriarch answered that the Serbian Orthodox Church was completely loyal to the state and the government of the state and did not concern itself with politics or political parties; and he added that there was no conflict between the government and the church. But his position enabled him to be unyielding on the questions of the Macedonian Church and the priests' associations, which the bishops considered would divide the unity of the Church and strike at their authority.

He died on May 6, 1950,[75] and his body lay in state in the cathedral until his funeral on May 11. During the Easter celebrations a month earlier there had been extraordinary manifestations of devotion in Belgrade; the cathedral and all the other churches had been packed and overflowing with worshippers.[76] In his Easter message the patriarch commended the efforts of the faithful to hand on the traditions of the faith to future generations; there was no people in the world whose past was so linked to the past of the church. Now great crowds filled the cathedral and overflowed into the streets, and representatives of the government and the Commission for Religious Affairs were present at his funeral,[77] but the customary procession with the coffin through the streets of Belgrade was not allowed.

The election of his successor was an ordeal which dragged on until the beginning of July. The procedure for the election of a patriarch was laid down in the new 1947 constitution; one of the most important innovations was the inclusion of the president

[73] Ibid.
[75] *SPC*, p. 476.
[77] *Vesnik*, 25.v.50.
[74] Ibid.
[76] RNS, 8.iv.50.

of the Union of Associations of Orthodox Priests in the Elective Sabor. A long article appeared in *Vesnik*;[78] it listed the names of all the eligible candidates (bishops of five or more years' seniority) and continued that the next patriarch must not be chosen by age or seniority but must be a proven patriot who could maintain the unity of the church, guard its authority and help the clergy and people to remain steadfast in working for all the people; during the war some bishops had been photographed with the occupiers, had lived quietly in Belgrade, and and had supported the Četniks; the bishops' Sabor, who would choose the three candidates to submit to the Elective Sabor, had a heavy responsibility to cast their votes wisely. This was directed particularly against Metropolitan Josif, whom neither the government nor the priests' association nor the Macedonian clergy for whom they also spoke was prepared to accept as the next patriarch.

The Elective Sabor was summoned for June 10 but only twenty-seven of the seventy-three members appeared in the cathedral, not enough for a quorum; the others had either failed to come or been prevented from doing so. The names of the three candidates chosen by the bishops were never published either in *Glasnik* or *Vesnik*, but it became known that they were Metropolitan Arsenije of the Montenegrin Littoral, Bishop Nektarije of Zvornik–Tuzla and Metropolitan Josif of Skopje.[79] According to *Vesnik*[80] Josif and his 'clique' had included a known collaborator, with the result that the majority of the Elective Sabor was unwilling to take part in the election and stayed away, 'siding with the union'. It seems more likely that measures had been taken to keep them away, and this was widely believed. The foreign press reported that Metropolitan Josif had been detained by the police.[81]

The Sabor met again on June 30[82] and chose three candidates, Metropolitan Damaskin of Zagreb, Metropolitan Arsenije of Montenegro, and Bishop Vikentije of Zletovo–Strumica. The Elective Sabor met the next day, July 1. This time fifty-nine members out of seventy-three turned up and two bishops sent substitutes to vote for them, Georgije of Budim, who was not allowed by the Hungarian government to travel, and Makarije of Budimlje, who was ill. Bishop Vikentije was elected patriarch with thirty-three votes, Metropolitan Arsenije followed with twenty-five votes and Metropolitan Damaskin with two;[83] one

[78] 7.vi.50.
[80] 25.vi.50.
[82] *Gl.*, 1.ix.50; *Vesnik*, 15.vii.50

[79] Serbian Orthodox source.
[81] RNS, 27.vi.50.
[83] Ibid.

paper was spoiled.[84] Vikentije had the absolute majority required by the church's constitution.

The new patriarch was installed on July 2. His sermon was brief:

you are waiting to hear from me what my programme will be...my programme is an old one; it is a short one. My programme is the Lord Jesus Christ. I believe that this programme includes everything...it is our whole faith, our love and our hopes. It includes the church, the fatherland, the people, the government and relations with the state and with the people.[85]

The occasion was solemn and official. The government was represented by three ministers, including the Rev. Vlada Zečević, the Partisan priest who was now minister of communications; there were two ministers from the Serbian government, the president of the State Religious Commission (Državna Verska Komisija), Miloje Dilparić, and the Rev. Milan Smiljanić in his capacity as president of the Religous Commission of Serbia. Both the British ambassador, Sir Charles Peake, and the United States chargé d'affaires were present.[86]

The new patriarch was interviewed by Tanjug, the government news agency, and expressed his wish for cooperation and a good understanding with the government. He was optimistic but non-committal about the other matters at issue with the government; the problem of the Macedonian was approaching a favourable solution, the Synod was studying the question of the bishops who had been absent from their dioceses for more than six months and expected to be able to resolve it, and the Sabor felt that it was necessary to come to an understanding about the priests' associations, both in the interests of the church and the general interest.[87] Courtesy calls were exchanged with Marshal Tito,[88] the president of the Serbian government and other government officials.[89]

Patriarch Vikentije was a striking contrast to his predecessor. Scholarly, somewhat phlegmatic, with a peaceable disposition (although he was capable of angry outbursts), he preferred to gain his ends by diplomacy and delay rather than by frontal assaults. He was born on August 23, 1890, in a small village in Bačka; his family belonged to the Serbian minority under Hungarian rule. After completing his studies at the theological

---

[84] *Vesnik*, 15.vii.50. (There was no interruption in the publication of *Vesnik* but *Glasnik* did not appear from June 1 to Sept. 1, 1950.)

[85] *Gl.*, 1.ix.50.
[86] *Borba*, 3.vii.50.
[87] Ibid. 6.vii.50.
[88] Ibid. 23 and 27.ix.50.
[89] Ibid. 8.vii.50.

faculty (as it then was) at Sremski Karlovci, he taught briefly in his own village and in 1917 took monastic vows. This was followed by several years of working in the church courts in the dioceses of Temešvar and Bačka and at Novi Sad, during which time he took a second degree, in history, at Belgrade University. He was ordained in 1929, and in 1930 was appointed general secretary of the bishops' Sabor and the Synod, a position which gave him an intimate knowledge of the inner workings of the church. He continued this work after his election as auxiliary bishop in 1936, until he was sent in 1938 to Sremski Karlovci as patriarch's vicar. The following year he became Bishop of Zletovo–Strumica in southern Serbia (Macedonia) and in 1940 he took over the administration of the neighbouring diocese of Ohrid–Bitola.

After the Bulgarian invasion in 1941, he was expelled to Belgrade and was immediately sent by the Synod to take charge of the diocese of Žiča, which had been left vacant by the arrest of Bishop Nikolaj Velimirović; he remained there until in 1947 he was elected first bishop of the new created diocese of Srem.

His experience, which lay entirely within the administration of the church – he was never a parish priest – gave full play to his shrewdness and cultivated his qualities of tact and diplomacy. The writer of a biographical note describes him as cultivated and witty, with a talent for paradox;[90] his enemies claimed that he was weak, but if this was so he had the obstinacy of some weak men. He came to the patriarchate after a crude electoral tussle, with the formidable disadvantage of having been the government's choice. The gentler manners which the Serbs of the Vojvodina acquired under the Austro-Hungarian Empire were not always to the taste of the fiery, violent Serbs of Serbia proper, and Metropolitan Josif, a popular figure about whom legendary stories circulated,[91] had been bundled unceremoniously out of

---

[90] *SPC*, pp. 476–8.
[91] The most famous and best-authenticated of these concerns on occasion shortly after the war when a mob collected in front of his house shouting 'Down with Josif!' He appeared on a balcony and called out: 'Quiet, quiet, my children; you must not rise against the temporal authority which is appointed by God. But in any case, which Josif do you mean [producing two large portraits], Josif Stalin or Josif Broz Tito?' He was passionately pro-Russian; of the Red Army forces which helped to liberate Belgrade in 1945 he said: 'Whatever they are that's how they are and they're ours.' In Serbian more neatly: 'Kakvi su, takvi su, naši su.'
   The writer was told, with considerable amusement, by a Serbian Orthodox priest the story circulating about a serious illness towards the end of his life. He was not expected to survive and his household had gathered around him, holding candles and waiting to light them as the soul left his body. As the

the way during the election. Vikentije's particular temperament was to serve the church well at this point in its history when it needed above all time to recover from the war. Under his rule the Synod did not give way on the two questions of radical importance to the church, Macedonia and the recognition of the priests' associations, while he succeeded at the same time in maintaining good relations with the government, a stance which required skill, luck and a capacity to speak fair but not actually do anything. The strain eventually killed him, but he had not given way.

Two new bishops and two new vicar-bishops were elected in the summer of 1951;[92] the two latter, the Rev. Hranislav Djorić, who took the monastic name German and was appointed general secretary of the Synod, and the Rev. Dositej Stojković, were later to become leaders of the opposing sides in the long struggle over the Orthodox Church in Macedonia, German as patriarch and Dositej as metropolitan of the Macedonian Orthodox Church.

In December 1951 Vicar-Bishop German, accompanied by Dr Glumac of the theological faculty, set off for Western Europe and the United States to visit the Serbian Orthodox communities in Europe, the World Council of Churches and the North American and Canadian diocese and its controversial bishop, Dionisije. The stated purpose of the trip was to 'strengthen the ties between the Serbian Orthodox Church and its outlying dioceses, weakened by the war, and to ask the World Council of Churches for much-needed material help'.[93] There were Serbian communities in Vienna, Trieste, Paris, London, Western Germany and Switzerland; there had been no personal contact since the war between the hierarchy in Yugoslavia and Bishop Dionisije, who had attacked the Yugoslav government on every occasion, and who was uncooperative when Bishop Irinej and Bishop Nikolaj Velimirović arrived in the United States after the war. Officially, the trip was pronounced a success: the Serbian Orthodox bishops abroad were solving the problems of the church in the right way, and the World Council of Churches had shown understanding of the needs of the church. Publicly the cracks were papered over, but the meeting with Dionisije was very unsatisfactory.[94]

moment appeared to be arriving a match was struck. Suddenly the bed-clothes stirred, his old hand slowly appeared, with two fingers raised in ribald gesture of defiance, and was then withdrawn. He survived for several years.

[92] *Gl.*, 1.viii.51. The two diocesan bishops were Longin Tomić, to be Bishop of Zahumlje–Hercegovina, and Simeon Zleković, to be Bishop of Gornjikarlovac.

[93] *Gl.*, 1.xii.51.   [94] Orthodox source.

Social insurance

Two events took place early in Vikentije's patriarchate which were important in the development of the relations of the church with the government; they concerned the social insurance of the clergy, and the legal status of the religious communities.

The church's pension fund had been expropriated in 1946 and responsibility for the pensioners taken over by the state; some of these however were removed from the list of beneficiaries.[95] Part of the fund was eventually returned to the church, but its value had diminished greatly because of devaluation. The Sabor decided that this remnant should be used to make payments to those who were not receiving pensions from the government.[96]

The whole question of social insurance for the clergy was acute, and was for many years to be a major preoccupation of the church's administration. The Serbian Orthodox Church had always looked after its own people, and provided pensions from the charitable foundations and other funds at its disposal. Now these were either nationalised or severely diminished by the change in the value of money. The government was prepared to draw up agreements for social insurance with various groups outside the social sector (i.e. various categories of self-employed people and the churches) and issued its regulations on the social insurance of priests on May 19, 1951.[97] These were accepted by the church as a basis for negotiation. Two opposing principles had to be reconciled: the state felt that priests and their families should have no special advantages over people in the social sector; the church was unwilling to surrender any of the rights acquired under its own pension scheme.[98] After several months of negotiation between the church and the National Council of Health and Social Policy a contract was signed on December 21 and came into force on January 1, 1952.[99]

The agreement provided insurance for bishops, priests, deacons and priest–monks regularly employed in the service of the church, on a basis which was slightly less favourable than for persons in the social sector; lay monks and monks working within their monasteries were not included in the agreement, although the church had tried to cover them at least for sickness. Married priests paid 16 per cent of their income, those without families 12 per cent. The agreement did not satisfy all of the church's requirements, but it was a beginning and was followed over

---

[95] *Gl.*, 1.iii.51.   [96] Ibid.
[97] *Služ. List* 25/51, quoted in *Gl.*, 1.i.52.   [98] *Gl.*, 1.i.52.
[99] Ibid.

the next few years by a series of agreements each of which represented a further step forward. The Union of Priests' Associations was delighted; it had been campaigning for state pensions for the clergy for the last seventy years.[100] The following June Patriarch Vikentije, with two bishops, called on Marshal Tito to thank him for having used his influence to help to resolve this question, and promised the support of the church in building up and developing the country. Tito replied that the government would look favourably on the constructive work of the church, especially its support for brotherhood and unity, peace and independence.[101] The phrases on each side were conventional but they indicated that the atmosphere, for the moment, was favourable.

The Law on the Legal Status of Religious Communities

The government published the draft of a proposed law on the legal status of religious communities early in 1953, and invited comment from the religious communities; the purpose of the law was to give precise legal definition to the relevant provisions of the constitution. The Catholic Church did not answer, but the Synod of the Serbian Orthodox Church made a detailed examination of the proposed law and submitted its suggestions; a delegation headed by Patriarch Vikentije called on Moše Pijade, the vice-president of the federal Executive Council, who assured them that their suggestions would be carefully considered.[102] The law came into force on June 4, 1954.[103]

Although the church was far from getting all it had asked for, it now had in theory a legal basis for protest when its constitutional rights were violated. It was a number of years before these rights began to be respected. The immediate effect was a tightening up of the ideological front against the churches; *Komunist*, the party journal, called on party members to intensify the fight against religious prejudices and superstititions. Local party members reacted angrily to any signs that the church was standing on its rights. *Borba*, reporting the incident in which Bishop Nektarije Krulj of Tuzla was violently set upon and driven out of the monastery at Ozren in Bosnia, where a religious gathering was to be held, wrote: 'The people were revolted when they heard that the reactionary clergy, led by Krulj, were telling the people of this district that the Law on the

---

[100] *Vesnik*, 1.i.52.   [101] Ibid. 7.vi.52.
[102] *Borba*, 20.x.53.   [103] *Gl.*, June 1953; see ch. 7.

Legal Status of Religious Communities expressly states that religious services can be held.'[104]

Another, in the end perhaps even more trying, consequence of the passing of the law was that the federal Commission for Religious Affairs informed the Synod that it could no longer deal with the sort of local complaints which the Synod had been bringing to them; these must be dealt with by the competent local authorities.[105] The Synod, in order to by-pass the delays of the local bureaucracies, had asked bishops and priests to send all complaints to it, and it had they taken them up directly with the Commission on Religious Affairs. It was obviously, from the point of view of the church, a much more satisfactory method, but it was not in accord with the practice of self-management and the growing decentralisation which had now been adopted as Yugoslavia's particular contribution to communism. The consequence was that priests, who had had no legal training, had to petition the local authorities for their rights in cases involving complicated legal points. The Synod issued a long circular to priests explaining the new situation and advising them to use a lawyer in difficult cases, or come to the patriarch's Administrative Committee, who would advise them on property law.[106]

Priests' associations II

Patriarch Vikentije's accession ushered in a period of several years when the Synod, starting from a position of weakness, managed by procrastination, administrative delays and a scrupulous attention to forms and regulations to fend off the increasing pressure from the union and the government for recognition of the priests' associations. The subject came up each year at the Sabor, and each year on one excuse or another recognition was either refused, or the subject was removed from the agenda. It is certainly going too far to suggest that the differences of opinion within the Sabor were nothing but an elaborate manoeuvre to mask a united determination not to give way. Many of the bishops were deeply conservative and some had learned from past experience habits of open defiance. There was genuine conflict within the Sabor, but the resulting deadlock was probably not entirely unwelcome. Patriarch Vikentije never voted against recognition, but he always succeeded in being outvoted. At the same time individual bishops made paternal

[104] *Borba*, 22.viii.53.
[105] Sin. 238/50, 13.ii.54: *Gl.*, Jan.–Feb. 1954.
[106] Sin. 291/59, 6.ii.54: *Gl.*, Jan.–Feb. 1954.

gestures. Bishop Irinej of Bačka, for example, attended the opening of a branch of the priests' association's cooperative in Novi Sad[107] and the newly elected Vicar-Bishop Dositej represented the patriarch at the opening of the First Congress of the Union of Associations of Orthodox Priests in the autumn of 1951.[108]

The union petitioned the Sabor for recognition in 1951 and was refused, on the grounds that the priests' associations were organised by republics and not by dioceses, which would be more suitable for a church organisation. In 1952 the union repeated its request. Its leaders also did a considerable amount of preliminary lobbying; according to them Metropolitan Josif said he would not vote for recognition but promised not to obstruct; Metropolitan Damaskin of Zagreb told them that the work of the association had been useful to the church and to him personally and promised to support the petition; Vladimir, Visarion, Nikanor and Simeon also promised their support, as did Longin and Emilijan, who had been members of the associations before their election.[109] However, the request of the leaders of the union for a meeting with the Legislative Committee of the Sabor was refused, and on June 2, the Sabor decided by secret vote to remove the question of the recognition of the associations from its agenda, as they had not yet met the Sabor's requirements concerning their rules. *Vesnik* reported that there were only four dissenting votes and one blank.[110] The *New York Times* reported that Patriarch Vikentije had abstained.[111]

The leaders of the union reacted angrily with renewed attacks on named bishops for their activities during and after the war,[112] and with further efforts to spread the associations, setting up local committees and holding conferences.[113]

It was a delicate position and Vikentije was under great strain. He was extremely irritated by a statement of the Catholic Bishops' Conference in Zagreb on September 23–5, 1952, justifying its prohibition (*non licet*) of priests' associations by referring to the decision of the Sabor.[114] In an interview published in the party daily *Politika* he strongly condemned 'this misplaced procedure . . . of the Catholic episcopate, which is inimical to our country. It looks as though the Catholic bishops wished to

---

[107] *Vesnik*, 28.iv.51. [108] Ibid. 1.xi.51.

[109] Ibid. 7.vii.52. [110] Ibid.

[111] *NYT*, 4.vii.52.

[112] *Vesnik*, 1.x.52, in an article signed by the Rev. Ratko Jelić, secretary of the union of associations.

[113] Ibid. 1.xi.52. [114] Ibid. 15.x.52.

conceal their blind obedience to the Vatican.'[115] The Orthodox priests' associations, he continued, had not yet been recognised *de jure* because of certain unresolved organisational questions; but the hierarchy were not in principle against them, and there was even provision for them in the 1931 and 1947 constitutions of the church. He listed the ways in which the bishops and the associations already worked together:

1 The Sabor had decided unanimously that the president of the union should take part in the election of the patriarch.
2 Some members of the associations had been elected to the episcopate.
3 There was regular contact between the bishops and members and officers of the associations.
4 Some bishops were present at conferences of the associations and when necessary collaborated with them.
5 There was no discrimination against members of the associations in appointments to parishes or in promotions.[116]

On its side the union from its inception took every opportunity to identify itself as a group of patriotic Serbs, both with the government and the church. It took part (in July 1950) in the Congress of the Yugoslav National Commission for the Defence of Peace in the World[117] and welcomed the presence of Bishop Vladimir Rajić of Raška–Prizren, representing the Serbian Orthodox Church. The church, added *Vesnik*, is not neutral towards the sufferings of its persecuted children in Hungary and Romania, and it went on:

The Serbian Orthodox Church has always been a national church and had the same interests as the people...The gospel teaches that all true Christians should be permeated with love and devotion towards their government. It was given to us by God, as all governments are; we are in duty bound to be faithful in fulfilling our obligations as citizens, not only from fear, but from conscience as we are taught by the Holy Apostles.[118]

This was a change from its attacks on the prewar government. At the Fourth Congress of the People's Front in March 1953 the Rev. Milan Smiljanić[119] addressed the delegates in the name of 1,800 Orthodox priests both Serbian and Macedonian (the latter in 100 per cent membership of their association):

[115] 9.x.52, quoted in *Vesnik*, 15.x.52.   [116] *Vesnik*, 15.x.52.
[117] Ibid. 1.viii.50: this was part of the government's efforts to rally support within the country and internationalise its opposition to the Soviet bloc after its expulsion from the Cominform.
[118] Ibid.
[119] Smiljanić shortly after became president of the union on the death of the Rev. Vitomir Vidaković, the first president.

You do not ask this of us but we want you to know that we are with you. The church is separated from the state, but we are sons of this country, and citizens of these social communities... The good of the country is our good. We do not look in your platform for the things which divide us, but for the things which unite us, which are much greater.[120]

The union held out over its rules for another year. It decided unanimously on June 26, 1953, that membership of associations should be based on republics.[121] The Sabor again refused to approve the rules of the union.[122] Finally at the end of the year the union gave way and agreed to alter the rules to provide for diocesan associations, without abolishing the republican ones.[123]

But nothing was done to implement this decision, and the muted form of the announcement in *Vesnik* (a brief announcement on an inside page) suggests that there must still have been some doubts or obstacles. The Sabor, meeting in 1954, again failed to recognise the union[124] and *Vesnik* commented editorially that on the one hand the church seemed to be waiting for signs of repentance among 'the chosen representatives of the clergy' while on the other hand no ecclesiastical punishments had been meted out to any of the leaders of the associations. The article concludes with the old grievances of the priests' associations against the hierarchy:

The fact is that the bishops persist in considering the ordinary priest as someone not yet grown up, who must be led by the hand... Our harsh history shows that it is only when he is a completely free man that the priest can be useful to his people and his church; examples from Austrian times show the influence and reputation the priest had when he was chosen by the people and did not fear either the bishops or the emperor himself.[125]

But there were indications that a change was beginning in the triangular relationship between the church, the associations and the authorities. The government was beginning to realise that it would get further by negotiating directly with the bishops, and that a union hostile to the hierarchy might become an embarrassment. In spite of the fact that the Sabor had again refused to recognise the priests' associations and had put off to the following year the request of the Macedonian priests for their own bishops, the Commission for Religious Affairs held a reception for it.[126]

[120] *Vesnik*, 1.iii.53.   [121] Ibid. 15.vii.53.
[122] Ibid.   [123] 20.xii.53: *Vesnik*, 15.iii.54.
[124] *Vesnik*, 27.vii.54, and RNS, 7.vii and 22.vii.54.
[125] *Vesnik*, 27.vii.54.   [126] RNS, 12.x.54, and *Vesnik*, 15.x.54.

There were difficulties also within the union, and the congress planned for October 1954 was postponed.[127] Instead the Administrative Committee called on Dobrivoje Radosavljević, the president of the Commission for Religious Affairs, who addressed them at length about their work. He discussed the taxation of priests and church property, social insurance for priests, the new Law on the Legal Status of Religious Communities and the relations of the clergy with the authorities, all subjects relevant to a professional association of clergy. He urged the clergy to take a more active part in social life and help to prevent excesses by irresponsible people; he admitted irregularities in taxation and asked the union to suggest improvements. He spoke about the role of the associations: 'Some think that the associations will lose their meaning as relations between church and state improve. But this is a mistake, as the associations are not a political body but serve only the clergy, which is why most of them are members.'

This was a signpost to a professional, non-political role for the associations, with no mention even of the reforming mission of the associations within the church. Radosavljević went on: 'It is normal that the association has tried to improve relations between church and state, but it might also try to improve its relations with the hierarchy.'[128]

From this time there began a slow change in the function of the associations; except in the matter of the Macedonian Church, where they acted in the closest cooperation with the government, they functioned increasingly as professional associations, concerned with the social welfare of their members.

The Second Congress of the union finally met in February 1955 and soon after it took Radosavljević's hint and began to set up diocesan associations.[129] The priests' associations were now organised on four levels, the local association or sub-committee, the diocesan association, of which priests were individual members, 'territorial' associations, in which diocesan associations were grouped by republics, and the union of associations which coordinated them all. The local association kept in touch with the local authorities, the diocesan associations worked with the bishop and the territorial associations with the republican

---

[127] RNS, 12.x.54.   [128] Vesnik, 15.x.54.
[129] Ibid. 10.iii and 1.iv.55. The congress was attended by 226 delegates, representing 1,759 out of a total of 2,301 priests (RNS, 23.ii.55). Some of the delegates faced with this change of policy reacted by attacking the bishops vigorously, but the leadership had made up its mind and warned any priests who might be considering voting against the change (ibid.).

authorities. The officers of the union maintained contact with the church leaders and leaders of the government and mass social organisations (i.e. the Red Cross, Socialist Alliance, etc.) The Assembly of the union consisted of delegates elected by the local associations, and it elected the officers of the union. The arrangements, commented *Vesnik*, kept in mind that its members were both priests and citizens.[130] By July, diocesan associations were established in all the dioceses, all with the knowledge and some with the blessing of the bishops. Two bishops attended Assemblies and eight sent representatives; the Socialist Alliance showed great interest in the new development.[131]

There were other indications that the leaders of the union were beginning to act more independently. A long article, 'unintentional conflicts with the Law', appeared in *Vesnik*[132] just before the Administrative Committee of the union met Radosavljević in October 1954; it described some of the injustices which priests suffered at the hands of the local authorities, the prosecutions for petty infringements of the law, the illegal expropriations of their houses, excessive taxation etc.; decentralisation, they pointed out, did not mean that local authorities could act against the laws passed by the government. *Vesnik* also published a glowing tribute to Bishop Irinej of Dalmatia by Dr Glumac of the theological faculty, three years after his death.[133] a remarkable departure from its former faithful echoing of the government's attitude to the Orthodox bishops abroad.

The Macedonian dioceses II

The struggle over the Macedonian Church became increasingly linked with the conflict over the priests' associations, as the latter were enlisted in the government's campaign to force the new patriarch to settle the question. The union had in any case supported the agitation of the Macedonian clergy for an independent Macedonian Church from its foundation (although there are hints that the national feelings of some of the Serbian priests made it hard for them to accept this, and a group of delegates to the congress of the union of associations in February 1955 applauded a priest who opposed the election of bishops on national grounds – it was immaterial whether

---

[130] *Vesnik*, 1.iv.55.
[131] Ibid. 20.vii.55. Some of the organisations no doubt existed largely on paper but there is evidence today to show that many diocesan associations are very much alive and perform useful functions (Orthodox sources).
[132] *Vesnik*, 1.x.54.   [133] Ibid. 15.iv.55.

they were Serbs or Macedonians, they should be good Yugoslavs).[134]

Pressures on the new patriarch to settle the Macedonian church question began at once, and he on his side made one statement after another announcing that the question was about to be resolved. In an interview immediately after his election[135] and again in December 1951[136] he repeated that the church was anxious to settle the question. Relations between the patriarchy and the Macedonian dioceses, he said, had never been totally severed: pensions and other claims on the church's central funds were still being paid, there were Macedonian students at the seminaries and the theological faculty, and representatives of the Macedonian clergy had taken part in the election of the patriarch. (This was a reference to the fact that the president of the Union of Associations of Orthodox Priests had been one of the electors.)

Representatives of the Macedonian Organising Committee called on the Synod on November 6, 1951.[137] According to Vikentije they made a favourable impression[138] and the Synod promised to refer the matter to the Sabor, with whom the final decision lay. The delegation recognised the jurisdiction of the Serbian Orthodox Church over the church in Macedonia 'insofar as it respects the national sovereignty of the Macedonian people'. They asked that the administrative language of the church in Macedonia should be Macedonian, while the liturgical language would continue to be Old Church Slavonic, and they asked for Macedonian bishops.[139]

This was a considerable change from the aggressive language and the behaviour of earlier years. The fact that they acknowledged the jurisdiction of the Serbian patriarchy was vital, and the other demands were not unreasonable and could be negotiated. In the end, this turned out to be a change of tactics and not of aims; there were always individuals among the leaders of the Macedonian priests who were determined to get complete independence. And on their side, Vikentije and the Synod played for time and procrastinated.

As they left, the delegation asked the Synod to allow Vicar-

---

[134] RNS, 24.ii.55.
[135] See above, p. 196.
[136] *Vesnik*, 1.xii.51.
[137] Ibid. 1.i.52.
[138] Ibid. 1.xii.51: interview with Tanjug.
[139] According to *Vesnik*, which on this occasion was certainly speaking for the Macedonian clergy, they did not want a presbyterian church; during the seven years when they had been virtually cut off from the hierarchy and clergy in other dioceses they had continued to nurture the Orthodox faith and to press the patriarch to give them bishops.

Bishop Dositej to visit them. Dositej Stojković had been consecrated in June 1951. He could, and later did, claim Macedonian nationality, since, although he was born in 1906 at Smederevo, not far from Belgrade, his parents were migrant Macedonian workers whose home was at Mavrovo.[140] He was educated at the seminary in Sremski Karlovci, and in 1924 took monastic vows at Kičevo in Macedonia and spent the next eight years at Hilandar, the Serbian monastery on Mt Athos. After his consecration he lived in the patriarchate, where he was known for his ascetic life and his charity.[141]

His visit to Macedonia turned into a triumphal progress. He arrived at Skopje on December 5, 1951, and at once celebrated the bishop's liturgy and preached in Macedonian. The Macedonian Commission for Religious Affairs put cars at the disposal of the party, and they drove the same afternoon to Bitola where he was received by all the clergy and large crowds of the faithful and again celebrated the liturgy; afterwards he distributed *nafora*, the blessed bread, for nearly two hours. It was Dositej's *krsna slava*, the anniversary of the family patron saint which is characteristic of Serbian and Macedonian Orthodoxy, and the traditional *žito* (wheatmeal cakes) and candles had been prepared for him. The following day he drove on to Ohrid where he was met with ringing church bells and crowds with their hands full of flowers and celebrated the liturgy.[142].

The Macedonians are a fervently religious people and they had been deprived of bishops for over ten years, during and after the war; moreover the authorities smiled on the celebrations and helped instead of putting obstacles in their way. The result was an outburst of national and religious enthusiasm which the leaders of the union hoped would be decisive: 'We who were with Bishop Dositej can only thank God for putting Patriarch Vikentije at the helm of the church, who has with his wisdom and goodness solved this painful Macedonian question. To be deaf to all this would be a sin towards the church.'[143] But the rejoicing was premature and the excitement died down; in the end nothing was changed.

[140] *Vesnik*, 1.ix.59.
[142] *Vesnik*, 1.i.52.
[141] Serbian Orthodox source.
[143] Ibid.

7

The constitution and the laws[1]

The constitutional and legal provisions concerning the position of the religious communities and the practice of religion by individuals apply equally to all believers, and therefore it seems appropriate to break off the narrative at this point to consider these provisions and their implementation as they affected both the Roman Catholic and the Orthodox Churches. We have reached a point where the material which follows can be seen in its context, and where it can help to throw light on the second part of this study.

The constitutional position

Under the constitutions of 1921 and 1931 there was no state church in Yugoslavia, but there was no separation of church and state. Religious confessions had a special status, and not all were treated equally.

Religious confessions which had been legally recognised before the creation of Yugoslavia were described as 'accepted', those which were recognised after 1931 were described as 'recognised', and there were a number of small religious communities which were never 'recognised' and in consequence suffered some discrimination.

The major churches performed certain functions for the state; they kept registers of birth, marriages and death, and had jurisdiction over matrimonial disputes. There was, for example, no civil marriage anywhere in Yugoslavia after 1921 except in the Vojvodina, where it had previously existed. The churches also maintained some primary and secondary schools. Freedom of conscience was guaranteed but religious education in schools was compulsory.

[1] The following definitions will be useful:
    Jutro (pl. *jutra*), usually translated 'acre': roughly 10,000 square metres. By origin it means the amount of land a man can plough in a morning.
    Kj: cadastral *jutro*.
    Hectare: 2.471 acres.

The basis for the future constitutional and legal provisions concerning the position of religion and the churches in Yugoslavia was laid down during the war, first by the Supreme Staff of the People's Liberation Army in Foča in February 1942 in the directive on the Organisation and Tasks of the People's Liberation Committee (The Foča documents),[2] secondly at the first session of AVNOJ at Bihać in 1942 and thirdly at the second session of AVNOJ at Jajce on November 27, 1945.

The Foča documents declared that all citizens were equal regardless of political, national or religious differences, and established the principle of the separation of the churches from the state. The first session of AVNOJ set up a department for religion attached to the Executive Committee elected at this meeting. It was concerned with religious matters in the Partisan units and among the population of the liberated and unoccupied parts of Yugoslavia.[3] The arrangement by which religious affairs were under the direct control of the Executive Committee of the federal and republican governments has continued to this day; there has never been a separate ministry for religious affairs.

The statutes of AVNOJ promulgated at Jajce enlarged the Foča declaration and made it more precise:

Art. 1   gave equal rights to all citizens without regard to nationality.
Art. 10   guaranteed freedom of religious belief and conscience.
Art. 11   guaranted freedom of speech, of the press, of association and assembly 'in the framework of the NOB' Narodno-Oslobodilačka Borba (National Liberation Struggle) to all except those who had served the enemies of the people.[4]

These basic rights were included in the declarations of the Regional Anti-fascist Councils, set up in the various regions of the country, as they were liberated.

The first constitution of the new Yugoslav state was promulgated in 1946. It contained the following provisions relating to religion:

Art. 25. a   Freedom of conscience and freedom of religious belief is guaranteed.
        b   The separation of the churches from the state is decreed.
        c   Religious communities whose teaching is not against the constitution are free in their religious affairs and to perform religious rites. They may establish religious schools to train their clergy, under the general supervision of the state.

---

[2] Leon Geršković, *Dokumenti o razvoju narodne vlasti.* [Documents on the Development of the People's Authority] (Belgrade, 1948), p. 31, quoted in *RIY*, p. 51.
[3] *RIY*, p. 51.   [4] *PDZA*, p. 242.

Art. 21

d It is forbidden to misuse the church and religion for political ends, or to establish political organisations on a basis of religion.

e The state may, at its discretion, give material assistance to religious communities.

All citizens are equal in rights and duties regardless of differences in nationality, race, religion, language, education or social position. It is unconstitutional to give special privileges or to restrict the rights of any citizen on the basis of nationality, race or religion, and to preach national, racial or religious hatred and intolerance.

Art. 23 All citizens without regard to sex, nationality, race, religious faith or degree of education and place of residence over the age of eighteen have the right to vote and to be elected to office in any organ of state power, including citizens in the army except for those who have been deprived of civil rights by the courts and those who have lost their civil rights on the basis of federal laws.

Art. 26 Marriage and the family are now under the protection of the state and are regulated by law. Only civil marriage has legal validity but a religious ceremony may take place after a civil marriage.

Art. 27 Freedom of the press, of speech, of association, of public assembly are guaranteed.[5]

The fact that so many judgments handed down by the courts carried not only prison sentences but a subsequent deprivation of civil rights for a further period of years meant that many priests and believers were effectively disfranchised and suffered various other civil disabilities.

A new constitution was promulgated in 1963; its provisions were generally similar to those of the 1946 constitution: clause 25 which decreed the separation of church and state was reworded; it now reads: 'Religious communities are separated from the state and are free in the performance of religious affairs and religious rites' (Art. 46). The activities of religious communities are more specifically defined, and in some respects restricted. The term 'religious affairs' (*verski poslovi*) has not yet been officially defined, and the interpretation placed on it varies in different parts of the country, and at different times. The 1963 constitution also declared explicitly that religious communities have the right to own real estate (Art. 46), a right which had always been implicit, since maximum holdings were laid down in the Law on Agrarian Reform.[6]

[5] *Ustav FNRJ: Zbirka Zakona* [*Constitution of the SFRY: Collection of Laws*] 22: *Služ. List*, 1949.

[6] *Constitution of the Socialist Federal Republic of Yugoslavia*, Federal Secretariat for Information, 1963. The 1974 constitution, Art. 174, continues these provisions. The new republican laws to implement Art. 174 have appeared in draft form

The Law on Agrarian Reform

One of the first acts of the new government after it had established its rule over the whole country was to pass the Law on Agrarian Reform and Colonisation.[7] It was designed to change the whole basis of land ownership, and was not aimed specifically at the churches; but it did in fact complete the land reform begun after the First World War which had left the possessions of the churches largely untouched. The following provisions principally affected the churches:

Art. 1   ...the law is based on the principle that the land belongs to him who cultivates it.

Art. 2   The land shall be distributed immediately and registered in the name of the new owner.

Art. 3   In order to create the necessary land fund the following are to be expropriated:

large holdings of over 45 hectares, or 25–35 best agricultural land if worked by tenants,

land held by banks, enterprises etc., except those portions intended by the owners for industrial, building, scientific, cultural and other socially useful purposes,

land held by churches, monasteries, church institutions and charitable foundations (either secular or religious),

any land over the maximum, held by farmers (*zemljoradnik*),

holdings over 3–5 hectares not worked by the owners as their main occupation, or their families, but by hired labour,

any land which became ownerless during the war or for which there is no legal succession.

Art. 4   Expropriated land becomes the property of the state with all buildings, livestock etc., with no compensation.

Tractors and farm machinery shall be given to the state machine tractor station.

Art 5   Holdings left in private hands shall be not less than 20 or more than 35 hectares, depending on local conditions, and are to be worked by one family. Local authorities shall have power to increase the maximum in the case of mountainous or very bad land.

Art. 8   Land over 10 hectares shall be expropriated from churches and monasteries etc. Churches of major importance and major historical worth may retain 30

and been discussed in the press, but have not yet been passed as this volume goes to press.

[7] *Služ. List*, no. 64, 27.v.45; see also pamphlet *Zakon o agrarnoj reformi i Kolonizaciji* [Law on Agrarian Reform and Colonisation] including a speech by Moše Pijade (Belgrade, 1945).

hectares of agricultural land and 30 hectares of woodlands.[8]

Art. 10 The following lands also go to the general land fund:

a land belonging to citizens of the German Reich and persons of German nationality confiscated by the decision of Sept. 21, 1944,

b land belonging to enemies of the people,

c land expropriated for the purpose of distribution to poor peasants.

It was left to the state to determine which religious establishments were 'major' or of 'historic importance'; many Serbian monasteries and churches were included, in particular the famous medieval frescoed churches, but few Catholic ones.

The law also provides that all church property within a parish belongs to the parish, which is a legal person. Thus various different kinds of church property, endowments, prebends and benefices (*nadarbina*) were included in one overall category.

Under this law 173,367 hectares of land belonging to religious communities, representing 85 per cent of their holdings[9] was expropriated,[10] of which about 70,000 hectares belonged to the Serbian Orthodox Church.[11] It has not been possible to obtain an overall figure for the Catholic Church, but assuming that the holdings of the Moslem religious community were not large, the bulk of the remainder, between 90,000 and 100,000 hectares, belonged to the Catholic Church.

The law was operated by the Agrarian Council of the provisional government of Yugoslavia, which coordinated the work of the republican ministries for agriculture and forestry.[12] Local commissions of poor and middle peasants were set up to discuss the distribution of expropriated land, and to hear appeals, 'so that the work of the Agrarian Council should be ultimately controlled by the revolutionary will of the people'.[13]

The pressing need at this time was for food production, and

---

[8] The original proposal had been 5 hectares for each parish or monastery and 20 hectares of arable and 20 of woodland for religious institutions of special historical or cultural importance; both the Catholic and the Orthodox Churches protested vigorously (Pattee, doc. LXVIII, p. 456; Gl., 1.v.46; Petranović, p. 287) and the provision was altered.

[9] Petranović, p. 291.

[10] See Appendix II, table 6.

[11] SPC, p. 243.

[12] Petranović, p. 293. The law was confirmed by the new parliament which met in November 1945 and established the Federal People's Republic of Yugoslavia (Auty, Yugoslavia, p. 107).

[13] Petranović, p. 293, quoting speech by Krsto Popivoda at the Fifth Congress.

a system of compulsory deliveries of agricultural produce was set up. Church lands could either be worked by the parish authorities (*župni ured*) or leased out or worked by sharecroppers (*napolice*). Directive 1522 (cl. 4) of the ministry of state supply of Croatia of August 13, 1949, sent out to all district People's Committees, laid down that church and monastery lands were not liable to compulsory deliveries unless the lands were entirely or partly leased out or share-cropped.[14]

The application of the regulations varied from region to region, and within the regions themselves, and it is impossible to give a detailed account of the way in which the law was applied within the scope of this study. Following are some examples taken from the Croatian and Slovenian dioceses.

Some parishes were more successful than others in their appeals to the commissions of peasants and to the district committees. The archbishopric of Zagreb pointed this out to the parish offices in a circular[15] and gave several examples: the parish of Mahićno had been exempted from compulsory deliveries of cereals, meat and milk by the district People's Committee at Karlovac (no. 9407, 4.v.50); the parish at Sisak had been exempted from compulsory deliveries of meat and milk by decree of the town People's Committee of Sisak (no. 3665, 6.vi.1950) and at Granešina a decree of the district Executive Committee of Zagreb (no. 2761, 9.iii.1950) exempted the parish from deliveries of cereals, but required deliveries of meat and milk.

The Commission for Religious Affairs of Croatia informed the regional ecclesiastical authorities (*duhovna oblast*) on September 24, 1950, that the ministry for state supply had issued a further decree in an attempt to introduce some uniformity into the practices adopted by local commissions.[16] The new decree stated again that the regulations did not require compulsory deliveries from church lands worked by the church itself, but that in the case of economically better-off church lands which produced a surplus which could be marketed, compulsory deliveries, with the prior consent of the regional People's Committees, might be required. Church lands, however, which were leased out or share-cropped were liable to compulsory deliveries in the same way as privately owned land.

It was often impossible for the priest or the parish office to cultivate the legal maximum of land; in many instances a part or a whole was either given to the commune or leased to an

[14] Circular 3690, 18.viii.50, archbishopric of Zagreb, quoting the directive.
[15] Ibid.
[16] Circular 5713, 7.xii.1950, archbishopric of Zagreb.

agricultural cooperative; in other cases the land was simply abandoned.[17] The Catholic Church authorities saw the danger in this piecemeal paring away of church lands and suggested other alternatives. They reminded the clergy who had asked permission to dispose of church lands that local People's Committees had the duty to help owners who were unable to work the land themselves, and gave them directions for applying to them.[18] But the disposal of land must have continued; in 1955 a circular forbade priests to alienate church lands without the consent of the archbishopric under threat of suspension.[19]

The dioceses of Zagreb[20] and Djakovo were great landowners, but many parishes on the Dalmatian coast and its hinterland, in Hercegovina and in the mountainous regions of Slovenia and Istria owned less than 10 hectares of land at the time of the reform; in these regions there were also many peasants with minimal holdings or no land at all. The churches were thus often left with less than the legal maximum and the available land distributed to landless peasants.

In some parishes (particularly around Karlovac in Croatia) the local commission demanded that the churches should receive less than 10 hectares;[21] the commissions in some Slovene parishes decided that 3 hectares was sufficient (Mirno, Peča, Gorišnica, Moskanci, Ljutomer, St Peter and Novo Mesto);[22] no land was expropriated in 533 Slovene parishes which all owned less than the legal maximum.[23] Peasants in Veleševac where the priest wished to share-crop the church land demanded that it should instead be distributed among the landless peasants.[24] The poverty and land-hunger around Varaždin were particularly severe: there were 15,000 landless peasants and a further 10,000 who owned less than a *jutro* while the church had 10,000 kj.[25]

The churches lodged many complaints about the application of the law; in Croatia alone 343 complaints relating to 48 per cent of church property had been lodged up to November 1946; of

---

[17] Memorandum to the writer from a Catholic legal source.
[18] Circular 2347/1950, 28.iv.50: *SVNZ*, no. 3, 1950.
[19] Circular no. 1, *SVNZ*, no. 2, 1955.
[20] According to Petranović (p. 286) direct Vatican pressure had ensured that the entire church estate of 8,012 kj of arable land, instead of the proposed 2,791 kj, remained in the possession of the archdiocese of Zagreb (together with 10,037 kj of woods) after the first land reform. This decision, taken in 1923, reversed an earlier one.
[21] *Vjesnik*, 6.i.46, quoted by Petranović, p. 293.
[22] *Slobodni Dom*, 4/1946, quoted by Petranović, p. 293.
[23] Petranović, p. 295.
[24] Petranović, p. 293.
[25] *Slobodni Dom*, 4/1946, quoted by Petranović, p. 293.

these 150 were allowed wholly or in part.[26] In Croatia 43 appeals to be considered as establishments of historic importance were received and 3 allowed, of which the diocese of Djakovo received 2, the first for the bishopric itself, because of the national and cultural work of Bishop Strossmayer, and the second for the cathedral at Djakovo as a cultural monument; the third went to the monastery of the Franciscan Third Order at Glavotok for its cultural work, especially its support for the use of *glagolica*.[27] In Slovenia the bishoprics of Ljubljana and Maribor were allowed the maximum holdings[28] but the claim of the bigger and more important archibishopric of Zagreb was disallowed.

The Serbian Orthodox Church was faced with a particularly difficult problem, as all its land holdings were registered in the name of the Serbian Orthodox Church, and not of particular parishes, dioceses or monasteries. A delegation from the patriarch's Administrative Committee called several times on the president of the Commission for Agrarian Reform and Colonisation and finally wrote a letter listing the various ways which, in their opinion, the law was being misapplied:[29]

a According to the constitution of the Serbian Orthodox Church a parish is a legal person (Art. 5) and it is also a church authority (Art. 19). The wording of Art. 8, cl. 2, of the law expressly states that church authorities are to receive the legal minimum, whereas local authorities are granting land only to the parish church.[30]

b Individual charitable foundations had not been allowed to keep any land at all; but according to the constitution of the church these foundations are legal persons and under Art. 8 of the law they should be allowed the legal minimum.

c The patriarch's Administrative Committee had been informed that religious institutions and church authorities would only be allowed to keep land which had been registered in their own names (no. 21737, 15.xii.45).[31] In a further letter (no. 1019, 11.ii.46) the ministry informed the patriarch's Administrative Committee that it would allow 15 hectares of arable land and 15

---

[26] Petranović, p. 294, quoting Archiv FNRJ ministry of agriculture, fasc. 601: yearly report on Agrarian Reform Law by the ministry of agriculture and forestry of the People's Republic of Croatia, 12.ix.1945–7.

[27] Petranović, p. 295. The glagolitic alphabet is the Western form of the Old Church Slavonic alphabet; *glagolica* is the term generally used for the Roman Catholic liturgy in Old Church Slavonic. The Slav clergy, particularly in Istria and Dalmatia, fought for the right to use this liturgy, as part of their efforts to withstand the Latinising pressure of the Italians; the communists approved of this as a manifestation of national feeling.

[28] Petranović, p. 295.

[29] No. 1748, 14.iii.46: *Gl.*, 1.vi.46.

[30] The Serbian Orthodox Church rather confusingly always refers to the legal maximum of 10 hectares as the 'legal minimum'.

[31] *Gl.*, 1.vi.46.

hectares of forest to each metropolitanate, and 10 hectares each to bishoprics, on condition that the land was registered in their names. The patriarch's Administrative Committee had answered that the Serbian Orthodox Church was a 'united legal person' and all lands owned by it were registered in the name of the Serbian Orthodox Church and not in the name of individual metropolitanates or bishoprics; the text of the law, in any case, made no stipulation about the registration of the land.

d The land on which a church or monastery stood, the churchyard and the approach to the church should not be included in the legal minimum of land left to religious institutions, but only land which could be worked, such as pastures, vineyards, orchards, and gardens. The law also stated that the proportion of buildings left to the monastery should be in proportion to the land left to it, and that buildings such as monks' dwellings etc. should not be used in calculating this, but only buildings used in connection with the working of the land. Some state organs were ignoring both these provisions.

e Some churches and monasteries had complained to the patriarchate that all their good land was being expropriated and they were being left with the worst; churches should be allowed to choose 50 per cent of the land apportioned to them.

f Mills on mill-streams should not be confiscated since they were a form of industry, not workable land.

In its answer (no. 16795, 16.iv.46) the ministry of agriculture and forestry of Serbia ignored the arguments about land registration; concerning the other points raised it answered:

a Art. 3, cl. 3, of the law provides that a proportion of the church buildings should be left to the church, but it does not stipulate that this refers only to buildings used in connection with working the land; the only buildings specifically excluded are those used exclusively for religious ceremonies.

b The right to choose 50 per cent of the land to be retained is given only to those institutions specified in Art. 3, cls. 5 and 6; these do not include monasteries, churches and other religious institutions. Local authorities, however, have been told to apportion to the churches, as far as possible, land lying in the vicinity of the church or monastery.

c Water mills are not to be regarded as industrial property, but form a part of the land they stand on; the water-mills will be apportioned with the land.

The Laws on Nationalisation and Expropriation

The new government looked upon nationalisation as 'a revolutionary economic act of the socialist state whereby the essential structure of the economy is changed through the abolition of private ownership of the most important means of production and the establishment of the title of state socialist ownership thereto'.[32]

The Law on the Nationalisation of Private Economic Enterprises was passed on December 6, 1946,[33] and applied to privately owned enterprises in forty-two different branches of the economy. It stipulated that compensation should not be paid for property serving social, charitable, cultural and similar purposes. This meant in effect that the churches would receive no compensation. They had enterprises in several of the industries designated, among them the graphic and printing industries, the insurance association for church property and the exploitation of spas and medicinal springs. Both the Catholic and the Serbian Orthodox Churches were severely affected by the expropriation, without compensation, of their printing presses; aside from the financial consequences it put the religious press at the mercy of presses controlled by the authorities. During the early years the printing of the few remaining religious journals was sometimes held up by protests of workers over the contents of journals. *Blagovest*, the Catholic monthly, and *Glasnik*, the official journal of the Serbian Orthodox Church, were both affected in this way.[34]

The law was amended in 1948[35] to include most of what remained in the private economic sector; all sanatoria, hospitals, public baths, spas and health resorts, together with all medical buildings and installations (Art. 2(a), cl. 8) and all printing lithographic and offset printing presses (Art. 2(a), cl. 9) were nationalised.

The Basic Law on Expropriation was enacted in 1947, amended in 1953,[36] and revised and considerably expanded in 1957.[37] It concerns the manner and extent to which real estate may be expropriated in the public interest, and fixes the amount of compensation payable. Church property is not excluded from compensation. The only specific reference to church property is in Article 56 of the 1957 revision, which provides that if church land, or a site previously occupied by a church which had been destroyed in the war, is expropriated, and no other building for public worship belonging to the same religious community exists in the same place, the beneficiary of the expropriation should be obliged to provide an equivalent suitable plot of land.

[32] *Collection of Yugoslav Laws*, vol. III, p. 3.
[33] *Služ. List*, no. 98, 1946: ibid, pp. 13, 3.
[34] *Blagovest* did not appear Jan.–July 1949, Oct. 1949–May 1950 and May 1953–Jan. 1954. *Glasnik* did not appear March–June 1951.
[35] *Služ. List*, no. 35, 1948: *Collection of Yugoslav Laws*, vol. III, pp. 4, 13.
[36] *Collection of Yugoslav Laws*, vol. III, p. 5.
[37] *Služ. List*, no. 12, 1957: ibid. p. 23.

The process of nationalisation was completed in 1958 with the Law on the Nationalisation of Dwelling Houses and Building Lots;[38] by this time social self-management had been introduced in Yugoslavia and 'the existence of private ownership of apartment houses and building land tended to obstruct the further promotion of socialist relations'.[39]

Art. 3 stipulated that legal persons etc. could own only business premises and buildings which served their own authorised activity;

Art. 11 specifically exempted from the provisions of the law buildings and premises 'serving the religious communities for their religious activities' (including seminaries and theological schools), as well as buildings and residences for the bishops and clergy;

Art 74 allowed the churches to retain or regain ownership of buildings which had previously served as residences for bishops and clergy, if at the time of the coming into force of the law they did not serve for health, social–educational, cultural and other activities, and to restore them to their previous use. Compensation for expropriated buildings would, in general, be paid in instalments over fifty years, or compensation might be given in kind.

Both the Catholic and the Serbian Orthodox Churches had real estate holdings in apartment buildings, the income from which was considerably larger than the small instalments of compensation. The Serbian Orthodox Church estimated that 1,180 buildings, worth 8,000m dinars, belonging to it were nationalised.[40]

The Criminal Code

Several provisions of the Criminal Code (1951)[41] affected religious communities either specifically (Art. 311) or in common with others (Art. 119).

Art. 119 forbids anyone to incite or exacerbate national, racial or religious hatred between peoples and nationalities in Yugoslavia; whoever commits the offence systematically or takes advantage of his special position to commit the offence, or if disorder and violence result from the offence, is liable to twelve years' close confinement;

Art. 311 forbids the misuse of freedom of worship and the carrying out of religious functions by the clergy for anti-constitutional purposes.

Article 119 deals with actions which strike at the unity of Yugoslavia by inciting fratricidal conflict, which is held to be among the gravest crimes a citizen can commit. This is referred to also in the constitution and the pre-constitutional declarations,

---

[38] *Služ. List*, no. 52, 1958: ibid. p. 60.
[39] *Collection of Yugoslav Laws*, vol. III, p. 7.
[40] *SPC*, p. 243; it is not clear from the text whether this represents old or new dinars, or when the valuation was made.   [41] *LSRCY*, p. 32.

and in the Law on the Legal Status of Religious communities. The two articles taken either separately or together covered a wide field, and many priests went to prison under their provisions. Not only the clergy but anyone offending against national or racial unity was severely punished; but it was rare for persons insulting priests or believers, or disturbing religious ceremonies, to receive more than the lightest punishment.[42] Examples of this have been seen in chapters 2, 4, 5 and 6.

Art. 313 provides that anyone preventing or obstructing the performance of religious rites will be punished by a fine or imprisonment for one year.

It is difficult to find any instance of punishment for the contravention of this clause, although the authorities sometimes intervened to stop interference with religious observance when the clergy complained.

The laws concerning the secrecy of the confessional were successively liberalised. Under the Code of Criminal Procedure of October 12, 1948, Article 165, priests and doctors were not among those relieved of the obligation to give evidence in criminal cases concerning matters learnt in the course of their professional duties or confessed in secret. This article was amended in 1951 as follows:

Cl. 4 Religious confessors concerning that which has been confessed in secret.
(2) The refusal must be given in before the examination and will be noted in the record.
(4) This relief does not apply when it is a question of criminal acts against the people and state.[43]

The archbishopric of Zagreb, in the same circular in which these amended provisions were communicated to the clergy, warns priests that nothing can relieve them of their obligation to observe the complete secrecy of the confessional.

On September 16, 1953, a revised Code of Criminal Procedures was issued; Article 221 (the former Art. 165) relieved priests entirely of the obligation to give evidence in criminal cases concerning matters confessed to them in secret.

In practice, no pressure was brought on priests to violate the

---

[42] 'It must be admitted that the authorities sometimes reacted incorrectly to the misuse of religion for political purposes, giving a handle to people who asserted that churches in Yugoslavia had no legal rights and were subject to arbitrary action of individual authorities' (*Review of International Affairs*, 1.iii.53, article on 1953 law).

[43] *SVNZ*, no. 126, 1951: circular concerning the new criminal laws, 25.vi.51.

secrecy of the confessional;[44] although there may have been isolated exceptions, there was general agreement on this point among all the persons consulted by the writer. However, there were occasional press reports of accusations brought against priests for advice given in the confessional which suggests either that *agents provocateurs* were used or pressures brought on individual believers to accuse priests.[45] Archbishop Stepinac warned his clergy not to let a single word about politics cross their lips either from the pulpit or in the confessional.[46]

Art. 312 provided that a priest who performed a marriage service before the civil marriage had taken place should be punished by a fine or a sentence of one year. However, a regulation of October 16, 1951, provided that in cases of emergency, baptism or funeral services might be performed before official registration if they were registered within forty-eight hours.[47]

The Basic Law on the Legal Status of Religious Communities

Early in 1953 the Basic Law on the Legal Status of Religious Communities was introduced; a draft was published in February[48] and individual religious communities were asked to make their comments and suggestions.

In accordance with its policy of refusing any overt official cooperation with the government while Archbishop Stepinac was in prison, the Catholic Church refused to make any comment or suggestions[49] but a number of unofficial comments were made.

The Serbian Orthodox Church, through the Synod, made a number of detailed suggestions to clarify and define the law more precisely.

Our presumption is that the purpose of the law is to create religious harmony in the country and remove all reasons for conflict between church and state. This is best done if all relations between them are precisely and exactly defined...in a word the law must be clear and it must regulate all these questions which up to now have led to misunderstandings in the relations between church and state.[50]

A number of its suggestions were adopted and some articles were

[44] Several Catholic sources.
[45] A woman reported that she had been questioned about her civil marriage and her husband's party membership; the priest had offered to perform a secret marriage (*Sl. Por.*, 21.ii.51).
[46] See above, p. 75.
[47] *Collection of Yugoslav Laws*, vol. XI, p. 141; *SVNZ*, circular 200, 1951.
[48] *Borba*, 12.ii.53.
[49] This also was immediately after the rupture of diplomatic relations with the Vatican.
[50] Sin. 473/35, 18.ii.53: *Gl.*, Feb.–March 1953.

reworded, but a request that men on military service should have
the same religious rights as other citizens was refused[51] and a
provision that priests should be allowed to visit persons in prison,
which appeared in the draft law (Art. 21), was removed before
the law was passed.

The law, as it was finally passed on May 22, 1953, coming into
force on June 4,

guarantees freedom of conscience and faith; makes religious worship
    a private concern; gives citizens the right to belong to any or no
    religious community;
gives citizens the right to found religious communities and gives
    equality to all religious communities;
allows the religious communities to publish and distribute religious
    printed matter in the context of the general laws on the press;
separates schools from the church and allows religious instruction in
    churches and other designated places; it also allows religious com-
    munities to found religious schools for the education of the clergy;
prohibits the abuse of religious functions etc. for political ends and the
    incitement to religious intolerance etc; it also prohibits the hindering
    of religious gatherings, instruction, rites etc. and prohibits anyone
    from being either forced to or prevented from exercising his
    religious freedom in any way;
protects the rights of citizens from being infringed because of their
    religious convictions or activities; but no religious community or
    believer may enjoy special privileges or protection, or be exempt from
    the general civil or military duties of citizens;
states that religious communities are legal persons; allows the clergy to
    found clerical associations;
states that the decisions of religious communities in civil matters
    (marriages, disputes etc.) shall only be operative within the
    community;
gives the government (later altered to social–political communities) the
    possibility (but not the obligation) to give material assistance to
    religious communities, who may dispose of the aid themselves unless
    it is granted for a specific purpose;
prohibits anyone from either forcing or preventing the giving of alms
    for religious purposes; and allows alms to be collected in churches and
    other specified places: the permission of the communal authorities
    must be sought for collections anywhere else; allows the clergy to
    accept payment for the performance of religious rites whether these
    are performed in churches, the homes of the faithful or other
    customary places.
allows the performance of religious rites in churches etc. and in

---

[51] The conviction that if a man was a believer and a member of a religious
community this automatically implied that his loyalty to the state was doubtful,
was firmly rooted in the minds of all secularists, not only the communists. It
is a conviction which is gradually weakening, and has been questioned by a
number of Marxist socialists (Frid, Ćimić, Roter), but it is by no means dead
today.

churchyards, cemeteries etc. but requires the permission of the communal authorities for religious rites, processions, litanies etc. outside these designated places, except for family celebrations (weddings etc.);

allows baptism and circumcision at the demand of one parent or guardian; the consent of a child over ten years old is also required;

allows a religious marriage ceremony only after civil marriage and baptism only after civil registration;

allows persons in hospitals, homes for old people, boarding institutions etc. freedom to worship and be visited by a priest;

allows religious communities to organise the teaching in religious schools themselves, subject only to general supervision; forbids pupils to attend religious instruction during school hours; requires anyone attending religious instruction to have the consent of both parents and the consent of the child; requires anyone attending a religious school to have completed compulsory primary schooling;

gives students attending religious schools the same rights as those in other schools, the federal Executive Council to decide what these rights are.

Article 21 states that infringement of the law, when it does not amount to a criminal act, is to be punished by a fine of 10,000 dinars or fifteen days' imprisonment; Article 22 states that abuse of religious instruction amounting to a criminal act will be followed, besides the penalties imposed by the law, by closure of the religious school for a period of one to ten years.[52]

Each republic passed its own implementing law, some after considerable delays; Serbia, for instance, did not pass its law until March 2, 1962.[53] It defined more precisely than the federal law the sphere of the religious communities: 'the performance of religious rites, the collection of alms for religious purposes, and religious instruction on the basis of the provisions of the law' (Art. 1). The places where religious rites could be performed were specified in detail in Article 2, including 'places where a church used to stand and where it has long been recognised practice to perform religious rites' (the decision to rest with the local authorities). Alms could be collected in all these places (Art. 6). Priests performing these rites must be Yugoslav citizens; permission from the local authorities must be sought for priests who are foreign citizens (Art. 5). Christenings and circumcisions, family religious celebrations etc. could be carried out freely and without previous notification in the homes of believers (Art. 4). Religious instructions might be given in places of worship and in other premises used by the religious communities (i.e. in parish houses); the permission of both parents in writing was required,

[52] *Služ. List*, 27.v.53.
[53] *Gl.*, May 1962, pp. 178ff.

but the consent of the child might be given orally (Art. 7). Regulations for the registration of religious seminaries with the local authorities were given, and seminaries were required to observe all public holidays, school holidays and Sundays as a day of rest (Art. 11). Infractions of all the regulations were punished by fines of 10,000 dinars or fifteen days' imprisonment.

The accounts of events between 1945 and 1953, and those which followed the passing of the law, given in chapters 2–6 and 8 and 9, give some idea of the extent to which the constitutional guarantees and later the 1953 law were observed. In general it could be said that religious communities and their clergy were severely punished for any infringements of the law, which was strictly interpreted, while infringements of the rights of believers and the religious communities were either ignored or lightly penalised. This situation gradually improved after 1955. The hierarchy encouraged the clergy to stand up for their legal rights and sometimes appeals to higher courts were successful. The offical gazette of the Zagreb archdiocese[54] quoted a case from the gazette of the diocese of Split and Makarska (no. IV, 1957); a priest in Vranice was fined 3,000 dinars for using 'school methods' (i.e. keeping attendance registers and giving marks to children) in religious instruction, and caning children. He appealed and won on the grounds that the first charge was no longer an offence since the passage of the 1953 law, and that, while caning children was a 'physical offence' the parents had not complained and so it was not punishable at law.

One of the harshest provisions of the law was the right, given in Article 22, to close a seminary if any of its staff or students was guilty of infringing the law in any serious degree. It put into jeopardy the training of a whole generation of ordinands. The seminary at Split was closed for eight years and the seminary at Rijeka for five years under this provision.

The provision giving pupils in religious schools the same rights as other students was never implemented in full; students in seminaries and theological faculties do not have the right to defer their military service or to serve a shorter term (the official reason is that the seminaries do not give the premilitary training which is given at secondary schools); they do not have reduced fares on public transport or for holiday travel; until recently they were not covered by social insurance, although now (1972) students in Croatia and Slovenia are insured.

[54] *SVNZ*, no. 4, 1957.

The right to freedom of conscience and belief and of worship has always been conditional for the armed forces and for teachers. For many years men in uniform were forbidden to go to church, but there were variations in practice, depending on the commanding officer, and after the middle 1960s it became steadily easier for men doing their military service to perform their religious duties. There has also been a growing tolerance towards the practice of religion by teachers, especially those in the universities and secondary schools, and those who teach 'non-sensitive' subjects.[55] The practice varies greatly from republic to republic and between town and country.

The Law on the Legal Status of Religious Communities was revised in 1965 to bring it into conformity with the 1963 constitution.[56] The great change in the climate was underlined by the deletion of Article 22, which had provided for the closing of a religious school as a punitive measure. Article 3 of the revised law provided that 'religious communities shall be separated from the state', which had not been stated specifically in 1953. The penal sanctions were altered (Art 21 deleted and Art. 20(a) substituted) to provide for a fine of up to 20,000 dinars or up to thirty days' imprisonment for the following offences:

1 Preventing another person from taking part in worship;
2 infringing the rights of another person because of his religious affilitation or his participation in religious rites;
3 collecting money for religious purposes outside designated places without the approval of the relevant authority;
4 holding litanies, processions etc. in unauthorised places without the permission of the authorities;
5 admitting a student to a religious school before he has finished his compulsory schooling.

Article 20(b) provided for a fine of 10,000 dinars for admitting a child to religious instruction without the consent of both parents.[57]

---

[55] Since the tightening of party control which began in 1972 the right of believers to teach in schools has again been under constant attack.
[56] Služ. List, no. 10/1965: LSRCY, pp. 13ff.
[57] LSRCY, pp. 13ff.

8

The Catholic Church
The change: why and how it took place

This account now returns to the chronological narrative which
broke off at the end of chapter 4 with the rupture of relations
between the Yugoslav government and the Vatican in December
1953 and the breakdown of conversations between the Catholic
bishops and the government in 1953, and anticipated the death
in 1960 of Cardinal Stepinac.

Causes of the change

The ten years or so which followed the rupture of diplomatic
relations were a time of almost invisible changes which could
only have been apparent to the far-sighted. The seeds of these
changes had been present long before, in the determination of
the Partisans, devoted to Stalin though they were, to make their
own revolution in their own way. This determination was to be
put to the severest test by the expulsion of Yugoslavia from the
Cominform, and the mettle of the Communist Party of Yugoslavia was shown by its refusal to comply with the wishes of
Moscow and change its leadership. Instead, with reckless courage
and from a position of great economic weakness, it defied the
colossus and embarked on a lonely course full of dangers. The
two years which followed were a time of severe material
privation and harsh dictatorship which might have set the
further course of the party along the road of closed, totalitarian
rule which its southern neighbour, Albania, later took. But
Yugoslav communism had never been monolithic; it was always
full of currents and stresses, the outcome of the need to hold
together a group of disparate nations with different historical
backgrounds, and this gave it an interior flexibility and a
generally pragmatic cast of mind.

From this fateful event, which transformed the development
of Yugoslav communism and influenced the history of communism all over the world, a number of other events followed
which had an important bearing on the relations between the

government and the religious communities in general, and the Catholic Church in particular.

In 1950 the Law on Workers' Self-Management was passed, setting up elected councils for workers in all enterprises (industries and commercial firms) and public bodies and establishing the framework for the later growth of liberalisation and decentralisation. It also established (as a Catholic theologian pointed out to the writer in 1970) the principle of the central importance of man, whether the architects of the law fully realised it or not.

Stalin died in 1953 and by 1955, under Khrushchev, the pressure from Moscow had lightened. By this time, also, economic and military aid was flowing in from the West, particularly the United States, and there was every incentive to show that the Yugoslav communists were practising what they had always preached about their attitude to religion.

In 1954 the long-drawn-out quarrel over Trieste was finally settled and there was no longer any need to beat the Vatican with that particular stick; as time went on it became clear that the solution was reasonably just and would last.

In September of that year Dr Franjo Šeper was appointed Archbishop Coadjutor of Zagreb.[1] Although Stepinac was the older man they had been students together in Rome, and later, before becoming rector of the theological seminary, Šeper had been secretary to Stepinac when the latter became archbishop coadjutor. He disliked politics and after the war his attitude to the new government had been unprovocative. Although he had been forced to resign the rectorship after the trial in 1950 of teachers and students at the seminary he had not been incriminated. The only serious count against him was the fact that in 1941, as rector of the seminary in Zagreb, he had gone, at the head of all his students, to pay an official visit of welcome to Pavelić. The government considered that he was less compromised by the past than many other leading Catholic figures and was satisfied by the choice. His appointment appeared to indicate that the Vatican accepted that Cardinal Stepinac could no longer function as Archbishop of Zagreb and acknowledged

---

[1] Titular Archbishop of Philippopolis, as Archbishop Coadjutor of Zagreb *sedi datus* with all rights of a residential bishop (but no automatic right of succession to the archbishopric) (*Šematizam*, p. 47). His appointment took the unusual form of coadjutor to the archbishopric, rather than to Archbishop Stepinac personally; this was done to make the appointment as unprovocative as possible (Catholic source). On March 23, 1958, he was appointed apostolic administrator 'ad nutum Sanctae sedis' (with the right of succession) (*Šematizam*, p. 47).

the need to restore visible leadership to the Catholic Church in Yugoslavia.

The decade ended with the deaths of Pius XII (in 1958) and Cardinal Stepinac (in 1960) and the election of Pope John XXIII. The attitude of the Yugoslav government towards the new papacy was at first cautious ('It is naive to expect that the death of one pope and the accession of another will change anything; the Vatican remains essentially the same')[2] but their ears were cocked for signs of a change. The Second Vatican Council, which opened in the autumn of 1962, the document *Gaudium et spes* which it issued, the papal encyclicals *Mater et magistra* and later *Pacem in terris* and *Ecclesiam suam* convinced the Yugoslav government that a profound change was taking place within the Catholic Church, and that, in particular, its views about international peace and the Third World corresponded closely with those of the Yugoslav government. The Vatican and the Yugoslav leaders both began to watch for openings leading towards a *rapprochement*.

These events were the causes; evidences of the change began to appear early.

A brief false dawn was the consecration in Pazin in July 1950 of Dr Dragutin Nežić as Bishop and Apostolic Administrator of Pazin and Poreč–Pula (Istria),[3] the first since the controversial consecrations during the war of Bishop Šimrak of Križevci and Bishop Čule of Mostar.[4] A more general straw in the wind was the abolition in October 1950 of special privileges (special shops, ration cards etc.) for party members, an action which helped to rally the mass of the population behind the party.[5]

The first major indication of a new attitude was given by Alexander Ranković, the vice-president, in 1951, in a speech to the Fourth Plenum of the League of Communists.[6] This speech was an important statement in which for the first time the extent of the excesses and misdeeds which had taken place, especially by the secret police, was admitted and deplored.[7]

---

[2] *Vjesnik*, 2.xii.58.   [3] *Šematizam*, p. 13.
[4] See p. 38, n. 150.   [5] Armstrong, p. 125.
[6] 3–14.vi.51: 'Za dalje jačanje pravosudja i zakonitosti' [Towards the further strengthening of the administration of justice and legality].
[7] Ranković made a sweeping attack on the party, UDBA (the secret police) and the courts. Local authorities and party members, he said, brought pressure on the courts; some judges had been dismissed for refusing to cooperate; the accused tended to be held guilty until he proved his innocence. Many judges, especially in the lower courts, were unqualified; in Bosnia and Hercegovina 110 judges out of 184 lacked sufficient qualifications. Their pay was too low and should be increased. UDBA made far too many arrests; in 1949 47 per

Two years later came Tito's speech at Ruma calling for a halt to physical assaults on the clergy. Other communist leaders followed and Kardelj called on members of the party to enlist the support of Christians of good will in building socialism – they must learn to distinguish between the hostile political activities of some clergy and the religious convictions of many workers.[8] This may have been an attempt to drive a wedge between the clergy and the laity, but it gave promise of a welcome relief for the ordinary practising believer.

How the change took place

The position of the church did not change over night. For several years attacks, pressures and harassment went side by side with a slow general improvement which it is easier to appreciate in retrospect. Relations between the authorities and the churches were wary but quiet, and from the outside very little seemed to be happening.

Priests' associations The government still attached great importance to the priests' associations and continued its efforts to induce priests to join, and to suppress the opposition of the hierarchy; there was now an appropriate organisation for every priest in Yugoslavia who wished to join one.

The Association of Catholic Priests in Croatia had no real roots among the clergy and was unrepresentative; it was entirely a creation of the authorities and in this sense was different from Dobri Pastir (The Good Shepherd), the Catholic priests' association in Bosnia and Hercegovina, Ciril–Metodsko Društvo, the Slovene association, and the Association of Orthodox Priests in Serbia. This, coupled with the opposition of the powerful Croat hierarchy, was successful in keeping the membership of Catholic priests in Croatia lower than any other in Yugoslavia.[9]

cent of all people arrested were released without being brought to trial and 23 per cent of people accused by UDBA were later found guilty of lesser crimes and should have been dealt with by the ordinary police. He attacked party members who thought they had more rights than non-party members and tried to instruct judges. The administration must stop being judges in their own cause; the principle must be established that the courts are not the organs of the party. UDBA was not above the law. By his assertion that methods of interrogation were taking more democratic and more decent forms, he implied that this had not been so in the past. The speech had a far-reaching effect and is an important landmark in the evolution towards the rule of law in Yugoslavia.

[8] RNS, 21.v.54.
[9] In 1962 an official publication gave the number as 190 (*PCY*, p. 115).

The Croatian clergy had in general been well disposed towards the NDH during the war, even when they had not actively supported or collaborated with the Ustaša, and the climate was more unfavourable for a priests' association than anywhere else in Yugoslavia. In Bosnia and Hercegovina, where there had been widespread support for the Ustaša among the clergy, there were special reasons for the early and pronounced success of Dobri Pastir.

The bishops had already pronounced the associations *non licet* (forbidden). The ban was enforced with varying degrees of severity in different dioceses; suspended priests usually found jobs either in the priests' associations or in state-supported learned institutions of various sorts.[10]

Education During this period there was a renewed effort to intensify Marxist teaching in schools; a new subject, moral and social education, was introduced which was to take the place of religious instructions.

In March 1952 Tito had told a delegation of Yugoslav students: 'We are not going to allow young people, under the guise of carrying out religious rites, to be politically corrupted,'[11] and in April, speaking to a delegation of teachers and professors, he said:

We can't allow people to be given over to superstitition...we don't persecute religion, but we can't allow children to develop in their most formative years not as we would wish but according to the wishes of these who are on a quite different path. The state has the right to educate children, and must do so...the struggle for children can only be effective when every teacher, every educator, is deeply conscious of his duty, and if they have absorbed the conceptions which every citizen of this country must have.[12]

The decision was taken by the Third Plenum of the Central Committee in 1952 and implemented by the Council of Science and Culture of the FNRJ, which authorised the introduction of the new subject in the scholastic year 1952-3.[13] Religious instruction, which had been legally permitted in primary schools (though often in practice made impossible) was now abolished in all schools.

Children were to be taught to develop the characteristics of socialist man: determination, self-control, independence, love of the truth, loyalty and devotion to the socialist community which

[10] Verbal information from Association of Catholic Priests in Croatia, 1970.
[11] Tito, *Govori*, vol. VII, pp. 21–2 (15.iii.52).
[12] Ibid. vol. VI, p. 45 (29.iv.52).

was built with the joint efforts of all people. Religious practices were used by primitive people to try to control the forces of nature, and later to maintain the class structure and the slavery of the working class. But now Marxism and science had taught men how to control their environment and reap the profits of their own labour. The intention was quite openly to try to create new atheists.[14]

A spate of books and articles appeared[15] and the argument between those who wanted to attack religious belief directly and those who believed that religion would wither away as socialism developed and would only be strengthened by attacks, appeared at an early stage.[16] The moral difficulties faced by pupils who were taught one thing at school and another at home were also recognised; parents needed education in this subject as much as children. Articles designed for older readers and written at a simple level appeared both in journals and the daily press.[17] The problem was particularly acute in the countryside where the village priest and the village teacher were often the only educated men. There the teacher must be a leader in the fight against religion and be prepared to face a certain amount of social opprobrium; the uncomfortable fact was that only a very small minority of children in a village might *not* be receiving religious instruction outside school.[18] On the other hand M. Kangrga, of the philosophical faculty of the University of Zagreb and later one of the editors of the controversial neo-Marxist journal *Praxis*, was already warning of the danger of identifying Marxism with atheism, the antithesis of religion but also in itself a kind of religious attitude.[19]

The passive years. Archbishop Šeper and Dr Bakarić, the head of the Croatian government, exchanged courtesy calls in December

[13] Quoted in 'Nastava društvenog i moralnog odgoja' [The Teaching of Social and Moral Education], *Prosvjetni Vjesnik* [Educational Herald], no. 4–5, 1952.

[14] Ibid.

[15] E.g. Milos Janković, *Škola i religija* [School and Religion] (Belgrade, 1952), pp. 46–60; Milan Bakovljev, *Vaspitanje i religija* [Education and Religion] (Belgrade, 1952); *Školske Novine* [School News], 6.vi.52.

[16] E.g. review of Bakovljev's book in *Savremena Škola*, 8 (1953), 189–97, accusing Bakovljev of a formal, aggressively anti-religious approach, with no answers to questions which pupils might ask, and *Glas Rada* (organ of the Croatian trade unions), 21.viii.54, concerning the courses at the Workers' University.

[17] E.g. *Kulturni Radnik*, 1950/7, pp. 307–17; *Oslobodjenje* (Sarajevo), 29–30.i.53, articles by Enver Redžić, who frequently dealt with religious questions.

[18] See e.g. *Život i škola* [Life and School] (Osijek), March 1954, p. 3; *Prosvjetni List* (Sarajevo), 1.i.53.

[19] *Naprijed*, 8.ii.1952: M. Kangrga, 'O Religiji' [Concerning Religion].

1954, shortly after Šeper's appointment.[20] It was normal for the head of the Croatian government and the leader of the Catholic Church to be in official contact, but it also accorded with the government's desire for a general relaxation of tensions as part of its policy of peaceful coexistence in the world. Bakarić began to play down the whole issues of the churches. In an interview with foreign journalists he said that the time was not yet ripe for a *modus vivendi* or a restoration of diplomatic relations with the Vatican, which had not yet shown sufficient signs of good will. He brushed aside the priests' associations as having no political significance; their chief importance was that priests by joining took a clear stand against hostile policies.[21] Speaking to communist youth leaders in April, he said that the church had been forced back on the defensive, not because of persecution, but because of the economic and social progress which the country was making. He advised them to concentrate on the further development of a socialist society and stop worrying about church problems; as for himself, it was a long time since he had given the church a thought.[22]

The next few years were relatively quiet. The number of trials began to diminish, sentences became shorter and pressure on the daily life of believers gradually became lighter. The public harassment of bishops and, on the whole, of the lower clergy ceased. It was still dangerous for public employees, particularly teachers in primary and secondary schools, to practise their religion openly[23] but this also was slowly beginning to change. Conditions, as always in Yugoslavia, varied greatly from city to village, from one district to another and between the different republics; all generalisations are riddled with exceptions. This period, however, could be characterised as one in which the principal difficulties with which the church had to deal, aside from its poverty, were the strict oversight of religious observances and religious instruction, heavy and often unpredictable taxation[24] and constant administrative vexations. Priests coming before the courts feared with some reason that the most unfavourable interpretation would be put upon their actions.

The authorities remained particularly sensitive where educa-

---

[20] RNS, 7.xii.54.   [21] Ibid. 10.ii.55.

[22] Ibid. 6.iv.55.

[23] *L'O.R.*, 16.x.55, confirmed by numerous verbal sources.

[24] The subject of taxation is complex and no attempt has been made to deal with it systematically. The archbishopric at Zagreb sent frequent circulars to the clergy to inform them about new laws and regulations, advising them about their rights and offering help and advice about appealing to the courts (e.g. 6588/1946; 5713/1950; *SVNZ*, no. 1, 1960, p. 23).

tion and young people were concerned; a number of examples of this occurred in 1955 and 1956. In May 1955 *Novine Mladih* complained about the number of intelligent boys who were going into seminaries.[25] A young woman teacher in the Vojvodina was expelled from the teachers' association for being married in church.[26] Nikola Rački, secretary of the League of Communists in Rijeka, attacked the revival of Catholic influence among young people, a great many of whom were receiving religious instruction.[27] The League of Communists district conference in Prijedor (Bosnia) complained about the growth of religious influence among all the communities, Catholic, Orthodox and Moslem; the Catholics were forming church choirs and organising spare-time activities for young people.[28] Communists in Djakovo (Slavonia) were reported to be disturbed about the Catholic influence in education, which was traditionally strong because of the continuing influence of the great nineteenth-century Bishop Strossmayer of Djakovo. Many high-school pupils attended classes in religious instruction or sang in church choirs, and several of the teachers had been pupils at seminaries in Zagreb; religious slogans were scribbled on classroom walls and were not erased. Reporting this, *Borba* added that it took the communists two months' struggle to clear up the situation, and it would be some time before the schools returned to normal.[29]

A sprinkling of trials for hostile propaganda continued.[30] The most damaging involved two seminaries which as a result were closed for a number of years. In June 1955 the Rev. Josip Kapš, rector of the seminary at Rijeka, which had been opened in 1947, was accused, together with other members of his staff, of hostile and pro-Ustaša propaganda. Kapš was sentenced to six years' imprisonment and the seminary was closed for five years and the lower seminary for three years.[31] In its report, *Vjesnik u Srijedu*

---

[25] *L'O.R.*, 16.x.55, quoting *Novine Mladih*.

[26] RNS, 20.vii.57, quoting *Drevnik*, a local journal.

[27] RNS, 4.iv.56.   [28] Ibid. 8.v.56, quoting *Borba*.

[29] RNS, 13.iii.56.

[30] The Rev. Franjo Jambreković, s.j., who had been Croatian provincial of the Order before the war, and was at the time teaching at the Jesuit seminary, was sentenced to fifteen months for hostile propaganda (RNS, 21.vi.58). Fra Petar Just in Split was sentenced to twenty months for hostile propaganda and tax evasion (RNS, 11.ii.58) and at Doboj in Bosnia the Rev. Feliks Bilenki received five years, the Rev. Mihajlo Juris three years and the Rev. Gregor Biljak one year for hostile propoaganda and distributing anti-government literature (RNS, 18.xi.57, quoting *Oslobodjenje*). The Rev. Andrija Majić, vicar-general to Bishop Čule of Mostar, was arrested for trying to prevent priests from attending meetings of the priests' associations (RNS, 16.ii.58).

[31] *VUS*, 1.vi.55.

commented unfavourably on the rigid discipline in seminaries; all letters were censored, visits from parents and friends were supervised and the pupils were only allowed into town in pairs. The discipline, said *VUS*, is the business of the directors, but basic constitutional freedoms must not be violated, e.g. by isolation from the world, prohibition of reading the press, censorship of letters. The following year a similar trial was held in Split; Dr Ante Pilepić was sentenced to five and a half years, Dr Zdravko Ostojić to four and a half years and two students to two years and one and a half years. The seminary was closed for eight years and the two lower seminaries, the Bishop's and the Franciscan, for six years.[32] The authorities in these two cases were not only using the device of 'hostile propaganda' to attack the church's influence on young people, but also exercising one of the most damaging provisions of the 1953 Law on the Status of Religious Communities, which gave them the power to close a seminary for 'abuse of religious instruction amounting to a criminal act', in addition to the other penalties imposed by the law. This was the last occasion on which this provision was used, and it was later removed, when the law was revised in 1965, after a good deal of negotiation and pressure from both the Catholic and the Serbian Orthodox Churches.

The Vatican continued to give publicity to the plight of the church in Eastern Europe. The publication by *L'Osservatore Romano* in 1954 of two extensive articles detailing the sufferings of the Catholic bishops in Yugoslavia[33] was followed in June 1956 by *Dum maerentes*, Pope Pius XII's pastoral letter to the three imprisoned archbishops in Eastern Europe, Archbishop Stepinac, Archbishop Mindszenty in Budapest and Archbishop Beran in Prague, encouraging Catholics in communist countries to hold out against persecution.

It was banned in Yugoslavia[34] and attacked by *Borba*[35] as an incitement to rebellion against the government, and evidence of the Vatican's fear that 'the centuries-old blind obedience to the hierarchy' was yielding before 'the progress of socialism which is liberating millions from conservatism and mysticism'.

Nevertheless foreign observers were beginning to sense an improvement in the atmosphere. It seemed to the correspondent of the *New York Times* that the church and the state were living quietly side by side, each waiting for the other to make the first

---

[32] *MG*, 2.viii.56, quoting *Slobodna Dalmacija* of Split; RNS, 31.vii.56 and 2.viii.56, quoting *Borba* and *Politika*.
[33] See p. 134, n. 64.   [34] *NYT*, 7.viii.56.
[35] RNS, 8.viii.56.

move.[36] The government was satisfied that the church had been 'neutralised', said Dr Bakarić, and he again repeated that religion could not be opposed by force. It was quite natural for Catholic parents to want their children to have a religious education, and in Croatia about 50 per cent of them did. As for the Vatican, he said, the government would like to negotiate questions at issue with it, but it would never again resume diplomatic relations.[37]

Renewal of church and state contacts with the Vatican

The situation had begun to ease even before the death of Pius XII. Auxiliary Bishop Lach of Zagreb went to Rome in 1957. His visit had been in the air as early as June of that year[38] but the death on September 4 of Mgr Magjerec, rector of the College of St Jerome of the Illyrians in Rome, and the anxiety felt by the church in Croatia that his successor should be another Croat and not an Italian brought him immediately to Rome, where he arrived on September 9. His visit was successful, and the following year Dr Djuro Kokša was appointed rector. He was an outstandingly able Croatian priest in his middle thirties who had come to Rome to study in 1943 and had remained there, while retaining his Yugoslav citizenship. Lach had an interview with Pius XII during which he also raised the question of the obligatory *ad limina* visits of the bishops to the Holy See, which had been interrupted since the end of the war; the next date for such visits was 1958. The pope simply reminded Lach that it was the duty of all bishops to come to Rome; when this was reported back the bishops decided to ask for their passports.[39] Archbishop Šeper travelled to Rome in May–June 1958[40] and by the end of 1959 most of the other bishops had followed.[41] Pope John XXIII was enthroned in November 1958 and one or two Yugoslav bishops who happened to be in Rome at the time were present, but there was, tactfully, no general request of passports for this occasion.

Although both sides were reticent about it, there were persistent rumours of contact between high government officials and the church.[42] At the beginning of April 1959 Archbishop Ujčić and Bishop Bukatko of Križevci left for *ad limina* visits to Rome. They were seen off at the airport by the secretary of the

---

[36] *NYT*, 18.iv.57.
[37] Ibid.
[38] Ibid. 4.vi.57.
[39] Catholic source.
[40] RNS, 27.vi.58.
[41] *Le Monde*, 20.xii.59.
[42] RNS, 17.ii.59.

federal Commission for Religious Affairs, Miloje Dilparić[43] and
soon after their return in the middle of May Ujčić had an
interview with Dobrivoje Radosavljević, the president.[44] He was
a man of high calibre who was respected by the government and
his position as president of the Bishops' Conference made him
an important figure; the courtesies extended to him by the
government were a reflection of this.

There was a good deal of speculation about the nature of the
visit and the messages he might be carrying, but relations
between the Vatican and the Yugoslav government had not yet
reached the stage of negotiations; Archbishop Ujčić's visit served
rather to convey the position of each side to the other and
to develop a favourable atmosphere for future talks. The
position of the Vatican was unchanged; it continued to be
concerned particularly with the questions of freedom of religion,
education and the religious press, and with the return of the
church's sequestrated property. On the other side, there were
several empty dioceses awaiting appointments, and the government was anxious that any new bishops should be men not openly
hostile to it.[45] But it would have been difficult for the government,
always financially hard-pressed, and with other susceptibilities to
consider, to make special concessions to the Catholic Church over
nationalised buildings; there would have been an outcry from the
Orthodox if similar concessions had not been made to them, and
the Vatican on its side resisted sharply any suggestion of
consultation over the appointment of bishops, a logical position
for it to adopt towards a country where church and state are
separated.

Archbishop Ujčić was received by the pope and on his return
conveyed to the government the pope's understanding of its
position; there may even have been a hint that the Vatican would
keep in mind the government's point of view when appointing
new bishops. The Pope himself was believed to be in favour of

---

[43] Ibid. 8.iv.59.   [44] Ibid. 10.vi.59.
[45] The decoration bestowed by the government on the eight-four-year-old Bishop
of Djakovo, Dr Akšamović, was an indication of where its sympathies lay (ibid.
26.v.59). He was a cheerful character who liked everyone around him to be
happy, and had managed to be on good terms with both the wartime
government of the NDH and the postwar Yugoslav government. He had been
decorated with the Order of Merit First Class with Star by the NDH
(*Dokumenti*, p. 199) and his diocese had been active during the period of the
forcible conversions of Serbian Orthodox. In the autumn of 1945 the Central
Committee of the Croatian Communist Party visited Djakovo. Akšamović
invited them all to lunch and established excellent relations with them. After
this he could always approach the authorities direct when difficulties arose in
his diocese (Catholic source).

normalising relations on a basis of mutual confidence, but other Vatican officials were more cautious, and awaited some concrete gesture on the part of the Yugoslav government.[46]

Attacks and blandishments

At the same time that these talks were proceeding several sharp attacks on the church were delivered in the press. *Vjesnik*[47] accused the Catholic Church of being alone among religious communities in refusing to respond to government efforts to normalise church–state relations. In April *Borba* accused the Vatican of combining its aims for religion and the church with a reactionary political attitude, as shown by the pope's decree forbidding Catholics to vote for left-wing parties.[48] A few days later the official spokesman of the foreign ministry joined in the condemnation; he said that the pope's decree was against the principle of freedom of conscience and religion and in contradiction to Article 18 of the United Nations Declaration of Human Rights.[49]

These attacks were accompanied by blandishments. Archbishop Ujčić was decorated by Tito on his eightieth birthday for his efforts to improve relationships between the Catholic Church and the government at a difficult time.[50] When Tito received a group of Slovene priests from the Ciril–Metodsko Društvo on December 18, 1959, he spoke of the improved relations between the government and the Catholic Church and said that there was growing realism among some bishops and church leaders, giving hope for the future; any disagreements between them could be settled by discussion.[51] Miha Marinko, a Slovene member of the Central Committee of the League of Communists of Yugoslavia, opening the Congress of the League of Communists of Slovenia in June 1959, said that the policy of the Slovene communists towards the church had given very positive results, though Boris Ziherl, another leading Slovene communist, warned against a

[46] RNS, 10.vi.59, reported this story much more positively. A reliable Catholic source told the writer that this was somewhat speculative.
[47] Quoted in RNS, 21.i.59.
[48] RNS, 14.iv.59.
[49] Ibid. 17.iv.59.
[50] *Nova Pot*, Feb. 1960. At the presentation Dobrivoje Radosavljević praised his merits and said that his example showed that believers could be faithful both to the church and the state. Ujčić answered: '...as a theologian I am loyal to my leader the pope in Rome and as a citizen I am loyal to the president of the republic. As a priest I pray for the greater progress of our state, and the increase of its reputation and for lasting peace at home and in the world' (ibid.).
[51] Ibid.

resurgence of clericalism in politics,[52] always a danger in Slovenia.

The government's annual report to the Assembly on foreign and internal events in 1959 praised the positive attitude of the Serbian Orthodox Church and the Moslem religious community, and said that the Catholic Church was showing that it realised the usefulness of maintaining normal relations with the government and developing its activities within the framework of the constitution and the laws.[53] About this time there was some relaxation of party discipline. Members were no longer expelled if their families went to church; Komunist, the party's ideological weekly, urged members not to incur social odium and isolation by refusing to attend family funerals where a priest was officiating,[54] and Bakarić repeated this in a speech to party members in February 1960.[55]

The Vatican on its side made a number of conciliatory gestures. It removed a long-standing cause of irritation to the Yugoslav government by appointing as residential bishops a number of apostolic administrators.[56] The Vatican had, since the end of the war, followed a policy of appointing apostolic administrators to vacant dioceses in order to avoid provoking possible dissension with the government over the appointments; in the case of the Ljubljana diocese there was the additional reason that Bishop Rožman, who had fled in 1945, survived abroad until 1959. The Yugoslav government on the other hand looked upon the appointment of administrators as an indication that the Vatican considered the postwar frontiers and the political situation as temporary, and in the case of Ljubljana, the continued recognition by the church of a convicted war criminal. In 1960 Krunoslav Draganović,[57] who had been living in the

[52] RNS, 23.vi.59.
[53] Ibid. 15.iii.60.
[54] Ibid. 28.i.60.
[55] Ibid. 16.ii.60.
[56] Bishop Nežić of Poreč–Pula, Bishop Bukatko of Križevci, Bishop Držečnik of Maribor, Bishop Alaupović of Sarajevo, Bishop Vovk of Ljubljana (SVNZ, no. 5, 1960, p. 67).
[57] Dr Draganović, a former professor at the Zagreb theological faculty, was an important figure in the Croatian emigration. He left Zagreb for Rome in 1942 and worked vigorously to enlist the support of the Vatican for the NDH, and after the end of the war to succour members of the NDH government who had fled, and Catholic priests who had left the country; his name crops up frequently in trials of priests in Yugoslavia. He was reputed to have had a hand in arranging the escape and subsequent sheltering of several Ustaša leaders. His later history took an unexpected turn. It was revealed without explanation that he had returned to Yugoslavia on Nov. 11, 1967 (Oslobodjenje, 13.xi.67). In an interview Magistrate Vlajsavljević stated that he had returned legally and of his own volition, having crossed the frontier at Sežana. He had written to the public prosecutor and was now in the Sarajevo district, undergoing an

(Croatian) College of St Jerome in Rome, thus associating it with the attacks of the Yugoslav government on his activities, removed himself.[58] The atmosphere was improved by these changes.

Although by the beginning of 1960 there was a general loosening of rigid positions and a movement at the top towards better relations, simultaneously several trials of priests were taking place in other parts of the country. The two phenomena were not necessarily contradictory. The government's desire for better relations was genuine and it was prepared to make some concessions, but at the same time it did not cease to support the sections of the clergy who were prepared to cooperate with it, and to attack centres of what it considered hostile activity; these included a seminary and one of the bishops.

At Osijek (Slavonia) a group of priests and students from the seminary at Djakovo, including Dr Ćiril Kos, professor of theology, and six others, were accused of hostile propaganda and spreading religious, national and racial hatred. Djakovo, it will be remembered, was the town whose local communists had been so much concerned by the strength of Catholic influence in the schools. The public prosecutor demanded the closing of the seminary, and it is noteworthy that for the first time the bishops and the priests' associations joined forces in defence of the seminary. Archbishop Ujčić, Bishop Alaupović of Sarajevo and other bishops approached the authorities and promised that if the seminary was reprieved there would be no further cause of complaint,[59] and the associations of Catholic priests in Serbia and Croatia sent delegations to the federal Commission for Religious Affairs. The pleas were successful and the seminary was allowed to remain open.[60]

At the same time an important political trial was taking place in Zagreb, at which the principal accused was a Franciscan, Fra Rudi Jerek. He and several other persons were accused of espionage and of organising terrorist groups between 1956 and 1959; the Franciscan monastery at Ksaver in Zagreb was named as the centre of this group.[61] The prosecutor asked angrily whether these activities were an attempt to sabotage the im-

examination under Art. 118, cl. 1, of the Criminal Code, concerning hostile propaganda. Although he was under surveillance he had some liberty of movement and had visited his sister (ibid.). The mystery of his return has never been divulged. He has since been living quietly in his own diocese, engaged in editing the new *Šematizam* (general register of the Catholic Church in Yugoslavia). He was the editor of the last general *Šematizam*, published in 1939.

[58] Catholic source.
[59] RNS, 2.ii.60.
[60] Ibid. 9.ii.60.
[61] Ibid. 14.i.60.

proving relations between the government and the church.[62]

Two months later Bishop Čekada of Skopje was arrested and put on trial, accused of currency offences, and smuggling cars and radio and television sets worth 37m dinars; it was alleged that they had been sent by Dr Krunoslav Draganović.[63] Dr Čekada admitted receiving money through irregular sources, since relations between the church and the state were not normal. But he stated that the money had come from the Vatican and not from any individual, and was intended for use in his very poor diocese. As the case proceeded the tone of the press reports moderated and at the trial there was no mention of the political aspects which had been stressed earlier; it apeared that an effort was being made to avoid implicating the Vatican. It was Bishop Čekada who, to clear himself of the imputation of connections with a man considered by the authorities to be a war criminal, insisted that this was the normal help which a poor diocese could expect from the Holy See, reaching him by abnormal sources because of the abnormal circumstances. He received an eighteen-month suspended sentence[64] which in the circumstances must be considered lenient; he was regarded as hostile, among other reasons, because he was believed to have been opposed to cooperating with the government in 1953 when the Catholic Church was asked for comments on the Law on the Legal Status of Religious Communities. But in 1960 Cardinal Stepinac's death had already begun to transform the relations between the government and the church.

The preliminaries to negotiations

The death of Cardinal Stepinac, and what has sometimes been referred to as his 'posthumous amnesty', the public funeral in the cathedral in Zagreb, with full honours, removed the last serious obstacle to an improvement in church–state relations and opened up a real possibility of normalising relations with the Vatican. At the special requiem mass which Pope John XXIII celebrated for the cardinal he spoke of his hope for 'civil and religious' peace with Yugoslavia;[65] this was interpreted by the government as a sign that further approaches would be welcome.[66]

[62] Ibid.   [63] Ibid. 16.ii.60 and 17.iii.60.
[64] Ibid. 19.iii.60.
[65] L'O.R., 18.ii.60; Benigar, pp. 860–3.
[66] NYT, 19.ii.60.

The bishops met in their annual conference September 20–3, 1960. The government had expressed its hope that normal relations with the church should be established as soon as possible, and in a long memorandum the bishops reciprocated this hope and promised to encourage the clergy and the lay faithful to fulfil their civil obligations and to cooperate with the civil authorities in building the future of the country; they asked the government on its side to show a benevolent attitude to the church and to ensure that the provisions of the constitution and the Law on the Legal Status of Religious Communities were applied in a liberal spirit. They listed many breaches both of the law and the constitution:

In many places public worship was hindered and schoolchildren were prevented from going to church; strong pressures were brought on schoolteachers not to marry in church, and some teachers were even dismissed for going to church; priests were prevented from visiting the sick and elderly in hospitals and institutions; men called up for military service were forbidden to go to church; priests were punished for hearing confessions in private houses in small villages where there was no church or chapel. (Writer's summary)

They further made a number of demands:

The sequestrated churches, monasteries, schools, seminaries and other church buildings should all be returned to the church, which could not carry on its work without them; the parish registers which were removed when the government took over the keeping of vital statistics should be returned; the church should have the right to repair existing churches and build new ones; cemeteries should be divided and each religious community assigned a portion;[67] students in seminaries should have the same rights (health and social insurance, subsidised travel, deferred military service) as other students.[68] (Writer's summary)

The government's reply was mollifying; it thanked the bishops for their views and promised to consider them carefully. It was signed by Dr Edvard Kardelj, the vice-president, a further indication that the government was now taking these exchanges seriously.[69] It still hoped that the bishops would negotiate directly with it (by this time it had abandoned its earlier intention of arriving at an agreement with the church through the priests' associations, which were now treated simply as professional

[67] This was later done in some localities, e.g. Sarajevo, by a decree on cemeteries of 3.xii.64 (*LSRCY*, p. 79).
[68] The memorandum was reported in the foreign press (*Le Monde*, 11.x.60; *NYT*, 17.x.60), which listed some of the demands. It was published in part in the *Christian Democratic Review*, June 1961, from which this summary has been made.
[69] Catholic source.

could be negotiated), but now accepted that this was impossible without the consent of the Vatican.

Archbishop Ujčić again set off for Rome in November, taking the government's reply with him; his chief purpose, aside from communicating this to the Vatican, was to obtain permission for the bishops to negotiate directly with the government, without prejudicing the rights of the Vatican, a course which they believed would now be fruitful.[70] Mgr Tardini, however, feared that direct conversations of this kind would end in a compromise such as the Polish bishops had accepted, which he considered to be in some respects unilaterally constraining to the church. He had repeatedly warned the Yugoslav bishops of the dangers of such a course and was now determined to keep any negotiations in the hands of the Vatican.[71]

The conversations were secret, but it was clear that the permission which the bishops sought was not given.

Archbishop Ujčić and his secretary were warmly received by the Yugoslav ambassador in Rome;[72] the fact that this news was released to the press is an indication of the attitude of the Yugoslav government.

After this the Yugoslav government accepted that it could not by-pass the Vatican, and there was no longer any effort to persuade or force the bishops to negotiate direct. But there was no return to earlier conditions; a propitious atmosphere had been established. The government realised that the bishops themselves wanted a peaceful accommodation, and although it was nearly four years before the conversations which were to lead to the signing of the protocol in 1966 were officially begun, contacts increased, both sides cautiously continuing to test the ground.

In the long run the decision of the Vatican to retain negotiations in its own hands was justified; in the interval the Second Vatican Council took place and the Yugoslav government had time to gauge the importance of the changes which were taking place in the Catholic Church. There is no doubt that better conditions were eventually secured for the Catholic Church than the bishops could have obtained in 1960, and these conditions were backed by the force of an international treaty.

[70] Ibid.   [71] Ibid.
[72] RNS, 9.xii.60.

The Second Vatican Council

The Second Vatican Council opened in October 1962. Several Yugoslav bishops had been appointed to preparatory commissions which were set up in 1960[73] and had taken full part in the preliminaries of the council. The *ad limina* visits, as we have seen, had been resumed in 1958, and the bishops serving on preparatory commissions travelled freely to Rome, so that by the time the council opened in 1962 the links between the Yugoslav hierarchy and the Vatican had been fully restored. Twenty-four out of twenty-seven bishops attended the council, the remaining three being prevented by age or illness. They encountered no difficulties in obtaining passports to travel to the council, although some of their advisers had to wait a little longer. Yugoslav bishops attended all four sessions of the council and served on various commissions. Some observers found them dour, and their attitudes old-fashioned,[74] a reflection perhaps of their long isolation from the West and the mainstream of Catholic thought. But some of them brought unexpected insights to the debates. Bishop Čule of Mostar, who had spent several years in prison,[75] spoke out against clericalism, caesaropapism and any trace of dominance.[76] During the debate on atheism Archbishop Pogačnik of Ljubljana pointed out to the fathers that Pope John's encyclical *Mater et magistra* was neglected by Catholics but had been carefully studied by the communist authorities in Yugoslavia – 'If God has permitted this great apostasy it is because of the cosmic dimension of sin, including our own sins, and with a view to their correction and a perfect conversion to God'[77] – and Archbishop Šeper called for the church to show that it understood atheism and did not simply condemn it: 'Christians who defend the established order, appealing to God's authority, are partly responsible for modern atheism.'[78] The Yugoslav government noted also that Schema 13 of the council did not contain any condemnation of communism.[79]

[73] Ujčić (Central Committee), Šeper (*disciplina sacramentum*), Franić (theological commission), Bukatko (lay apostolate) (*SVNZ*, no. 1, 1960, p. 67).
[74] Rynne, *Third Session*, p. 90.
[75] He emerged with his health much impaired as a result of a railway accident in which he and a wagonload of other prisoners, including the Orthodox Bishop Varnava Nastić, were seriously injured while being transferred from one prison to another.
[76] Rynne, *Third Session*, p. 144.
[77] Ibid. p. 133.
[78] Rynne, *Fourth Session*, p. 71.
[79] *Godišnjak* [Yearbook] of the Institute of International Politics and Economics, Belgrade, 1965. In 1964 and the years following, the full and excellent section

Bishop Franić of Split, drawing on the painful experience of disunity among Yugoslav Christians, called for a true dialogue with the Orthodox, based on truth and mutual understanding, and a full recognition of the fact that an excessive zeal for Latinisation of the church was responsible for the continuation of the separation.[80]

The debate on Christian unity at the Second Vatican Council gave an opening for a dialogue with the Serbian Orthodox Church which was long overdue, but still fraught with difficulties. In 1963 a group of students from the theological faculty at Belgrade paid a visit to the theological faculty in Ljubljana, and this was followed early in 1964 by a second visit to Ljubljana and a visit to the theological faculty in Zagreb.[81]

The visit to Zagreb was not a success and was not repeated.[82] The fate of the 1963 Christmas message of the Bishop of Banja Luka was significant. Mgr Alfred Pichler, whose see was the scene of the murder of the Orthodox Bishop Platon in 1941 and of many crimes against the Serbian population, is a leader of practical everyday ecumenism in his own diocese, and his relationship with the Orthodox Bishop Andrej is brotherly. Pope Paul VI had opened the Second Session of the Vatican Council with a statement that in the past the Catholic Church had sinned against love and quarrelled with brother Christians, and he begged their forgiveness. Spurred by this example, Bishop Pichler issued a Christmas message to his diocese, acknowledging that in the last war their brothers of the Orthodox faith had been killed simply because they were Orthodox and not Catholics and Croats, by men who called themselves Catholic and carried Catholic baptismal certificates. 'We acknowledge with anguish the terrible crimes of these misguided men and we beg our Orthodox brothers to forgive us as Christ on the Cross forgave all men. We in our turn forgive all those who have wronged or hated us. Today, gathered around Christ's cradle, let all debts be cancelled and may love reign.'[83]

on the Vatican noted with sympathetic objectivity the council documents concerning international peace, the developing world, the tendency to separate the church from capitalism and the possibility of a dialogue with atheists.

[80] Rynne, *Letters*, p. 209.   [81] *Glas Koncila*, 29.iii.64.

[82] Catholic and Orthodox sources. However, in 1974 an ecumenical symposium was held at Maribor, in Slovenia, for the Orthodox faculty in Belgrade, the Catholic faculties in Ljubljana and Zagreb and a number of Orthodox and Catholic higher seminaries; an Evangelical pastor was also present. This was so successful that a second one was held in 1976 at Lovran near Rijeka and a third one is planned for 1978 to be held in Belgrade (information from AKSA, Catholic news service published in Zagreb).

[83] Official gazette of the diocese of Banja Luka, Dec. 1963.

Eighteen years after the end of the war and over twenty years after the terrible events of 1941 it might have been considered that this was none too soon; but it provoked deep anger among Catholic Croats, and in his own diocese some priests refused to read it from the pulpit, or read only extracts.[84] The only Catholic paper, aside from the diocesan gazette, in which the message appeared was *Danica*, published by the Association of Catholic Priests in Croatia.

It was not until 1967 that Archbishop Šeper and Patriarch German of the Serbian Orthodox Church met officially.

The changing climate of opinion in the Catholic Church expressed by the Second Vatican Council was paralleled in Yugoslavia by the promulgation of the 1963 constitution, which gave legal expression to the development of liberalism and decentralisation in Yugoslavia.

It is from this time that one can date the real rebirth of the Catholic press. It had never been entirely extinct; the monthly *Blagovest* [Annunciation] of the Belgrade diocese, after an interval during the war, continued to appear several times a year; the longest interval between issues was from May 1953 to the spring of 1954.[85] In October 1962 a fortnightly, *Glas Koncila* [Voice of the Council], made its first appearance under the auspices of the Zagreb archdiocese. It was intended, as the name indicates, to be a bulletin of information about the Second Vatican Council and was to be discontinued at the close of the council, but its success, under the skilful and enterprising editorship of two young priests, who were given a remarkably free hand by their superiors, was so great that it was allowed to continue. In 1970 the circulation had climbed to between 170,000 and 180,000. In the period following, many other Catholic papers appeared (see appendix iv).

The protocol

Official conversations concerning a treaty between the Vatican and the Yugoslav government began in 1964; informal conversations were believed to have been proceeding since 1962. Both sides were now eager for an understanding. The government welcomed the trend to ecumenism shown at the council. On its side the Vatican was now convinced that Yugoslavia was genuinely detached from the Soviet bloc; its interest in the former

[84] Catholic source.
[85] File of issues in Zagreb University Library.

colonial territories in Africa and Asia, which had been stimulated by the Second Vatican Council, caused it also to welcome Yugoslavia's identification with the Third World and its policy of non-alignment. Discussions were held in Rome from June 26 to July 7, 1964, continued in Belgrade from January 5 to 23 and May 29 to June 8, 1965, and concluded in Belgrade April 18 to 25, 1966.[86] On June 25, 1966, the 'Protocol of Discussions between the Representatives of the Socialist Federal Republic of Yugoslavia and the Representatives of the Holy See' was signed in Rome.[87] It guaranteed, among other things, the free performance of religious functions and religious rites, and admitted, within the framework of the law, the jurisdiction of the Holy See over the Catholic Church in spiritual, religious and ecclesiastical matters, while the Vatican accepted that the clergy would not abuse their functions for political ends, and 'condemned every act of political terrorism or similar criminal forms of violence, whoever its perpetrators be', promising to look into any case of terrorist activity brought to its notice by the Yugoslav government.[88]

The protocol provided for a mutual exchange of envoys, an apostolic delegate and a representative of the Yugoslav government, who had at first no formal diplomatic rank, although they were accorded diplomatic courtesies; in 1970 the missions were raised to diplomatic status, and the envoys are now an ambassador and a pronuncio (i.e. a nuncio who is not doyen of the diplomatic corps). This did not imply, however, that the protocol had become a concordat.

The negotiations were carried out directly between representatives of the Yugoslav government and the Vatican, and no members of the Yugoslav hierarchy took part. The inclusion of the clause on terrorism was a bitter pill for them to swallow. The activities of some priests among émigré circles, especially in Germany, gave the government serious concern. The government wanted a clear statement from the Vatican that it disapproved of such activities and would take sanctions against them, and the Vatican satisfied it on this point.

---

[86] *LSRCY*, p. 84.
[87] Ibid. A protocol is an agreement between governments of a less formal nature than a treaty. The protocol is not a concordat, which as a rule establishes a juridical position for the Catholic Church within a state, and defines its privileges and duties. In this case the protocol defined the relations between the Catholic Church and a country where church and state are separated, and set out an agreed formula for the manner of their mutual dealings.
[88] *LSRCY*, pp. 84–6. See also appendix V for full text.

On the other hand, there was no mention in the protocol of the appointment of bishops, which the Vatican considered to be an internal matter of church administration in a country where church and state are separated. The government, however, takes an understandable interest in the matter. A position satisfactory to both sides appears to have been reached; the Vatican now informs the government of its appointments shortly before they are publicly announced,[89] and there have been no controversial appointments. The protocol expresses the real interests of both sides and there is every indication that both sides intend that it shall work.

Commenting four years later, *Borba* wrote that when the agreement was signed some Yugoslavs felt a certain reserve about it; those outside the church because they feared that this represented only a change of tactics on the part of the church, and those inside the church because they felt that the protocol simply stated the constitutional position and offered the church nothing new. Events had proved that the protocol had in practice gone beyond the limits of a formal legal act and had inaugurated a new period of relations between the Yugoslav government and the Catholic Church.[90]

It was not the protocol alone which opened the door to a new era, but it gave the sanction of an act of state to tendencies which had been growing on both sides; on the part of the government towards a more whole-hearted and liberal interpretation of the constitutional and legal provisions concerning the status of the church, and on the part of the church, opposition to 'clericalism and chauvinism' and a 'differentiation between religion and politics, religion and national adherence...and a re-examination of the attitude of the Catholic Church towards other religious communities, atheism and socialist society'.[91]

A difficulty which has not yet been overcome is that the term 'religious affairs' (*vjerski poslovi*) which are the province of the churches has never been defined, and thus there is no clearly understood and agreed demarcation line between religious affairs and political matters.[92] The government welcomes the involvement of the Vatican in international peace-making and help to the Third World; but within the country its definition of 'political matters' which the churches must keep out of tends

---

[89] Yugoslav official source.   [90] *Borba*, 9.iv.70.
[91] Ibid.
[92] As this volume was being prepared for the press (1977) new republican laws were being considered, which it appears will define the term much more narrowly.

to vary with the internal political situation, especially with regard to expressions of nationalism. Pronouncements and actions which would pass without comment at periods of relatively easy internal relations are sharply attacked by the authorities during periods of nationalist resurgence.

The protocol introduced a slight varying of emphasis in the relations between the state and the Catholic religious community. The relations between the government and the Vatican are those between sovereign powers, and while this must have a profound influence on the relations between the authorities and Yugoslav Catholics, their interests are not necessarily identical. The ideological discussion has been removed from the sphere of international and official relations, and is carried on between Yugoslav Catholics and Yugoslav Marxists. While the Catholic Church will certainly be safe from any basic attack while Yugoslav–Vatican relations remain good, the influence of the Vatican and the pronuncio are only one of the factors affecting the relations between the authorities and the church.

9

The Serbian and Macedonian Orthodox Churches

Schisms and accommodations

The Serbian Orthodox Church now also entered a period when relations with the state began to improve. The changes were gradual, and the unsettled question of the Macedonian Church continued to be a constant irritant. The improvement was chiefly noticeable at the top, and took place side by side with continuing harassment, administrative vexations and, in communist phraseology, 'departures from legal norms' at the local level.

The patriarchate I, 1950–4

Some of the improvement was due to Patriarch Vikentije; he took many opportunities of saying a mollifying word, of pointing out the things which were improving, or going well, and occasionally slipping in a veiled reproach. Towards the end of the interview with *Politika* cited in chapter 6, he spoke of 'certain misunderstandings with lower organs of the ministry of the interior', perhaps because some of them, out of excessive zeal, applied regulations unjustly, or possibly because some priests were not obeying the new regulations with sufficient care; the higher church and state authorities were at pains to smooth these over. On the other hand, the church received a subvention from the state, priests received social insurance, and the state had made it possible for the Serbian Orthodox Church to maintain contacts with sister Orthodox Churches and other Christian bodies abroad.

In 1952, for the first time since the war, Christmas was openly celebrated in Belgrade, and the patriarch's Christmas message appeared in full in *Politika*.[1] He appealed to the faithful to cherish the spirit of national unity and harmony which was 'essential for the progress of the country in peace and indispensable for the defence of its independence and freedom'. In October 1953, accompanied by members of the Synod, Vikentije called on Tito to express formally the Serbian Orthodox

[1] 6.i.53.

249

Church's support of the government in its dispute with the great powers over Trieste[2] and he appealed to the heads of churches in both the East and the West to support Yugoslavia in this question.[3] It was easy for the Synod to pledge its support; although it was not Serbia's frontiers which were in question, Slovenes and Croats were brother Slavs and the territory had been claimed by Yugoslavia in 1918.

Shortly before Radosavljević's pointed remarks to the Executive Council of the Union of Priests' Associations in October 1954 there had been a ceremonial reopening of the Orthodox Church Museum in the presence of members of the commission for Religious Affairs, and a gathering of representatives of Belgrade cultural life, academics and intellectuals.[4] There was a similar gathering the following year at the celebration of St Sava's Day at the theological faculty.[5]

The patriarch began to appear on official occasions; in 1955 he attended President Tito's birthday reception and other government and diplomatic receptions.[6] The head of the Moslem religious community, the Reis-el-Ulema, called on him.[7]

After a break of several years, a series of visits to sister Orthodox Churches was undertaken – the Greek, Russian and Romanian – and these were returned. There were visits from the World Council of Churches: Dr Visser t' Hooft, the general secretary, and Dr Robert Tobias, one of the secretaries, had visited both the Serbian Orthodox and the Evangelical Churches at the beginning of 1952;[8] this was a friendly visit to establish contact, since the Serbian Orthodox Church did not finally become a member of the World Council of Churches until 1966. From 1955 onwards there were regular visits from representatives of Inter-Church Aid; Raymond Maxwell came in June 1955[9] and again in the autumn of 1956,[10] John Metzler of Church World Service in May 1959.[11] The secretary of the British and Foreign Bible Society came in April 1956 to discuss the supply of Bibles[12] and in August Dr Franklin Fry of the World Council of Churches arrived at the head of a delegation to visit the patriarch.[13] In the same month President Tito decorated Patriarch Vikentije on his sixty-seventh birthday for his work in strengthening friendship with other countries.[14]

[2] *Borba*, 27.x.53.
[3] Jugopress, 20.x.53.
[4] *Gl.*, June 1954.
[5] 27.i.55: *Gl.*, Jan.–Feb. 1955.
[6] *Gl.*, June 1955.
[7] Ibid.
[8] *Vesnik*, 15.i.52.
[9] *Gl.*, June 1955.
[10] Ibid. Sept. 1956.
[11] Ibid. June 1955.
[12] Ibid. May 1956.
[13] Ibid. July–Aug. 1956.
[14] Ibid.

But while these easier relations were developing at the top, the situation at other levels was still difficult. During 1953 there had been violent demonstrations against a number of bishops in Bosnia and Hercegovina; these seem to have been the result of the tightening of ideological discipline after the passage of the Law on the Status of Religious Communities. Bishop Vasilije and the Roman Catholic bishop Dr Ćelik were forced by mobs to leave Banja Luka, and Bishop Vasilije was nearly lynched.[15] Bishop Nektarije of Tuzla was driven out of his diocese. Although the premier of Bosnia and Hercegovina, Djuro Pucar, called for a halt to these assaults on priests[16] the prelates were not allowed to return to their dioceses until February 1954.[17] The following month Dobrivoje Radosavljević, the president of the federal Commission for Religious Affairs, said that the government was taking steps to correct the excesses of the previous autumn. He also gave the number of priests in prison: 124 Catholics, 32 Serbian Orthodox, 2 Protestants, mostly for wartime offences.[18]

The trial of Metropolitan Arsenije

The second major trial involving an Orthodox bishop took place in 1954; Metropolitan Arsenije Bradvarović of the Montenegrin Littoral was arrested early in July and tried at the end of the month.

His arrest was preceded by the trial in Cetinje, the old capital of Montenegro, of a group of four priests, Luka Poček, Luka Vujas, Mihajlo Gazivoda and Marko Kuševac, for hostile activities.[19] They admitted having discussed the possibility of a change of government, criticising the authorities and saying that the laws for the protection of religion existed only on paper. This admission was built up into a wide-ranging accusation; they expected a change of government to be brought about by a Cominform attack leading to intervention from the West and an eventual return of the monarchy; the Vatican would help reactionary elements such as Nikolaj Velimirović, Irinej (who had died two years earlier), Dionisije and the Archbishop of Canterbury; even the possibility of Tito's assassination was mentioned. Metropolitan Arsenije was implicated in the evidence. He had written and circulated a pastoral letter in 1952

---

[15] *Politika*, 24.viii.53.
[16] RNS, 16.ix.53; this was three weeks earlier than Tito's speech at Ruma.
[17] Ibid. 9.ii.54.
[18] Ibid. [no day] March 1954.
[19] *Pobjeda* (a Titograd daily), 31.i.54.

forbidding priests and the faithful to join the People's Front, and had used all his influence to prevent his clergy from joining the priests' associations. One of the priests described how Arsenije had initiated their meetings in 1947 and encouraged them in their hostile activities. Considering the nature of the accusations the sentences were surprisingly light: Poček was sentenced to two years, Vujas (who had tried to protect Arsenije) to four years, Kuševac to eighteen months and Gazivoda (who had admitted his guilt and said: 'The fifth one [i.e. Arsenije] should be here with us') to fifteen months.[20]

Metropolitan Arsenije was arrested on July 6[21] and tried on July 27 and 28 at Cetinje. There were no foreign press representatives present in the remote town, and the Yugoslav papers reported the case only briefly,[22] but the case nevertheless aroused considerable interest abroad.

Arsenije was accused of serious offences against the people and state leading to the overthrow of the people's authorities (Criminal Law, Art. 117, para. 1); arousing religious hatred and intolerance (Art. 119, para. 2); and bringing into disrepute the representatives of the highest organs of authority (Art. 174). The charges against the four priests were repeated; he was accused of spreading demoralising propaganda after the expulsion of Yugoslavia from the Cominform, weakening the resolution of the people to resist; he had used his influence against the growing improvement of relations between the Orthodox Church and the state; 'he called order in our country dictatorship'. By writing to Blažo Jovanović, Prime Minister of Montenegro, complaining of the attitude of local authorities towards the church and priests, he had been guilty of slandering high officials.[23] Three of the four priests who had been tried earlier were freed and testified against him; the fourth refused and remained in prison.[24] Arsenije was sentenced to eleven and a half years' imprisonment.[25]

The church was shaken at the severity of the sentence, which came at a time when relations with the state seemed to be improving, and foreign observers were surprised, contrasting it

[20] Ibid.
[21] Times, 26.vii.54; NYT, 25.vii.54.
[22] Borba, 31.vii.54, quoting Pobjeda, 30.vii.54; but Tanjug reported (30.vii.54) that Pobjeda would carry a report on the case on 31.vii.54.
[23] Times, 28.vii.54. RNS reported that Jovanović's wife had led a strong anti-religious campaign and been incensed by Arsenije's protest; it was unofficially reported that Arsenije had been told some weeks previously that if he would vacate his see and live elsewhere in Yugoslavia, charges against him would be dropped, but he refused (RNS, 24 and 27.vii.54).
[24] NYT, 28.vii.54.   [25] Borba, 31.vii.54.

with the lenient treatment of Metropolitan Josif, who had been sent to live in a monastery.[26] Arsenije, who by then was over seventy, had undoubtedly been opposed to the patriarch's policy of conciliation and cooperation with the authorities, and was an uncompromising opponent of the priests' associations. It is possible that the government wanted to give the churches a sharp warning, but also possible that the local authorities in Montenegro – not a land known for gentleness or compromise – had taken matters into their own hands and gone further than the Belgrade authorities might have wished; the comparatively muted reporting of the trial lends support to this theory. The correspondent of Agence France-Presse was allowed to visit Metropolitan Arsenije in prison and reported that his conditions were decent. He was allowed books, newspapers and medicines; he vigorously denied that he was guilty and said that he had no intention of resigning his diocese.[27] An appeal was lodged and his sentence reduced to five and a half years.[28] The following year the bishops, meeting at their annual Sabor, sent a formal appeal for pardon to President Tito.[29] Arsenije was released from prison in August 1956, suffering from severe asthma, and sent to live in the monastery of Ozren,[30] but he did not appear in public or attend a meeting of the Sabor until his sentence had formally expired at the beginning of 1960.[31] In June of that year he petitioned the Sabor to release him from his duties as Metropolitan of Montenegro (since it was obvious that the government would not allow him to return) and he was appointed to the now virtually titular see of Budim.[32]

The priests' associations

The Sabor met from May 23 to June 4, 1955,[33] after the union of priests' associations had decided to yield on the question of diocesan associations, and after several had already been set up. But the imprisonment of Metropolitan Arsenije seems to have hardened the mood of the bishops instead of frightening them. In spite of the fact that Rodoljub Čolaković, a senior member of the federal Executive Council, was present at the government's reception for the bishops (the highest government official so far to have attended these receptions, and an indication that the government was putting itself out to woo them) the bishops again

[26] Times, 30.vii.54.
[28] NYT, 19.ix.54.
[30] RNS, 29.ix.56.
[32] Ibid. 22.vi.60.

[27] RNS, 5.x.54.
[29] Gl., June 1955.
[31] Ibid. 9.vi.60.
[33] Gl., June 1955.

failed to put the priests' associations on the agenda, but advised them to continue their efforts to revise their rules.[34]

The Macedonian clergy were also fobbed off. There had been reports the previous autumn that a settlement of the Macedonian question had been reached at an unofficial meeting between Vikentije and the leaders of the priests' associations. The church had conceded the appointment of Macedonian bishops and the use of the Macedonian language, and the priests had agreed to an autonomous status under the Serbian patriarch instead of autocephaly, with one Synod and one Sabor.[35] This was repeated publicly by the Rev. Nestor Popovski when he addressed the Second Congress of the Union of Priests' Associations in February 1955.[36] Now it was told that while there was no objection to Macedonian bishops and language, the list of candidates for bishops it had submitted did not satisfy canonical requirements.

The same events were repeated in 1956. The Macedonian problem was referred to the Synod, and the priests' associations were not discussed. It was reported that the union had not even made its usual request for recognition.[37] Radosavljević made a friendly and conciliatory speech at the government reception for the bishops, and Ranković was present. It looked as though the government wanted to reduce tension and improve relations with the church.[38]

The patriarchate II, 1955–7: visits to other Orthodox Churches

In February 1955 the patriarch received an invitation to visit the Patriarch of Moscow[39] and later in the year he was invited to visit the Romanian patriarch;[40] the latter invitation clashed with his forthcoming visit to Greece, but the first was refused on a plausible excuse. The reconciliation with the Soviet Union had not yet taken place and the government evidently did not feel that the time was ripe for a visit to the Soviet Union. Nevertheless the Moscow patriarchate continued its overtures. It resumed the sending of its journal, which had been stopped in 1948, and it asked the Serbian Orthodox Church to take over the remaining Russian parishes in Yugoslavia, with the exception of the one in Belgrade.[41] There were five of them, the remnants of the émigré Russian Church which had established itself in Yugoslavia after

[34] Ibid. June 1955; RNS, 5 and 14.vi.55.   [35] RNS, 29.x.54.
[36] *Vesnik*, 10.iii.55.   [37] RNS, 20.vi.56.
[38] Ibid.   [39] *Gl.*, May 1955.
[40] RNS, 30.ix.55.   [41] Ibid. 8.iii.55.

the First World War. Most of its members had left Yugoslavia in 1944 before the advancing Soviet and Partisan forces.

At the end of October Patriarch Vikentije travelled to Greece to visit the Serbian cemetery for the war dead at Salonika, Athens and Mt Athos; he was accompanied by his two auxiliaries, German and Visarion, and seven priests, including the Rev. Milan Smiljanić. The visit was to be a quiet, semi-private one, but naturally included a courtesy visit to Archbishop Dorotheos of Athens; the government provided 'moral, material and diplomatic support'.[42] On the way to Athens the train stopped at Skopje, and the Rev. Nestor Popovski, president of the Organising Committee, accompanied by several other priests and a member of the Macedonian Commission for Religious Affairs, invited the patriarch to pay a visit to Skopje on his way back. Vikentije accepted and returned with his party on November 12; the first day was spent in long discussions. The following day eight Macedonian priests joined the three bishops in celebrating the liturgy before a great crowd which overflowed into the churchyard. At the official lunch which followed toasts were exchanged; Nestor Popovski assured the patriarch that there was no separatism in the Macedonian Church – it only wanted its own bishops; and Vikentije answered that the visits would be a turning point in their relations and the broken thread of unity would be restored. He concluded: 'There have been great changes in the country; the church is not concerned with political questions but it cannot be indifferent to them; the church must do its duty loyally on the principle that all governments are from God.'

The delegation visited the president of the Executive Council, Ljupčo Arsov, and left for Belgrade the following morning.[43]

Archbishop Dorotheos returned Patriarch Vikentije's visit the following September.[44] He was received with honours both by the church and the authorities[45] and decorated by Tito.[46]

A second invitation was now received from the Russian Orthodox Church and this time was accepted. The patriarch left for Moscow on October 5, 1956, accompanied by four bishops, Nektarije, Valerian, Hrizostom and Visarion, and by the Rev. Milan Smiljanić, the Rev. Petar Kapičić (who had led the unrest in the church in Montenegro at the end of the war and was a prominent member of the priests' association of Montenegro), the Rev. Tihomir Popović, the Rev. Nestor Popovski and the

[42] 28.x–14.xi.55: Gl., Jan.–Feb. 1956. [43] Ibid.
[44] 4–19.ix.56. [45] Gl., Sept. 1956 and Oct.–Nov. 1956.
[46] Jugopress, 12.ix.56.

patriarch's *chef de cabinet*, Archdeacon Djordje Žunić.[47] At the special request of Patriarch Alexei, the Rev. Vitalij Taraseyev of the Russian Orthodox Church in Belgrade was included. The patriarch's personal physician, Dr Jovan Nenadić, and Miloje Dilparić, secretary of the federal Commission for Religious Affairs, completed the party.[48]

They were received at the airport by an equally official party headed by Patriarch Alexei and including Archbishop Boris of Odessa, several priests, a representative of the city government, and the president of the government's Council for Russian Orthodox Church affairs, as well as two members of the Yugoslav embassy in Moscow. The first week was spent quietly in conversations and church visits; the visitors wrote later that they felt 'not like guests, but at home, brothers of one blood, one faith and one spirit'.[49]

The second two weeks were crowded with the customary round of official sightseeing. They visited the Kremlin, the University of Moscow and Lenin's tomb, an automobile factory, and the Military Museum; in Leningrad they saw the Hermitage, the observatory and the metro, and were taken to visit a hut where Lenin once hid for two months as 'a common worker'; then on to Kiev to see a collective farm, a children's nursery and a textile factory; they were received by Bulganin, the president of the Council of Ministers, and entertained by other government representatives.[50]

It was a packed and rather exhausting three weeks, but both the churches and the two governments must have thought the exercise worth it. As far as the Yugoslavs were concerned, the church and the government were each, quite legitimately, using the other. It was important for the Serbian patriarchate, for reasons both of brotherly love and ecclesiastical politics, to knit up its relations with other Orthodox Churches. This and other similar visits could not have been made without the approval and financial aid of the government. The government, on its side, found it convenient to use the church as an adjunct to its foreign policy without directly involving it. Both Patriarch Vikentije, and his successor, Patriarch German, on his later and even more extensive travels, were careful not to make any political pronouncements, or to refer to Yugoslavia's foreign policy except in the most general terms of international peace and good will. From the government's point of view it was unnecessary that they should do so; the fact that good relations between Orthodox Churches were being cultivated was in itself useful for Yugo-

[47] *Gl.*, Oct.–Nov. 1956.   [48] Ibid. Jan.–Feb. 1957.
[49] Ibid.   [50] Ibid.

slavia's foreign relations. The price paid by the church could be discerned in the composition of the patriarch's accompanying suite, and in the heavy programme of official visits and sightseeing which had to be gone through in addition to the business of the churches. But the government also paid a price: the travels of the patriarch enhanced the prestige of the church both at home and abroad and built up for it the kind of external constituency which gave it some of the protection the Catholic Church enjoyed through the existence of the Vatican.

There was an unplanned, and as it turned out, very agreeable break on the return journey. The party missed the train connection in Bucharest and found itself unexpectedly with time on its hands. A telephone call to the patriarchate brought the patriarch's vicar posthaste to the station with an invitation to spend the rest of the day with Patriarch Justinian. They exclaimed in wonder at the rich interior of the patriarch's palace and were surprised to learn about the size and strength of the Romanian Orthodox Church: 14 million believers, 1,700 priests and 7,500 monks and nuns, whose salaries were all paid by the state.[51] It was all very different from conditions at home. The opportunity was taken to invite Patriarch Justinian to visit the Serbian Orthodox Church the following year.[52]

When the Romanian patriarch arrived he was accompanied by three metropolitans, two other bishops and several priests, and he was received in appropriate style; government representatives at the railway station included senior members of the foreign ministry.[53] The usual pattern for these visits was followed: a mixture of private conversations and ceremonial occasions. Patriarch Justinian called on President Tito, and on Ranković, who was present also at the official reception given in honour of the patriarch by the government and the Synod.[54]

Patriarch Alexei of Moscow paid a three-week-long return visit;[55] it was equally ceremonious, equally official, equally warm. The two patriarchs issued a joint communiqué which emphasised the historic friendship of the two churches and the two peoples, especially during the last war when both had showed their patriotism and national character, and their willingness to share all the burdens of the people.[56]

Patriarch Vikentije had already spoken on this theme in a New Year message which he gave to Jugopress:[57]

[51] Ibid.
[52] Ibid. The visit took place on June 2–11, 1957; *Vesnik*, 16.xi.56.
[53] Ibid. July–Aug. 1957.   [54] Ibid.
[55] 11–31.x.57.   [56] *Gl.*, Nov. 1957.
[57] Ibid. Jan.–Feb. 1957.

Our Holy Church is national and independent, and throughout its history has always been with its people, with whom it shared good and evil...The church nurtures and fights for the holy, God-given truths of Orthodoxy: this is an obligation as much as patriotism. But this is possible because our country is free, independent and autonomous, and the church is not only formally, but in fact, separated from the state.

During this time the problems of the patriarchate continued to press hard on Vikentije, who was no longer young and who suffered from diabetes and other ailments.[58] In April 1957 a delelgation from the Macedonian Organising Committee headed by Nestor Popovski arrived to negotiate further concessions from the patriarch and Synod.[59] Bishops' deputies (*zamenici*) and members of church courts were appointed for all the Macedonian dioceses, and in a statement to Jugopress Vikentije said that the Macedonian clergy had now been authorised to use their own language for preaching, and to alter their church seals, which would now read: 'P.R. [People's Republic] Macedonia, Orthodox diocese *M* with see at *N*'. But when it came to the point the Sabor again rejected the proposed candidates for bishop. The Rev. Nestor Popovski, who had appeared on every list, was a married man with four children, a deacon not yet ordained priest; and the bishops found this quite unacceptable.[60]

There were also difficulties and unrest in Montenegro, and Patriarch Vikentije, accompanied by Vicar-Bishop Dositej, spent ten days there in July.[61] The church in Montenegro suffered in an acute form from all the problems of the Serbian Orthodox Church: it was very poor and the material circumstances of the clergy were bad, vocations for the priesthood were inadequate, there were almost no monks and too many priests were still in public service (for the most part in organs of social welfare).

The shortage of priests in Montenegro was chronic. Under the independent Kingdom of Montenegro before the creation of Yugoslavia, they had been paid by the state; when this changed

---

[58] *SPC*, pp. 478–9.   [59] 10.v.57: *Vesnik*, 1.v.57.

[60] He was ordained priest on Dec. 11, 1957, with three other Macedonian priests by the patriarch at the Vavedenje monastery in Belgrade. This was the first ordination of Macedonian priests since the war (RNS, 11.xii.57). It is interesting to speculate why the Macedonian priests persisted so obstinately in choosing canonically unacceptable candidates. Did they suppose that the Synod would easily consent to a return to the church's early practice of appointing married men as bishops, or was this a wilful disregard for canon law in which they were encouraged by the authorities who considered that canon law was a reactionary relic of the past, used as an excuse to be obstructive? No one with whom the writer discussed this point was able to offer a satisfactory explanation.

[61] 10–20.vii.1957: *Gl.*, Sept. 1957.

priests had to look for support to the patriarchate and to their parishioners, who were for the most part themselves very poor, and not used to putting their hands in their pockets for this purpose.

The patriarch pleaded with the priests to forget their differences, stop quarrelling about who was a member of the priests' association and who not, and to live in harmony; other eyes were watching them and unless they could unite they would never get what they wanted. He visited Cetinje, the old capital, Titograd, Bar and Kotor and was received by the republican and local authorities. Both sides were extraordinarily conciliatory. The patriarch continually stressed that the laws concerning religion and the church were good laws, and relations at the top were good, but that the law must be observed everywhere and relations at the local level improved. The presidents of the two councils at Cetinje and Kotor referred to the historic role of Montenegrin bishops, who had been both spiritual and temporal heads of the nation, and had led the people in battle; they acknowledged Vikentije's efforts to settle relations between the state and the church and the value to world peace of his trips abroad. Blažo Jovanović, the prime minister, admitted the excesses of some young people who wanted to prove what good revolutionaries they were; they were punished for this, but in the long run it was better to educate and to persuade than to punish.[62] The president of the Bar town council similarly deplored local excesses.[63] All this may have been a manifestation of Montenegrin natural hospitality and national pride in their past, but it would not have been said unless there was a real wish to improve relations.

The crowded progress took place in the blazing heat of a Montenegrin July, and was suddenly interrupted on the last day by an attack of acute appendicitis which put Vikentije into hospital for two weeks;[64] but he made a quick recovery and was well enough to attend an official reception for the President of Mongolia on August 27.[65]

The Macedonian dioceses, 1958

The Macedonian question continued to preoccupy the church and the authorities. Vikentije, accompanied by Bishop Hrizostom, Bishop Jovan of Niš and Vicar-Bishop Dositej, left on March 25, 1958, for a ten-day visit to Macedonia. They called on

---

[62] Ibid.
[63] Ibid.
[64] Ibid. July–Aug. 1957.
[65] Ibid. Sept. 1957.

Radosavljević before leaving and brought up the question of financial assistance, which had not yet been settled for that year; nothing was promised and it was obvious that much would depend on the outcome of the patriarch's visit to Macedonia. He urged them to come to a final settlement of the question.[66] The financial position, as always, was difficult and the church complained that aid from the World Council of Churches had also been reduced, and had to be shared with the Yugoslav Red Cross.[67]

The visit to Macedonia was described as a canonical visitation,[68] the first by a patriarch since before the war, to enable him to see conditions in Macedonia for himself and decide what was necessary to implement the new agreement with the Macedonian priests,[69] but it at once took on the character of a formal state visit.[70] He was met and fêted everywhere by government representatives, and had a long interview with Lazar Koliševski, the president of the Executive Council.[71] Huge crowds of the faithful welcomed him and overflowed into the streets when he celebrated the liturgy. They shouted 'Give us bishops.' as they had done seven years earlier during Dositej's visit; the Macedonian Organising Committee made it clear that it was Macedonian bishops they wanted.

After his return Vikentije gave an interview in which he confirmed that the Serbian Orthodox Church had agreed that Macedonian should be the language of preaching and administration, while Old Church Slavonic would be retained for the liturgy. After the church had been reorganised Macedonian bishops would be appointed; in the meantime bishops' vicars had been appointed to all three dioceses.[72]

The annual Sabor assembled on May 26, 1958, and two days later Tito received the bishops. The patriarch thanked him for his interest in church affairs and particularly for the agreement on social insurance; in his reply Tito again urged the bishops to resolve the question of the Macedonian Church.[73] Relations with Bulgaria were strained and the government feared that Bulgaria might use it as an excuse to interfere.[74] But the bishops refused to accept the candidates, Nestor Popovski, Spira Popovski and Vladimir Zefirov-Popovski, who were all married men, deferred

[66] RNS, 28.iii.58.   [67] Ibid.
[68] Vesnik, 1.v.58.
[69] Statement to Tanjug at the end of the visit: Gl., May 1958.
[70] Vesnik, 1.v.58 for details.   [71] Statement to Tanjug, 1.v.58.
[72] Borba, 19.iv.57.   [73] Gl., June 1958.
[74] RNS, 23.vi.58.

the question again and sent it back to the Synod.[75] Nestor Popovski offered to divorce his wife, but this was rejected; it was, said the bishops, contrary to church regulations and might make trouble with other Orthodox Churches. Only two bishops voted for the list and seventeen against it.[76] The Yugoslav press was silent about the meeting with Tito and did not report the outcome of the Sabor meeting.[77]

The patriarchate III, 1958–9

Three weeks later Vikentije was taken seriously ill; the strain of the previous year, the taxing visits to Montenegro and Macedonia, had weakened his never robust health, and he died in hospital in Belgrade on July 5. His death was immediately reported on the radio and was front-page news in the national press; *Politika* published a sympathetic obituary.[78]

Condolences were received from every quarter, from the government and social bodies, ambassadors of foreign powers and other churches. President Tito sent a wreath to the funeral, which was attended by many government representatives and delegations from the Greek and Russian churches; the message from Archbishop Ujčić of Belgrade, who was acting president of the Catholic Bishops' Conference, was much more than formal.[79]

Vikentije left his successor with an unenviable task. The question of the Macedonian Church could not be deferred any longer; the first of the two climatic turning points was approaching.

The Synod met at once and called a meeting of the Electoral Sabor for September 13, 1958. The bishops' Sabor met on September 9 and deadlocked; but at a second meeting it succeeded in choosing three candidates, Hrizostom of Braničevo, Visarion of Banat and German of Žiča.[80] Pressure from the government was never far away, and Radosavljević was reported to have had several conversations with members of the Sabor during the meeting,[81] but the bishops now felt sure enough of

[75] *Gl.*, July 1958.
[76] RNS, 23.vi.58. The correspondent added that the dissenting bishops had declared that they would rather have Greek bishops than accept such candidates.
[77] Ibid.
[78] Ibid. 6.vii.58.
[79] 'I remember always his sincere friendliness and our friendly conversations on theological matters' (*Gl.*, July 1958).
[80] *Vesnik*, 15.ix.58, and RNS, 11.ix.58. [81] RNS, 11.ix.58.

themselves to react more firmly. During the meeting of the Sabor Bishop Vasilije of Banja Luka was removed by the police and put under house arrest; the bishops at once threatened to suspend their sitting until he had been released. Three days later he returned to the patriarchate and took part in the election, installation and receptions for the new patriarch, but he was subsequently detained again, taken to Banja Luka and interrogated.[82]

At the Electoral Sabor German received thirty-seven votes, Hrizostom seventeen and Visarion none; two blank papers were returned. The following day German was installed as '43rd Patriarch since the foundation of the patriarchy under Tsar Dušan, and fifth in succession in the restored patriarchate' at a service attended by many government representatives and foreign ambassadors, as well as representatives of other religious communities in Yugoslavia, and foreign churches.[83]

The new patriarch's experience fitted him particularly for the tasks before him. By 1958 (in spite of Macedonia) the earlier threat to the very existence of the unified patriarchate had disappeared, and the church could turn its attention to strengthening its pastoral work. German had spent many years both as a parish priest and an administrator.

He was born in 1899 in a small village near Studenica and trained as a priest at the theological faculty in Belgrade; afterwards he studied law at the Sorbonne. He spent eleven years as a parish priest in Serbian villages, at the same time studying, writing and editing the diocesan journal of Žiča. In 1938 he was transferred to the office of the Synod, and in 1951 he became general secretary of the Synod and the Sabor, as well as editor of *Glasnik*, the official journal of the patriarchate. In the same year, having become a widower, he took monk's vows and was elected auxiliary bishop. The following year he became Bishop of Budim and in 1955 administrator of Žiča. When Bishop Nikolaj Velimirović of Žiča died in 1956 in the United States, he was elected to succeed him. He had travelled extensively; in 1951 he visited the United States and the World Council of Churches in Geneva and he accompanied Patriarch Vikentije on his visits to Greece and Moscow.[84] He had worked closely with Vikentije, he understood the need for cooperating with the government, and from Vikentije had learned much about the means of doing so. It was reported that the government considered him the most moderate candidate and that Radosavljević had urged his

[82] Ibid. 23.ix.58.   [83] Gl., Sept. 1958.
[84] SPC, pp. 479–83.

nomination; Hrizostom, in the eyes of the government, was too much in the tradition of Velimirović.[85]

Among the first tasks which the new patriarch undertook was to strengthen the church's relations with the other Orthodox Churches. In April 1959 he set off for a three-week journey to the Holy Land,[86] accompanied by Bishop Nikanor of Bačka, Bishop Hrizostom of Braničevo, Bishop Emilijan of Pakrac, several members of the theological faculty and of his own staff, and inevitably, the Rev. Milan Smiljanić, and the Rev. Kliment Malevski of Bitola. In his speech at the airport German underlined the traditional nature of this visit to the holy places, and especially to the Holy Sepulchre, a visit which has been made by all Serbian patriarchs up to the time of Patriarch Arsenije Čarnojević III in 1683. Historical circumstances subsequently interrupted the tradition which he was now restoring.[87] In addition the good relations which existed between Yugoslavia and the Middle Eastern countries were favourable for strengthening the ties between the Orthodox Churches of these countries and the Serbian Orthodox Church, which in their turn would contribute to developing friendly international ties.[88] The party returned on May 18, having visited the Patriarchs of Constantinople, Alexandria, Antioch and Jerusalem, the Archbishop of Athens and the Metropolitans of Beirut and Salonika[89] and had conversations with government representatives with whom they discussed the position of churches in their own countries and ways of strengthening friendly relations so as to preserve world peace.[90]

Patriarch German also showed his willingness to cooperate, at any rate formally, with the union of priests' associations. He sent Vicar-Bishop Dositej to represent him at the opening of the Third General Congress of the union on September 24, 1958, and attended the government reception for the union;[91] on October 15 he received members of the Executive Committee.[92] The following spring German, Hrizostom and Longin attended an official reception at the union[93] and in October German attended the annual meeting of the diocesan association at Žiča, his former diocese.[94]

[85] RNS, 13.ix.58.
[87] Gl., June 1959.
[89] Ibid.
[91] Vesnik, 1.x.58.
[93] Ibid. 1.iv.59.

[86] 29.iv–18.v.59.
[88] Ibid.
[90] Ibid. Aug.–Sept. 1959.
[92] Ibid. 15.x.58.
[94] Ibid. 15.x.59.

The autonomous Macedonian Church, 1959

Meanwhile the Macedonian question was pressing. The Macedonian priests had reacted angrily to the decision of the Sabor in May 1958 to reject their list of candidates; they declared that the Sabor, by failing to appoint Macedonian bishops, had not fulfilled its part of the April agreement. Immediately after Vikentije's death and without waiting for the election of his successor they announced that they would call an Assembly of the Macedonian Church and People. Two hundred and ninety delegates, both clergy and laity, met at Ohrid on October 5, 1958.[95]

Their first action was to proclaim the re-establishment of the historic archbishopric of Ohrid and elect Auxiliary Bishop Dositej as the first metropolitan. He was installed the same day at the church at St Kliment before a great crowd of the faithful; the president of the Macedonian Commission for Religious Affairs, Strahil Gigov, the secretary of the federal commission, Miloje Dilparić, and representatives of the local authorities (but not, of course, of the Serbian Orthodox Church) were also present.[96]

The Assembly council published a constitution for the new church,[97] which provided that it should remain in canonical unity with the Serbian Orthodox Church through the patriarch, who would also be Patriarch of the Macedonian Orthodox Church. It also provided (Art. 50) that the head of the church on taking office should swear to uphold the motherland and the people's authorities, to whom he would be loyal. It elected Nikola Trajkovski to be Bishop Kliment of Prespa–Bitola and Toma Dimovski to be Bishop Naum of Zletovo–Strumica. (Neither name had appeared on the lists previously submitted to the Serbian Sabor.)[98] Nestor Popovski, whose name had appeared on every list and who was one of the leaders of the Macedonian clergy, was not elected.

The presence of Dositej at the Assembly had not been authorised by the Sabor. Less than a fortnight earlier he had represented the patriarch at the opening of the Third General Congress of the Union of Orthodox Priests' Associations; he had left Belgrade without informing the Synod or getting its

[95] Slijepčević, Mac. 1959, p. 56; Vesnik, 15.x.58 and 1.viii.59; RNS, 24.vii.58.
[96] Vesnik, 15.x.58.
[97] Ustav na Makedonskata Pravoslavna Crkva, signed by Dositej, Archbishop of Ohrid and Skopje, Metropolitan of Macedonia, 6.x.58 (Copy in the U.S. Library of Congress).
[98] Borba, 6.x.58, quoted in Slijepčević, Mac. 1959, p. 62; Vesnik, 5.x.58; RNS, 7.x.58.

permission.[99] The patriarchate, in fact, would not have opposed his election; it was from its point of view a great improvement on previous suggestions, and German was reported to favour it.[100] It objected strongly, however, to the manner in which it had been done, and to the fact that Dositej had been elected uncanonically, by a mixed group of clergy and laity. The government appears to have seized on Dositej as an acceptable alternative to Nestor Popovski when it saw that the election of the latter would make more trouble than it was worth, and would leave the question of the canonical validity of the Macedonian bishops unresolved; the arrangement for the unity of the two churches under a common patriarch was good enough to counter any Bulgarian accusations that the Macedonians were being oppressed, and avoided the ultimate challenge to the Serbian patriarchate of a complete schism. The Macedonian clergy also compromised by discarding their list of episcopal candidates and accepting Dositej (of Macedonian origin but born in Serbia) and two fresh names.

The establishment of the semi-independent, or autonomous, Macedonian Orthodox Church, as it became known, was marked by an exchange of official receptions between the church and the Macedonian government; telegrams of greeting were sent to Tito and to German, assuring the latter that the unity of the church would be preserved in his person as head of both churches.[101]

The government now earnestly pressed the patriarch to accept the *fait accompli* and avoid a serious crisis; Tito himself appealed to German when the latter called on him in October[102] and later that month the patriarch had conversations with Ranković, Petar Stambolić and Jovan Veselinov, president of the Serbian government.[103] Other pressures were discreetly hinted at; the government offered to give a subvention of 30m dinars to cover the current deficit of the church and a further 30m to the social insurance organisation to be used to finance insurance of the clergy, but it was reported that payment would depend on a settlement of the Macedonian question.[104]

[99] RNS, 5.x.58, and Serbian Orthodox source. Dositej's motives remain problematical. He had been elected vicar-bishop in 1951 with the intention of sending him to Skopje (Serbian Orthodox source) but the authorities were not at that time ready to allow a Serbian bishop to go to Macedonia. He was noted for his charity and monastic asceticism, but after seven years as a vicar he was chafing for a diocese and ripe for persuasion by the authorities (Serbian Orthodox source).

[100] RNS, 3.x.58.　　　　　　　　　　[101] *Vesnik*, 15.x.58.
[102] RNS, 10.x.58.　　　　　　　　　　[103] Ibid. 31.x.58.
[104] Ibid. 17.i.59.

During his trip to the Middle East in the spring of 1959 Patriarch German saw the Ecumenical Patriarch Athenagoras in Istanbul; it was reported that Athenagoras advised against recognition of the Macedonian Orthodox Church, principally because of the uncanonical way in which it had been established, and the precedent which this would set.[105] On his way to Greece, the patriarch's train had stopped at Skopje and Dositej had invited him to visit the Macedonian Church on the way home; German now refused the invitation and returned straight to Belgrade.[106]

A decision could not be deferred much longer. The Sabor met in July and, it may be supposed reluctantly, accepted the situation.[107] On July 18 Patriarch German went to Skopje and the next day he and Metropolitan Dositej together consecrated the new elected Bishop of Prespa–Bitola. 'Tears of joy could be seen in the eyes and on the cheeks of Metropolitan Dositej and the newly consecrated Bishop Kliment and many of the faithful when the patriarch appeared after the consecration at the royal gates of the iconastasis with the new bishop and when the latter gave his first episcopal blessing.'[108] At the official lunch which followed Kliment and Dositej thanked the Sabor and in particular German for giving the faithful in Macedonia what they had so long desired; in his answer German left no doubt that he had gone as far as he was prepared to: 'It would be a great mistake if all of us and all others involved would consider that this is a turning point and that there is no more to be done. On the contrary we must fight with all our strength to fend off attacks and to resist all the forces which come at us from all sides and try to meddle in our affairs.'

The next day the patriarch accompanied the new bishop to his see at Bitola. Although it was a working day the church bells were ringing and the church itself and the streets around were packed with a crowd of six to seven thousand people; the patriarch and the bishop could hardly push their way through to the altar. People pressed up to kiss the patriarch's hand and get his blessing, and greeted their new bishop with delight.[109] The religious ceremonies were followed by a civic lunch and visits to local factories, and that evening the party travelled to Ohrid. The programme was repeated; at the civic lunch the patriarch was greeted by a member of the republican government as head of the Macedonian Orthodox Church and thanked for the part he

[105] Ibid. 5.v.59.   [106] Ibid.
[107] Ibid. 20.vii.59; *Glasnik* did not report this decision; *Vesnik*, 1.viii.59.
[108] *Gl.*, July 1959.
[109] Ibid.

had played in bringing about this happy solution ('Leaving behind us a period which lasted a long time...we now enter a new epoch of just relations between the Serbian and Macedonian Orthodox Churches. We consider this action a very important and useful contribution to strengthen unity among our people.')[110] and in his reply the patriarch hoped that this unity would serve the interests not only of the church but also of Yugoslavia.

There were further visits to churches and public works, a reception by the president of the Assembly, Lazar Koliševski, and finally, on July 24, the visit ended and the patriarch returned to Belgrade.

After the North American schism, Bishop Dionisije published two letters which Patriarch German had written him about the Macedonian question. The earlier, dated February 12, 1955, before he became patriarch, stressed the point he always insisted on, that this was an internal church matter, and that the difficulties were due to the fact that it had been linked with political questions. 'They want the church to recognise the Macedonian people. Our position is that this is a matter for the state and is not within the church's competence. The church recognises today's government and its authority, because it is a part of that state, but it is not required to take part in political questions.'[111] And after the declaration of autonomy he wrote, on September 30, 1959: 'Last October's decision at Ohrid placed us before a dilemma: either to take strong canonical measures and an open schism leading to a canonical separation or to accept the principle of church economy and save as much as we can. We felt we must do everything possible to stop the further unwished-for course of events.'[112]

But by consecrating a second Macedonian bishop, the patriarch had finessed with his last trump; he had given away the power which so far had been under the control of the Sabor to consecrate bishops in the apostolic succession, and made a gesture of trust in the hope that the trust would be reciprocated. He did not have to wait long before the Macedonian Church showed that it intended to manage its own affairs. On July 26 Metropolitan Dositej and the newly consecrated Bishop Kliment together consecrated Toma Dimovski, who had been elected by the Assembly of the Church and People as Bishop Naum of

[110] Ibid.
[111] Slijepčević, Mac. 1969, p. 70, quoting Dionisije, *Izdajstvo srpskoga naroda i Srpske Pravoslavne Crkve* [Betrayal of the Serbian People and the Serbian Orthodox Church] (Libertyville, Ill., 1968), p. 98.
[112] Ibid. p. 69.

Zletovo–Strumica. *Vesnik,* which in the Macedonian question had been the mouthpiece of the Organising Committee, commented:

Thus is accomplished the principal part of the restoring of the Ohrid archbishopric and the forming of the Macedonian Orthodox Church, which remains faithful and devoted to the spiritual and canonical unity of the Serbian Orthodox Church and so linked ever more closely in brotherly community with all our people in the Federal People's Republic of Yugoslavia...Macedonia now has three native-born bishops...three spiritual leaders to order church and religious life in Macedonia...so that the Macedonian Orthodox Church will flourish and help the Macedonian people in their struggle for a better and happier life. The Union of Associations of Orthodox Priests, which has sincerely and unselfishly helped and supported the demands of the faithful and clergy in Macedonia, is happy to see the question solved in this just and auspicious way.[113]

The following summer Bishop Naum headed a delegation, whose composition had been agreed with the patriarch, which visited Australia and consecrated a church in Melbourne, built by Macedonian émigrés.[114] The main purpose of the visit, however, was to encourage the forming of separate Macedonian Orthodox Church parishes;[115] these developed and in 1967 became a separate Macedonian diocese. The forms of unity were carefully observed by the Macedonians and the authorities; Patriarch German was always referred to as the head of the Serbian and Macedonian Orthodox Churches. The Macedonian Orthodox Church protested when German continued to sign himself Patriarch of the Serbian Orthodox Church.[116]

The two churches continued in an uneasy relationship until 1967; but ultimate control of the situation passed out of the hands of the Serbian Orthodox Church in 1959, and the postponement of autocephaly probably owed as much to Ranković (an aspect of the situation which was revealed in 1967 when the Macedonian Church made the final break) as to the desires of the two hierarchies.

The patriarchate IV, 1960–4

Visits inside Yugoslavia The resolution of the Macedonian question, however, had an excellent effect on relations between the Serbian Orthodox Church and the government; these now

[113] *Vesnik,* 1.ix.59.   [114] Ibid. 1.ii.61.
[115] RNS, 31.viii.60.
[116] During a visit to Patriarch Alexei of Moscow, although Bishop Kliment of Ohrid was with him (*Gl.,* Jan. 1962); when he visited Romania in 1962 he signed himself Patriarch of Serbia and Macedonia (*Gl.,* Feb. 1963).

entered into a comparatively unclouded period.[117] The patriarch began a series of visits which took him all over Yugoslavia, and the tradition, which had been interrupted by the war, of enthroning the patriarch at the historic archbishopric of Peć, in the district of Kosovo, 'the cradle of the Serbian nation', was revived with exceptional splendour.

In September 1959, accompanied by Nikanor of Bačka and Vladislav of Zahumlje–Hercegovina, he visited Bosnia and Hercegovina; it was the first patriarchal visit since the war. He had talks with Djuro Pucar, the president of the Assembly, and the head of the Moslem religious community, the Reis-el-Ulema Suleiman Hadji Kemura, and consecrated churches at Čajniče and Rudnik.[118]

The Sabor was summoned to meet in May 1960 at Peć patriarchate. The patriarch, who had received a high decoration from the government a few days earlier,[119] and all the bishops, accompanied by Miloje Dilparić, the secretary of the Commission for Religious Affairs, set out from Belgrade on May 27 and stopped over night at Studenica monastery.[120] The next day they passed through Raška, where a big crowd lined the road, stopped at Kosovska Mitrovica where the patriarch preached to a congregation which included Catholic friars and Moslem hodžas, whom he specially welcomed, and finally arrived at Peć where again crowds met him and he was welcomed at the gates of the patriarchate by the vice-president of the town council.[121] One of his first actions was to summon the two Macedonian bishops, Kliment and Naum, to the altar of the central church and present them with a large parcel of holy myrrh[122] for the use of their dioceses.

The next day, Sunday, May 29, early in the morning, the Sabor met; all the bishops except Arsenije, who was confined to a monastery, and Dionisije of North America, were present. (Varnava, who was also in forced residence in a monastery, was a vicar-bishop and not a member of the Sabor.) After approving

---

[117] Not entirely, however. Earlier in the year one issue of *Glasnik* had been confiscated for publishing a sermon by Dr Lazar Milin of the theological faculty calling for Serbian unity and lauding the Serbian Orthodox Church. The government interpreted this as chauvinism and accused Dr Milin of spreading national hatred (RNS, 18.iii.59). This touched the state's sorest point, on which it proved most suspicious of the Serbian Orthodox Church as national tensions revived in the sixties and early seventies.

[118] *Gl.*, Nov.–Dec. 1959.   [119] *Vesnik*, 1.vi.60.

[120] *Gl.*, June 1960.   [121] Ibid.

[122] This is used for confirmations and is given by the head of the church; the gift was thus a symbol that the Serbian patriarch was head of the Macedonian Church.

the resolution of the Synod that the patriarch should be installed at Peć, the Sabor rose, and the ceremonies began. The liturgy was said in the presence of the Orthodox congregation, many high government representatives[123] and Moslem leaders. The patriarch and Metropolitan Damaskin of Zagreb both spoke of the unity and continuity of the Serbian Orthodox Church in territories which were united at the time of the formation of the Peć patriarchate, and the freedom of conscience and worship which believers enjoyed today. The reference to the unity of Serbian territories was welcomed not only by the faithful; the Albanian government was eyeing the large Albanian minority living in Kosovo and Metohija and the government's support of this massive manifestation of Serbianism was possibly caused by the need to counter this.

The installation was followed by an official lunch given by Fadil Hodža, president of the provincial Assembly, after which the patriarch and his retinue set off to visit the great monasteries and churches of the district, Dečani, the Church of the Holy Mother of God at Prizren, Gračanica, and the monastery of the Holy Archangels. At the final official lunch given by the provincial government the patriarch spoke of the example which Yugo-slavia, as a country of many nations and many religions living together in amity, could give to the world.

It had been, as it was intended to be, an impressive display of unity and tradition: the unity and continuity of Serbian Ortho-doxy, the rejection of any further threats to the unity of Serbian territories, and the unity of Yugoslavia, the last of these the principal concern of the Yugoslav government.

In the second half of July the patriarch paid an extensive visit to western Yugoslavia and the Dalmatian coast, and was received by Tito on the island of Brioni.[124]

In July 1961 another opportunity to assert the unity of the church came when the patriarch, accompanied by three bishops, Damaskin, Vasilije and Hrizostom, went to Cetinje to instal the new Metropolitan of the Montenegrin Littoral, Bishop Danilo

---

[123] Dobrivoje Radosavljević, president of the federal Commission for Religious Affairs, Slobodan Penezić, vice-president of the Serbian government, Fadil Hodža, president of the provincial government of Kosmet, Isa Jovanović, president of the Serbian Commission for Religious Affairs, Strahil Gigov, of the Macedonian government, Miloje Dilparić, secretary of the federal Commission for Religious Affairs, Boško Jovanović, president of the Peć People's Committee. Photographs of the occasion also show the hereditary Albanian Moslem guardians of the Peć patriarchate in attendance (*Vesnik*, 1.vi.60).

[124] *Gl.*, Oct. 1960.

Dajković, who had been consecrated in Belgrade at the end of June.[125] The see had been empty since Arsenije's arrest in 1954. The clergy, desperately poor and leaderless for so many years, had been torn by strife and dissension and many had left the priesthood; in 1957 Patriarch Vikentije had spent ten days with them to try to settle their differences and appeal for unity. Now Dilparić, the secretary of the Commission for Religious Affairs, accompanied the patriarch, a visible guarantee that the period when the government had encouraged divisions within the church on republican lines was over.[126] The appointment of Bishop Danilo was a happy one; he was a Montenegrin by birth, educated at the seminary at Cetinje, and had spent his early years as a parish priest among his own people.[127] The patriarch's visit lasted a fortnight and covered the whole diocese; everywhere he and the metropolitan were enthusiastically welcomed by the faithful and feasted by local officials;[128] it was an overt recognition by the authorities as well as by the church of the historic role of Montenegrin bishops as leaders of the people.

Visits abroad The patriarch continued his heavy programme of visits to other Orthodox Churches. He went to Moscow for a fortnight in October 1961,[129] and Patriarch Alexei returned the visit in May 1962;[130] both events were heavily buttressed with official support and representation. German and his suite were received by Brezhnev, Alexei and the other members of his delegation were received by Tito, and both Alexei and Bishop Nikodim, who accompanied him, were given decorations. Flattering references were made to Alexei's sharing the hardships of the siege of Leningrad and all the speeches embroidered the themes of world peace and disarmament. Alexei's visit included three days in Macedonia, during which he was showered with honours and festivities by both the Macedonian authorities and the bishops and clergy of the new Macedonian Church, and fulsome praises of the unity of the Russian, Serbian and Macedonian people were sung.

Catalogues of these visits quickly become tedious but they serve to illustrate the way in which the government, which had 'privatised' religion, continued to watch over, control and make use of it in its institutional form; the public life of the state was no longer permeated by religious formulas but these formulas nevertheless continued to play an acknowledged although

---

[125] Ibid. July–Aug. 1961.
[127] *SPC*, p. 534.
[129] Ibid. Jan. 1962.

[126] See above, pp. 190, 204, 205.
[128] *Gl.*, July–Aug. 1961.
[130] Ibid. July–Aug. 1962.

restricted part in public life. The patriarch was supported by his own men; the state saw to it that he was also accompanied by theirs, government officials, priests from the associations and Macedonian priests. It must have been a strain, but it is also not too far-fetched to suppose that the Orthodox 'theology of forgiveness' and the peculiar strain of sweetness which in Orthodoxy exists side by side with the most Byzantine intrigues helped to lubricate the complex relationships within these ecclesiastical progresses.

The visits to Moscow continued and became almost routine; German attended the celebrations of Patriarch Alexei's fiftieth anniversary as bishop in July 1963,[131] and in September 1965 a Serbian Orthodox delegation, headed by Bishop Jovan of Šabac and Bishop Andrej of Banja Luka, visited Moscow to continue the strengthening of relations between the two churches.[132] There was a ceremonial visit to the Romanian Orthodox Church in October 1962[133] to which enough importance was attached for German to be received by President Maurer, and for a joint official communiqué to be issued supporting world peace and unity among Christians. When the Bulgarian patriarch visited Yugoslavia in June 1963 he was received by Ranković[134] and when German returned his visit in September 1964 he was accompanied by Archbishop Dositej of the Macedonian Church[135] to underline the continuing unity of the Serbs and Macedonians within the Yugoslav federation.

The Pan-Orthodox Conference and the Second Vatican Council, 1961–5

Shortly before going to Moscow the patriarch had led a delegation to the Pan-Orthodox Conference which met on the island of Rhodes from September 24 to October 1, 1961.[136] It was the first gathering of all Orthodox Churches since the Council of Nicea in A.D. 787. A long catalogue of theological theses, which the Synod later published, was discussed, and continuing committees set up. But the most important question which the Conference considered was the appeal to reconciliation which had been issued by Pope John XXIII. Patriarch German had been very non-committal at an interview[137] shortly after the pope had spoken; the Serbian Orthodox Church, he said, had not itself received any communication and so far there had been no official

[131] Ibid. Aug.–Sept. 1963.
[133] Ibid. Feb. 1963.
[135] Ibid. Jan. 1965.
[137] Ibid. June 1960.

[132] Ibid. Jan. 1966.
[134] Ibid. Aug.–Sept. 1963.
[136] Ibid. Feb. 1962.

consultation, although he admitted that 'the matter had arisen during conversations'.

Ecumenical Patriarch Athenagoras had already declared himself in favour of sending Orthodox observers to the Council; he hoped that the Orthodox Churches would be a bridge between Rome and the Protestant Churches. But Patriarch Alexei of Moscow opposed the idea vigorously; an article in the journal of the Moscow patriarchate in 1961 described the invitation of the Council simply as a fresh attempt to bring the Orthodox Churches under the domination of Rome.[138] However, Mgr Willebrands, who was later to head the Secretariat for Christian Unity, paid a visit to Moscow shortly before the Council opened[139] and appears to have reassured the Moscow patriarch. When the Council opened there were two observers from the Moscow patriarchate, the only Orthodox Church to be represented.[140]

The position was more difficult theologically for the Orthodox Church than for the Protestants. For the latter an ecumenical council called by the Roman Catholic Church had no theological or ecclesiastical authority; an invitation to send observers was simply an opportunity to observe and to exchange ideas. But the Orthodox had to make it plain that they did not consider this a true ecumenical council but simply one called by the Patriach of the West, and without authority over the other patriarchs. In addition there were political factors, among them the first signs of an easing of the Kremlin's attitude to the Vatican, such as Khrushchev's telegram to Pope John XXIII on his eightieth birthday; these were not the only considerations but they undoubtedly gave the Moscow patriarchate more room to manoeuvre. A second Pan-Orthodox Conference met in September 1963 to discuss the appeal of Pope Paul VI to end the long schism, and to decide its future attitude to the Second Vatican Council.

The Serbian Orthodox Church was in a particularly difficult position; it had to consider not only the political climate and Yugoslavia's non-aligned status but also the deep-seated hostility of most of the laity and clergy to the Catholic Church. The leadership, many still bearing the scars of the war years, could not afford to go too far ahead of them. The pope's visit to Jerusalem and his meeting there with the Ecumenical Patriarch Athenagoras in January 1964 gave Patriarch German the opportunity to make a statement to *Le Monde* welcoming this as an

---

[138] Rouquette, pp. 149–52.
[139] Ecumenical Press Service, 12.x.62, quoted by Fletcher, pp. 107–8.
[140] Ibid.

event of historic importance for all Christianity and the first step towards ending 'the age-long isolation of the Catholic Church'.[141] Bishop Emilijan called on Cardinal Koenig of Vienna in November 1964 on his return journey from a visit to Prague[142] and Mgr Willebrands, secretary of the Vatican Secretariat for Christian Unity, visited the patriarch in June 1965 during a tour which took him to the Ecumenical Patriarch in Constantinople and other Eastern patriarchs.[143] Finally, in the autumn of 1965, Dr Lazar Milin of the theological faculty and Dr Dušan Kašić, director of St Sava's Theological Seminary in Belgrade, went to the Council as observers;[144] their encounters there with Western European Catholics, especially the French, were reassuring and happy.[145]

The life of the church

In common with the rest of Yugoslavia, the everyday life of the church and of believers gradually became more relaxed during this period. There had been a constant struggle since the war to build new churches to replace those which had been destroyed during the war, and to serve the new communities which were springing up around the big cities. In spite of the difficulty of obtaining building permits for churches, 181 churches and 8 monasteries were built during the twenty-five years after the war and 841 churches and 48 monasteries were repaired and restored. Many of these were classed as cultural monuments, and the expense of renewing 450 of them was borne by republican or local authorities;[146] these included the outstandingly successful restoration of the famous medieval frescoed churches and monasteries of Macedonia and the southern part of Serbia, some of which work had already been started before the war.

The religious education of children in the parishes had never been as vigorous in the Orthodox Church as it was in the Catholic Church, but now at least two dioceses, Bačka under Bishop Nikanor, and Belgrade–Karlovci under the patriarch, could boast that there were classes for the religious instruction of children in every parish.[147]

The training of boys for the priesthood also expanded; since the war this had been one of the church's chief preoccupations. In 1966 there were only about 500 students in the seminaries and

[141] Gl., April 1964.   [142] Ibid. May 1965.
[143] Ibid. July–Aug. 1965.   [144] Ibid. Nov. 1965.
[145] Conversation with Dr Milin, Jan. 1972.
[146] SPC, p. 254.
[147] Verbal information from the patriarchate, 1971.

faculty as compared with 1,000 before the war, and many of them failed to proceed to ordination.[148] The former theological faculty at Sremski Karlovci in the Vojvodina, which had been closed by the Ustaša, had not been reopened after the war; now it was decided to establish a branch of the Belgrade St Sava seminary there in March 1964,[149] and this became an independent institution in May 1967.[150] In 1964 Bishop Stefan of Dalmatia reopened the historic seminary at Krka, inland from Šibenik on the Dalmatian coast, with an imaginative scheme for a two-year shortened course to train older men for the priesthood;[151] in May 1966 a normal five-year source was started which ran parallel with the short course.[152] The same year a monastic school was established at the monastery of Ostrog in Montenegro.[153] This brought the total number of seminaries up to four, together with one faculty and one monastic school; in 1970 they had a total of 767 students,[154] still short of the numbers which were needed but at any rate a step forward.

A remarkable phenomenon was the increase in the number of nuns during the whole postwar period; it was a continuation of the resurgence of women's monasticism which started in the early 1920s. Women's religious vocations had gradually disappeared under Turkish rule, and when the Serbian Orthodox Church was reunited in 1920 only one convent, with ten or so nuns, existed in its territory.[155]

In 1925 a group of Russian nuns, refugees from the Russian revolution, had been given permission to come to Yugoslavia; they settled in the monastery of Hopovo, north of Belgrade in the hills of the Fruška Gora. Their arrival, bringing with them the rich tradition of women's monasticism in Russia, coincided with the beginnings of the religious revival (the so-called *bogomolski pokret*) in the Serbian Orthodox Church.[156] By the following year four new convents had been established, bringing the total number to 73 nuns (including the 21 Russians) and 35 novices. The movement continued to grow and in 1941, just before the war, there were 27 convents in the twelve dioceses, with 286 nuns and 111 novices.[157] War and the occupation scattered them and a number of convents were ravaged and left empty, but the nuns gradually returned and the growth which

[148] *Gl.*, May 1966.   [149] Ibid. Jan 1964.
[150] Ibid. June 1967.
[151] Ibid. Jan. 1964, and conversation with Bishop Stefan.
[152] *Gl.*, July 1967.   [153] Ibid.
[154] *RIY*, p. 11.   [155] *SPC*, p. 337.
[156] Ibid. p. 333.   [157] Ibid. p. 337.

had been interrupted by the war was resumed. In 1969 there were 81 convents with 658 nuns and 187 novices;[158] this figure does not include the Macedonian dioceses which had in the meantime declared their autocephaly.[159] Several monasteries which had formerly been occupied by monks were turned over to women (Žiča, Gomionica, Rakovica and others).[160] The nuns who had formerly run schools now earn their living mainly by farming and market-gardening, weaving, rug-making and knitting; they also look after about a hundred mentally handicapped children.[161]

The schism in North America, 1962–3

Before returning to the developments in the Macedonian situation, a brief account must be given of another schism, in the American–Canadian diocese, which, painful though it was, did not deal the fundamental blow to the unity of the church which the Macedonian schism was to do.

Bishop Dionisije Milivojević of the American–Canadian diocese had been a virulent opponent of the postwar government in Yugoslavia from the beginning, and was the subject, immediately after the war, of a number of complaints to the patriarchate by the government. There had also been a growing number of private complaints, reaching the patriarchate from both priests and the laity in the emigrant community, about the bishop's conduct of diocesan affairs and about his private life.[162] Dionisije had, as a young priest, taught at one of the seminaries and directed the monastic school at Dečani. He was one of the founders of the *Bogomolski* movement of spiritual revival within the church, and was a candidate for the episcopacy who could not be disregarded. The movement, however, was marred in its early days by the familiar excesses of 'enthusiasm' – spiritual indiscipline, visions and dabblings in spiritualism; Bishop Nikolaj Velimirović of Žiča, a man of charismatic personality, took control and by his energetic direction and powerful preaching brought the movement back to more orthodox channels of expression. Dionisije, now something of an embarrassment, was elected vicar-bishop in 1938 and in 1939 was sent to the United States as bishop of the American–Canadian diocese.[163]

---

[158] Ibid. p. 339, quoting the Statistical Review of Dioceses, 1969.
[159] Women's monasticism continues to be weak in Macedonia. *RIY* gives no figures for nuns, though *CFPRY* in 1959 gives fifteen.
[160] *SPC*, p. 337.   [161] Ibid. p. 342.
[162] *Gl.*, April 1964; *Vesnik*, 1.xi.63.   [163] *SPC*, p. 496.

After the outbreak of war in Yugoslavia in 1941 the American–Canadian diocese was cut off from direct contact with the patriarchate for nearly ten years. In 1946 Bishop Irinej of Dalmatia and Bishop Nikolaj Velimirović arrived in the United States as refugees, but the encounter between them and Dionisije was difficult; Velimirović was a commanding personality and Dionisije guarded his episcopal prerogatives jealously. As a result Irinej left the United States and spent the rest of his life in England, and Velimirović retired to live in one of the institutions of the Russian Orthodox Church Abroad in the United States. Although many of the bishops shared Dionisije's anti-communism, all of them resented his treatment of Velimirović, whom they greatly admired. Dionisije on his side was irritated when Patriarch Gavrilo reasserted his control over the handful of Serbian priests in Europe (there were two in Britain) who had come under the American–Canadian diocese during the war.[164] It was not until 1951 that personal contacts were restored by the visit of Bishop German and Dr Glumac. But by then habits of independence had been established.

Matters came to a head in 1962. The previous year the administration of the diocese had been reorganised; it was divided into four deaneries (*namesništvo*) and the Central and South American parishes added to its jurisdiction.[165] Dionisije now proposed that the diocese should be raised to a metropolitanate and two or three auxiliary vicar-bishops appointed.[166] The Sabor decided to look into this on the spot and at the same time to investigate the complaints against Bishop Dionisije, and commissioned Metropolitan Damaskin of Zagreb, who had served briefly before the war as Serbian Orthodox bishop of America and Canada, Bishop Nikanor of Bačka and another priest to visit the United States.

They arrived in Libertyville, Illinois, on September 14, 1962, for a meeting of the diocesan council, and according to the first accounts were warmly welcomed and invited to be the guests of the council.[167] Four days of official discussions with Bishop Dionisije followed, after which the delegation set off for a tour of the diocese. The visit lasted until November 26, a full month longer than had been intended,[168] by which time signs of conflict had begun to come into the open; the deans of the Middle West district had already announced that they were resolved to remain in canonical unity with the Serbian Orthodox Church and

[164] Serbian Orthodox source.
[166] Ibid. April 1964.
[168] Ibid. April 1964.

[165] *Gl.*, June 1961.
[167] Ibid. April 1963.

rejected 'the provocative and unfounded allegations about the delegation made in some émigré publications'.[169]

There is no official record of the events between the return of the two bishops and the next meeting of the Synod, although it is not difficult to infer from what followed that Dionisije must have realised that he was in serious trouble and set about preparing a counter-attack.

At its meeting on April 4, 1963, the Synod considered the report of the two bishops and a letter from Dionisije; the gravity of the situation became apparent when it was decided to call an extra-ordinary meeting of the Sabor on May 10. The Sabor dealt first with the reorganisation of the diocese. Disregarding Dionisije's suggestions, they divided it into three new dioceses, the Middle Eastern and Canadian, the Middle Western and the Western.[170] The Rev. Stefan Lastavica, parish priest of Windsor, Ontario, was elected bishop of the Middle Eastern diocese and immediately consecrated in the United States; the Rev. Grigorije Udicki was appointed temporary administrator of the Western diocese. The Sabor then turned to Dionisije, and in the light of the situation which the bishops had found, and of Dionisije's own letter, decided to suspend him from his episcopal duties as bishop of the new Middle Western diocese, while the complaints about him were investigated. The Rev. Firmilijan Ocokoljić, the secretary of the former diocese, was appointed temporary administrator, and the diocesan clergy informed of the actions which had been taken.[171] Bishop Hrizostom of Braničevo and Bishop Visarion of Banat were appointed to investigate the case, and together with the Rev. Mladen Mladenović, secretary of the Synod, and the Rev. Božidar Tripković, secretary of the Church Court of Belgrade, went to the United States.

They met Dionisije on July 5, not at his home, but at a nearby holiday resort. Dionisije, who had refused to accept his suspension (this can be inferred from the report of the whole case in *Glasnik* of April 1964), now refused to answer questions, or to carry out the Sabor's decision to divide his diocese into three.[172]

[169] Ibid. April 1963.
[170] Ibid. June 1963; *Vesnik*, 1.vi.63. The Middle Eastern and Canadian diocese, see Cleveland, Ohio (22 eastern states and the whole of Canada), had 36 parishes, 36 priests, 1 monk, 80,000 faithful (*SPC*, p. 522). The Middle Western diocese, see Monastery of St Sava, Libertyville, Ill. (15 states and southern Africa) had 26 parishes and St Sava, 26 churches, 20 priests, 1 monk and 50,000 faithful (*SPC*, pp. 529–30). The Western American diocese, see Alhambra, Calif. (13 western states, Central and South America), had 13 parishes, 9 priests, 2 monks, 20,000 faithful (*SPC*, p. 516).
[171] *Gl.*, April 1964; *Vesnik*, 1.vi.63.   [172] *Gl.*, April 1964.

A further extraordinary session of the Sabor was called on July 26; Visarion flew home to attend it. The bishops deprived Dionisije of his see on the grounds that he had disobeyed the Synod and thus broken his bishop's vow; the Rev. Firmilijan Ocokoljić was elected bishop in his place on July 27, and at the same time the Rev. Grigorije Udicki, administrator of the Western diocese, was elected its bishop. Both men were consecrated within the next few days by Bishop Hrizostom and the new Bishop Stefan of the Middle Eastern diocese.[173] The Sabor sent a message to Serbs abroad explaining their actions, appealing for unity and concluding with a solemn warning of the spiritual dangers facing them from Dionisije:

Dionisije is now trying to take you with him. We ask you not to let yourselves be deceived, to think carefully before you separate yourselves from the body of the church. Whoever separates himself from the church separates himself from God's angels and saints at whose head stands the Holy Mother of our Lord, separates himself from St Sava, St Tsar Lazar and all the Serbian saints and martyrs. The curse of God, the curse of St Sava and all the Serbian saints before the throne of God falls on those who separate themselves from the church. Hold fast to your legal bishops, listen to them and hold them in respect.[174]

Dionisije retorted by summoning the Tenth Assembly of the Church and People which met at Libertyville on August 6–8 and again on November 12–14. The assembly declared the diocese separated from the mother church and autonomous, and elected the Rev. Irinej Kovačević vicar-bishop. He was consecrated at Libertyville on December 3 by 'two self-styled, non-canonical, unrecognised Ukrainian bishops, Genadije and Grigorije'.[175]

A formal indictment was sent to Dionisije on October 15, 1963, and he was asked to reply within thirty days. In return, he asked that the period should be extended to six months and that all the declarations, complaints and depositions connected with the indictment should be sent to him, properly certified. The Synod answered on December 10, giving him a month instead of the six he had asked for and refusing his second request, since he already had a list of the accusations with full details. Dionisije then returned the indictment and announced that he would refuse to reply to it.[176]

He was tried by the Sabor on March 5, 1964, in his absence, and accused of breaking his bishop's oath by disobeying the highest church authorities, causing a schism in the church, and

[173] Ibid.
[175] Gl., April 1964.
[174] 27.vii.63: Vesnik, 1.ix.63.
[176] Ibid.

'personal misuse of material goods and behaviour unbecoming to his priestly calling'. The details of the accusations concerning Dionisije's private conduct were not published officially, though rumour had already made them notorious and *Vesnik* published a savage attack on him making precise charges.[177] The Sabor sentenced him to be 'deprived of his episcopal and monastic functions', that is, he was defrocked. He was not, however, excommunicated, as Patriarch German made clear in his Easter message, so as not to close the door to repentance and a return to the church.[178]

The schism was the first in the history of the Serbian Orthodox Church and as such a great shock, particularly to the hierarchy, who were acutely aware of the threatened dangers of divisions at home. There was also real distress at the nature of the dirty linen which was aired. But the break was peripheral; it did not concern canon law, or touch the basic unity of the Serbs. It was due far more to personalities and in-fighting between old political enemies in the emigrant community, between former Četniks and followers of Ljotić, the Serbian fascist who was an admirer of Nazi ideology and had strongly opposed the national-ist mystique of the Četniks. The majority of the accusations of misconduct against Dionisije came from followers of Ljotić in the United States. But even here the lines were not sharply drawn; some Četnik groups continued to support the patriarch and although in the end probably about half the emigrant community followed Dionisije, the majority of the clergy re-mained faithful to the patriarchate.[179] The exiled King Peter of Yugoslavia, who at first supported Dionisije, withdrew his support in 1967 in a message which appealed for Serbian unity in the Serbian Orthodox Church.[180] Among the consequences of the schism have been a series of lawsuits over church property which have wasted the substance of the church and have only recently been concluded.

The Macedonian Orthodox Church, 1962–8

The difficulties with Dionisije preoccupied the bishops in the early sixties and the Macedonian question receded temporarily into the background. There were efforts on both sides to patch up relations after the unilateral proclamation of autonomy. In February 1962 Dositej paid an official visit to the patriarch in

[177] *Vesnik*, 1.ii.64.   [178] *Gl.*, April 1964.
[179] Serbian Orthodox source.
[180] *Diakonia* (New York), III, no. 1 (1968), pp. 84–5.

Belgrade.[181] Together they visited the dioceses in the Vojvodina and Srem and called on Radosavljević, the president of the Commission for Religious Affairs, who expressed the satisfaction of the government at this evidence of growing unity between the two churches. In August German accompanied Patriarch Alexei to Macedonia during his visit to Yugoslavia and the following month returned for a short holiday as Dositej's guest.[182] He went to Skopje shortly after the great earthquake in the summer of 1963[183] and returned the following year with Bishop Emilijan of Timok and Bishop Visarion of Banat to observe the progress of rebuilding; they were received by the Macedonian government and entertained by the priests' association.[184] When German visited the Patriarch of Bulgaria at the end of 1964 Dositej accompanied him, an important gesture of solidarity.

The Macedonian Church during this period was consolidating its position. There is mention of new churches at Kočani and Kolešino, and the rebuilding of the monastery church at Negotino; the amended church constitution of 1961 provided for courses in Macedonian language and literature to be taught in the seminaries (which at that time did not exist) and the Macedonian priests' association ran a Macedonian language course for priests during the winter and spring of 1965–6.[185]

One can still only speculate why the Macedonians finally chose to push the matter to its final conclusion in 1966–7. The leaders of the Macedonian clergy had undoubtedly always intended that Macedonia should have its own church. They were increasingly irritated by the failure, as they saw it, of the Serbian Orthodox Church to interpret the terms of Macedonian autonomy in the sense which they gave to it: Patriarch German continued to sign himself, with rare exceptions, as Patriarch of the Serbian Orthodox Church and not the Serbian and Macedonian Orthodox Churches, and in relations with sister Orthodox Churches to treat the three Macedonian dioceses as an autonomous part of the Serbian Orthodox Church instead of as a separate and equal ecclesiastical organisation, united to the Serbian Orthodox Church by a common head. Matters may have come to a head in 1967 because of two immediate factors, the Brioni Plenum of the Yugoslav League of Communists in July 1966 followed by the overthrow of Ranković, the vice-president and until then Tito's likeliest successor, and a resurgence of tension between Yugoslavia and Bulgaria which gave the Yugoslav government reason to wish to strengthen Macedonian loyalty to Yugoslavia. Crven-kovski, the Macedonian party leader, said at Ohrid in October 1967 that if it had not been for Ranković the question of the Macedonian Church would have been settled long since.[186] Ranković, a Serb, had previously been minister of the interior and head of the secret police, and had been succeeded by one of his own men. He was therefore strongly inclined by his bureaucratic training to centralise, and by his national feelings to favour Serbian institutions and, perhaps only partly consciously, Serbian hegemony. In the early postwar years he had been looked upon by the Serbian Orthodox Church as a persecutor, but later he began to take it under his – rather rough – protection, and when he fell the church felt that it had lost a protector.[187] Outside Serbia his fall released a flood of relief, and throughout Yugoslavia tension relaxed; the activities of the secret police were sharply curtailed and administrative measures of repression virtually disappeared.

According to the official gazette of the Macedonian Orthodox Church, the Sabor had refused in May 1966 to present the Macedonian Orthodox Church to the sister Orthodox Churches, leaving them with no recourse except to break the link with the Serbian Orthodox Church.[188] The two Synods met on November 18 in Belgrade, and the Macedonians, in an angry mood, demanded 'full independence' – that is, autocephaly[189] – threatening to call a meeting of the Assembly of Church and People and declare their own autocephaly if their demands were not met.[190] The Serbian Synod continued to insist that the constitution of the Macedonian Orthodox Church, and thus its status, could only be changed with its consent; it refused to summon an immediate meeting of the Sabor but asked the Macedonian bishops to put their demands into writing.[191]

On December 3 the Macedonian Orthodox Church sent the Sabor a formal demand for autocephaly, repeating its threat to act unilaterally if it was not granted.[192] It was five months before the Serbian Sabor answered. In the meantime Dositej was building up the image of an independent church. He sent Christmas greetings to the Serbian (*sic*) patriarch[193] and early in

[186] *Politika*, 29.xi.67.   [187] Serbian Orthodox source.
[188] *VMPC*, July–Aug. 1967, p. 103.   [189] *Vesnik*, 15.ix.67.
[190] Slijepčević, Mac. 1969, p. 71, quoting sin. no. 1026, minute 144, 10.iii.67, report of a visit by Patriarch German and two other bishops to Petar Stambolić, president of the Federal Executive Council, a photocopy of which is in Dr Slijepčević's possession.
[191] *Vesnik*, 15.ix.67, and Slijepčević, Mac. 1969, p. 71.
[192] *Gl.*, Sept. 1967.   [193] *VMPC*, Jan–Feb. 1967.

January received a call from the Roman Catholic bishop of Skopje, Mgr Čekada, and the apostolic delegate, Mgr Mario Cagna.[194] The twenty-second anniversary of the consecration of Patriarch Alexei of Moscow was made the occasion for a long article about his visit in 1962 together with a photograph of the patriarch taken with Archbishop Dositej.[195] Another long article discussed the historical and canonical requirements for autocephaly in the Orthodox Churches.[196]

Private discussion between the two churches and the government continued. Patriarch German, Metropolitan Danilo of the Montenegrin Littoral and Bishop Stefan of Dalmatia called on Petar Stambolić, the prime minister, on March 7.[197] Dositej, with Vicar-Bishop Metodij and the Rev. Nestor Popovski, president of the Macedonian Priests' Association, called on Patriarch German and on Stambolić on April 17.[198]

The Sabor held its ground in spite of pressure; some of the more far-sighted bishops had felt that it would have been wiser, as well as more brotherly to help the Macedonian clergy instead of frustrating their desires,[199] but now they closed ranks. On May 24 at an extraordinary session of the Sabor, the request of the Macedonian Church was refused[200] on the grounds first that its organisation and personnel were not sufficient to qualify it for autocephaly[201] and secondly that the Macedonian Church had behaved uncanonically: Dositej, its metropolitan, had broken his oath to preserve canonical unity with the Serbian Orthodox Church taken at his installation as metropolitan in 1958, and the

---

[194] Ibid. This was an ordinary courtesy call; the protocol with the Vatican had recently been signed and Mgr Cagna had arrived to take up his post as Vatican representative. It was normal that he should call on Orthodox bishops during his visits to Catholic bishops, but for Dositej the call came at a convenient moment.

[195] Ibid. [196] Ibid. May–June 1967.

[197] Slijepčević, Mac. 1969, p. 71. [198] VMPC, May–June 1967.

[199] Serbian Orthodox source. [200] Gl., Aug. 1967.

[201] The reasons given were: the Macedonians had only three bishops, including the metropolitan, whereas canonically they should have had three in addition to the metropolitan; they appeared to have insufficient clergy to sustain an autocephalous church, although their numbers were not clear – they listed 334 priests, 54 priest–monks, monks and nuns and 34 diplomaed seminary students, but monks and nuns were not priests and there was no guarantee that all the seminarians would proceed to ordination. It appeared that out of 953 churches and 66 monasteries, 619 were without a priest and 32 monasteries were empty. The Macedonian Church had no seminary and since it made no mention of one it seemed that it intended to continue to use the Serbian Orthodox seminaries to train its priests (ibid.). In February 1967, in answer to an enquiry from abroad, the metropolitanate supplied the figure of 'about 400 parishes', adding that a general regrouping of parishes was in progress (Pavlowitch, ECR, 1(4)).

decision had been taken by an Assembly which contained only four bishops out of thirty-four members, whereas a decision of this magnitude could only be taken by a bishops' Sabor. Moreover Dositej had told the Serbian Synod that the Macedonian government had been consulted and had approved the move; this was government meddling in church affairs, which was both uncanonical and against the Yugoslav constitutional principle of the separation of church and state. In view of all this, if the Macedonian Church proclaimed its autocephaly, it would be regarded as a schismatic religious organisation.

The Assembly of the Macedonian Church and People met at Ohrid July 17–19, 1967, 'under the protection of St Kliment and St Naum'. It proclaimed an autocephalous Macedonian Orthodox Church and reaffirmed the restoration of the archbishopric of Ohrid which had first been proclaimed in 1958; the ruling body of the new church was to be a Synod consisting of five diocesan bishops. Two new dioceses, Velika and America–Canada–Australia, were established (July 17), the former with its see at Ohrid but with only a vague territorial definition, and the latter consisting of the parishes established among Macedonian emigrants; Vicar-Bishop Metodij was elected diocesan bishop of Velika and Vicar-Bishop Kiril[202] diocesan bishop of America–Canada–Australia. Metropolitan Dositej was installed as head of the new church with the revised title of Archbishop of Ohrid and Macedonia. The addition of 'Macedonia' to the title followed the practice of other local churches.

The new church based its right to autocephaly both on its claim that it was the successor of the independent archbishopric of Ohrid which had been abolished in 1767 by the Ottoman Turks and was now restored and on the right of every nation to have its own local church (*mesna crkva*). The explanatory statement which was joined to the proclamation, and which was also signed by the five bishops, referred to the long struggle of the Macedonian people for their national freedom, which had always been combined with a struggle for an independent church and which the liberated Macedonian people affirmed as well through their own language and culture. It retraced the history of the postwar struggle of the Macedonians for their own church and

[202] Kiril, who had worked at the metropolitanate in Skopje since 1962, took monk's vows in 1964 at the age of thirty, with the rank of deacon; a few months later he became archdeacon. In 1967 he was elected vicar-bishop by the Synod; on July 9 he was ordained priest by Dositej, who immediately after the liturgy advanced him to archimandrite. On July 12 he was consecrated vicar-bishop, and on July 19 he was referred to officially as Bishop of the America–Canada–Australia diocese (*VMPC*, Sept.–Oct. 1967, pp. 166, 201).

claimed that the Serbian Orthodox Church by accepting in 1958 the separation of the three Macedonian dioceses, governed by their own constitution, had, by implication, sanctioned the 1958 Assembly of the Church and the People and given the Macedonian Orthodox Church a canonical release (*otpust*); this amounted to a recognition by the Serbian Orthodox Church of a limited autocephaly. The unity of the two churches, under a common patriarch, was not a jurisdictional unity but one founded on the dogmas and canons which unite all Orthodox Churches. In spite of this the Serbian Church, in its dealings with other Orthodox Churches, persisted in behaving as though the Macedonian Church was an autonomous part of the Serbian Church instead of an equal and independent body, united to the Serbian Church through a joint head. This fact, the statement concluded, was the reason why the Macedonian Orthodox Church, which had demonstrated over the last nine years that it was capable of existing fruitfully and successfully, had asked the Serbian Orthodox Church to grant it formal autocephaly. Faced with the Serbian refusal, the Macedonian Church had no recourse other than to declare its own autocephaly, following the example of other local churches. (The reference here was to the breakaway of the Greek and Bulgarian Churches from the patriarchate of Constantinople.) It referred to Rule 17 of the Fourth Ecumenical Council to support the claim of the liberated Macedonian people to have their own church in their own state.[203] The Union of Associations of Orthodox Priests supported the Macedonian Orthodox Church in a letter to the Serbian patriarchate – couched in the respectful and conciliatory tone which it had adopted some years earlier – pleading for recognition of the Macedonian Orthodox Church.[204]

The Serbian Sabor met again on September 14 and refused recognition in uncompromising terms:

acting in its now established pattern the Macedonian Synod ignored this decision [or the Serbian Synod of May 24] and proclaimed the autocephaly of the Macedonian Orthodox Church...the Sabor decided that since the Macedonian hierarchy had unilaterally and uncanonically decided to separate from the mother church and form a schismatic religious organisation, the Sabor will sever its liturgical and canonical communion with them and believes its duty is to take proceedings against those guilty of schism.

It will not, however, cut itself off from the faithful but will continue to serve their religious needs and to educate Macedonian students at the seminaries and theological faculty.[205]

---

[203] *VMPC*, July–Aug. 1967, for this whole account.
[204] *Vesnik*, 15.ix.67.   [205] *Gl.*, Sept. 1967, for this whole account.

The Sabor reminded the Macedonian Church that it had not been limited in any religious or national sense by the Serbian Church; it had its native-born bishops and used its own language, and the Serbian Church trained its priests and negotiated social-insurance agreements in which the Macedonians shared.[206]

This decision in its turn was vigorously rejected by the Macedonian Synod on October 17. It published the statement of the Serbian Orthodox Church in full – the first time either of the protagonists had published in its own journal the text of a communication from the other – and refuted it point by point. The break was now irrevocable.

The Macedonian Church was, as was to be expected, fully supported by the Macedonian authorities. A long article explaining the church's position appeared in *Nova Makedonija* on September 20, 1967; the Serbian Orthodox Church was sharply attacked for saying that Macedonia was not a state but only a part of a federated state, with limited sovereignty. If one followed this argument, said *Nova Makedonija*, there was no reason for an independent Serbian Church either, since Serbia and Macedonia were equal members of the Yugoslav federation. It shrewdly picked out a further sentence from the Serbian document: 'What would happen to the Orthodox Church if every ethnic group decided out of its own will to declare its independence from a section of the church?'

This, of course, was the fear which had dogged the Serbian Orthodox Church since the war, but the use of the expression 'ethnic group' was unguarded and was seized on both by the authorities and the Macedonian Orthodox Church[207] as proof that the Serbian Orthodox Church still supported Serbian pretensions to hegemony.

The new church, with the fullest cooperation from the Macedonian authorities, applied itself immediately to establishing its position. The latter had already given permission for a new and imposing archbishopric to be built in the centre of Skopje, and the foundation stone was laid on June 14, 1967.[208] A new seminary at the monastery of Sv. Ilija (St Elijah) in the mountains outside Skopje was opened on October 30 in the presence of government officials.[209] The seminary was later

---

[206] See e.g. agreement of 14.vii.66 signed by the patriarch of Serbia and Macedonia German (*VMPC*, Nov.–Dec. 1966).

[207] Ibid. Sept.–Oct. 1967; *Politika*, 19.ix.67.

[208] *VMPC*, Sept.–Oct. 1967.

[209] *Politika*, 1.xi.67, quoted in Slijepčević, Mac. 1969, p. 82; *VMPC*, Sept.–Oct. 1967.

transferred to Dračevo, a suburb of Skopje.[210] At the end of July Dositej travelled to Canada to visit Macedonian parishioners in Toronto and Montreal, and he was followed in June 1968 by Bishop Kiril, who made his first canonical visitation to his flock in Canada and the United States.[211] The newly appointed Yugoslav consul-general in Toronto called on Dositej at the end of August before taking up his post.[212] The federal government conferred a high decoration on the archbishop to mark his sixtieth birthday in August, and he was among the official guests at the gathering on October 19 when the Macedonian Academy of Arts and Sciences was founded.[213] A translation of the New Testament into Macedonian appeared, under the auspices of the British and Foreign Bible Society.[214]

Great efforts were made to establish communications with sister Orthodox Churches, who were somewhat uncertain about the correct response (and had to take into account political as well as canonical considerations). The Rev. Dr Vasil Valjanov, a member of the cabinet of the Patriarch of Bulgaria, called on Archbishop Dositej on September 26, 1967,[215] and early in October a group of priests from Bitola, on a visit to Istanbul, were received by the Ecumenical Patriarch Athenagoras.[216] Metropolitan Kliment, Bishop Metodij and the Rev. Klime Malevski visited Patriarch Athenagoras, and Bishop Naum, Bishop Kiril and the Rev. Nestor Popovski visited Patriarch Justinian of Romania and continued their journey with visits to the Russian and Bulgarian Churches.[217] The following New Year Dositej received messages of greetings from the heads of both the Bulgarian and Romanian Churches, and from Metropolitan Nikodim of Leningrad.[218]

None of these exchanges, however, resulted in formal recognition of the new church. The Serbian patriarch continued to ignore the greetings of the Macedonian Orthodox Church, but there has been no anathema, or severing of relations with the faithful, and Macedonian students continue to be trained at the theological faculty in Belgrade.

The Archiepiscopal Assembly of the Church and People (as it has become known) of the Macedonian Orthodox Church took

---

[210] The writer visited this seminary in 1970.
[211] *VMPC*, July–Aug. 1968.
[212] Ibid. Sept.–Oct. 1967.   [213] Ibid.
[214] Ibid. March–April 1968.   [215] Ibid. Sept.–Oct. 1967.
[216] Ibid.   [217] Ibid. Nov.–Dec. 1967.
[218] Ibid. In addition Dositej congratulated Cardinal Šeper, Archbishop of Zagreb, on his appointment as prefect of the Sacred Congregation in Rome and was thanked (ibid. Jan.–Feb. 1968).

a further step to give the church weight and authority in October 1968 when it raised all five dioceses to the rank of metropolitanates.[219] The somewhat amorphous diocese of Velika, whose territory had never been defined, was renamed metropolitanate of Debar–Kičevo. The Assembly also adopted the Gregorian calendar, which came into use on Christmas 1970. Dositej referred to this in an interview with the Catholic fortnightly *Glas Koncila* as an indication that the new church wished to collaborate with the ecumenical movement, adding that Christmas would now be celebrated on the same day by the Catholics and Orthodox, and it would be easier to ask the authorities to declare it a public holiday.[220]

During the early months of 1968 both sides paid a number of calls on the authorities, without breaking the deadlock. Finally the Serbian Orthodox Church started proceedings in the ecclesiastical court against Dositej and the other Macedonian bishops; on September 23, 1968, a solemn summons was sent to them to return to the way of the holy canons. When this summons was disregarded, the Synod, on December 12, sent Bishop Makarije of Srem and Bishop Nikanor of Bačka to Skopje; their mission was equally unsuccessful.[221]

Here the matter now rests. According to canon law, the invitation must be repeated three times. There is no doubt that the government would prefer the matter to rest and not be brought to a head, but it would also like to maintain reasonable relations with the Serbian Orthodox Church. It can be assumed that the authorities have persuaded the patriarch to delay action.

---

[219] 7.x.68: ibid. Sept.–Oct. 1968.   [220] *Glas Koncila*, 3.xi.68.
[221] *Pravoslavlje* (journal of the patriarchate, Belgrade), 19.xii.68, quoted in Slijepčević, Mac. 1969, pp. 85–6.

Epilogue

This work is a preliminary study of a recent historical period, for which many essential documents are still not available; its principal advantage is that it has been written when many people who are still alive can give their differing versions of events. The relations between the churches and the state in Yugoslavia continue to develop and there have been rapid changes during the last few years; these, however, must wait for further detailed study. This epilogue gives a few indications of the direction of these changes.

The relaxation of tight party control which had been growing slowly during the second half of the 1950s and the early part of the 1960s took a sharp spurt forwards after the fall of Ranković. The change was most marked in the Catholic areas, especially in Croatia, coinciding as it did with the signing of the protocol between the Yugoslav government and the Vatican. At the same time Croatian nationalism, never far below the surface, began to manifest itself more openly. This nationalism had many liberalising tendencies, which were shared by the leaders of the Croatian League of Communists, who enjoyed widespread popular support. The nation found itself in growing unity and the church found itself increasingly sharing in this unity. But the Serbian inhabitants of Croatia were apprehensive, not without reason. In Slovenia the old suspicions of clericalism were still present, but there was remarkable freedom for the expression of divergent ideas; there was more reality in the separation of the republican government from the republican party organisation than in any other republic. In Serbia the old guard of the party was approaching retirement and new liberal men were coming in. The relations between the Serbian Orthodox Church and the state were strained by the Macedonian schism, but this did not erupt into open conflict. The federal and republican governments were determined that the Macedonian Orthodox Church should at last achieve autocephaly, but they avoided as far as possible any open humiliation of the Serbian Orthodox Church; and the church did not push its opposition to the final break of excommunicating the Macedonian hierarchy.

A change in the atmosphere of church–state relations took
place, however, after December 1971 when President Tito,
speaking to a specially summoned meeting of the party Presidium
at Karadjordjevo, condemned Croatian nationalism, which
during 1971 had begun to assume proportions which appeared
to endanger the unity of the federation. The leadership of the
Croatian League of Communists was removed from office, and
during the course of the following year a number of prominent
liberal Serbian, Slovene and Macedonian communists were
replaced by more conservative men and party discipline was once
more tightened. These moves, which were part of Yugoslavia's
tight-rope walking between the two power blocs, were intended
partly to fend off any threat of interference by the Soviet Union
in a situation where it might feel itself threatened by excessive
liberalisation and westernisation in Yugoslavia, and partly to
reassert the leading role of the party and counteract the
dangerously divisive forces of nationalism which had been
awakened within the country. The reappearance of conservative
party figures was accompanied by a renewal of attacks on the
churches, both for excessive nationalism and for exceeding their
constitutional rights to concern themselves with 'religious
affairs'. These began to be much more narrowly defined. There
was constant sniping at the churches, but, at the time of writing
(1974) there has been no all-out attack on religious belief.

The tone of the period 1966–71 was exemplified by a special
session of the Executive Committee of the Central Committee of
the League of Communists of Croatia.[1] It condemned 'political
meddling' by the church in the work of social organisations, but
it also condemned 'bureaucratic elements in society' which
endangered the unity of society by attacking believers, especially
in the regions of mixed nationality. It encouraged individual
believers to express their political feelings by working as equal
citizens within the Socialist Alliance, and it reminded the leaders
of the Socialist Alliance that the majority of its members were
believers.

But the authorities found themselves in a dilemma of their own
creation. They approved of the Vatican's new attitude to world
affairs, particularly to peace and the Third World, but inside
Yugoslavia they wanted the churches to confine themselves
strictly to 'religious affairs'; in theory they wanted individual
believers to behave like fully participating citizens and self-
managers, but in practice there was a good deal of resistance,
especially at the local level. Above all they were determined to

[1] *Komunist*, 2.iii.67.

keep the churches as institutions out of Yugoslav internal politics, and they were always nervous of the churches' activities among young people.

The dilemma was never satisfactorily resolved. It represented the two contradictory attitudes in the party towards religion which had been present since the beginning: the humanist and Marxist, which expected that religion would gradually wither away as men became disalienated and in the meantime must be tolerated, and the impatient, hard-line opposition to religious belief and the churches, which was eager to attack them at every opportunity.

On the one hand religion became a subject for objective and often sympathetic study among Marxist sociologists and philosophers, and a dialogue sprang up between them and Catholic theologians; and on the other hand any sign of nationalism, or of excessive activity by the churches in matters outside the religious sphere, was severely censured. It was, nevertheless, a time of hope and opening horizons. The progressive elements in the party and the elements in the Catholic Church which had welcomed the Second Vatican Council supported each other; the church saw that it was not in its interest to give a handle to the conservatives in the party. This policy was paralleled by the wise and conciliatory diplomacy of the pro-nuncio, Mgr Mario Cagna.

Dr V. Bajsić, later dean of the theological faculty at Zagreb, wrote at this time:

Today the freedom of the church includes: worship, preaching, religious instruction in parishes, a religious press, religious seminaries and ordination, and charitable works. At present the opportunities open to the church are even greater than it is able to seize, because there is so much lost time to make up after twenty years of freeze. The church is not and must not be politically active, but the category of politics is ambiguous and can be defined differently... It is not only a question of the clergy and the exercise of the ministry; it is a question of the whole church. It is a question of ensuring that the faithful can profess their religion freely and under no compulsion, no matter which social category they belong to, and at the same time can fulfil their duties to the state and to society as citizens with full rights. It is not so much a judicial question... it is a question of getting rid of old taboos, of wiping out the lasting effects of fear (and the faithful are sometimes full of fear and inhibitions), of developing patiently a reciprocal trust... Today in Yugoslavia the Christian as a citizen has all the rights of his compatriots but not the same possibilities... We have arrived at a point at which not much more can be expected from the law. A change is only possible with a change in men. We are dealing with a moral question which weighs heavily on the church, on Christians in their relations to the gospel and on communists in their relation to humanism... in other words it is a

common task. Any country would be proud to succeed in carrying this
out.[2]

In a wider field, relations between the Yugoslav government
and the Vatican continued to improve and full diplomatic
representation was resumed in 1970. The Yugoslav government
put no obstacles in the way of 50,000 pilgrims from Croatia who
flocked to Rome in June 1970 for the canonisation of the first
Croatian saint, Nikola Tavelić, and welcomed the international
Mariological and Marian Congresses held in Zagreb in the
summer of 1971 and attended by prominent church dignitaries
and leading European theologians. President Tito and other
Yugoslav leaders called on the pope during official visits to the
Italian government and both Mgr Willebrands and Mgr Casaroli,
the Vatican secretary of state, visited Belgrade. The government
also clearly approved of official gestures of friendship between
the Roman Catholic and Serbian Orthodox Churches, of which
the most notable was the visit of Cardinal Šeper, Archbishop of
Zagreb, to Patriarch German in 1967.

This halcyon period, full of hope for the future, was not
suddenly extinguished, but gradually faded out. Relations today
are still correct, and between the Yugoslav government and the
Vatican they are good; both sides have much to gain from
keeping them so. But anything which could be interpreted as
an expression of nationalism is severely censured; for the first
time in a number of years several Catholic priests have been
imprisoned for nationalist activities, and, much more unexpectedly, a senior Serbian Orthodox bishop was sentenced to one
month in prison in 1972 for an injudicious sermon. Above all,
the need to give children a sound Marxist education to counter
the influence of religion again preoccupies the authorities.

Yugoslavia remains an unpredictable country, the despair of
tidy minds, and no one can safely forecast the future. This study
has shown, however, a slow but never completely reversed
movement towards greater toleration by all the elements in
this situation – the government and Marxist intellectuals, the
churches and Christian intellectuals, the Vatican, and even –
though this remains in some ways the most difficult factor – the
ordinary Catholic and Orthodox believers who are still deeply
scarred by centuries of conflict and suffering. It must be the hope
of everyone who knows this brave and beautiful country that the
toleration which had begun to develop in the face of all historical
precedents will not be entirely extinguished in the difficult period

[2] *Svesci*, Sept.–Oct. 1969.

through which the country is now passing, and in the uncertain future; and that Yugoslavia, which has accomplished in its time a number of impossible things, will still give an example of how Marxist humanism and religlious belief, the churches and a communist government, can exist side by side and learn from each other.

For readers who would like to study this period further, the following books, journals and articles are suggested:

AKSA (Aktualnosti Kršćanska Sadašnjost) [Current News: Contemporary Christianity].

Biblija (The Bible), Zagreb, 1968. A new translation by a group of writers and scholars, Catholic and Marxist, under the chairmanship of Dr Jure Kaštelan, writer and poet, and the Rev. Dr Bonaventura Duda, O.F.M.

Borba, 26.vi.66. A general survey of religion and the churches in Yugoslavia.

Bošnjak, B. (ed.), Religija i društvo [Religion and Society], Zagreb, 1969. Articles by Zdenko Roter, Zlatko Frid, Branko Bošnjak etc.

Čekada, Čedomir, Proigrana šansa: fenomen glasa koncila u svjetlu činjenica i dokumenata [Opportunities Gambled Away: the Phenomenon of Glas Koncila in the Light of Facts and Documents], Djakovo, 1971. A polemical attack on the post-Second Vatican Council movement in Croatia by an influential conservative Catholic publicist.

Ćimić, Esad, Drama ateizacije [The Drama of Atheisation], Sarajevo, 1971.

　　Socialističko društvo i religija [Socialist Society and Religion], Sarajevo, 1966. A full-length study written with sympathetic insight by a professor of sociology at the University of Sarajevo.

Drašković, Čedomir, 'A Yugoslav view of the church in modern society', Sociological Translations in Eastern Europe, 25.vii.67, original in Encyclopaedia Moderna, I, nos. 3–4 (March–June 1967), 52–3. Dr Drašković is a member of the theological faculty of the Serbian Orthodox Church in Belgrade.

Frid, Zlatko, Religija u samoupravnom socijalizmu [Religion in Self-Management Socialism], Zagreb, 1971. A collection of essays and papers by the former president of the Commission on Religious Affairs on Croatia.

Glas Koncila [Voice of the Council]. Published under the auspices of the archbishopric of Zagreb but independently edited. A lively fortnightly with a circulation of over 110,000. See in particular articles by the Rev. Dr T. Šagi-Bunić and the satirical column signed 'Don Jure'.

Godišnjak: Institut za Medjunarodnu Politiku i Privredu [Yearbook: Institute of International Politics and Economics], Belgrade. See section on the Vatican from 1964 onwards.

Kavčič, Stane, Promjene u katoličkoj crkvi [Changes in the Catholic Church], Ljubljana, 1967.

Komunist (Belgrade), 2.iii.67. Report of a session of the Executive

Committee of the Central Committee of the League of Communists of Croatia on 6.ii.67.

Moyzes, Paul, 'Christian–Marxist encounter in the context of a socialist society', *Journal of Ecumenical Studies* (Philadelphia), 9, no. 1, 1–27.

Naše Teme [Our Themes] (Zagreb), no. 6 (June 1967), no. 12 (1972). Journal of the Union of Croatian Youth. Two complete numbers with papers on religion, the church and atheism.

Odgoj, Škola/Religija, Crkva [Education, School/Religion, Church], Zagreb, 1969. Proceedings of a conference of educationalists published by *Školske Novine* [School News].

Politika, 18.i.69. Report on a consultation of educationalists from Serbia, Croatia and Slovenia.

Roter, Zdenko. See Bošnjak, B. (ed.).

Šegvić, Petar, 'Ideološki problemi statusa crkve u našem društvu' [Ideological problems of the status of the church in our society], *Socijalizam*, March 1968, pp. 358ff. Šegvić is a member of the Federal Executive Commission and writes extensively on religion.

Školski Vjesnik [School Herald] (Split), year 19, nos. 5–6 (May–June 1969). Papers presented at a conference of educationalists in Split.

Svesci [Notebooks], Kršćanska Sadašnjost, Zagreb. Articles on the Christian–Marxist dialogue, the place of believers in a self-management socialist state, ecumenism etc. in nos. 3 (April–May 1967), 6 (Sept.–Oct. 1967), 7–8 (Nov.–Dec. 1967), 9 (1968), 10 (1968), 12 (Dec. 1968), 13 (Feb.–March 1969), 14 (May–June 1969), 15 (Sept.–Oct. 1969), 16 (Nov.–Dec. 1969), 17–18 (May–June 1970), 19–20 (July 1970–Dec. 1971). Nos. 21–4 (Jan. 1972–Dec. 1973) contains the results of a questionnaire sent to all Catholic clergy by the Council on the Clergy of the Bishops' Conference of Yugoslavia in 1971 and an analysis of the sociological, economic and other aspects of the clergy.

Teorija in Praksa – Revija za Družbena Vprašanja [Theory and Practice – Review of Social Questions] (Ljubljana). Occasional articles.

Životić, Mladen, *Aktualni problemi odnosa prema religiji* [Contemporary Problems in Relations with Religion], Belgrade, 1961.

Appendix I

Value of the Yugoslav dinar in terms of the United States dollar

1939	50 dinars (= $1.00)
1945	50 dinars
1952	300 dinars
1961	750 dinars
1965	1,250 dinars
1968	(Monetary reform)
1970	15.00 dinars
1971	17.00 dinars

Appendix II

Statistical tables

For a number of reasons statistics about churches and religious communities are unreliable: inexperience or incompetence in gathering statistical data, the need for concealment, reliable data not available or non-existent. The 1953 census was the only one in which questions about religious adherence were asked (see table 1); the great majority of people declared a religious adherence, but it is probable that many of them were indicating their nationality as much as their religious belief. A good source of information about the situation today, *Religions in Yugoslavia* (whose statistics are provided by the religious communities themselves), gives no membership figures. The Vatican yearbook, *Annuario Pontificio*, gives figures based on diocesan returns, and the annual statistical review of the dioceses of the Serbian Orthodox Church gives figures based on the returns of parish priests; these must be considered to be estimates. The 1973 figures from each have been used in table 3.

The statistics in this appendix have been drawn from the following sources: *CFPRY*; *RIY*; Eterovich and Spalatin; *Annuario Pontificio*, 1944–73; *SPC*; the Serbian Orthodox Church Statistical review of dioceses for 1973; and Pavlowitch, *ECR*, 1(4).

Table 1. *Size of religious communities*

	Total population	Roman Catholic	Serbian Orthodox	Moslem	Other	Without religious affiliation
1953[a]	16,936,573	5,370,760	6,984,686	2,080,380	362,872	2,127,875
1973	21,500,000	6,537,348[b]	6,692,541[c]	—	—	—

[a] 1953 census, quoted by Eterovich and Spalatin.
[b] *Annuario Pontificio*, 1973. The figure has been reached by totalling the diocesan figures.
[c] Statistical review of dioceses, Serbian Orthodox Church, 1973. This figure does not include the Macedonian Orthodox Church; *RIY* gives 600,000/1,000,000 for it.

Table 2. *Comparative statistics in 1959*

	Dioceses	Priests	Monks	Nuns	Churches	Monasteries	Seminaries	Faculties	Students
Serbian Orthodox Church	20[a]	1,720	600			2,980	2	1	500[b]
Macedonian Orthodox Church	3	212	31	15	210	50			
Roman Catholic Church	24[c]	3,365		5,700	6,000+		17	2	1,400

[a] In addition two dioceses abroad: the American–Canadian and the Buda.
[b] 300 in the seminaries and 200 at the faculty.
[c] Four of these were apostolic administrations.
Source: *CFPRY.*

Table 3. *Comparative statistics in 1973*

	Believers	Dioceses	Parishes	Priests	Monks	Nuns	Churches	Monasteries	Seminaries	Faculties	Students
Serbian Orthodox Church	6,692,541	21[a]	2,415[b]	1,400[c]	276[d]	704	3,368[e]	83 72 convents[e]	5[e]	1[e]	767[f]
Macedonian Orthodox Church	600,000/ 1,000,000[e]	4[g]	—	250[h]	—	—	953[i]		1	—	—
Roman Catholic Church	6,547,348	21[j]	2,438	2,419	2,360[k]	6,334		247 575 convents[e]	30[e]	2[e]	1,663[l]

[a] Includes the portion of the Skopje diocese remaining after the 1967 schism. There are also three dioceses in North America and one in Europe/Australia.

[b] 1,384 parishes have full-time priests, 883 parishes are visited by a neighbouring priest and 120 by an ordained monk, and 26 are not served at all (SPC).

[c] Includes 1,379 parish priests and 21 priests doing administrative work. In addition there are 508 retired priests who give occasional assistance in parish work.

[d] 208 in monasteries, 68 outside monasteries.

[e] Source: RIY.

[f] 120 at the theological faculty, 647 at the seminaries.

[g] There is also one diocese abroad: Canadian–American–Australian.

[h] Source: RIY. There are also 50 retired priests. Pavlowitch gives 334 priests, the figure supplied in 1967 by the metropolitane of Skopje.

[i] Obviously includes chapels and shrines, including those no longer in religious use.

[j] There are also two apostolic administrations (Banat; Koper); a third, Pazin, is included in the diocese of the Poreč. In October 1977 the Istrian apostolic administrations and the diocese of Poreč–Pula were incorporated into the archdiocese of Rijeka, thus unifying all the Catholics of Istria into one diocese.

[k] Includes 1,354 ordained monks, many of whom carry out parish duties.

[l] 651 at the two theological faculties, 477 at the 8 major seminaries, 535 at the 22 minor seminaries.

Sources: *Annuario Pontificio*, 1973 (diocesan figures totalled); Serbian Orthodox Church statistics review of dioceses for 1973; *RIY*.

Table 4. *Changes between 1944 and 1973 in four Catholic dioceses*

The source for this table is the *Annuario Pontificio*. Diocesan figures appearing in this official publication are provided by the dioceses themselves. For a number of years after the war *AP* gave the last prewar or wartime figures. Between 1951 and 1953 new figures appear which show the situation as it then was, but do not record the changes of the immediate postwar situation. It is difficult to get an accurate overall picture of that period, and it is misleading to add up the figures given for each diocese; firstly, because circumstances made it difficult to compile accurate statistics, and, secondly, because a number of dioceses on the Italian frontier were divided by the disputed postwar frontiers, whereas the figures in *AP* continue to refer to the whole diocese.

The table shows the changes which took place in four important and representative dioceses; Zagreb, the largest Croatian diocese; Ljubljana, the largest Slovenian diocese; Sarajevo, a diocese whose inhabitants are nationally and religiously divided between Catholic Croats, Orthodox Serbs and Moslems, and where the majority of the Catholic parish priests are regular (Franciscan), not diocesan, clergy; and Split, the most important Dalmatian diocese. The years 1944 (which represents prewar figures), 1951, 1956, 1961, 1964 and 1966 have been taken to chart the changes; the year 1973 gives the contemporary situation.

	Population	Roman Catholics	Parishes	Diocesan priests	Men's Orders		Women's Orders		Seminarians
					Houses	Numbers	Houses	numbers	
				Zagreb					
1944	2,038,000	1,900,000	384	826	41	538	124	1,603	111
1951	2,353,000	1,900,000	385	612	28	359	35	1,298	66
1956	2,130,000	1,850,000	390	498	31	386	98	1,383	105
1961	2,130,000	1,850,000	391	500	37	490	101	1,483	120
1964	2,130,000	1,850,000	393	493	31	582	113	1,448	97

	570,293	276	336	14	119	13	794	26
1961	586,000	278	320	17	208	20	746	47
1964	590,000	281	312	30	220	40	677	61
1966	643,000	286	302	33	245	53	651	95
1973	714,000	292	344	[a]	303	[a]	623	165
Sarajevo (Vrhbosna)								
1944	1,225,000	108	113	14	228	42	605	30
1956ᶜ	1,300,000	99	68	10	295	3	31	15
1961	1,200,000	105	94	10	211	5	208	37
1964	1,349,000	108	106	10	133	4	240	40
1966	1,349,000	115	107	11	215	5	255	39
1973	1,450,000	112	84	[a]	340	[a]	364	58
Split								
1944 (1946)	300,000	149	173	16	140	39	330	97
1956ᶜ	306,340	156	153	11	51	22 (1957)	207	21
1961	320,000							
1964	327,000	154	160	13	98	34	260	51
1966	360,000	157	146	13	89	31	256	48 (1965)
1973	368,000	172	155	[a]	187	[a]	519	67

[a] Not given in *Annuario Pontificio*.
[b] The change to postwar figures comes two or three years later than in other dioceses.
[c] Figures for 1951 omitted as they show no significant change.
[d] Increase due to boundary changes.

Table 5. *Distribution of priests within Serbian Orthodox dioceses*

Table 3 showed the overall shortage of priests in the Serbian Orthodox Church today. Table 5 shows how unevenly the shortages are divided among the twenty-one dioceses.

	Parishes	Priests	Retired priests[a]
Belgrade–Karlovci	94	60	59
Banat	132	88	28
Banja Luka	121	69	12
Bačka	101	74	17
Braničevo	127	96	38
Gornjikarlovac	144	24	9
Dabar–Bosnia (Sarajevo)	66	47	8
Dalmatia	82	45	6
Žiča	173	137	56
Zagreb	44	12	5
Zahumlje–Hercegovina (Mostar)	47	18	3
Zvornik–Tuzla	92	54	6
Niš	276	142	115
Raška–Prizren	66	28	7
Skopje (portion)	50	29	22
Slavonia	78	36	7
Srem	147	106	8
Timok	90	44	21
Crnogorsko–primorje (Montenegrin Littoral)	184	18	24
Šabac–Valjevo	147	120	35
Šumadija	154	132	22

[a] Some carry out parish duties.

Source: Statistical review of dioceses, Serbian Orthodox Church, 1973.

Table 6. *Land expropriated under the Law on Agrarian Reform*

The following table gives the amount of land expropriated from the churches in each republic (the Vojvodina is listed separately) and the number of owners expropriated.

	Hectares	Average hectares per owner	Owners
Serbia	18,696	133.5	140
Vojvodina	34,522	50.7	679
Croatia	48,328	69.6	694
Slovenia	48,657	112.9	431
Bosnia and Hercegovina	55,607	46.3	121
Macedonia	14,010	20.5	684
Montenegro	3,547	161.2	22
Total for FNRJ	173,367	62.2	2,771

Source: Petranović, p. 291, quoting Vladimir Stipetić, *Agrarna reforma i kolonizacija u FNRJ 1945–48* [Agrarian Reform and Colonisation in the SFRY 1945–48], table 5, p. 439.

Petrović adds that M. Mirković (cited by Stipetić) gives 165,000 hectares of land expropriated from the churches but he inclines to accept Stipetić's figures, 'which are based on researches in the archives'. He adds (p. 291, n. 105) that the ministry of agriculture of Yugoslavia did not differentiate between the various religious communities in its statistical tables and that 'church publications on the status of owners before and after the agrarian reform, insofar as they exist', were not available to him. The landholdings of the Catholic Church were much less centralised than those of the Serbian Orthodox Church; the writer was told in 1971 by Zagreb diocesan officials that no central register of expropriations was kept or has since been compiled.

Table 7. *Breakdown of land expropriations in Croatia*

A second table gives a breakdown of expropriations in Croatia, district by district, with the overall amount in Church hands.

District	Owners	Total (cadastral *jutra*)	*Jutra* left to the church
Osijek	96	8,514	1,385
Slavonski Brod	77	27,509	1,537
Daruvar	47	3,116	841
Bjelovar	51	4,281	877
Varaždin	100	6,893	1,482
Zagreb	72	5,664	933
Zagreb City	72	2,032	194
Banija (Sisak)	21	3,212	310
Kordun (Karlovac)	35	4,319	609
Primorje (Sušak)	27	5,563	495
Lika (Gospić)	1	29	17
Dalmatia (district)	120	15,081	4,414
Total	728	86,213	13,094

Source: FNRJ Archives, fasc. 601, annual report on the implementation of the Law on Agrarian Reform of the ministry of agriculture and forests of Croatia, 12.ix.45–7; quoted by Petranović, p. 292.

The tables do not differentiate between the holdings of the different churches but according to Petranović the greater part of the land belonged to the Catholic Church.

There were three principal categories of large landowners: private persons, the churches and the banks. In Serbia and Montenegro churches and monasteries had larger holdings than any other category, the result of the fact that there were no feudal holdings with right of inheritance. In Croatia banks and firms had somewhat larger holdings than the churches, while in Slovenia church holdings were considerably greater than those of banks and firms. In Macedonia, Vojvodina, and Bosnia and Hercegovina private large landowners were predominant (Petranović, p. 292, quoting Stipetić (see table 6), p. 436).

Appendix III

The British and Foreign Bible Society in Yugoslavia[1]

The connection of the British and Foreign Bible Society with Serbia began in 1818 when it agreed, together with the Russian Bible Society, to finance the first translation of the Bible into Serbian from Church Slavonic; the Russian Bible Society paid Vuk Karadžić's translator's fee and the British and Foreign Bible Society gave a grant of £500 to cover the cost of printing.

Before the Second World War a depot had been established in Belgrade and in 1938 the circulation of Bibles, New Testaments and portions of the scriptures was 82,562. During the war years, 1941–5, 80,613 copies were distributed, a remarkable feat in view of the conditions in the country. In 1945 a consignment was sent through the Red Cross, and 17,601 copies were distributed. The 1946 annual report records that Mr Vladimir Jeremić, the secretary, and his assistant were alive and well, although they had been imprisoned by the Gestapo for six months. The depot was closed in 1949 and Mr Jeremić was imprisoned by the Yugoslav authorities from April 1949 to March 1950; but no charge was brought against him and he was eventually released. A representative of the society visited Belgrade in 1951; the depot was reopened and in spite of the poor condition of the books, which had been stored in damp cellars, distribution was resumed.

The depot remained open for nine months in 1952 and there was a considerable increase in circulation, but this fell sharply in 1953 when a heavy import duty on books was imposed. President Tito's visit to Britain in 1953 brought about an easing of the situation and circulation again increased. In 1955 customs charges were reduced and there were no difficulties about importing copies of the scriptures. Mr Jeremić travelled extensively through all the republics, and found that the Catholic Church in Croatia and Slovenia was anxious to obtain supplies; in Skopje he met the translators of the Bible into Macedonian. The situation changed again in 1956 when import duty was raised steeply and two large consignments of books were refused entry; nevertheless an unusually high number of complete Bibles was distributed that year, and colportage, the peddling of Bibles from village to village by individual colporteurs, began to increase; in spite of severe taxation and a new restriction by which books could only be sent in small packages by post, the circulation was over 60 per cent of the previous year's. In 1958 a representative of the society visited Belgrade and in 1959 Mr Jeremić and his wife were able to visit London. The improving conditions in

[1] Source: Annual reports of the British and Foreign Bible Society, 1946–73.

Copies of the scriptures distributed (Bibles, New Testaments, portions of the scriptures) in Yugoslavia by the British and Foreign Bible Society

1938	82,562	1958	25,401
1941–5	80,613	1959	31,565
1946	17,601	1960	34,220
1947	45,838	1961	32,324
1948	23,716	1962	44,359
1949–50	No figures	1963	16,388
1951	9,097	1964	404
1952	13,062	1965	65,426
1953	No figures	1966–70	No figures
1954	15,006	1971	15,000
1955	64,697		(local production begins)
1956	22,988	1972	157,000[a]
1957	14,101	1973	42,064[b]

[a] Figures inflated by the inclusion of 20,000 scriptures for children and many portions of scriptures. Bibles, 3,000; N.T.s, 5,000.

[b] Bibles, 16,315; N.T.s, 10,305.

Yugoslavia were reflected in the work of the society and Mr Jeremić travelled widely through the country distributing books.

An official of the society visited Yugoslavia in 1961 and reported that a small but steady stream of books was entering the country with the permission of the authorities; it was far from sufficient to meet the needs of the people but there were no important hindrances. The translation of the New Testament into Macedonian was ready for printing and work on the Old Testament was proceeding. Hungarian and other Protestant minorities were receiving the scriptures in their own languages: 'there is much to be thankful for in Yugoslavia', concludes the report.

History repeated itself in 1962. In the nineteenth century a press law had made the importation of books difficult, and the press law of 1962 aimed at restricting the import of foreign political propaganda made it illegal for anyone except a recognised Yugoslav agency to import and distribute books; the depot was closed in June. But the atmosphere was friendly, and diplomatic negotiations were started and continued throughout 1963. In May 1964 an official of the society visited Belgrade to work out a *modus operandi*; Mr Jeremić had prepared the ground well and it was arranged that a Yugoslav commercial firm should import the books and that they should be distributed by the priests' association from the society's headquarters; Mr Jeremić continued as liaison officer. The work, which had been closed down for two years, was resumed with government permission.

No circulation figures appear in the reports from 1966 to 1970, probably owing to the fact that Mr Jeremić was seriously ill; but distribution continued. In 1970 the report speaks warmly of the publication of the splendid new Croatian translation of the Bible, which was available in many bookshops, and acknowledged the 'disappearance of the former dogmatic Roman Catholic treatment' in the translation. During the following year, 1971, the printing of Bibles and other scriptures began inside Yugoslavia; as a trial run 15,000 New Testaments in Serbian were printed in Ljubljana. The experiment was successful and now all books in the main Yugoslav languages are printed in Yugoslavia. New translations and revisions of old translations have been undertaken and seminars held for translators. Relations with the Roman Catholic Church are good, and a new version of the New Testament in Slovene was produced in cooperation with it.

Appendix IV

The religious press[1]

Before the Second World War there was a large Roman Catholic and Serbian Orthodox press. The Serbian patriarchate and the principal Serbian Orthodox and Roman Catholic dioceses published their official gazettes; newspapers, journals and periodicals were published by the diocesan authorities and the various religious orders. Both churches owned printing presses.

During the war the Catholic press with some exceptions in the occupied areas continued to appear, but the Serbian Orthodox press disappeared, with the exception of *Glasnik* (the official gazette of the Serbian Orthodox Church), which managed to continue publication in spite of great difficulties. It did not appear from April to October 1941, nor from April to December 1944, and it appeared irregularly during 1945, but since then it has been published monthly, with a few brief interruptions. *Glasnik* has an official section which publishes decisions of the Synod and the Sabor (Assembly), legislation affecting the church, and anything concerned with church–state relations, as well as official news about the patriarchate and the dioceses. Its unofficial section contains articles of general religious interest. Its circulation in 1955 was 2,100; in 1960, 2,400; and in 1970, 3,000.

At the end of the war the Catholic press disappeared, with the exception of the official diocesan gazettes (Zagreb, Split, Djakovo, Ljubljana). The only other exception was *Blagovest* [The Annunciation] a bimonthly[2] founded in 1931 and published in the diocese of Skopje, which resumed publication in 1946, after having been closed under the Bulgarian occupation; it is now published by the diocese of Belgrade. It has appeared regularly since 1946 except for a number of short breaks and one longer one between May 1953 and January 1954. Its circulation is 23,000.

The postwar press

A fortnightly *Gore Srca* [Lift Up Your Hearts] was founded in April 1946 by the Literary Society of St Mor in Istria (Književno Društvo Sv. Mora za Istru) and edited from the seminary in Pazin. The seminary, the first Croatian one in Istria, had just been opened, and since the Slav clergy in Istria sided with the Yugoslav authorities in the dispute with Italy over the frontier, the paper's way was made easier. Its circulation at the

---

[1] Sources: *RIY*; a list of the Catholic press supplied to the writer in 1970 by the secretariat of the Bishop's Conference of Yugoslavia; and *SPC*.

[2] Throughout this appendix 'bimonthly' means every two months.

beginning was 6,000 and grew to 12,000 by the middle of 1947; although it was never very large or important it was at that time the only religious paper in Croatia other than the official diocesan gazettes. *Gore Srca* continued to appear until the issue of October 26, 1952, when it ceased publication without any explanation. (There is a file of copies in the University Library, Zagreb.)

Oznanilo [Church Notices] was founded by the diocese of Ljubljana; the first issue appeared on November 1, 1945, but only a few numbers came out. Both these papers appear in a list of the religious press in Yugoslavia, given in *SRCY* in 1953, although by then they had ceased publication.

Verski List [Religious Gazette] was founded by the diocese of Maribor in 1946, and *Družina* [The Family], a fortnightly magazine of news and features about religious life, was founded in 1952 and is now published by the diocese of Ljubljana. *Verski List* still appears and *Družina* has become the leading popular religious magazine in Slovenia, with a circulation of 130,000.

The various Catholic priests' associations with two or three minor exceptions all publish their own papers; the first number of each recorded the founding of its association. *Bilten* [Bulletin], the journal of the first, abortive Slovenian priests' association, appeared during 1947–8; it was succeeded by *Nova Pot* [New Way], the journal of the Association of Cyril and Methodius (Ciril–Metodsko Društvo) of Catholic Priests in the People's Republic of Slovenia. The first number appeared in November 1949 with an introductory article by the Rev. Dr S. Cajnkar, who later became its editor. This has continued to appear and is a serious and respected publication.

Dobri Pastir [The Good Shepherd] is the journal of the Dobri Pastir Assocition of Catholic Priests in Bosnia and Hercegovina; it appeared first in February–March 1950. The membership of the association was and remains largely Franciscan and the editor is a Franciscan. The journal now appears twice yearly as *Nova et Vetera*.

Vesnik [The Herald], the fortnightly paper of the Union of Associations of Orthodox Priests in Yugoslavia, appeared on March 1, 1949. It reflected faithfully the opinions of the Yugoslav authorities concerning church–state relations until about 1955. The Union of Orthodox Priests' Associations then began to take a more independent line, although it continued to support the cause of the Macedonian clergy, and this was reflected in the policy of *Vesnik*. Today it is concerned with the professional life of the clergy and its articles continue to show a certain independence from the views of the hierarchy which has been characteristic of the Association of Orthodox Priests since its founding at the end of the nineteenth century. Its circulation today is 3,500. The Union of Associations also publishes a theological journal, *Pravoslavna Misao* [Orthodox Thought], twice a year. It was founded in 1958; circulation 2,000.

These, together with the *Glasnik* of the Serbian Orthodox patriarchy, already mentioned above, the *Službeni List Nadbiskupije Zagrebačke* [Official Gazette of the Archbishopric of Zagreb] and the official gazettes of the dioceses of Ljubljana, Djakovo and Split, and some smaller diocesan gazettes, composed the religious press of Yugoslavia until the beginning of the 1960s. The gazette of the diocese of Djakovo, the *Djakovački Vjesnik*, has a much wider range of articles than most diocesan gazettes. It began to appear in 1943 in this expanded form.

Printing presses belonging to the Catholic and Orthodox Churches were nationalised after the war, and religious publications had to depend on secular printing presses. This gave rise to many difficulties, often caused deliberately as a means of bringing administrative pressure on the publication; on a number of occasions printers refused to print material to which they took objection. Newsprint, moreover, was in short supply and the churches' publications suffered; the publications of the priests' associations did not have this difficulty.

The 1960s and after

While the Second Vatican Council was in session a small weekly mimeographed bulletin of information about the Council was establi-shed under the auspices of the Zagreb archbishopric. It was called *Glas s Koncila* [Voice from the Council]; the first number appeared on October 4, 1962. This was the small beginning of what has developed into the largest-circulation religious paper in Yugoslavia, and one of the largest circulations of any periodical. The decision to continue publi-cation after the end of the Council was taken with some hesitation by the archdiocesan authorities but since then there has been no looking back. In 1964 the paper, renamed *Glas Koncila* [Voice of the Council], assumed its present printed, tabloid format, and now appears fort-nightly. Its circulation climbed rapidly and in 1970 stood at between 170,000 and 180,000. Today (1974) it is about 110,000. The archbishopric, having established the paper, left its editors free to make their own policy. The result has not always been what the ecclesiastical authorities would have wished, and it has often also been attacked and criticised by the government; a number of individual issues have been banned. But it has maintained its independence and a high standard of lively, controversial and occasionally pugnacious journalism; it runs an occasional satirical column, Diary of a Village Priest, by 'Don Jure', in the wide-eyed vein of *The Good Soldier Schweik*. It also publishes *Mali Koncil* [The Little Council], a monthly for children, circulation 80,000.

In 1966 Cardinal Archbishop Šeper of Zagreb authorised the establishment of Krśćanska Sadašnjost [Contemporary Christianity], a centre for post-Second Vatican Council research, documentation and information. It publishes a number of journals and periodicals:

Svesci [Notebooks], a theological journal one of whose purposes is to acquaint Yugoslav Catholics with the theological thought of the West from which they had been cut off for many years; it was a bimonthly but now tends to appear irregularly; circulation, 4,500.

Kana [Cana], a monthly family journal in colour with features on the home, fashion, children etc.; founded 1970; circulation, 120,000.

AKSA [*Aktualnosti Krśćanska Sadašnjost* – Current News: Contem-porary Christianity], a weekly mimeographed news service, with news of church and religious affairs in Yugoslavia, a digest of items on these subjects from the Yugoslav secular press and religious news from other parts of the world; founded 1970; circulation, 400.

Svjedočenje [Witness], a bulletin on the life of the Church.

Effatha, a bulletin for nuns; founded 1969; circulation, 1,500.

Upoznajmo Bibliju [Let's Get to Know the Bible], for Bible study.

Služba Riječi [Service of the Word], a series of pamphlets on liturgical renewal; founded 1969; circulation, 3,000.

The Catholic Church in Slovenia has a considerable output of publications; besides *Družina* and *Verski List*, already mentioned, there are:

Ognjišče [The Hearth], a monthly for young people, published by the diocese of Koper; founded 1966; circulation, 70,000.

Cerkev v Sedanjem Svetu [The Church in Today's World], a monthly pastoral review; founded 1967; circulation, 2,300.

Bogoslovni Vestnik [Theological Messenger], a scholarly theological review appearing from time to time; founded 1940; circulation, 2,200; ceased publication some years after the war.

Znamenje [The Sign], a serious quarterly journal of contemporary theological and religious thought, in the spirit of the Second Vatican Council; founded 1972.

Both the Hungarian and the Albanian national groups have their own publications: *Drita* [Light], monthly in Albanian published by the parish of Prizren, circulation, 3,000, and *Hitelet* [Life of Faith], founded in 1963, published by the parish of Novi Sad, circulation, 16,000.

There are in addition a considerable number of other Roman Catholic magazines and publications, issued by religious orders, students at the theological faculties and higher seminaries, and dioceses. Following is a comprehensive selection of these:

Bakarska Zvona [The Bakar Bell], published by the parish of Bakar; founded 1963.

Betanija [Bethany], a paper for the sick, published by the archbishopric of Zagreb; founded 1969; circulation, 2,500.

Bogoslovska Smotra [Theological Review], a philosophical–theological journal published by the Zagreb theological faculty; founded 1910; ceased publication for some years after the war.

Crkva u Svijetu [The Church in the World], quarterly on contemporary religious and philosophical questions; published by the diocese of Split; founded 1966; circulation, 2,000.

Glasnik Srca Isusova i Marijina [Herald of the Heart of Jesus and Mary], monthly; published by the Society of Jesus in Zagreb; founded 1963.

Gospino Ognjište [Our Lady's Hearth], published by the Jesuit College, Zagreb, for secondary-school pupils; founded 1967.

Katehist, periodical founded in 1963 by the Catechical Institute of Zagreb.

Služba Božja [Service of God], bimonthly founded in 1961 by the Franciscan Divinity School of Makarska.

Veritas [The Truth], illustrated monthly review; founded 1962; published by the Franciscan conventuals of Zagreb.

Marija [Mary], ten issues yearly; concerned with the veneration of Mary; published by the Order of the Most Holy Redeemer, Split; founded 1963; circulation, 15,000.

In an article which appeared on July 7, 1969, *Borba* estimated that the total circulation of the Catholic press in Yugoslavia had grown from 260,000 in 1961 to 11 million in 1968.

The Serbian Orthodox Church publishes, in addition to the papers mentioned above, some diocesan gazettes and parish magazines, and the following periodicals and journals.

Pravoslavni Misionar [Orthodox Missionary], published by the Serbian Orthodox Church. Founded in 1958 as a quarterly for the religious education of the laity, it began with a circulation of 4,000; in 1959 it became a bimonthly and by 1968 had attained its present citculation of 50,000.

Pravoslavlje [Orthodoxy], a fortnightly newspaper published by the patriarchate; founded 1967; circulation, 24,000. It is the principal non-official church publication. A number of books and pamphlets have appeared under *Pravoslavlje*'s imprint.

Svetosavsko Zvonce [The Bells of St Sava], monthly for children and young people, published by the patriarchate; founded 1968; circulation, 30,000.

Bogoslovlje [Divinity], founded before the war but ceased publication during the war and not resumed until 1957; twice yearly; published by the Orthodox theological faculty.

Teološki Pogledi [Theological Outlook], published periodically by the Belgrade–Karlovci diocese to discuss new developments in religious and theological thinking; circulation, 2,000.

There are also several calendars appearing yearly, with statistics and information about the churches. The Serbian Orthodox Church's pocket calendar appears in an edition of 800,000. Serbian dioceses in North America and Europe also publish calendars and papers.

The Macedonian Orthodox Church publishes its official journal *Vesnik* [Messenger] every two months. It was founded in 1959 at the time of the declaration of the autonomy of the Macedonian Orthodox Church. Circulation is between 2,000 and 3,000.

In addition to these the Moslem religious community and the various Protestant religious communities have their own publications; none of them has the circulation or importance of the Catholic and Orthodox press.

There is no pre-censorship in Yugoslavia. Occasional issues of a journal have been banned by the courts. On a few occasions the decision of a lower court has been reversed on appeal. Religious journals are not sold on newspaper stands or bookshops (except for a brief period at the end of the 1960s in Slovenia) but may be bought in churches or by subscription. This is one of the minor points at issue between the churches and the authorities.

In spite of repeated appeals the churches have not been allowed time on radio or television, and with a very few exceptions, religion and the churches are not discussed on them.

Appendix V

Protocol of discussions between the representatives of the Socialist Federal Republic of Yugoslavia and the representatives of the Holy See

With a view to the settlement of relations between the Socialist Federal Republic of Yugoslavia and the Catholic Church, the representatives of the government of the Socialist Federal Republic of Yugoslavia and of the Holy See held discussions in Rome from June 26 to July 7, 1964, in Belgrade from January 5 to 23 and from May 29 to June 8, 1965, and again in Rome from April 18 to 25, 1966.

Within the general cadre of subjects which came up for discussions, the representatives of the Socialist Federal Republic of Yugoslavia presented the following attitudes of the Yugoslav government:

1. The principles upon which the regulation of the legal status of religious communities is based in the Socialist Federal Republic of Yugoslavia and which are guaranteed by the constitution and laws of the Socialist Federal Republic of Yugoslavia are as follows: freedom of conscience and freedom of religion; separation of the church from the state; equal status and equal rights for all religious communities; equality of rights and duties of all citizens whatever their creed and religious worship; freedom to found religious communities; recognition of the status of a legal person to the religious communities.

Within the cadre of these principles, the government of the Socialist Federal Republic of Yugoslavia guarantees to the Catholic Church in Yugoslavia the free performance of religious functions and religious rites.

The responsible organs of the social–political communities (the commune, the district, the republic, the federation) ensure to all citizens, without any discrimination, the consistent application of the laws and other regulations serving to safeguard respect for the freedom of conscience and the freedom of religious worship guaranteed by the constitution of the Socialist Federal Republic of Yugoslavia.

The government of the Socialist Federal Republic of Yugoslavia is prepared to consider the cases which the Holy See may deem necessary to indicate to it in connection with this matter.

2. The government of the Socialist Federal Republic of Yugoslavia admits the competencies of the Holy See in the exercise of its jurisdiction over the Catholic Church in Yugoslavia in spiritual matters and in matters of ecclesiastical and religious character insofar as they are not contrary to the internal order of the Socialist Federal Republic of Yugoslavia.

Also in future bishops of the Catholic Church in Yugoslavia shall have

313

guaranteed to them the possibility of maintaining contacts with the Holy See, deeming that such contacts have an exclusively religious and ecclesiastical character.

The Holy See – while adhering to the demands which it presented for its part in the course of the discussions in connection with the complete regulation of relations between the Catholic Church and the Socialist Federal Republic of Yugoslavia – noted the declarations on the attitudes of the government of the Socialist Federal Republic of Yugoslavia expressed in points 1 and 2 above.

Within the general cadre of subject which came up for discussions, the representatives of the Holy See presented the following attitudes of the Holy See.

1. The Holy See reaffirms the principled attitude that the activity of Catholic priests, in the performance of their clerical duties, should proceed within the religious and ecclesiastical framework and that, consequently, they may not abuse their religious and ecclesiastical functions for ends which would actually have a political character.

The Holy See is prepared to consider the cases which the government of the Socialist Federal Republic of Yugoslavia may deem necessary to indicate to it in this respect.

2. The Holy See – consistently with the principles of Catholic ethics – does not approve and condemns every act of political terrorism or similar criminal forms of violence, whoever its perpetrators be.

Consequently, should the Yugoslav government appraise that Catholic priests have participated in an action of such a kind to the detriment of the Socialist Federal Republic of Yugoslavia, and should it deem necessary to indicate such cases to the Holy See, the Holy See is prepared to consider such indications with a view to instituting proceedings and eventually taking appropriate measures provided for by canon law for such cases.

The government of the Socialist Federal Republic of Yugoslavia – while adhering to the demands which it presented for its part in the course of the discussions in connection with the complete regulation of relations between the Catholic Church and the Socialist Federal Republic of Yugoslavia – noted the declarations on the attitudes of the Holy See expressed in points 1 and 2 above.

Both sides express their readiness for mutual consultation also in future, whenever they deem it necessary, on all matters affecting the relations between the Socialist Federal Republic of Yugoslavia and the Catholic Church.

With a view to facilitating further mutual contacts, the government of the Socialist Federal Republic of Yugoslavia is prepared to facilitate the stay in Belgrade of an apostolic delegate who would simultaneously possess the function of envoy to the said government, with the proviso that it reserves the right to designate its envoy to the Holy See.

For its part the Holy See is prepared to receive the envoy of the government of the Socialist Federal Republic of Yugoslavia and to send its apostolic delegate to Belgrade.

Drawn up in Belgrade on the 25th of June, 1966, in two original texts, in the Serbo–Croatian and Italian languages with the proviso that both texts shall be equally authentic.

For the government of the SFRJ   For the Holy See
MILUTIN MORAČA (signed)   AGOSTINO CASAROLI (signed)

Bibliography

(Periodicals are listed separately at the end)
Akten zur Deutschen Auswärtigen Politik, ser. E, vol. 1 (Dec. 12, 1940–Feb. 28, 1942). Göttingen, 1969.
Annuario Pontificio, 1944–1968. [Vatican yearbook]
Apostolski, M. et al. (eds.), *From the Past of the Macedonian People*, Skopje, 1969.
Armstrong, H. F., *Tito and Goliath*, London: Gollanz, 1951.
Auty, Phyllis, *Tito: A Biography*, London: Longman, 1970.
Yugoslavia, London: Thames and Hudson, 1965.
'The Post-War Period', in *Short History* (q.v.), pp. 236–65.
Baerlein, Henry, *The Birth of Yugoslavia*, 2 vols., London: Leonard Parsons, 1922.
Barker, Elizabeth, *Macedonia and its Place in Balkan Power Politics*, London: Chatham House, 1950.
Basta, Milan, *Agonija i slom Nezavisne Države Hrvatske* [Last Days and Fall of the Independent State of Croatia], Belgrade, 1971.
Benigar, A., *Alojzije Stepinac Hrvatski Kardinal*, Rome: ZIRAL, 1974.
Benković, T., OFM, *The Tragedy of a Nation*. [Pro-Croat pamphlet; wartime; no publisher]
Bičanić, R., *Kako živi narod – život u pasivnim krajevima* [How the People Live – Life in the Passive Regions], Zagreb, 1936.
Bociurkiw, B., 'Lenin and Religion', in *Lenin the Man, the Theorist, the Leader* (London: Pall Mall Press, 1973), pp. 107–34.
Bošnjak, B., 'Reflections on Religion', in *Religion and Atheism in the USSR and Eastern Europe*, ed. B. Bociurkiw and J. Strong (London: Macmillan, 1975), pp. 18–36.
Bročić, M., 'The Position and Activities of the Religious Communities in Yugoslavia', in *Religion and Atheism in the USSR and Eastern Europe*, ed. B. Bociurkiw and J. Strong (London: Macmillan, 1975), pp. 351–67.
Buchan, J. (ed.), *Yugoslavia*, London: Hodder and Stoughton, 1923.
Cavalli, F., s.j., 'Al processo dell' Arcivescovo di Zagabria', *Civiltà Cattolica*, 7.xii.46, 318–38.
Četniks (The), G2 (PB) AFHQ, 1944. Confidential. [Political Branch, Allied Forces H.Q.: a survey of Četnik activity in Yugoslavia, 1941–4].
CFPRY = The Church in the Federal People's Republic of Yugoslavia, Belgrade: Information Service, Yugoslavia, 1959.
Ciano, Count G., *Diaries 1939–42*, London: Heinemann, 1947.
Diplomatic Papers, London: Odhams, 1948.
Clissold, S., *Whirlwind*, London: Cresset Press, 1949.
'Occupation and Resistance', in *Short History* (q.v.), pp. 208–35.

CNS = *Cerkev na Slovenskem* [The Church in Slovenia], Ljubljana, 1971. [Register of the Roman Catholic Church in Slovenia]

Collection of Yugoslav Laws, ed. B. Blagojević, Belgrade: vol. III, *Nationalization and Expropriation*, 1962; vol. v, *Execution of Criminal Sanctions*, 1962; vol. XI, *Criminal Code*, 1964. [In English]

Constitution of the Socialist Federative Republic of Yugoslavia, Belgrade: Federal Secretariat for Information, 1963.

Dedijer, V., *With Tito through the War*, London: Alexander Hamilton, 1951. [War diaries]

Tito Speaks, London: Weidenfeld and Nicolson, 1954.

Denitch, B., 'Religion and Social Change in Yugoslavia', in *Religion and Atheism in the USSR and Eastern Europe*, ed. B. Bociurkiw and J. Strong (London: Macmillan, 1975), pp. 368–88.

Dimevski, S., *Crkovna istorija na makedonskiot narod* [Church History of the Macedonian People], Skopje: Macedonian Orthodox Church, 1965.

Dokumenti = *Dokumenti o protunarodnom radu i zločinima jednog dijela katoličkog klera* [Documents concerning the Anti-National Activity and Crimes of a Part of the Catholic Clergy], Zagreb, 1946.

Dragoun, T., O.P., *Le dossier du Cardinal Stepinac*, Paris, 1958.

Enciclopedia Cattolica, Rome, 1951.

Eterovich, F. H. and C. Spalatin, *Croatia: Land, People and Culture*, vol. I, University of Toronto Press, 1964.

Falconi, C., *The Silence of Pius XII*, London, Faber and Faber, 1970. [First published in Italy, 1965. The writer was given access to the wartime correspondence between the NDH and its diplomatic representatives at the Vatican]

Fletcher, W. G., *Religion and Soviet Foreign Policy*, Oxford: Chatham House, 1973.

Fotitch, C., *The War We Lost*, New York: Viking Press, 1948.

Frankel, J., 'Communism and the National Question in Yugoslavia', *Journal of Central European Affairs*, April 1954.

Godišnjak: Institut za Medjunarodnu Politiku i Privredu [Yearbook: Institute for International Politics and Economics], Belgrade, 1964 et seq. [Sections on the Vatican]

Hoptner, J. B., *Yugoslavia in Crisis 1934–41*, New York: Columbia University Press, 1952.

Ilevski, Done, *The Macedonian Orthodox Church: The Road to Independence*, trans. James Leach, Skopje: Macedonian Review Editions, 1973.

Italian Genocide Policy against the Slovenes and Croats, Belgrade: Institute of International Politics and Economics, 1954.

Jones, Major William, *Twelve Months with the Partisans*, London: Bedford Books, 1946.

Kardelj, E., *Problemi naše socialistične graditve* [Problems of our Socialist Construction], Ljubljana, 1956. [Collected speeches and articles]

Kidrič, B., *Zbrano delo: govori, članki in rasprave* [Collected Works: Speeches, Articles and Interviews], vol. 2, Ljubljana.

Kocbek, E., *Tovarišija* [Comradeship], 2nd edn, Ljubljana, 1967.

Kocijančič, B., Speech, February 1964, on the twentieth anniversary of the setting-up of the Commission for Religious Affairs in Slovenia

(19.ii.44), by the first president of the commission. [Copy supplied by the commission]

Lendvai, P., *Eagles and Cobwebs*, London: Macdonald, 1970.

Liberté du culte dans la République Fédérative Populaire Yougoslave (*La*), Belgrade, 1947. [Official publication; some documents included]

Lisac, A. J., 'Deportacija srba iz hrvatske 1941' [Deportation of the Serbs from Croatia 1954], in *Istorijski zbornik* [Historical Anthology], Zagreb, 1956.

LSRCY = *Legal Status of Religious Communities in Yugoslavia*, Belgrade, 1967. [Laws, constitutional provisions, specimens of social contracts and protocol between the Vatican and the Yugoslav government, with introductory note]

Maček, V., *In the Struggle for Freedom*, State College, Pa., 1957.

Maclean, Fitzroy, *Eastern Approaches*, London, Cape, 1949.

Disputed Barricades, London: Cape, 1957.

Magnum Crimen, see Novak, V.

Marx, K. and F. Engels, *Basic Writings on Politics and Philosophy*, ed. L. S. Feuer, London: Collins/Fontana, 1969.

Mousset, Jean, *La Serbie et son église*, Paris: Librarie Droz, 1936.

MPG = *Memoari Patriarha Srpskoga Gavrila* [Memoirs of the Serbian Patriarch Gavrilo], Paris, 1974.

National Liberation Movement of Yugoslavia: A Survey of the Partisan Movement April 1941–March 1944, Confidential PIC/276, PICME, June 1944. [Political Intelligence Centre Middle East; pamphlet]

Neal, F. W., *Titoism in Action*, Berkeley: University of California Press, 1958.

Novak, B., *Trieste*, Chicago: University of Chicago Press, 1970.

Novak, V., *Magnum Crimen*, Zagreb, 1948.

O'Brien, A. H., *Archbishop Stepinac: The Man and his Case*, Westminster, Md.: Newman Bookshop, 1947.

Ostović, P. D., *The Truth about Yugoslavia*, New York: Roy Publishers, 1952.

Pattee, R., *The Case of Cardinal Aloysius Stepinac*, Milwaukee: Bruce Publishing Co., 1953. [A work commissioned by members of the American Catholic hierarchy; includes a large number of documents not otherwise easily available]

Pavlowitch, S. K., *Yugoslavia*, London, Benn, 1971.

'The Orthodox Church in Yugoslavia', *Eastern Churches Review*, 1, 4 (Winter 1967–8): 'The Problem of the Macedonian Church', 374–86; 2, 1 (1968): 'A War Casualty', 29–35; 2, 2 (1968): 'Rebuilding the Fabric', 165–74; 2, 3 (1969): 'Looking Out to the World', 275–85.

PCY, see Vidić, R.

PDZA = *Prvo i drugo zasedanje AVNOJ-a* [First and Second Sessions of AVNOJ], Zagreb, 1953. [Documents]

Petranović, B., 'Aktivnost rimokatoličkog klera protiv sredjivanja prilika u Jugoslaviji: mart 1945–septembar 1946' [Activity of the Roman Catholic Clergy against the Normalising of Conditions in Yugoslavia: March 1945–September 1946], in *Istorija XX veka: zbornik radova* [History of the Twentieth Century: A Collection of Essays] (Belgrade, 1963), pp. 263–313. [An important source;

Petranović had access to Croatian state archives and archives of the ministry of justice of Croatia including the stenographic report of Archbishop Stepinac's trial]

Petrovich, Michael, 'Religion and the Tensions of a Multi-National State', *East Europe Quarterly*, 6, 1 (March 1972).

Proces proti vojnim zločincem in izdaljcem Rupniku, Röseneru, Rožmanu, Kreku, Vizjaku in Hacinu [The Trial of War Criminals and Traitors Rupnik, Rösener, Rožman, Krek, Vizjak and Hacin], Ljubljana, 1946. [Official account]

Putovi revolucije [Roads to Revolution], Zagreb: Institut za Istoriju Radničkog Pokreta [Institute for the History of the Workers' Movement], 1963.

Rhodes, Anthony, *The Vatican in the Age of the Dictators 1922–1945*, London: Hodder and Stoughton, 1973.

RIY = *Religions in Yugoslavia*, ed. Z. Frid, Zagreb: Binoza, 1971. [Collection of essays by Catholic, Marxist, Moslem, Orthodox and Protestant scholars and religious leaders; statistics and other factual information provided by the religious communities]

Roberts, W. B., *Tito, Mihailovich and the Allies 1941–1945*, New Brunswick, N.J.: Rutgers University Press, 1973.

Rootham, Jasper, *Miss Fire*, London: Chatto and Windus, 1956.

Rouquette, R., *Vatican II: la fin d'une chrétienté*, Paris, 1968.

Runciman, S., *The Orthodox Churches and the Secular State*, Oxford: University Press, 1971.

Rusinow, D., *Italy's Austrian Heritage*, Oxford: Clarendon Press, 1969. 'Italy's Austrian Heritage 1919–1946: The Place of Venezia Giulia and Venezia Tridentina in Italian History', D.Phil. thesis, University of Oxford, 1962. [Unpublished appendixes]

Rynne, Xavier, *Letters from Vatican City*, London: Faber and Faber, 1963.

The Second Session, London: Faber and Faber, 1964.

The Third Session, New York: Farrar, Straus and Giroux, 1965.

The Fourth Session, London: Faber and Faber, 1966.

Saint-Siège et la guerre en Europe juin 1940–juin 1941 (Le), Rome: Libreria Editrice Vaticana, 1967.

Schuster, G., *Religion behind the Iron Curtain*, London: Macmillan, 1954.

Šematizam Zagrebačke Nadbiskupije 1966 [Register of the Zagreb Archdiocese], Zagreb, 1966. [Cited as *Šematizam*]

Short History = *A Short History of Yugoslavia*, ed. S. Clissold, Cambridge: University Press, 1966.

Shoup, P., *Communism and the Yugoslav National Question*, New York: Columbia University Press, 1966.

Slijepčević, Djoko, *Istorija Srpske Pravoslavne Crkve* [History of the Serbian Orthodox Church], vol. 2, Munich, 1966. [Cited as Slijepčević]

Pitanje Makedonske Pravoslavne Crkve u Jugoslaviji [The Question of the Macedonian Orthodox Church in Yugoslavia], Munich, 1959. [Cited as Slijepčević, Mac. 1959]

Makedonsko Crkveno pitanje [The Macedonian Church Question], Munich, 1969. [Cited as Slijepčević, Mac. 1969]

Slovenskim duhovnikom [Appeal to the Slovene Clergy], Propagandni Odsek pri Izvršnem Odboru OF. [Underground pamphlet published during the war]

SPC = *Srpska Pravoslavna Crkva 1920–70: spomenica o 50-godnišnjici vaspostavljanja srpske patriaršije* [The Serbian Orthodox Church 1920–70: A Commemoration of the 50th Anniversary of the Re-Establishment of the Serbian Patriarchate], ed. Metropolitan Vladislav of Dabar–Bosnia, Belgrade, 1971. [An official history of fifty years of the Serbian Orthodox Church]

Spinka, M., 'Modern Ecclesiastical Development in Yugoslavia', in *Yugoslavia*, ed. R. J. Kerner, (U.N. series, Berkeley: University of California Press, 1949), pp. 244–60.

Spomenica Pravoslavnih sveštenika 1941–1945 [Commemoration of the Orthodox Clergy 1941–1945, 'victims of fascist terror and those who fell in the people's liberation struggle'], ed. Dušan Strbac, Belgrade: Savez Udruženja Sveštenstva FRNJ [Union of Associations of Orthodox Priests in the SFRY], 1969.

SRCY = *Situation of Religion and the Church in Yugoslavia Today*. [Mimeographed document; no publisher; no date; but internal evidence suggests Yugoslav Information Service, 1952]

'Statistički pregled eparhija za 1973 godine' [Statistical review of dioceses, 1973], Belgrade: Serbian Orthodox Church. [Mimeographed sheets]

Stavrianos, G., *The Balkans since 1943*, New York: Holt, Rinehart and Winston, 1965.

Stefanović, J., *Odnos izmedju crkve i države* [Relations between Church and State], Zagreb, 1953.

Stojadinović, M. J., *Ni rat, ni pakt* [Neither War nor the Pact], 2nd edn with introduction by Dušan Biber, Rijeka, 1970.

Stranjaković, D., *Pre deset godina* [Ten Years Ago], Belgrade, 1951. [Pamphlet, no publisher]

Sudjenje = *Sudjenje Lisaku, Stepincu, Šaliću i družini: ustaško–križarskim zločinima i njihovim pomagačima* [The Trial of Lisak, Stepinac, Šalić and Others: Ustaša–Crusader Criminals and their Helpers], Zagreb, 1946. [The official account of the trial of Archbishop Stepinac]

Tajni dokumenti o odnosima Vatikana i ustaške NDH [Secret Documents concerning the Relations of the Vatican and the Ustaša NDH], Zagreb, 1952. [Official publication]

Tito, J. B., *Govori i članci* [Speeches and Articles], vols. I–X, Belgrade, 1959.

Nacionalno pitanje u Jugoslaviji u svjetlosti narodno-oslobodilačke borbe [The National Question in Yugoslavia in the Light of the National Liberation Struggle], in *Proleter* [wartime newspaper], no. 16, Dec. 1942.

Tochitch, D., *Totalitarisme et droits de l'homme*, Paris, 1949.

Tomasevich, J., *Peasants, Politics and Economic Change in Yugoslavia*, Stanford, Cal.: University Press, and Oxford: University Press, 1955.

'Yugoslavia during the Second World War', in *Contemporary Yugoslavia*', ed. Wayne Vucinich (Berkeley: University of California Press, 1969), pp. 59–118.

Ude, L., Speech by Dr Lojze Ude to clergy and party activists of the Bela Krajna at Crnomelj on September 13, 1944, in *Slovenski zbornik* [Slovene Anthology], Ljubljana, 1945.

U ime Hrista – svetinje u plamenu [In the name of Christ – churches in flames], 1944. [Pamphlet; no publisher; list of destroyed and desecrated Serbian Orthodox churches]

UPSJ = Udruženje Pravoslavnog Sveštenstva Jugoslavije 1889–1969 [Association of Orthodox Priests in Yugoslavia 1889–1969], Belgrade, 1969. [Official history of the association]

Ustav na Makedonskata Pravoslavna Crkva [Constitution of the Macedonian Orthodox Church], Skopje, 1958.

Ustav Srpske Pravoslavne Crkve (1949) [Constitution of the Serbian Orthodox Church], 2nd edn, Belgrade, 1957.

Vatican Docs., see *Saint-Siège et la guerre en Europe (Le)*.

Vidić, R., *Position of the Church in Yugoslavia*, Belgrade, 1962.

Vucinich, W., 'Interwar Yugoslavia', in *Contemporary Yugoslavia*, ed. W. Vucinich (Berkeley: University of California Press, 1969), pp. 3–58.

Ware, Timothy, *The Orthodox Church*, Harmondsworth: Penguin Books, 1963.

Woolf, R. L., *The Balkans in our Time*, Cambridge, Mass.: Harvard University Press, 1956.

World Council of Churches: Material from archives concerning relief sent to Yugoslavia.

Yugoslav Communism: A Critical Study. Prepared for the subcommittee to investigate the administration of the Internal Security Act, of the Committee on the Judiciary, U.S. Senate, 87th Congress, 1st session, Oct. 18, 1961. [Useful bibliography]

Zakon i Ustav Srpske Pravoslavne Crkve (1931) [Law and Constitution of the Serbian Orthodox Church], Belgrade, 1931.

Zakon o agrarnoj reformi i kolonizaciji [Law concerning Agrarian Reform and Colonisation], Belgrade, 1945. [Pamphlet, including a speech by Moše Pijade. Extracts from this law also in *LSRCY*, p. 23]

Zeman, Z. A. B., *Break-up of the Habsburg Empire 1914–1918*, Oxford, 1961.

Periodicals

Bilten [Bulletin]. [Monthly journal of the Association of Slovene Priests; 1949 only]

Blagovest [Annunciation]. [Catholic monthly; formerly diocese of Skopje, now archdiocese of Belgrade]

Borba [Struggle], Belgrade and Zagreb. [Daily]

CSM = Christian Science Monitor, Boston, Mass. [Daily]

Daily Telegraph, London.

Delo [Work], Ljubljana. [Daily]

Dobri Pastir [The Good Shepherd], Sarajevo. [Monthly journal of the Dobri Pastir association of Catholic priests in Bosnia and Hercegovina]

Gl. = Glasnik: Službeni List Srpske Pravoslavne Crkve [The Messenger: Official Gazette of the Serbian Orthodox Church], Belgrade. [Weekly]

Glas Koncila [Voice of the Council], Zagreb. [Catholic fortnightly]

Gore Srca [Lift Up your Hearts], Pazin, 1946–52. [Catholic monthly]

Hrvatska Revija [Croatian Review], formerly Madrid, now Buenos Aires. [Croatian émigré monthly]

Il Popolo, Rome. [Daily]

Katolički List [Catholic Newspaper], Zagreb. [Weekly; ceased publication 1945]

Komunist, Belgrade. [Weekly LCY ideological journal]

Le Monde, Paris [Daily]

L'O.R. = *L'Osservatore Romano*. [Vatican daily]

MG = *Manchester Guardian*. [Daily; now *The Guardian*]

Narodni List [People's Newspaper], Zagreb. [Daily; ceased publication]

Nova Makedonija [New Macedonia], Skopje. [Daily]

Nova Pot [New Way], Ljubljana. [Monthly journal of the Ciril–Metodsko Društvo – Catholic association of Slovene priests]

NYHT = *New York Herald Tribune*. [Daily; ceased publication]

NYT = *New York Times*. [Daily]

Oslobodjenje, Sarajevo. [Daily]

Oznanilo [Church Notices], Ljubljana. [Catholic fortnightly, 1945–7]

Politika, Belgrade. [Daily]

RNS = Religious News Service, New York. [Its Belgrade correspondent, a Serb, had reliable sources of information in the Serbian Orthodox Church]

Slobodna Dalmacija [Free Dalmatia], Split. [Daily]

Sl. Por. = *Slovenski Poročevalec* [Slovene Herald], Ljubljana. [Daily; ceased publication]

Služ. List = *Službeni List FNRJ* [Official Gazette of the SFRY].

Svesci [Notebooks]. [Catholic bimonthly journal of theological thought; now appears irregularly]

SVNZ = *Službeni Vjesnik Nadbiskupije Zagrebačke* [Official Gazette of the Zagreb Archdiocese], Zagreb. [Weekly]

The Times, London. [Daily]

Vesnik [Herald], Belgrade. [Monthly journal of the Union of Associations of Orthodox Priests in Yugoslavia]

Vjesnik [Herald], Zagreb. [Daily]

VMPC = *Vesnik na Makedonskata Pravoslavna Crkva* [Herald of the Macedonian Orthodox Church], Skopje. [Weekly official gazette and journal of the Macedonian Orthodox Church]

VUS = *Vjesnik u Srijedi* [Wednesday Herald], Zagreb. [Weekly edition of *Vjesnik*]

Index

Ačimović, Milan, 17

agrarian reform, 74, 212–17; started before end of war, bears hard on churches, 63; Stepinac protests to Tito about, 67 & n; dispossesses Italian landlords, 82 & n; welcomed by Istrian clergy, 87; helps reduce Catholic Church to poverty, 121f; welcomed by CMD, 130; extent of Serbian Orthodox Church, land nationalised, 156, 213; financial position of church after, 168f; administration of law on, 214; some churches receive less than minimum holding, 215; complaints lodged by churches, 215f

Akšamović, Bishop of Djakovo, 39n, 71n, 74, 108n, 144; unfavourable comments on Stepinac's staff, 143; character and decorations, 236n

Alajbegović (NDH minister), 110, 114

Alaupović, Bishop of Sarajevo, 139, 144

Albania, 226, 270; Kosovo and western Macedonia joined to, 9

Albanian minority, 270; in southern Serbia, 1; in Macedonia, 2; Albanian Catholics in southern Serbia, 2; religious publications for, 311

Alexander, Field-Marshal: refuses to concede Trieste to Partisans, 53f

Alexander, King, 3

Alexei, Patriarch of Moscow, 179, 256, 283; denies hegemonistic aims, 193; visits to Serbian patriarch, 257, 271; visits Macedonian church, 271, 281; opposes Orthodox presence at Second Vatican Council, 273

Andrej (Frušić), Bishop of Banja Luka, 244, 272

Apostolov, the Rev. Nikola (Macedonian Orthodox), 183, 184

Arsenije (Bradvarović), Bishop of the Montenegrin Littoral, later of Budim, 195, 269, 271; trip to Sremski Karlovci, 153; search for war orphans, 153n; administrator of four Croatian dioceses, 155; press attack on, 174; prevented from travelling to Budapest (Budim), 180; appointed Metropolitan of the Montenegrin Littoral, 180; arrest and trial, 251–3

Arsov, Ljupco, 255

Artuković (NDH minister), 29, 36, 76

ASNOM (Anti-fascist Council for the National Liberation of Macedonia), declaration on Macedonian language, 183

Athenagoras, Ecumenical Patriarch of Constantinople, 273; advises against recognition of Macedonian Orthodox Church, 266; receives Macedonian bishops and priests, 287

Austrian military frontier, 2

AVNOJ (Anti-fascist Council for the National Liberation of Yugoslovia): 2nd meeting, 44; 1st and 2nd meetings, 48; Serbian Orthodox priests and Catholic laymen among delegates to, 50; 1st AVNOJ decrees religious instruction in schools in liberated territory, 50; 2nd AVNOJ, 50; constitutional bases for church–state relations laid down, 50f, 210f; approves intended annexation of prewar Italian territory, 53; affirms equality of Macedonia with other Yugoslav nations, 182

Bačka: annexed by Hungarians, 9

Bajić (NDH official), 37

Bajsić, the Rev. Dr V. (Zagreb theological faculty), 66n, 291

Bajt, the Rev. (Catholic), 128, 129; excommunicated, 131

Bakarić, Dr V., 57, 60 64, 75, 238; on relations with Catholic clergy, 52; Stepinac calls on, 59; Stepinac calls on again, 61; answers Stepinac's letter, 66; acknowledges irregularities and excesses, 66; deplores visions and miraculous apparitions, 66n; on links between church and ustaše, 79; government not destroying the church, but separating it from the state, 118; interview on position of the church, admits errors, 122f; calls on Archbishop Šeper, 231f; time not yet ripe for renewed relations with Vatican, 232; interview with New York Times, 235

Bakšić, Canon Professor, 57n

Baranja: annexed by Hungarians, 9

Bauer, Archbishop of Zagreb, 19, 108n; dies, 20

Bauerlein, Bishop of Djakovo: house-arrest, 133; press attack on, 134

Bebler, Dr Aleš, 140, 141n

Bela Garda (White Guard) (see also Domobran), 45, 90, 92; regrouped as Domobran, 41n; crimes denounced by Slovene priests' association, 129

Belgrade agreement, 81

Bellato, Fra (Franciscan), 91n

Beninca, Fra (Franciscan), 91n

Bevk, the Rev. Dr (Catholic), 92n

Bičanić, Dr Rudolf: describes prewar regional poverty, 4

Bilenki, the Rev. F. (Catholic), 233n

Biljak, the Rev. G. (Catholic), 233n

Bilten, 127, 129, 309; banned by Vatican, 127; demand for lifting of ban, 128; ceases publication, 129

Bitenc: spy-ring, 91, 92

Blagovest, 218, 245, 308

Blatnik, Dr Stanislas, 91, 92; tried in absentia, 90

Blažević, Jakov (public prosecutor), 96, 100, 105, 108, 109n & f, 112n; announces Stepinac will be brought to trial, 102; opens case, 102, 104; enraged by Stepinac, 106; states purpose of the trial, 117

Bogdan, Ivo, 103, 114

bogomolski pokret (movement of spiritual renewal in Serbian Orthodox Church), 275, 276; Bishop Nikolaj Velimirović one of leaders, 11

Bojanović, Father (Ustaša town prefect), 28

Bonifačić, Bishop of Split, 51, 71n; attacked in press, 134 & n

Borba, 169, 189, 209; deplores attack on Bishop Vovk, 90; attacks bishops over priests' associations, 134; attacks Synod, 167; on religious influence in schools, 233; attacks Dum maerentes, 234; attacks Vatican, 237; comments on Protocol, 247; estimates size of Catholic press, 311f

Borić, Canon, 57n; gives shelter to unknown sick man and suffers the consequences, 79 & n; action defended by Stepinac, 80

Bosnia–Hercegovina (after 1945 Bosnia and Hercegovina), 10, 27; under Turks and Austro-Hungarians, 2; Jewish community in, 2; prewar poverty in Hercegovina, 4; Moslems in assumed by NDH to be Croats, 22; Franciscans in, 31; Catholics in, 33; Moše Pijade appeals to all faiths in, 49n

Brašić (Četnik), 101

Brecelj, Dr Marijan, 85n

British and Foreign Bible Society, 305–7; secretary visits Yugoslavia, 250; publishes New Testament in Macedonian, 287; welcomes new Catholic–secular translation of Bible, 307; yearly statistics of distribution, 306

British Broadcasting Corporation: uses Stepinac's sermons in wartime broadcasts, 36, 113

Brkljačić, Father (Ustaša officer), 28

Budak, Mile (NDH Minister of Education): anti-Serb pronouncements, 22; leading Croat writer, 22n

Budanović, Bishop of Subotica, 71n; assaulted, press attacks on, 134; attacked by mob, 136

Bukatko, Bishop of Križevci, 238n, 243n; press attack on, 134; visits Rome, 235

Buletić, the Rev. M. (Catholic): killed by mob, 134

Bulgaria, 2; treaty of friendship with Yugoslavia, 7; annexes eastern Macedonia, 9; occupation of Macedonia increasingly unpopular, 182 & n; strained relations with, 260

Bulgarian Communist Party: unsuccessful attempt to take over Macedonian Communist Party, 182

Bulgarian Orthodox Church: assumes jurisdiction over three Macedonian dioceses, 12f, 182; patriarch visits Yugoslavia, 272

Buratović, the Rev. Andjelko (Catholic), 50

Burić, Bishop of Senj, 34, 37, 71n, 144; member of Committee of Three, 107

Byzantine empire, 1

Cagna, Mgr Mario, 283 & n, 291

Cajnkar, Dr S. (Ljubljana theological faculty), 309; member of Slovene Commission for Religious Affairs, 46n; thinking anticipates Second Vatican Council, 47n; helps to found moderate priests' association, 129; becomes vice-president of CMD, 129; respected by hierarchy, his character, 131 & n; elected dean of theological faculty, 131

Canki, Dr Pavao, 114

Cantala, the Rev. M. (Catholic), 91

Canterbury, Archbishop of: deplores attacks on Serbian Orthodox Church, 172

Carević, Bishop of Dubrovnik, 133; disappears and presumed killed, 62 & n

Casaroli, Mgr, 292

Catholic Action, 103, 105

Catholic Church (national): Ude denies that party wishes to create, 47; Tito on, 58; Stepinac convinced Tito wants, 60; Stepinac accepts that this is not so, 66

Catholic Church (Roman) (see also church–state relations, Commission for Religious Affairs, priests' associations, Protocol, religious education, religious press, Stepinac, trials of priests), 53–94, 221, 226–47, 238; welcomes establishment of NDH, 19; looks forward to many conversions, 26; rejects NDH rules on conversions, 27; attitude of bishops to conversions and atrocities in NDH, 33f; bishops' conference meets November 1941, 33; committee to regulate conversions, 34; pastoral letter of March 1945, 39f; mass for 4th anniversary

of NDH, 40; affirms willingness to cooperate with new government, 57; circular on Christian marriage, 63f; pilgrimage to the shrine of Marija Bistrica, 64; government does not interfere in church internal affairs, 66n; pastoral letter of Sept. 20, 1945 and accompanying circular to clergy, 69ff; deplores introduction of civil marriage, 70; charitable work put under government supervision, 70; circular to clergy accompanying pastoral letter, 71n & f; some bishops oppose open publication of pastoral letter, 74; considered defence of wartime actions published in official gazette of Zagreb archdiocese, 75ff; charitable work of Caritas authorised by government, 78; poverty of church and clergy, 78; position of church begins to change after signing of London agreement, 84; relations with new authorities in Ljubljana easier than in Zagreb, 85f; division of three dioceses on Italian border, 87; pilgrimages resumed, 87; confessional: priests advised to be gentle, 89, Bishop Vovk accused of misusing, 89, secrecy of clarified, 137, (legally affirmed) 220f; government believes church is only serious potential focus for opposition, 119; policy affected by Stepinac's uncompromising attitude during imprisonment, 120; government policy to restrict role of church, 121; declares membership of priests' associations non expedit, 125 & n; sets up diocesan insurance fund, 125; bishops decree priests' associations non licet, 131, 139 & n, 202; persecution of bishops and clergy, 131–6; sharp decrease in women's religious orders in Bosnia and Hercegovina, 132; material help from abroad, 132f; harassment of bishops touring dioceses, 133f; bishops attacked for forbidding priests to join associations, 134; pressures against increase in 1951–2, 135; 30 pupils in Maribor expelled for going to church, 135; does not respond to violent pressures, 136; pressure against begins to die down in 1953, 136; six dioceses without bishops, 136; bishops write to Tito, 139;

Catholic Church (Roman) (cont.)

Catholic organisations closed, 142n; abortive negotiations between bishops and government, 144f; bishops appeal to constitution against persecution, 146; effect of Stepinac's trial and imprisonment on development of, 150; reactions to communist attacks on, 178; refuses to comment on the Law on the Legal Status of Religious Communities, 200; slow general improvement in position, 219; public harassment of bishops and clergy diminishes, 232; chief difficulties of the church, 232; pope encourages church to hold fast, 234; attacks in the press, 237; further trials, 239f; bishops' memorandum to government listing breaches of law, 241; bishops at Second Vatican Council, 243f & n; dialogue with Serbian Orthodox Church opens, 244; pilgrimage to Rome, 292; Marian Congress in Zagreb, 292; statistical material, 298, 299, 300, 301, 303, 304

churches and church property (see also agrarian reform, laws concerning religion and religious communities), 65 & n, 78, 92; many schools and buildings requisitioned, 63; arbitrary expropriation a sin punishable by excommunication, 72 & n; repairs urgently needed for many war-damaged churches, 78; land holdings and possessions, 122n; convents expropriated in Slovenia and Bosnia and Hercegovina, 132; estimated extent of church lands nationalised, 213; clergy forbidden to alienate church lands without permission of bishops, 215; concern over sequestrations, 236; demand for return of sequestrated churches, 241; printing presses nationalised, 310

dioceses: Ljubljana: most clergy collaborate with Italians, 41; bishop and clergy call on Italian high commissioner, 42; first contact with Partisans, 84; initiative for contact comes from church, 85; 67 parishes empty, 87; becomes archbishopric in 1961, 88n; diocesan and regular priests in, 132; under apostolic administrator, 136n; allowed maximum land holdings, 216; statistics, 301; official gazette of, 306. Maribor: some clergy join OF, 42. Sarajevo: under apostolic administrator, 136n; diocesan and regular priests in, 132; statistics, 301. Split: diocesan and regular priests in, 132; official gazette, 308. Zagreb, 34n, 154, 214, 215; circular on rules for conversion, 26f; very few priests from flee, 56; relatives of missing persons appeal to for help, 64; wartime connections with Partisans, 67n; publishes seven articles in official gazette defending Stepinac, 75f; circulars to clergy reveal circumstances of everyday life, 78; police searches of palace, 79, 80; diocesan and regular priests in, 132; land claim disallowed, 216

priests (see also trials of priests): some implicated in atrocities against Orthodox Serbs, 27; in Ustaša movement prewar, 29; Slovene, in OF, 43, 44; church fears socialist tendencies of some Slovene priests, 47; some join Partisans, 49; some bishops suspend those who join Partisans, 49f; killed with retreating forces, 55, 56n; estimates of numbers killed, 56n; young priests who believe in idea of Yugoslavia, 58; many killed just before and after end of war, 62 & n; priests and nuns sentenced to imprisonment, 62; arrested, sentenced to death after war, 65; removed after war at instance of authorities, 69n; numbers dead, missing, arrested, imprisoned, 70, 91, 111, 131f, 142n, 251, imprisoned for unauthorised contacts with Nunciature, 132n, imprisoned for nationalist activities since 1970, 292; some in mixed population areas refuse to read pastoral letter, 74; authorities assert only those guilty of crimes tried, 80; trials of as object lessons, 81; some support government over Trieste, 82; difference between collaborating Slovene clergy and those supporting resistance, 85; Istrian clergy welcome agrarian reform, 86f; advised to be

Catholic Church (Roman) (*cont.*)
gentle in confessional, 89; press articles denounce, 92; amnesties in 1953, 93n, 136; interference in placing of in Slovenia immediately postwar, 94; priest fined for teaching without a licence, 94; 150 sign statement refuting charges against Stepinac, 116; material help to in prison, 133; courts deal with several, 232
 seminaries and theological faculties, 142; money needed for, 78; requisitioned seminaries returned, 86; seminary at Pazin opened, 86, 124; Stepinac alleges work of made impossible, 111; church influence in education reduced to seminaries and theological faculties, 122; drop in numbers of seminarians, 132; 13 students and two priests from Zagreb tried but seminary not closed, 135; seminary at Koper not closed, 135; theological faculties separated from universities, 137; fees increased and funds sought to educate boys, 138; eight seminaries closed, 142n; trial of Dr Kos and seminarians from Djakovo, 147,239; legal rights of seminarians, 224; legal provisions for closing of, 224; demand for equal rights for seminarians, 241

Catholics, Greek, 2, 27, 33
Catholics, Roman, 1; a minority in the whole country, 3f; Slav consciousness shared with Orthodox, 4; prewar conversions to Orthodoxy, 26 & n; some Roman Catholic delegates to 1st AVNOJ, 50
Cecelja, the Rev. Vilim (Ustaša military vicar), 103, 107, 111
Čekada, Bishop of Skopje, 282; trial of, 240
Čelik, Mgr (Apostolic Administrator of Banja Luka): assaulted, expelled from diocese, 134; attacked by mob, 136; forced to leave Banja Luka by mob attack, 251
census (1953): on religious affiliation, 135, 297
Černetić, the Rev. August (Catholic), 46n
Četniks, 53, 87, 92, 175, 195, 280; begin to disintegrate, 18; cooperation with Italian army, 33; Slovene

groups supporting, 41n; attitude of Četniks to south Slav nations, 48; retreat across frontier, 55; Slovene Četniks, 91; accused of atrocities against Croatian Catholics and planning to extend Greater Serbia, 109; Montenegrin Četniks collaborate with Italians, 180; some Orthodox priests join, 187
Christian Socialist movement, 4, 41, 45, 131; part of Slovene Liberation Front, 43; appeals to Bishop Rožman, 44; uneasy alliance with communists, 44f; anti-clericalist, 44; pressures on individual members to join Communist Party, 44; behaviour of Partisans towards, 47f; cooperate with OF, 49; CMD springs from, 126
church–state relations (general) (*see also* social insurance of clergy): constitutional basis for laid down at 2nd AVNOJ, 50f; government's determination to separate church and state, 121
 Catholic Church: government more concerned to reach settlement than, 69 & n; bishops' circular to clergy rejects separation of church and state, 71n; government takes over official registers of births, marriages, deaths, 78; Bakarić on, 79; Stepinac replies, 80; influence of Trieste question on, 81f; nature of relations determined by Stepinac trial, 120; three main points at issue, 122; government wish to change church, 123; contradiction in attitude of government, 139; joint commission of bishops and government set up, talks break down, 144f; bishops declare they are not competent to make agreements, 145; Boris Kraiger declares relations depend entirely on attitude of church, 145; government declares it is ready to negotiate directly with Vatican, 145; enter quieter phase, 146; permission for Stepinac's public funeral a turning point in, 149; quiet but wary, 229; rumours of contacts, 235f; improved relations and further trials, 239; Stepinac's death removes last obstacle to improvement, 240; preliminaries to negotiations, 240–5;

church–state relations (*cont.*)
effect on of Protocol, 247f; definition of 'religious affairs', 247f; change at end of 1971, 290; dilemma of authorities, 290f; present state, 292

Macedonian Orthodox Church: government greets new church, 265, 266

Serbian Orthodox Church, 199; government subventions as lever, 158; usefulness of church to government, 164; Vicar-Bishop Varnava's opinion of, 176; democracy as a tool to manipulate church, 181; state enables church visits abroad, 193; good under Patriarch Vikentije, 198; shift in government position, 204; begin to improve 249; mutual usefulness of patriarch's travels, 256f; financial assistance in question, 260, 265; government pressure to accept autonomous Macedonian Church, 265; enter into quiet period, 268f; government makes use of church, 271f; strained by Macedonian schism, 288, 289

Ciano, Count G., 10n; signs treaty of friendship with Yugoslavia, 7; conversation with Pavelić, 28

Čimić, Esad, 111n

CMD (Ciril–Metodsko Društvo) (including first Slovene priests' association), 229; founded 1949, 124; signs agreements for health and social insurance and taxation, 125; curious incident in connection with, 126n; 60% of Slovene priests belong, 126; account of founding, 127f; denounces Ustaša crimes, attacks hierarchy, 127; reformed by moderate clergy, 129; sets up *zadruga*, 129; concerns set out, 129f; programme anticipates thinking of Second Vatican Council, 130; numbers in, 130; tries to be objective, 131; visits Tito, 237

civil rights, deprivation of, 93

Čolaković, Rodoljub (Partisan leader and government), 52, 253

Cominform, 80, 93, 121, 136, 137n, 180, 251; expulsion of Yugoslavia from, 81, 83, 193, 226

Comintern, 182

Commission for Religious Affairs, 85, 113, 126, 168, 210, 214, 239, 255;

first commission, 46; constitution, 46n; set up in Slovenia in 1944; 67; federal and republican commissions established, 67; Croatian Commission for Religious Affairs set up, 68; authorises work of Caritas, 78; close links with Slovene priests' association, 127; becomes official body, 143; bureau of religious affairs set up by Macedonian High Command, 183, 186; no longer deals with local complaints, 201; holds reception for Sabor, 204; Orthodox priests' associations committee lectured by chairman of, 205

Committee of Three, 107

Communist Party (later LCY), 44f, 45, 67n, 226, 237; dominates Slovene OF, 4; supports overthrow of regency, 9; in Slovene OF, 43; uneasy alliance with Christian Socialists, 44; determined to drive the church our of politics, 44f; wartime membership of Christians in Slovene party, 45; Edvard Kocbek comments on, 45f; attitude towards religious belief, 47f, 173; controlled OF, 49; Stepinac's words to, 111; tasks facing after the war, 121; Slovene party orders systematic struggle against hierarchy and clericalism, 135n; attitude to Yugoslav nations, 178; Yugoslav party jurisdiction over Macedonian party, 182; abolition of special privileges, 228; disturbed by growth of religious influence, especially in schools, 233; discipline on religion relaxed, 238; Brioni Plenum, 281; relaxation of party control after fall of Ranković, 289; shift in leadership towards harder line, 290; session of Croatian party Executive Committee, 290; contradictions in attitude towards religion, 291

confessional, secrecy of, 137, 220f

Constantinople, Orthodox patriarchate: wary of Slav liturgical nationalism, 47

constitution: constitutional basis for church–state relations established at 2nd AVNOJ, 50f; articles relating to religion, 50f; constitutional and legal status of the religious communities, 209–25;

constitution (*cont.*)
prewar constitutional position of religious bodies, 209; basis in Foča documents and 1st and 2nd AVNOJ, 210; Art. 25 of 1946 c. lays down rights and duties of religious communities, 210f; provisions of 1963 c., 211; promulgation of 1963 c., 245

Corfu negotiations, 4

Council of Foreign Ministers, 82

Crnković, Josip (catechist), 96n, 97; arrested, 79

Croatia, 19–32, 56–81, 149; Orthodox Serbs in, 2; autonomous banovina established, 6; Croatian nationalism manifested, 289, condemned by Tito, 290

Croatia–Slavonia, 10, 12; Protestant groups in, 2; Catholic majority in, 3

Croatian ministers (in wartime government-in-exile); protest anti-Croat use of smuggled memoranda, 15n

Croatian Orthodox Church, 39, 61, 62, 154, 174; creation of, 25; step towards Uniate Church, 31n; priests sentenced to be shot, 62; Synod resolution cancels all acts of, 179

Croatian Peasant Party (HSS), 9, 74, 104; anti-clerical, 3; Stepinac voted for in 1938, 112

Croats, 4, 10, 20, 49n, 52, 65, 73, 178; in Bosnia–Hercegovina, 2; in southern Serbia and Macedonia, 2; resistance to King Alexander's dictatorship, 3; prewar regional poverty explodes into religious and national conflict, 4; Croat extremism fuelled by dispute over concordat, 6; welcome defeat of Yugoslavia, 19; killed by Serbs, 30n; 'ante-murale Christianitatis': position within Yugoslavia, 31; historic desire for independence, 40; oppressed in Istria and Julian region, 41; Tite speaks as a Croat, 57 & n

Crvenkovski, Krste (Macedonian leader), 282

Čučkov, Emanuel (Macedonian government), 185

Ćuk, the Rev. Ilija (Orthodox), 49; member of ZAVNOH, 50

Čule, Bishop of Mostar, 71n, 133, 228; length of sentence, 93n; injured in railway accident, 176; at Second Vatican Council, 243

Cvetković, Dragiša (prewar prime minister), 7

Czechoslovak Orthodox Church, 179

Dalmatia, 10, 59; inhabitants Catholic, 2; Catholic majority in, 3; prewar poverty in, 4; Italian province, 9; determined Italians should not return, 52

Damaskin (Grdanički), Bishop of the Banat, 161, 176, 195, 202, 270, 277

Damjanović, General (Četnik), 52

Danilo (Dajković), Bishop of the Montenegrin Littoral, 270f, 283

Dankelmann, General (German military commander in Serbia), 15 & n

Dedijer, Dr V. (Partisan; later government and historian), 29f, 102n

Demokracija, 83

Democratic Federated Yugoslavia: proclaimed at Jajce, 48

Didović, the Rev. Franjo (Catholic), 50

Dilparić, Miloje (secretary of Serbian Commission for Religious Affairs), 196, 236, 264, 270n; accompanies patriarch to Moscow, 255; accompanies patriarch to Peć, 269; accompanies patriarch to Montenegro, 271

Dimevski, Toma, *see* Naum, Bishop of Zletovo–Strumica

Dionisije (Milivojević), Bishop of America–Canada, 168, 177, 198, 251, 267, 269, 277, 280; government complains about activities, 167; attacked by priests' associations, 192; opponent of postwar Yugoslav government, 276; life and character, 276f; proposes metropolitanate in North America, 277; suspended from episcopal duties, 278; refuses to accept suspension, 278; summons Assembly of Church and People at Libertyville, Ind., 279; defrocked but not excommunicated, 279f

Djaković, Mitar (secretary to Patriarch Gavrilo), 164

Djilas, Milovan (Partisan leader; later government), 51, 123n, 176

Djorić, the Rev. Hranislav, *see* German (Patriarch)

Djumandžić (NDH minister), 29

Djurić, Major-General (Partisan): calls at patriarchate, 151

Dobrečić, Bishop of Bar, 71n; refuses to allow bishops' pastoral letter to be read in his diocese, 74

Dobri Pastir, 229, 230, 309; founded 1950, 124; 80% of Catholic priests in Bosnia and Hercegovina belong, 126; account of founding, 126f

Domagoj, 103

Domobran (see also Bela Garda): regrouped, 41n; retreat into Austria, 55; turned back at frontier, majority killed by Partisans, 55f; take oath of allegiance, 88

Dorotheus, Archbishop of Athens, 255

Dositej (Stojković), vicar-bishop, Metropolitan of Skopje, 198, 202, 263, 265 & n, 287; early life, 208; visits Macedonia, 208, 259ff; accompanies patriarch to Montenegro, 258; elected metropolitan of restored Archbishopric of Ohrid, 264, 265f; presence at Macedonian Church Assembly not authorised by Sabor, 264; Patriarch German and D. consecrate second Macedonian bishop, 266; consecrates third Macedonian bishop, 267; accompanies Patriarch German to Sofia, 272; visits Patriarch German, 280f; accompanies patriarch to Bulgaria, 281; builds image of independent church, 282f; installed as head of Macedonian Orthodox Church, 284; visits parishioners in Canada, 287; decorated by government, 287

Dositej (Vasić), Metropolitan of Zagreb: ill-treatment and expulsion, 6, 11; dies from after-effects of ill-treatment, 24

Draganović, the Rev. Dr Krunoslav (Catholic, associated with NDH), 26; activities and unexpected return to Yugoslavia, 238 & n

Drljić, the Rev. Ratislav (director of Francisan seminary, Bosnia), 127

Družina, 309

Državno Ravnateljstvo za Ponovu, 22f, 116

Držečnik, Bishop of Maribor, 42 & n, 134 & n, 139, 238n; assaulted, 134n

Dum maerentes, 234

Dvoršak, Sister Brigitta (Catholic): acquitted at trial, 91n

Ecclesiam suam, 228

education, moral and social: intro-

duced by authorities, 230f; again preoccupies authorities, 292

Ehrenberg, Ilya, 28

Ehrlich, Dr (Ljubljana theological faculty), 42

Emilijan (Marinović), Bishop of Slavonia (Pakrac), 202, 263, 274

Emilijan (Piperković), Bishop of Timok, 281; member of Synod in 1941, 12; visits Moscow patriarchate, 163; press attacks on, 174

Evangelical Church, 33, 39

Fajfar, Tone (Slovene Partisan): goes to Otočac to meet Slovene priests, 44; delegate to 2nd AVNOJ, 44; delegate to 1st AVNOJ, 50

Fazinić, the Rev. Andjelko (Dominican provincial), 69n

'50–50' agreement, 53n

Firmilijan (Ocokolić), Bishop of the Middle West (USA), 278f

Foča documents: first declaration of position of religious communities, 210

food deliveries, compulsory, 78; application to church lands, 214

forced conversions (see also NDH, Orthodox Serbs, Stepinac), 76, 116, 153

Fotitch, Konstantin (wartime Yugoslav ambassador to USA), 168

Franciscans, in Bosnia–Hercegovina, 28, 31 & n; Evelyn Waugh's report on conduct of, 32; Bosnian Franciscans during the war, 52; two groups tried in Ljubljana and Pula, 90f; found Dobri Pastir, 126; see also individual Franciscans: Bellato, Beninca, Glavaš, Gomiero, Jerek, Just, Karla, Kocijančič, Krešo, Margetić, Martinčić, Mattielo, Medić, Ostojić, Planišek, Prejić, Rižner, Šuhac, Tiburcije, Tovčar, Valenčak, Vinko.

Franić, (Arch)Bishop of Split, attacked by mobs, 134 & n, 136; at Second Vatican Council, 243n, 244

Frid, Zlatko, 111n

Fry, Dr Franklin (WCC): visits Patriarch Vikentije, 250

Fulgosi, Vicar-General (of Split), 351

Gačinović, the Rev. Vojislav (Orthodox), 168

Garić, Bishop of Banja Luka, 24, 39n, 55, 119

Gaudium et spes, 228

Gavrilo, Patriarch (Mihajlo Dožić), 164, 165, 166, 167, 176, 191, 277; Metropolitan Gavrilo of the Montenegrin Littoral elected patriarch 1937, 6; protests signing of Tripartite Pact, 7; leaves Belgrade for Ostrog, 10; supports King Peter's decision to leave the country, 10; tried and imprisoned by Germans, 11; gives informal support to Metropolitan Josif, 12; visited by Synod, 17; receives visitors, 17; convinced Nedić acting honourably, 17; moved to Vojloviča monastery, 17; transported to Dachau, liberated by U.S. Army, 18; travels after liberation, 164; government informs Synod that he is in Italy, 165; returns to Belgrade, 165ff; determined to work with new government, 168f; calls on Tito and other officials, 169; speaks to Pan-Slav Congress, Christmas message, 169f; receives delegation of priests, 190; visit to Moscow, 193; blunt speaking to Patriarch Alexei, 193f; interview with Associated Press, 194; death and funeral, 192, 194

Gazivoda, the Rev. (Catholic), 118

Gazivoda, the Rev. Mihajlo (Orthodox), 251

Georgije (Zubković), Bishop of Budim, 195

German, Patriarch (Hranislav Djorić) (vicar-general; Bishop of Budim, later of Žiča), 159, 180, 255, 256, 265, 268, 274, 277, 281, 283; elected vicar-bishop, visits Europe and USA, 198; meets Archbishop Šeper, 245, 292; elected patriarch, 261f; life and character, 262; visits other Orthodox Churches and Holy Land, 263f; willingness to cooperate with priests' associations, 263; sees Patriarch Athenogoras, 266; refuses invitation to visit Macedonian Church, 266; two months later visits Skopje to consecrate Bishop Kliment, 266f; analyses Macedonian Church question, 267; visits Bosnia and Hercegovina, 269; progress through Serbia to Peć patriarchate,

269; installation at Peć, 270; visits western Yugoslavia, 270; received by Tito, 270; instals Metropolitan of Montenegro, 270f; visits Moscow patriarchate, 271; further visits to Moscow, 272; visits Romanian Orthodox Church, 272; at the Pan-Orthodox Conference, 272; welcomes meeting of the pope and Patriarch Athenagoras, 273f; several visits to Macedonia, 281

Germans, in the Vojvodina, 2, 4; leaders of German minority tried, 61

German security police reports, 29, 30

Gigov, Strahil (president, Macedonian Commission for Religious Affairs), 264, 269n

glagolitic (alphabet), 216 & n

Glas Koncila, 245, 310; interview with Metropolitan Dositej, 288

Glasnik (official journal of Serbian patriarchate), 177, 185, 195, 218, 262, 269n, 278, 308

Glavaš, the Rev. Radoslav (NDH minister; Franciscan), 27, 29, 39n, 97, 101, 113, 114n

Glina (scene of Ustaša massacre), 29

Globnička, Captain (Partisan), 79

Glumac, Dr (Serbian Orthodox theological faculty), 159, 198, 206, 277

Godrić, Father (Cather), 92n

Gogov, the Rev. Metodije (Macedonian, Orthodox), 183, 184

Gomiero, Fra (Franciscan), 91n

Gore Srca, 86, 308

Goričan, the Rev. H. (Catholic), 92n

Grazioli, Emilio (wartime Italian high commissioner), 42

Grema (Catholic student): sheltered by Canon Borić, 79

Grigorije (Udicki), Bishop of Western America, 278f, 279

Grisogono, G. (prewar government minister), 31

Grol, Milan (postwar non-communist government minister), 73

Guberina, the Rev. Ivo (Catholic; Ustaša ideologue): sentenced to hanging, 61 & n

Gulin, Dr Pavle (Slovene Četnik), 96n, 97, 100, 101, 104; accusation against, 97; condemned to death, 117

gypsies: Stepinac defends, 76

Habsburgs, 1, 117

Hacin, Dr (wartime Ljubljana police chief), 87

Harrison (British consul), 101 & n

hatred, inciting to national, racial or religious, 269n; constitutional provisions against, 51; legal provisions against, 219, 222

Hercegovina, see Bosnia–Hercegovina

Hermogen (Maksimov) (bishop of the Russian Church Abroad), 26; becomes head of Croatian Orthodox Church, 25; consecrates Spiridon Mifka, 25; sentenced to be shot, 61f; all acts of cancelled by Synod, 179

Hodža, Fadil (president of Kosovo provincial assembly), 270 & n

Hrizostom (Vojinović), Bishop of Budim, later of Braničevo, 180, 255, 259, 261f, 262, 263, 270, 278, 279

Hungarian Orthodox Church, 193f

Hungarians, in the Vojvodina, 2; round-ups and killings of Serbs in the Vojvodina, 13n; religious publications for, 311

Hurley, Mgr (chargé d'affaires at Nunciature), 104n, 119n; present at Stepinac trial, 102 & n; disagreeable interview with members of the Slovene priests' association, 128

Ilc, the Rev. Anton (Slovene Catholic; spiritual vicar in liberated territories), 42, 46n

Independent State of Croatia, see NDH

Inter-Church Aid (see also World Council of Churches): aid to Serbian Orthodox Church, 158; aid to Yugoslavia, 159; regular visits paid to Yugoslavia, 250

Internal Macedonian Revolutionary Organization (IMRO): contacts with ustaše, 3

Irinej (Ćirić), Bishop of Bačka, 180, 202; member of Synod in 1941, 12; beaten by mob, 166

Irinej (Djordjević), Bishop of Dalmatia, 155, 166, 167, 168, 198, 251; arrested and interned, 24; in exile, dies in England, 165, 277; press attacks on, 173; attacked by priests' associations, 192n; tribute to, 206

Islam, see Moslems

Istria, 49, 82, 84–94; mixed population, 2; Italian oppression feeds Slav nationalism, 41; many priests sympathise with resistance, 42; determination to cast off Italian rule, 52; Italian democratic groups seek assurances from Allies about, 53; in Zone B, 82; Istrian clergy welcome land reform and support Yugoslavia's claim to Istria, 86f; priests' association in, 124; virtually all Istrian priests members, 126

Italian Communist Party: supports Yugoslavia over Trieste issue, 82; withdraws support after 1948, 83f

Italian minority: in Julian region, 2; dispossessed by agrarian reform law, 82; rights protected under London Agreement, 84

Italian peace treaty (1947): redraws zonal boundaries, 82

Jambreković, the Rev. F., S.J. (professor, Jesuit seminary), 233n

Jasenovac (NDH concentration camp), 24, 28, 37, 76

Jerek, Fra Rudi (Franciscan), 239f

Jeremić, Vladimir (secretary, Belgrade branch, British and Foreign Bible Society), 250, 305, 306, 307

Jerić, the Rev. Ivan (Vicar-General of Prekmurje), 118

Jesuits of Ljubljana: tried and property confiscated, 92 & n

Jews: community in Bosnia, 2; Stepinac defends Jews, 36, 76, 113

Joanike (Lipovac), Metropolitan of the Montenegrin Littoral: killed by Partisans, 180

John XXIII, pope, 148, 228, 235, 240, 272, 273

Jones, Major (attached to Slovene Partisan unit): describes mass for Partisan units, 43n

Jonić (minister in wartime government of Serbia), 16

Josif (Cvijović), Metropolitan of Skopje, 166, 168, 169, 176, 181, 184, 186, 193, 202, 253; put under house-arrest by Bulgarians, expelled from Macedonia, goes to Belgrade, 11; assumes leadership of church, 12; obtains informal approval of imprisoned patriarch, 12; at Arandjelovac, 14; visits patriarch, 14; Easter message, 1942, 15f; stands up to Nedić, 16; organises

Josif (*cont.*)
collection for Partisan and Russian wounded, 151; permission to return to Macedonia refused, 153f; starts reconstruction, 156; complains about obstacles to religious education, 160; visits Moscow patriarchate, 163f; urges Patriarch Gavrilo to return, 165; press attacks on, 173, 192; twice arrested, 173f; administrator of diocese of Montenegro, 180; warns Macedonian clergy, 184; refused permission to travel to Skopje, 185; refuses to transmit government grant to Macedonian clergy, 185; arrested, 186; again refused permission to return to Skopje, 186; visits Moscow, 193; detained by police, 195; anecdotes about, 197f & n

Jovan (Ilić), Bishop of Niš, 157f, 176; member of Synod in 1941, 12; visits Moscow patriarchate, 163f; press attacks on, 174; attacked by priests' associations, 192; visits Macedonia, 259

Jovan (Velimirović), Bishop of Šabac, 272

Jovanović, Blažo (premier of Montenegro), 252 & n; admits excesses, 259

Jovanović, Isa (president, Serbian Commission for Religious Affairs), 270n

Julian region (*see also* Trieste), 87; mixed population, 2; suppression of Slav population in, 2; Italian oppression feeds Slav nationalism, 41; many priests sympathise with resistance, 42; determination to cast off Italian rule, 52; Italian democratic groups seek assurances about, 53; agreement to divide, 55

Juris, the Rev. Mihajlo (Catholic, Bosnian), 233n

Just, Fra Petar (Franciscan), 233n

Justinian, Patriarch of Romania: entertains Patriarch Vikentije, 257; visit to Serbian patriarchate, 257; receives Macedonian bishops, 287

Kangrga, M. (Zagreb philosopher): on danger of identifying Marxism with atheism, 231

Kapičić, the Rev. Petar (Orthodox, Montenegrin), 180; accompanies patriarch to Moscow, 255

Kapš, the Rev. Josip (Catholic, rector of Rijeka seminary), 233

Karamatijević, the Rev. Jevstatije (Orthodox): delegate to 1st AVNOJ, 50; visits Moscow patriarchate, 163

Kardelj, Dr Edvard (Slovene; Partisan and government leader), 29, 60, 241; expresses regret for assault on Bishop Vovk, 90; admits excesses, 123n; statistics on priests' associations, 129; accuses Vatican of supporting Italian irredentism, 141; Christian support in building socialism solicited, 229

Karin, the Rev. Dr Karlo (Catholic, Bosnian; professor of theology), 127

Karla, Fra H. (Franciscan), 91n

Kašić, Dr Dušan (director, Sv. Sava theological seminary): at Second Vatican Council, 274

Katičić, Dr (Zagreb lawyer), 94; appointed to defend Stepinac, 102; speech in defence of Stepinac, 116

Katolički List (prewar, wartime semi-official Catholic journal), 37; welcomes attack on Soviet Union, 37; quoted in Stepinac trial, 105, 106

Kemura, Reis-el-Ulema Suleiman Hadji (head of Moslem religious community), 269

Kidrić, Boris (Slovene; Partisan leader; postwar government), 86; member, Commission for Religious Affairs, 46; condemns pastoral letter of Sept. 1945, 74; receives church delegation, 85; view of Slovene Catholic masses as part of OF, 87

Kiril, vicar-bishop, Bishop of America–Canada–Australia (Macedonian Orthodox), 284f, 287; career, 284n

Kliment (Trajkovski), Bishop of Prespa and Bitola, 264, 266, 267, 269, 287

Kocbek, Edvard (Slovene writer; Partisan and Catholic), 85n; delegate to 2nd AVNOJ, 44; war memoirs, 45f; delegate to 1st AVNOJ, 50; Commissioner for Education, 50; travels to Vatican, 51; conversation with Stepinac, 60

Kocijančič, Fra (Franciscan), 91n

Koenig, Cardinal, 148, 274

Kokša, the Rev. Dr Djuro (Catholic), appointed rector of St Jerome's College, Rome, 235

Kolarek, Canon Nikola (Zagreb), 34n, 57n

Koliševski, Lazar (head of Macedonian government), 260, 267

Komunist, 200, 238

Korošec, Mgr (deputy premier of prewar Yugoslavia), 4

Kos, the Rev. Dr Ćiril (Djakovo seminary), 147; trial of, 239

Košak (NDH minister), 110

Kosovo: annexed to Albania, 9

Kostić, the Rev. Slobodan (Orthodox), 180

Kovačević, the Rev. Irinej (vicar-bishop of schismatic Orthodox diocese in USA), 279

Kragelj, the Rev. Josif (Catholic), 83 & n

Kragujevac: several priests shot in October 1941 killings, 17

Krajger, Boris (Slovene; Partisan leader; government), gives numbers of priests arrested, 91; admits excesses, 123n; chairs joint commission of bishops and government, 144; comments on breakdown of talks, 145

Kralj, the Rev. Mother Marija (Catholic), 92

Krek, Dr (prewar Slovene minister), 164; tried *in absentia*, 87

Krešo, Fra K. (Franciscan), 96n

križari (prewar youth section of Catholic Action; postwar underground Ustaša groups), 56n, 96f, 104, 105, 108, 115; flag for secretly blessed, 79, 100

Kršćanska Sadašnjost, 310

Kuševac, the Rev. Marko (Orthodox), 251f

Kvaternik, Slavko (commander, Ustaša forces), 20, 103, 105, 112; proclaims establishment of NDH, 19; receives Stepinac, 19

Labor, the Rev. Dr Marcel (director, Koper seminary), 135

Lach, Auxiliary Bishop of Zagreb, 27, 57n, 98, 143; visits Rome, 235

Lacković, the Rev. S. (Catholic; secretary to Archbishop Stepinac), 67n, 79, 100, 114n

Lampret, the Rev. Jože (Catholic; Partisan), member of Slovene Commission for Religious Affairs, 46n; delegate to 2nd AVNOJ, 50; suspended *a divinis*, calls on Mgr Hurley, 128f; calls with delegation on Tito, 130; his headlong approach discarded, 30; excommunicated for ignoring suspension, 131

Lastavica, the Rev. Stefan (Orthodox), *see* Stefan, Bishop of (U.S.) Middle Eastern diocese

Law on Workers' Self-Management, 83

laws concerning religion and religious communities, 144; 1953 Law on the Legal Status of Religious Communities, 122, 146, 200, 205, 221–5; revised in 1965, 225, 240, 241, 251; 1939 law on support of the Orthodox Church abrogated, 157; constitutional and legal status of the religious communities, 209–25; Law on Agrarian Reform, 212–17; provisions affecting churches, 212f; Law on Nationalisation and Expropriation, 217–19, no compensation for churches, 218; Criminal Code, 219–21; Serbia, law implementing federal law, 223; constitution and Law on Legal Status, observance of, 223f; statistics: land expropriated, by republics, 303, land expropriated in Croatia, by districts, 304

League of Communists of Yugoslavia (LCY), *see* Communist Party

Lederhas, the Rev. L., S.J. (Catholic, superior of Ljubljana Jesuits), 92

Lenić, Canon Dr S. (Ljubljana), 88n, 92; tried and sentenced, 91

Leopold, the Rev. Dr Edgar (superior, Pleterje Carthusians), 44, 130

Letica, Dušan (minister of finance, Nedić government): orders priests' salaries to be paid by government, 14

Liberation Front, *see* OF

Lisak, Col. Erih (Ustaša police chief), 79, 80, 94, 96 & n, 97, 98, 102, 104, 107, 108, 115; escapes and returns to Yugoslavia, 79; put on trial, 96f; evidence at trial, 98ff; condemned to be hanged, 117

Ljotić, Dimitrije (Serbian fascist), 18n, 281

Ljubljana: annexed by Italians, 9

Ljubostinja (monastery): Bishop Nikolaj Velimirović interned in, 11
Lobkowicz, Prince (NDH representative in Rome), 31n, 38, 110
Logar, Cene (member, Slovene Commission for Religious Affairs), 46n
von Lohr, General (commander, German forces in NDH), 55
Lončar, Canon (of Zagreb), 57n
London Agreement, 84
Longin (Tomić), Bishop of Zahumlje–Hercegovina, later of Zvornik–Tuzla, 202, 263

Macedonia and Macedonians, 10, 178, 182; divided in 1912, 1; Croats and Slovenes in, 2; violent discontent in, 3; western parts annexed to Albania, 9; eastern parts annexed by Bulgaria, 9; Bulgarian Orthodox Church takes over three dioceses, 12; acquires statehood and language, 52; expelled bishops and priests not allowed to return, 154; resistance in led by Vukmanović-Tempo, 182; equal status of affirmed at 2nd AVNOJ, 182
Macedonian Orthodox Church (including events leading up to): 49, 154, 169, 181, 182–7, 194, 196, 198, 206–8, 259–61; first demand or, 151; government encourages separatist priests, 169; Macedonian language allowed to clergy for first time, 171; origins of concept of an independent church, 183; priests demand liturgical use of Macedonian language, 183; wartime meeting of priests at Izdeglavje sets up church administration, 183; Independent Macedonian Orthodox Church proclaimed, 184; complains to Synod, 185; were the Macedonian clergy fellow travellers? 186; question of independence temporarily lapses, 186; obtains concession over language, 187; not prepared to accept Metropolitan Josif as patriarch, 195; request for own bishops deferred, 204; pressures mount for solution, 207; Organising Committee calls on Synod, 207; Patriarch Vikentije visits, 253; triumphal visit of Vicar-Bishop Dositej, 208; Macedonian clergy fobbed off by Sabor, 254; further

concessions secured, 258; first ordinations since the war, 258n; Patriarch Vikentije makes canonical visitation, 259f; further concessions granted, 260; Macedonian priests call Assembly of the Macedonian Church and People, restore Archbishopric of Ohrid, elect Dositej metropolitan, 264; constitution published, 264; autonomous Macedonian Orthodox Church, 265; Ecumenical Patriarch advises against recognition, 266; rejoicing in Bitola, 266f; consecration of second bishop to ensure independence, 266; third bishop consecrated, 267f; parishes in Australia, 268; Patriarch Alexei of Russian Orthodox Church visits, 271; consolidates position, builds and repairs churches, 281; speculation on reasons for breakaway, 281; Serbian and Macedonian Synods meet, 282; formal demand for autocephaly, 282f; demand refused by Sabor, 283f; proclaims autocephaly and establishes two new dioceses, 284f; explanatory statement justifying action, 284f; supported by Macedonian authorities, 286; seminary opened, 286f; no recognition from other Orthodox Churches, 287; five dioceses become metropolitanates, 287f; Velika renamed Debar–Kičevo, 288; adopts Gregorian calendar, 287; disregards summons of Synod, deadlock, 288; statistics, 298, 299; religious publication, 312
Maček, Dr V., 103, 105, 107, 115; rebuffs German advances, 9; joins Simović government, 19; Stepinac supports in 1938 election, 20; visited by Stepinac, 101 & n; Stepinac voted for prewar, 112; meets Patriarch Gavrilo, 164
Mačura, the Rev. Milan (Orthodox), 124n
Magjerec, Mgr (rector, St Jerome's College, Rome), 235
Majić, the Rev. A. (Vicar-General of Mostar), 233n
Majstorović-Filipović (commandant, Jasenovac concentration camp), 28; expelled from Franciscans, 28; sentenced to hanging, 61

Makanec (NDH minister), 36
Makarije (Djordjević), Bishop of Budimljan–Polim, later of Srem, 195, 288; press attack on, 174
Malevski, the Rev. Kliment (Orthodox, Macedonian), 263, 287
Mančevski, the Rev. Veljo (Orthodox, Macedonian), 183
Mandić, Dr Nikola (president of NDH), 114n
Manzoni, Archbishop of Zadar: pledges loyalty to peoples' authorities, 52
Marcone, Abbot Ramiro (apostolic visitor to the Catholic Church in the NDH), 38n, 51, 59, 60 & n; appointed apostolic visitor, 21f; calls on Tito, 59f
Margetić, Fra Mamerto (Franciscan), 96n, 101; accusation against, 97f
Margotti, Archbishop of Gorizia, 42, 93n, 131n; attacked in Yugoslav press, 86, 92n; excommunicates journalists for anti-Vatican campaign, 118
Marić, the Rev. Dr (Zagreb theological faculty), 137
Marić, the Rev. Djuro (Catholic; Ustaša), 96n
Marinko, Miha (premier of Slovenia), 135, 237
Marković, the Rev. Blažo (Orthodox): delegate to 1st AVNOJ, 50
Martinčić, Fra Modesto (Franciscan provincial in Croatia), 28, 91, 96n, 112; length of sentence, 93n; put on trial, 96n; accusation, 97; behaviour during trial, 98f; examined during trial, puts blame on Stepinac, 101; refusal to sign pastoral letter of March 1945, 107; condemned to five years, 117
Masucci, the Rev. Giuseppe Carmelo (secretary to Abbot Marcone), 34n, 38n, 97, 99
Mater et magistra, 288, 243
Matica Mrtvih (Slovene death register), 56n
Mattielo, Fra (Franciscan), 91n
Maxwell, Raymond (Inter-church Aid): visits Yugoslavia, 250
Medić, Father (Franciscan; Ustaša military chaplain), 28
Medjumurje, 9, 59
Medvešček, the Rev. (Catholic), 129
Merc, Dr Ivan, 56n

Meštrović, Ivan (sculptor; Croat), 20n, 22, 67n
Metodij, vicar-bishop, Bishop of Velika, 283, 287; elected Bishop of Velika, 284
Metzler, John (Church World Service): visits Yugoslavia, 250
Mifka, Spiridon, the Rev. (Croatian Orthodox Bishop of Sarajevo), 25, 26, 179; sentenced to hanging, 61
Mihailović, General Draža (Royal Yugoslav Army; leader of Četnik forces), 18, 49, 52, 91, 164, 165, 168
Miklavčič, the Rev. Dr M. (Ljubljana theological faculty), 84, 85; intermediary between church and government, 86; helps to found moderate priests' association, 129; respected by hierarchy, 131 & n
Mikulček, Prebendary (Zagreb): links with Partisans, 67n
Mikuš, the Rev. Dr Metod (archivist to Bishop Rožman of Ljubljana): joins Partisans and appeals to Bishop Rožman, 44; suspended, 44n; delegate to 2nd AVNOJ, 44, 50; member, Slovene Commission for Religious Affairs, 46n; regrets bishops' pastoral letter of Sept. 1945, 74n; unfavourable opinion of Bishop Rožman, 88
Milanović, Dr Bozo (dean, Pazin seminary), president of Istrian priests' association, 124
Mileta, Bishop of Šibenik, 71n; meets Partisan leaders, 51, 52
Milin, Dr Lazar (Belgrade theological faculty), 269n; at Second Vatican Council, 274
Miodragović, Dr Jovo (Orthodox), member of ZAVNOH, 50
Mišić, Bishop of Mostar: realises Ustaša methods harming the church, 23; refuses absolution to murderers, etc., 32; reports and deplores atrocities, 32f
Mitrovica, Mitra (Minister of Education, Serbian government), 160 & n
Mladenović, the Rev. Mladen (Orthodox), 278
Montenegro: inhabitants Orthodox, 1; Montenegrins settled in the Vojvodina, 2; governor installed by Italians, 9; rising against occupation in 1941, 13; church life strictly controlled by Italians, 13; Serbian

Montenegro (*cont.*)
refugees crowd into, 13; separatist priests in, 169; shortage and unrest among priests in, 258

Moscatello, Mgr Nicolo (counsellor of Yugoslav legation to Vatican), 118

Moškov, General (Ustaša leader), 96, 97, 100, 101n, 104, 108, 115

Moslems, 1, 39, 61, 126, 144, 250, 270; Albanian, 1; Slavs become Moslems, 2; Albanian, in Macedonia, 2; of Bosnia and Hercegovina assumed by NDH to be of Croatian origin, 22; acquire mosque in Zagreb, 22; Serb retaliations against, 29; AVNOJ appeals to, 49; positive attitude praised by government, 238

Muftić, Ismet (mufti of Zagreb), sentenced to be shot, 61

Nadrah, Vicar-General of Ljubljana, 85n

Nastasević, the Rev. Milan (Orthodox), 188

National Commission for the Defence of Peace in the World, 203 & n

National Liberation Committees: set up before end of war to administer territory, 84

nationalisation of church property, *see* Catholic Church (Roman): churches and church property; Serbian Orthodox Church: churches and church property; laws concerning religion

Naum (Dimovski), Bishop of Zletovo–Strumica, 264, 268, 269, 287; consecrated, 267f; visits Australia, 268

NDH (Independent State of Croatia), 51, 65, 76, 103, 104, 106, 113, 120, 155; established, 9; estimates of population, 10n; Serbs flee or are expelled from, 13; Bishop Nektarije administrator of four dioceses in, 13; proclaimed on April 10, 1941, 19; Stepinac criticises, 20; issues anti-Serb decrees, 22; treats Moslems as brothers and allies, 22; 'nation of two religions', 22; sighs agreement with Germans for deportations of Serbs, 22; deportations of Serbs, 23f; and the Catholic Church, 26–40; passes new law simplifying conversions, 26 & n; rules governing conversions, 27;

enlists parish priests for conversions, 27; atrocities against Orthodox Serbs, 27ff; estimates of numbers of Serbs who perished in, 29; considers arresting Stepinac, 34n; press censorship, 37; chances of recognition by Vatican disappear, 37f; 4th anniversary celebrated by thanksgiving mass, 40; hopes of keeping independent state, 52; government prepares to flee, 53; fighting retreat across frontier, 55; remnants turned back at frontier, majority killed by Partisans, 55; never recognised *de jure* by the Vatican, 59; archives deposited at archbishopric, 61

Nedelja, 83

Nedić, General (head of Serbian government under Germans): leads Serbian puppet government, 13; summons hierarchy, 16; Germans complain to about priests, 16; visits Patriarch Gavrilo, 17

Nektarije (Krulj), Bishop of Zvornik–Tuzla, 169, 170, 176, 184n, 186, 195; expelled from Tuzla, goes to Belgrade, 11; member of Synod in 1941, 12; administrator of four NDH dioceses, 13; expelled from diocese, 24; visits Bosnian and Hercegovinian dioceses, 155; beaten up, 174; press attacks on, 174; set upon and ejected from monastery, 200; driven out of diocese, 251; visits Russian Orthodox Church, 255

Nešković, Dr Blagoje (president of Serbian government), 169

Nežić, Bishop of Pazin and Poreč–Pula, 238n; approves rules of priests' associations, 124; called up for military service, 134f; consecration, 228

Niedzielski, Dr (president of prewar *križari*), 105

Nikanor (Iličić), Bishop of Bačka, 202, 263, 269, 274, 277, 288

Nikolaj (Jovanović), Bishop of Zahumlje–Hercegovina, expelled from Mostar, goes to Belgrade, 11; expelled from diocese, 24

Nikolaj (Velimirović), Bishop of Žiča, 13, 164, 165, 166, 167, 168, 197, 198, 262, 276; interned in Ljubostinja monastery, 11; joins Patriarch

Nikolaj (Velimirović) (*cont.*)
Gavrilo in Vojloviča monastery, 18; transported to Dachau, liberated by U.S. Army, 18; outstanding political leader but compromised by friendship with Ljotić, 18n; press attacks on, 173; attacked by priests' associations, 192n; difficulties with Bishop Dionisije, 277

Nova Makedonija, 286

Nova Pot, 309; founded 1949, 129; explains actions of church and government each to other, 131

Novine Mladih: complains about intelligent boys going to seminaries, 233

Nunciature (*see also* Hurley, Mgr), 137

Oberški, the Rev. Dr (Zagreb theological faculty), 137

Ocokoljić, the Rev. Firmilijan, *see* Firmilijan, Bishop of the Middle West

Oddi, Mgr (cardinal), (chargé d'affaires, Vatican legation to Yugoslavia), 139; severing of diplomatic relations between Yugoslavia and Vatican, 140f

OF (Osvobodilna Fronta), 41, 43, 94, 127, 128; Christian Socialists join, 4; attempt to win over clergy, 43; communists in, 43; controlled by Communist Party, 43, 49; invitation to Bishop Rožman to visit, 44; attitude to religion sincere? 44; Catholics in Slovenia part of, 74; church authorities make contact with, 84; close links with Istrian and Slovene clergy, 124

Old Catholics, 36n

Orlovi (Eagles) (later *križari, q.v.*), 56n

Orthodox Churches' leaders meet in Moscow, 193

Orthodox Serbs, 2, 111; in Bosnia-Hercegovina, 2; in the Vojvodina, 2; Slav consciousness shared with Catholics, 4; numbers and dioceses in NDH, 10n; must convert to Latin not Greek rite, 27; atrocities against Orthodox Serbs in NDH, 30; estimated numbers perished in NDH, 15n, 29, 32; estimated numbers converted, 30; attitude to large Catholic minority in Yugoslavia, 31; forced conversions of explained in official Zagreb archdiocese gazette, 76f;

conversions annulled by ZAVNOH, 78; reference to forced conversions in Stepinac trial, 102, 103, 104, 112, 116; court examines Stepinac on forced conversions of, 106f; accused of atrocities and planning forced conversion of Croat Catholics, 109; Stepinac defends himself on forced conversion charges, 110, 111; Pope Pius XII asserts that those forcibly converted could not be accepted by Catholic Church, 118; displeased by Stepinac's 'posthumous amnesty', 149

Orthodox Slavs in Macedonia, 2

Osservatore Romano, L', 62, 80, 89; publishes messages of protest about Stepinac's sentence, 117; publishes decree excommunicating all those who took part in Stepinac trial, 118; publishes Vatican answer to Yugoslav government's letter severing diplomatic relations, 142; sufferings of bishops, two articles on, 134n, 234

Ostojić, Fra Bono (Franciscan): founder and elected president of Dobri Pastir, 127

Ostojić, the Rev. Dr Z. (Split seminary), 234

Ostrog (monastery): patriarch takes refuge in, 10

Ottoman Turks, 1

Oznanilo, 86, 309

Pacem in terris, 228

Pallua, Dr E. (Catholic layman; secretary, Croatian Commission for Religious Affairs), 68

Pan-Orthodox Conference, 272f, 273

Pope Paul VI, 273

Partisans, 18, 39, 43, 44, 48–52, 53, 62, 90, 92, 114, 123, 153, 154, 163, 164, 174, 180, 226; fight way back to Serbia, 18; enter Belgrade, 18; use Stepinac's sermons in clandestine propaganda, 36; proclaim government in 1943, 38; opposition to, 38f; shoot Dr Ehrlich, 42; Slovene units had chaplains, 43; hidden and nursed by Carthusians at Pleterje, 44; attitude and behaviour towards church when in power, 47f; Macedonian clergy make contact with, 49; some bishops sus-

Partisans (*cont.*)
pend priests who join, 49f; priests with, 50; contacts with (Catholic) bishops, 51f; administer large parts of Yugoslavia in 1944, 52; free Dalmatia, 52; suspicious of Allied intentions in Trieste, 53 & n; kill majority of surrendered forces, 55; enter Zagreb, 56; Stepinac aids those who appeal for help during war, 67; wartime connections between Partisans and Zagreb archbishopric, 67n; Mgr Rittig joins, 68; forced to withdraw from Trieste, 81; liberate large portions of Slovenia before end of war, 84; enter Ljubljana, 84; enter Belgrade, 151; relations with Macedonian clergy, 183; some Orthodox clergy join, 188

patriarchate, Serbian, *see* Serbian Orthodox Church

Paul VI, pope, 244, 273, 292

Paul, prince regent, 7, 20; conflict over concordat, 5; introduces relaxation of centralism, 6; regency overthrown, 9

Pavelić, Ante (the Poglavnik, Ustaša leader), 19, 20, 29, 33, 36, 37 & n, 38n, 64, 77, 79, 96, 99, 103, 105, 106, 107, 112, 114, 174, 227; establishes Ustaša centres in Italy and Hungary, 3; wanted the Sandjak included in the NDH, 10n; connections with Germans and Italians during exile, 19; receives Stepinac and bishops, 19; goes to Italy, 21; private audience with Pius XII, 21; Vatican anxiety not to appear to recognise officially, 21n; decrees establishment of Croatian Orthodox Church, 25; nominates second Croatian Orthodox bishop, 25; conversation with Ciano, 28; asks Stepinac to head provisional government, 39; orders withdrawal to Austria and flees, 55; angered by Stepinac's activities, 113n

Pavlišić, Bishop of Senj: called up for military service, 135

Peć patriarchate, 269f

Petar (Simonjić), Bishop of Dabar–Bosnia: Synod enquires after his fate, 15; arrested, put in concentration camp where he dies, 24

Peter, King of Yugoslavia: majority proclaimed, 9; escapes into exile, 9; leaves the country, 10; appeals for unity of Serbian Orthodox Church, 280

Phanariots, Greek, 4

Pichler, Bishop of Banja Luka: 1963 Christmas message offends many Croat Catholics, 244f

Pijade, Moše, 176, 200; speech at AVNOJ, 48f

Pilepić, the Rev. Dr A. (Split seminary), 234

Pius XII, pope, 141, 149, 228, 234, 235; receives Pavelić, 21; offers house to Patriarch Gavrilo, who refuses, 164

Planišek, the Rev. J. (Franciscan), 91n

Platon (Jovanović), Bishop of Banja Luka, 244; brutal murder of, 6; news of murder reaches Belgrade, 11; patriarch informed of murder, 17 & n; circumstances of murder, 24f

Poček, the Rev. Luka (Orthodox), 251f

Pogačnik, Archbishop of Ljubljana: at Second Vatican Council, 243

Politeo, Dr (Zagreb lawyer), 37n, 95, 109n; appointed to defend Stepinac, 102 & n; speech in Stepinac's defence, 112–16; defence obstructed by court, 112

Politika: attacks Synod, 167; interview with Patriarch Vikentije, 202f, 249; Patriarch Vikentije's 1952 Christmas message published in, 249; sympathetic obituary of Patriarch Vikentije, 261

Popović, the Rev. Tihomir (Orthodox, Macedonian): accompanies patriarch to Moscow, 255

Popovski, the Rev. Nestor (Orthodox, Macedonian), 254, 255, 260f, 264, 265, 283, 287; accompanies patriarch to Moscow, 255; heads delegation to patriarch, 258; candidacy for bishop unacceptable, 258 & n

Popovski, the Rev. Spira (Orthodox, Macedonian), 260

Popp (Evangelical bishop), 33n

Praxis, 231

Prejić, Father (Ustaša military chaplain; former Franciscan), 28

Prekmurje, annexed by Hungarians, 9

priests (*see also under* Catholic Church (Roman), Serbian Orthodox Church): engaged on two warring

priests (*cont.*)
sides, 18; unfavourable position before law courts, 232; numbers in prison, 251
priests' associations: publications, 309, 310
Catholic (*see also* CMD, Dobri Pastir): 86, 94 & n, 123, 124–31, 134, 142, 144, 229f, 233n; in Slovenia, 86; encouraged by the state, 122; bishops oppose, 124; Istrian, 124; Croatian founded 1953, 125; associations in Serbia, the Vojvodina, Montenegro founded 1953, 125; bishops pronounce *non expedit*, 125 & n; professional aspects of emphasised after 1953, 125; material benefits to members, 125; Croatian, signs agreement for social insurance, 125; pressure on clergy to join and on bishops for disciplining those who did, 126; statistics at end of 1952, 126; curious incident in connection with, 126n; Dobri Pastir founded, 127; founding of Slovene described, 127ff; bishops attacked for forbidding priests to join, 134; Radio Vatican broadcasts ban on, 136; decree *non expedit* applied with varying firmness, 138; provisional opinion on canon-law applicability, 138; Vatican asks bishops to oppose, 138f; bishops declare *non licet*, 138 & n; Vatican broadcast warning Croatian clergy not to join, 145; in Croatia, 229; *non licet*, variations in enforcement, 230; Bakarič brushes aside, 232; association defends accused priest, 239; changed status of, 241f; Croatian association journal *Danica* publishes controversial Christmas message of Bishop Pichler, 245
Orthodox (includes Union of Associations of Orthodox Priests), 49n, 158, 159, 163, 167, 173, 174, 181, 187–92, 190, 194, 196, 200, 201–6, 263, 264, 281, 307, 309; Association of Serbian Priests in Croatia founded, 124n; clergy in Montenegro begin to press for, 180ff; early example of, 187; obscure links between pre- and postwar, 188; first wartime meeting of Orthodox priests, 188; republican associations founded, 188; active in rebuilding country, religious arm of government, 189;

numbers of priests joining and active, 189; Serban declared uncanonical, 190; joint commission with Serbian Orthodox Church to examine differences, 190f. Union of Associations of Orthodox Priests in Yugoslavia founded, 191f; attacks bishops by name, 192; president of, a member of Elective Sabor, 194f; not prepared to accept Metropolitan Josif as patriarch, 195; recognition of by bishops postponed by administrative delays, 201; recognition, angry reaction to Sabor refusal of, 202; Serbian patriotism, 203; diocesan as well as republican associations agreed, 204; Administrative Committee lectured by chairman of Commission for Relations with Religious Communities, 205; associations increasingly become professional, 205; Second Congress, reorganisation, 205f & n; growing independence, 206; linked to struggle for independent Macedonian church, 206; opposed by Bishop Arsenije, 253; Sabor fails to discuss, 253f; associations welcome autonomous Macedonian Orthodox Church, 268; supports autocephaly of Macedonian Church, 285
prison conditions: religious observances in prison, 93; easing of conditions as reward for joining priests' association, 126
Protestants, 273; in the Vojvodina and Slavonia, 2
Protocol (1966), 242, 245–8, 313–15 (text)
Protulipac, Dr Ivan (head of prewar *križari*), 56n
Pušar, Djuro (premier of Bosnia and Hercegovina), 269; calls for halt to attacks on priests, 251
Pušić, Bishop of Hvar, 71n, 134 & n; meets Partisan leaders, 51; fined, 134

Rački, Nikola (secretary of LC in Rijeka): attacks Catholic influence on young people, 233
Radić, Stjepan (prewar Croatian political leader): on bishops and politics, 119
Radosavljević, Dobrivoje (president, Commission for Religious Affairs),

Radosavljević (*cont.*)
204, 205, 236, 237n, 250, 251, 254, 260, 261, 262, 270n, 281

Rakovica (monastery): Patriarch Gavrilo takes refuge in, 10; Patriarch Gavrilo imprisoned in, 11; Synod visits patriarch in, 14

Ramšak, the Rev. F.(Catholic, Slovene), 91

Ranković, Aleksander, 93n, 136, 144, 254, 257, 265, 268, 272, 281, 289; admits excesses, 123n; gives numbers of priests in prison, 132; speech to IVth Plenum on strengthening legality reveals illegal arrests and unjustified prosecutions, 135, 228 & n; influence on question of Macedonian Orthodox Church, and effect of fall, 282

religious education, 85, 142, 232f, 236; stopped in schools after war, 62; Stepinac's instructions to clergy concerning, 63; Stepinac complains about restrictions on, 65; neither side prepared to yield, 69; Catholic bishops complain about hindrances to, 70f; circular to clergy refers to, 71n & f; secondary school at St Vid, 88n; Bishop Vovk's advice to parents, 89; Bishop Vovk's alleged views on catechism classes, 89; Catholic priests allowed to give, 89; Bishop Vovk fined for circular on, 90; laws and regulations affecting, 94 & n; licence needed to teach, 94; Stepinac alleges r.e. hampered, 111; last traces of Catholic Church influence on education removed, 112; permission to teach r.e. only to members of priests' associations, 126; discontinued in primary schools, 137; obstacles to, 142; Serbian Orthodox Church faces difficulties over, 159ff, 169; abolished in schools, 230; 50% of children in Croatia receive, 235; religious instruction of children in Serbian Orthodox parishes, 274

religious press (general), 308–12; confiscation of printing presses puts at mercy of authorities, 218; printing presses nationalised, 310

Catholic, 37, 85, 103, 105, 115, 127, 128, 236, 308, 309, 310, 311, 312; fervently Ustaša during war, 37; virtually suppressed postwar, 62f; muzzled, 65; bishops complain about suppression, 70; circular to clergy demands freedom for, 72n; *Oznanilo*, 86; *Verski List*, 86; *Gore Srca*, 86; *Bilten*, 127ff; *Nova Pot*, 129; 152 Catholic publications, 24 publishing houses closed, 142n; rebirth of, 245

Serbian Orthodox, 309, 310, 312; disappears during the war except for *Glasnik*, 308

Rihar, the Rev. Franc (Catholic), 308

Rittig, Dr Josip, 74n

Rittig, Mgr Svetozar (of St Mark's Church, Zagreb; joined Partisans; postwar member of government), 61; member of ZAVNOH, 50; delegate to 2nd AVNOJ, 50; accompanies clergy delegation calling on Tito, 57n; first president of Croatian Commission for Religious Affairs, 68; previous career, 68f; becomes member of Croatian government, 74; thanks Stepinac in 1943 for his help in saving lives, 113; president of Croatian Catholic priests' association, 125; tries to effect settlement between bishops and government, 137; loses influence, 143

Rižner, Fra J. (Franciscan), 91n

Roman Catholics, *see* Catholics, Roman

Roman empire, 1

Romanian Orthodox Church, 275

Romero, General (commander, Italian occupation forces, Slovenia), 42

Rösener, General (commanding German forces in Slovenia), 87, 88

Roter, Zdenko, 111

Rožman, Bishop of Ljubljana (prewar and wartime), 41, 44, 46n, 55 & n, 56, 85 & n, 239; calls on Italian high commissioner, 42; friendly relations with Italians and Germans, 42; character described, 42f; ignores invitation from OF, 44; leaves Ljubljana with defeated forces, 55; put on trial *in absentia*, 87f; Vatican unwilling to deprive of title to see, 88n; discredited by flight, 119, 148; dismissal demanded by members of priests' association, 128

Rupnik, General (president, wartime civil government of Ljubljana), 87

Rušinović, Dr Nikola (wartime NDH representative at the Vatican), 28, 31n, 38, 110

Russian Orthodox Church (Moscow patriarchate), 51, 163, 179, 180, 193, 254, 255f, 273

Russian Orthodox Church Abroad, 27

Salać, the Rev. Dr (Zagreb seminary), 135

Šalić, the Rev. Ivan (secretary to Archbishop Stepinac), 61, 67n, 79n, 98, 99, 100, 101, 102, 104, 108, 115; arrested, 79; length of sentence, 93n; put on trial, 96; sentence, 96n; accusation, 97; takes fright and avoids meeting Lisak, 99; allows Lisak to stay overnight in the palace, 100; receives letters for Stepinac, 100; refuses to bless križari flag but allows chapel to be used, 100; harried and bullied by court, 100; states he was well treated in prison, 101; puts blame on Stepinac, 101; contradicts Stepinac's testimony, 108; condemned to 12 years, 117

Salis Seewis, Count, auxiliary bishop of Zagreb, 78, 132, 133, 138, 143; instructed to accompany Pavelić to Rome, 22; explains circumstances in later interview, 22; heads delegation to meet Tito, ensuing discussion, 57ff; gives provisional opinion on priests' associations, 138

Samuilov, the Rev. Stefan (Orthodox), 180

Santin, Bishop of Trieste, 93n, 143; leader of anti-Yugoslav sentiment over Trieste, 83; opens seminary in Pazin, 86; attacked in Yugoslav press, 92n

Šarić, Archbishop of Sarajevo, 33 & n, 39; flies with Ustaša forces, 55 & n; discredited by flight, 119, 148

Sava, Sv., 3, 16

Sava (Trljajić), Bishop of Gornjikarlovac: Synod enquires after his fate, 15; declared hostage, imprisoned, killed, 24

Schröder, General (German military commander in Serbia), 15n

Second Vatican Council, 47, 130, 228, 243–5, 273, 291, 310; Yugoslav bishops appointed to, 243n; no condemnation of communism, 243;

material concerning in Godišnjak, 243n & f; gesture of repentance towards other Christians, 244; two Russian Orthodox observers at opening of, 273; Serbian Orthodox observers at, 274

Šegvić, Dr Kerubin: Stepinac protests death sentence on, 65 & n

Sekulić, Dr Miloš: brings detailed list of murdered Serbs and damaged churches to London, 15n

self-management, 201; Law on Workers' Self-Management, 227

Šenk, the Rev. Ferdo (Catholic; member of ZAVNOH), 50

Šeper, Archbishop (Cardinal) Franjo, 102n, 310; resigns as director of seminary, 135; negotiates over Stepinac's funeral, 147f; conducts solemn requiem, 140; appointed Archbishop Coadjutor of Zagreb, 227f & n; calls on Bakarić, 231f; visits Rome, 235; at Second Vatican Council, 243n; meets Patriarch German, 245, 292

Serafim (Jovanović), Bishop of Raška–Prizren: interned in Tirana and dies, 11

Serbia and Serbians, 1, 2, 9, 10; inhabitants Orthodox, 1; Serbian culture, 2; Croat and Slovene catholics in southern Serbia, 2; Albanian Catholic minority in southern Serbia, 2; during the war, 10–18; Germans set up government under General Nedić, 13; refugees crowd into, 13; Commissariat for Refugees set up, 14; tide of war turns in, 18; German command in refuses to accept further NDH transports, 23; attitude of Serbian Orthodox Church to, 173, 178; attitude of communists to, 173; implementing law for Law on Legal Status of Religious Communities, 223; new liberal men in government, 289

Serbian Orthodox Church (see also church–state relations, Commission for Religious Affairs, priests' associations, religious education, religious press, trials of priests), 144, 151–77, 172, 178–208, 249–88, 289; patriarchate established in 1919, 3; constituent ecclesiastical organisations, 3n; objects successfully to concordat between Vatican and Yugoslavia, 5; strained

Serbian Orthodox Church (*cont.*)
relations with government in 1937, 5f; supports overthrow of regency, 9; patriarchate damaged in bombing, 10; movement of spiritual revival in, 11 (*see also bogomolski pokret*); church structure in NDH destroyed, 12; Bulgarian Orthodox Church takes over three Macedonian dioceses, 12f; appeals to Serbs to receive refugees, 14; priorities under the occupation, 14f; position worsens as internal resistance springs up, 18; under NDH, 22–6; greets liberation, 151; government representatives at solemn requiem for fallen, 153; reduced financial circumstances of, 156f & n; government subventions to, 157, 158; financial help from abroad, 156n, 158f; objections to laicising marriage and divorce, 162f; first postwar contact with other Orthodox churches, 163f; widespread harassment of priests, believers; evictions, assaults, imprisonment, 166f & n; as embodiment of Serbian people, 173; view of Yugoslavia, 178; identifies itself with Serbia, 178; difficulties arising in dioceses outside Yugoslavia, 179f; two dioceses in Czechoslovakia transferred to Moscow patriarchate, 179; difficulties with Budim diocese, 179f; difficulties with Temešvar diocese, 180; bishops withstand attacks on their authority from within and manipulation from without, 181; attack on church unity from Macedonia, 182; constitutional concession to Macedonian clergy, 187; the patriarchate, 193–8; links with other churches resumed, 193; death of Patriarch Gavrilo, 192, 194; election of Patriarch Vikentije, 194ff; installation of Patriarch Vikentije in the presence of government representatives, 196; visit of Vicar-Bishop German to dioceses in Europe and N. America, 198; constitutional rights established by new law but at first not observed, 200; positive attitude praised by government, 138; dialogue with Catholic Church opens, 244; supports government over Trieste, 249f; museum ceremonially reopened, 250; visits to sister churches, 250; demonstrations against bishops, 251; Moscow patriarchate, overtures from, 254, first visit to, 255f; objections to uncanonical election of Vicar-Bishop Dositej as Archbishop of Skopje, 264f; loses control over Macedonian church events, 267f; installation at Peć patriarchate, 270; attitude to Second Vatican Council, 273f; growth of women's religious orders, 275f, 286; schism in North America, 276–80; attacked by *Nova Makedonija* over Macedonian schism, 286; fear of schism, 286; starts proceedings against Macedonian bishops, 288; deadlock over Macedonian church, 288; bishop imprisoned for one month, 292; statistics, 298, 299, 302, 303

churches and church property, 68; patriarchate building confiscated by Germans, 12; property in Sremski Karlovci confiscated by NDH, 16; patriarchate building returned but under Gestapo supervision, 17; estimate of churches and monasteries destroyed, 25, 29; numbers destroyed, buildings and funds nationalised, 155f & n; pension fund expropriated, 199; extent of church lands expropriated, 213; church's case against application of Agrarian Reform Law, 216f; reply of Ministry of Agriculture, 217; value of buildings expropriated, 219; numbers of churches and monasteries built and repaired, 274

dioceses: American–Canadian, 179, 182, 198, 277ff; visit of Sabor delegation, 277; Middle West deans loyal to Serbian patriarchate, 277; diocese divided into three, 278 & n; defrocking of Bishop Dionisije and consequent schism, 279f. Montenegrin Littoral: divided by Italian occupation, 13; unrest among Orthodox clergy in, 180f; poverty of, 258f

priests: expelled from Macedonia, 11; seven killed in the Vojvodina, 13; training of virtually stops, 16; butchery of, 17; arrested in many districts, perish in reprisals, 17; numbers deported from NDH, 23; three imprisoned with Bishop

Serbian Orthodox Church (*cont.*)
Sava, 24; murdered with Bishop
Platon, 25; estimates of numbers
killed, deported, fled, 25n, 29; few
remaining in NDH cooperate with
Croatian Orthodox Church, 25f;
come out of hiding, 37; some join
Partisans, 49; some delegates to
2nd AVNOJ, 50; Croatian sentenced to be shot, 62; need government permit to travel, 154; some
reluctant to return to ruined
parishes, others missing or imprisoned, 154f; numbers killed in
Gornjikarlovac, Zvornik–Tuzla,
Dalmatia, 155; weakness of clergy,
161 & n; harassment of priests and
bishops, 166 & n, 169, 173; government encouragement of unrest
among in Montenegro and Macedonia, 169, 180ff; those who had
collaborated with Croatian Orthodox Church forgiven, 179; activities of in liberated territories, 188
& n; bishops forbid conferences
of, 190; social insurance, 199f;
injustices suffered by, 206; 32 in
prison, 251; four tried in Cetinje,
251f; shortage of in Montenegro, 258
Sabor, 11, 167, 170, 176f, 192,
196, 199, 201, 270; creates two
new dioceses, elects six new bishops,
170; promulgates new constitution, 170f; decrees new procedure
for election of patriarch, 171;
amends new constitution in 1967,
171f; cedes parishes to Romanian
Orthodox Church, 180; Elective S.
meets, 195f; fails to recognise
priests' associations, 202, 204; appeals to Tito for pardon for Bishop
Arsenije, 253; refuses to discuss
priests' associations, 253f; refuses
to accept Macedonian nominations
for bishop (May 1958), 258, 260;
meets after patriarch's death, 261;
elects German as patriarch, 262;
accepts autonomous Macedonian
Church, 266; summoned to meet
at Peć, 269; investigates situation
in North America, 277; divides
North American diocese into
three, 278; deprives Dionisije of
his see, 279; appeals for unity
among Serbs abroad, 279; tries
and defrocks Bishop Dionisije,
279f; refuses to present autonomous Macedonian Orthodox
Church to sister Churches, 282;
refuses to accept its demand for
autocephaly, 283 & n, 284; reaffirms refusal to recognise, 285f
seminaries and theological faculty:
all five seminaries closed, 16; seminary in Cetinje reopened, 16;
examinations held at Niš, 16; lack
of fuel causes winter closure, 158,
162; difficulties in reopening, 161;
reopening of at Prizren and Rakovica, 161f; legal rights of seminarians, 223, 224; regulations
governing, in Serbia, 224; legal
provisions for closing of, 224; at
Sremski Karlovci, Krka, Ostrog,
274f; continues to train Macedonian students after schism, 287
Synod, 167, 177, 196, 198, 279;
defined, 12n; membership in 1941,
12; occasionally meets in Novi Sad,
12; visits patriarch in Rakovica, 14;
issues messages to people, 14f;
appeals to German authorities to
stop persecution in NDH, etc., 15;
concern for training of future
priests, 16; minutes censored, 17;
visits Patriarch Gavrilo, 17; 1945
Easter message, 18; pronounces
Croatian Orthodox Church uncanonical, 27; reasserts control, 151;
orders priests and bishops to
return to dioceses, 153; keeps lists
of imprisoned priests, 155; financial assistance to clergy and impo-
verished dioceses, 157; complains
about Serbian government policy
on religious education, 150f; on
civil marriage, 162f; tries to find
Patriarch Gavrilo, 164, refused
permission to visit him, 165;
formal protest to government
about ill-treatment of clergy, 166f;
answers government complaints,
167; attacked in press, 167; meets
returning patriarch at airfield,
168; five questions to be discussed
with government, 168f; sends two
memoranda to Tito, 169; seeks
Bishop Varnava's release, 176f;
faces challenge to authority, 179;
attacked by some Montenegrin
priests and reacts vigorously, 181;
asks Macedonian clergy to com-

Serbian Orthodox Church (*cont.*)
municate directly with Metropolitan Josif, 184; declares Macedonian Peoples' Committee uncanonical, 184f; statement on position of Macedonian dioceses, 185f, further appeal to Montenegrin and Macedonian clergy and complaint to government, 186; conversations with priests' associations, points at issue between them, no agreement reached, 190f; submits suggestions to government on Law on Legal Status of Religious Communities, 200, 210f; informed by Federal Commission for Religious Affairs that it can no longer deal with local complaints, 201; puts off recognition of priests' associations by administrative delays, 201; receives delegation of Macedonian priests, 207; indicts Bishop Dionisije, 279; meets Macedonian Synod, 282

Serbs (*see also* Orthodox Serbs), 4, 49n, 64; Catholic Serbs, 2; prewar poverty in Croatian border regions explodes into national and religious conflict, 4; tension with Croats fuelled by dispute over concordat, 6; expelled from the Vojvodina and Macedonia, 10; rounded up and killed in the Vojvodina, 13n; agreement for deportation of Serbs in Croatia; arrests begin, 22; inefficiency causes chaos, 23; numbers deported and fled from NDH, 29; estimated numbers who perished in NDH, 29; ask Mussolini for protection, 32f; Stepinac defends, 36, 76, 113

Šimecki, Josip (catechist), 79n, 96n, 104, 108; arrested, 79; accusation, 97; asks Šalić to bless *križari* flag, eventually does so himself, 100

Šimenc, the Rev. J. (Catholic), 91

Simeon (Stanković), Bishop of Šabac, 184n, 202; press attacks on, 174

Šimić, Father (Catholic), 28

Simonović, the Rev. Jagoš (Orthodox), 50

Simović, General Dušan: heads government after 1941 coup, 9

Šimrak, Bishop of Križevci, 34, 39n, 103, 114n, 133, 228; arrested and dies, 62; member of Committee of Three, 107

Širaj, the Rev. J. (Catholic), 92

Široki Brijeg: Franciscan friary and school at, 29

Slapšak, the Rev. Dr (secretary to Bishop Rožman), 86

Slovene People's Party: led by prelates, 4

Slovenes, 52; in southern Serbia and Macedonia, 2; expelled from Slovenia, 10; protest against forced conversions, 32; appeal to Stepinac, 36; Stepinac protests arrest of priests, 37; oppressed in Istria and the Julian region, 41; thousands deported, 48; appeal to by AVNOJ, 49; Catholics in Slovenia part of OF, 74; indignation over status of Slovene language in Zone A, 83; Slovene Catholic groups take refuge in Zone A, 83

Slovenia, 10, 49, 74, 84–94, 289; inhabitants Catholic, 2, 3; southern part taken over by Italy, 9; during the war, 41–8; Commission for Religious Affairs set up in, 67

Slovenska Demokratska Zveza, 83

Slovenski Poročevalec: comments on trials of priests, 92

Slovenski Primorec, 83

Smiljanić, the Rev. Milan (Orthodox), 49 & n, 169, 197; joined Partisans, 49 & n; calls on patriarch, 190; declares church support for government, 203 & n; accompanies Patriarch Vikentije on official visits, 255; accompanies Patriarch German on visits to Orthodox Churches, 263

Smole, Viktor (member, Slovene Commission for Religious Affairs), 46n

Smolić, the Rev. Jože (Catholic), 92

SNOS (Slovene National Liberation Council), 46

social insurance of clergy, 124, 125, 158, 199f, 205, 249, 286

Socialist Alliance, 290

Sokols, 45; part of OF, 43

soldiers: rights as believers, 225

Spellman, Archbishop of New York, 84, 143

Spoleto, Duke of (member, Italian royal family): invited to accept crown of Croatia, 21; accepts but remains in Italy, 21; received privately by Pius XII, 21n

Sporazum (Agreement) signed in 1939, 6

Srebrnić, Bishop of Krk, 37, 71n; imprisoned for two months, 133

Stambolić, Petar (Prime Minister of Yugoslavia), 265, 283

Stefan (Boca), Bishop of Dalmatia, 275, 283

Stefan (Lastavica), Bishop of (U.S.) Middle Eastern diocese, 278; elected bishop, 279

Stepinac, Alojzije (Aloysius), Archbishop of Zagreb (cardinal), 31, 32, 39n, 42, 61n, 70, 79n, 88, 93n, 95, 97, 100, 123, 133, 173, 221, 227, 228; welcomes establishment of NDH, 19; calls on Kvaternik, 19; received by Pavelić, 19; shows lack of caution, 19; early life and career, 19f; appointed archbishop coadjutor, 19; becomes archbishop, 20; supports Maček in 1938, 20; circular of welcome to 'young Croat state', 20; growing doubts and tensions, 21; instructs Bishop Salis Seewis to accompany Pavelić to Rome, 21; realises Ustaša methods harming church, 23; receives first reports of atrocities against Orthodox Serbs, 27; attitude to forced conversions and atrocities, 30f, 32; urges Pavelić to allow conversions to Greek Catholic rite, 33; writes to Pavelić stating attitude of church to forced conversions and protesting against atrocities, 33f; appoints Committee of Three to oversee conversions, 34; public protests, 34ff; never took oath of allegiance to NDH, 34n; letters of protest to NDH, intervenes in individual cases, 36f; places 7,000 Serbian children in private families, 36; visits to Rome, 37; maintains formal relations with NDH, 38; circulars to clergy reflect mounting chaos, 38; refuses to head government, 39; attitude to swearing and to church in politics, 39n; speech to students, 40; remains in Zagreb, 55; releases cathedral clergy from obligation to remain, but all stay, 56; taken into preventive custody, 56; wartime record defended by Bishop Salis, 59; released from custody, calls on

Bakarić and Tito, urges concordat or modus vivendi, 59; charmed by Tito, 60n; convinced government wants national Catholic Church, 60; conversation with Edvard Kocbek, 60; insists only Vatican can negotiate relations with state, 60; second visit to Bakarić, 61; reports NDH archives deposited at archbishopric, 61; complains to Bakarić about trials, 62; exhorts clergy to courage and faith, 63; orders closing of all religious associations except Caritas, 63; attacks new legislation on marriage and sets out Catholic doctrine uncompromisingly, 63f; letter to Bakarić (July 1945) with numerous and vigorous complaints, 65f; second letter to Bakarić, 66f; brother killed by Germans for Partisan activity, 67n; mother supplied food to Partisans, 67n; letter to Bakarić on schools, 67; telegram to Tito on confiscations and Law on Agrarian Reform, 67; attacks on him increase, 74; attack on at Zaprešić, 75; warns clergy to keep off politics, 75; actions defended by official gazette of Zagreb archdiocese, 75ff; angry letter to Pavelić, 75f; defends Jews, Serbs, gypsies, 76; appeals for charitable gifts, 78; circular to clergy defending his actions, 79f; pressure against builds up, 80; trial, 95–120, note on sources, 95, encounter with Lisak, 99f, tells Šalić to destroy letter from Moškov, 100, visits Dr Maček, 101, arrested, 102, details of accusation, 102ff, pleads not guilty and refuses to answer questions, 105, speech on occasion of Sabor opening, 1942, 106, questioned on forced conversions, 106f, denies that pastoral letter of March 1945 was drafted by Ustaša officials, 107, received NDH archives and handed them over to new authorities, 107 & n, calls on Maček on own initiative, 107, refuses to head Regency Council, 107f, his mediocre entourage and personal dignity, 108, document alleged to be personal letter from him to the pope detailing Serbian

Stepinac (*cont.*)
atrocities, 108f, 109n, diaries hidden, discovered in 1950, 109n, denies authenticity of document, 109 & n, speech in his own defence, 110ff, prewar member of Committee for Aid to Refugees from Hitler, 112, attitude to NDH authority based on Gregory XVI's *Sollicitudo ecclesiarum*, 112 & n, defense plays down his authority, 113 & n, sermons used as Allied propaganda, 113, alleged letter to the pope analysed by Dr Politeo, 113, people pray for during trial, 116 & n, condemned to 16 years, 117, worldwide protests, 117, alleged to be leader of all priests on trial, 118, government attitude to trial analysed, 119f, his bearing reinforces church, 120, treated by authorities with comparative leniency, 120n; released from prison to live in Krašić, press interview, 137; created cardinal, 140ff; interview with *New York Times*, 144; last days and death, 146–50; receives visitors, health deteriorates, 146; refuses to ask any favours, 146f; summoned to court at Osijek, refuses angrily to appear, 147; dies Feb. 10, 1960, 147; funeral arrangements, 147f; funeral, 148; character and influence, 149f; 'the bolshevik archbishop', 150; 'posthumous amnesty', 149, 240; warned priests to keep off politics, 240

Stifanić, the Rev. Srečko (Catholic): member of ZAVNOH, 50

Stjepevac, Mgr, 133

Stojadinović, Dr Milan (prewar prime minister): crisis over concordat, 5

Stojanov, the Rev. Kiril (Orthodox, Macedonian), 183, 184

Stojković, the Rev. Dositej, *see* Dositej, Metropolitan

Strossmayer, Bishop of Djakovo (19th century), 58 & n, 68, 119n, 123, 216, 233

Šubašić, Dr Ivan (wartime premier of Yugoslav government-in-exile, postwar Foreign Minister): resigns from government, 73

Suhač, Fra F. (Franciscan), 91n

Taraseyev, the Rev. Vitalij (Russian Orthodox Church, Belgrade), 256

Tardini, Mgr (under-secretary of state, Vatican), 140; warns bishops not to make any agreement without Vatican approval, 144; determined to keep negotiations in the hands of the Vatican, 242

Tavčar, Fra F. (Franciscan), 91 & n

Tavelić, Sv. Nikola, 292

taxation, 78, 205, 232 & n; tax for support of patriarchate repealed, 157

teachers: rights as believers, 225 & n; open practice of religion still difficult, 232; woman teacher expelled from teachers' association for church-going, 233

Tiburcije, Fra (Franciscan), 96n

Tisserant, Cardinal, 28, 31n

Tito, 59, 65, 66, 74n, 137n, 139, 141, 143, 144, 146, 147, 148, 176, 250, 253, 255, 257, 261, 265, 266, 271, 281, 305; concludes agreement with Russians to enter Yugoslavia, 18; sends letter to Vatican, 51; meets delegation of higher Catholic clergy, 57ff; urges a more national Catholic Church, 58f; wishes to create a Slav community embracing both Catholic and Orthodox, 58f; promises excesses will be investigated, 59 & n; condemns visions and miraculous apparitions, 66n; letter to Stepinac on agrarian reform, 67; bishops' conference writes to, 70; angered by pastoral letter of September 1945, 73; asks Mgr Hurley to urge withdrawal of Stepinac, 104n; warns Vatican of Stepinac's arrest and asks for his removal, 119n; offers twice to release Stepinac on condition he leave Yugoslavia, 120; admits excesses, 123n; receives visit from CMD, 130; in Ruma speech deplores violence against priests and calls for attacks to cease, 136, 146, 229; angered by Stepinac's elevation to cardinal, 141; Catholic hierarchy in Britain protests visit of, 143; negotiates with bishops, 143f; invites Patriarch Gavrilo to return, 164; on the patriarch's return, 166; receives visit from patriarch, 169; article on nationality question,

Tito (cont.)
178; on religious teaching of children, 230; receives Slovene priests, 237; urges Orthodox bishops to resolve Macedonian question, 260; receives Patriarch German, 270; condemns Croatian nationalism, 290; calls on Pope Paul, 292
Tobias, Dr R. (World Council of Churches): heads mission of fellowship to churches of Yugoslavia, 159; visits Orthodox and Evangelical Churches in Yugoslavia, 250
Tomasevich, Dr Jozo (historian), 15n
Tomažič, Bishop of Maribor, 42, 71n, 86
Tome, the Rev. Aloyz (Catholic, Slovene): tried for collaboration with Četniks, 91
Topalović, Dr Živko (member, Četnik Central National Committee), 48
Toroš, the Rev. Dr M. (apostolic administrator of Slovene part of Gorizia), 129
Trajkovski, Nikola, see Kliment, Bishop
trials of priests, 233n & f; immediate postwar, 61; a number sentenced to imprisonment, 62; procedure described by Stepinac, 62; fresh arrests daily, 65; show trials, 80; many priests in Istria and Slovenia tried, 90; the Rev. Dr Blatnik tried in absentia, 90; Franciscans tried in Pula and Ljubljana, 91 & n; trials in Slovenia of Ramšak and Tome, 91 & n, 92; trials of Ljubljana Jesuits, 92; Salesian seminarians tried in Ljubljana, 92 & n; trials of Široj and Smolič, 92; trial of Jesuits Lavh, Prijatelj, Preac, Koncilja, Pate, the Lazarist Trontelj, 92n; sentencing policy, 93 & n; sentences coupled with deprivation of civil rights, 93; priests tried with Archbishop Stepinac, 96n; further trials, 118; later trials linked to struggle over Italian frontier, 122; 300 Catholic priests awaiting trial, 131; trial of the Rev. J. Kapš, 233; four Serbian priests tried at Cetinje, 251f
Trieste (see also Julian region), 81–4, 87, 143, 227, 250; mixed population, 2; Partisans reach, 53f; divided into Zones A and B, 81 82

Tripartite Pact: Yugoslavs sign in 1941, 7
Tripković, the Rev. Božidar (Orthodox), 278

UDBA (Department of State Security): attacked by Ranković, 228n
Ude, Dr Lojze (Catholic, Slovene; fought with Partisans): member of Slovene Commission for Religious Affairs, 46n; speech at Črnomelj, 46; states party attitude to religion and atheism, 47
Udicki, the Rev. Grigorije (Orthodox), see Grigorije, Bishop of Western America
Ujčić, Archbishop of Belgrade, 32, 71n, 139, 140, 143, 144, 239, 243n, 261 & n; asks Stepinac to intervene for Serbs, 36; press attack on, 134; acting president of bishops' conference, 136; visits Rome, 253f; decorated on 80th birthday, 237 & n; further visit to Rome, 242; warmly received by Yugoslav ambassador, 242
Ukmar, Mgr, 134
Uniates, see Catholics, Greek
Union of Associations of Orthodox Clergy in Yugoslavia (Udruženje Pravoslavnog Sveštenstva Jugoslavije), see under priests' associations
Ustaša (movement, forces), ustaše, 11, 17, 19, 53, 61, 67n, 73, 79, 90, 91, 99, 104, 106, 107, 119, 149, 164, 179, 230, 275; aim of independent Croatia, 3; contacts with Internal Macedonian Revolutionary Organisation, 3; brutalities drive people into resistance, 23; Catholic priests join before the war, 29; agents contact Franciscans, 32; not all ustaše forces fled after Axis defeat, 56; estimate of numbers of remaining in the country, 56n; the Rev. Djuro Marić, ustaše captain, 96n; fugitives, ustaše underground, 100; alleged links of Catholic Action with, 103; crimes denounced by Slovene priests' association, 128; pillage church treasury in Sremski Karlovci, 153
Ustaša leaders (see also Alajbegović, Budak, Canki, Glavaš, Guberina, Lisak, Makanec, Mandić, Moškov, Pavelić): Stepinac gives benefit of

Ustaša leaders (cont.)
doubt to, 20; local U. chief murders Bishop Platon, 25; angered by Stepinac, 136; arrange denunciation of Partisan atrocities by religious bodies, 31; many educated in seminaries of Bosnia–Hercegovina

Valenčak, Fra Anton (Franciscan), 91 & n

Valerian (Stefanović), vicar-bishop, Bishop of Šumadija, 153, 184n; visits Russian Orthodox Church, 255

Valjanov, Dr Vasil (member, Bulgarian patriarchate), 287

Varnava (Nastić), Vicar-Bishop, 166, 174ff, 243n, 269; administrator of Dabar–Bosnia, 170; early life and character, 174; arrested and tried, 175f; sentenced to prison, hurt in railway accident, pardoned, 176f; last days, death, obituary, 177 & n; attacked by priests' associations, 192

Varnava (Rosić), Patriarch: death in 1937, 5; struggle over succession, 6

Vasilje (Kostić), Bishop of Banja Luka, 270; press attack on, 174; attacked by priests' associations, 192; attacked by mobs and forced to leave Banja Luka, 251; house-arrest during election of Patriarch German, 262, 270

Vatican (see also Protocol, Second Vatican Council), 28, 32, 80, 90, 92, 110, 121, 123, 128, 132, 135, 136, 140, 144, 172, 173, 226, 227, 232, 234, 257, 273, 290, 292; Italianising tendencies, 4; recognises new state, 4; concordats in force in 1919, 5n; negotiations for new single concordat, signed in 1935, never ratified because of Serbian Orthodox opposition, 5f; precautions over reception of Pavelić and the Duke of Spoleto, 21n; begged by Slovenes to forbid further conversions, 32; well informed about events in NDH, 37; attitude to NDH, 38n; wary of Slav tendency to reject Latin in liturgy, 47; asked to send representative to liberated territory, 51; never recognises NDH de jure, 59; Stepinac asserts it is responsible for church's relations with government, 60, 80, 112; in alliance with Italy, 81; Yugoslavia accuses of helping Italian expansionism, 84; first reaction to Stepinac trial, 102; mentioned in accusation of Stepinac at trial, 104; urged to withdraw Stepinac, 105n; excommunicates all those participating in Stepinac trial, 118; Stepinac trial determined nature of its relations with Yugoslavia, 119f; refuses to allow bishops to negotiate agreement, 124; urges bishops to oppose priests' associations, 138f; answers Yugoslav government note severing diplomatic relations, 142; Radio Vatican warns Croatian clergy not to join priests' associations, 145; attacked by Boris Krajger, 145; V. and government both watch for openings to negotiate, 228; position of towards negotiations with government, 236; makes conciliatory gestures, 238; beginning of improvement in relations after Stepinac's death, 240; decision to retain control of negotiations with government justified, 242; negotiations with Yugoslav government begin, 245f; relations with Yugoslav government improve, 292

Velimirović, Bishop, see Nikolaj, Bishop of Žiča

Venjamin (Taušanović), Bishop of Braničevo, 184n, 189; attacked by priests' associations, 192; visits Moscow, 193

Verski List, 86, 309

Veselinov, Jovan (president of Serbian government), 265

Vesnik (journal of the Union of Orthodox Clergy of Yugoslavia), 173, 202, 204, 206, 309; founded, 191; attacks bishops, 192; on election of new patriarch, 195; Christians should support government, 203; exasperated comment on failure to recognise priests' associations, 204; article on legal injustices suffered by priests, 206; tribute to Bishop Irinej, 206; welcomes autonomous Macedonian Orthodox Church, 268; attacks Bishop Dionisije, 280

Vidaković, the Rev. Vitomir (Orthodox), 203n

Vidali (leader, Italian Communist Party in Trieste), 84

Vikentije (Prodanov), Patriarch, Bishop of Zletovo–Strumica, later of Žiča, Srem, 186, 201, 207, 254, 262; expelled by Bulgarians, goes to Belgrade, 11; administrator of diocese of Žiča, 13; welcomes WCC delegation, 159; Tanjug interview, 174; elected patriarch and installed, 194ff; press interview, 196; life and character, 196ff; calls on Tito, 200; calls on Moše Pijade, 202; abstains in vote on priests' associations, 202; irritated by Catholic bishops' statement, 202f; interview with *Politika*, states hierarchy not in principle against priests' associations, lists points of cooperation, 203; on claims of Macedonian clergy, 207; responsibility for improved relations, 249; supports government over Trieste, 250; attends Tito's birthday celebrations, 250; decorated by Tito, 250; refuses invitation to visit Moscow patriarchate, 254; visit to Greece, 255; visits Macedonian clergy, 255; visit to Russian Orthodox Church, 255f; unplanned visit to the Romanian patriarch, 257; joint communiqué with Patriarch Alexei, 257; New Year message, 257f; visits Montenegro, 258f; appendicitis, 259; canonical visitation to Macedonia, 259f; taken ill and dies, 261

Vilfan, Dr Joža, 43n

Vimpulšek, Dr Žarko (president of court at trial of Stepinac et al.), 96, 99, 105; questions Stepinac, 105, 106, 107

Vinko, Fra M. (Franciscan), 91n

Visarion (Kostić), Bishop of Banat, 202, 254, 255, 261f, 278, 279, 281

visions and miraculous apparitions, 66n

Visser t' Hooft, Dr (general secretary, WCC): visits Orthodox and Evangelical Churches, 250

Vjesnik: attacks Catholic Church, 237

Vjesnik u Srijedu, 233f

Vladimir (Rajić), Bishop of Mukašev-Prijašev, later of Raška–Prizren, 184n, 202, 203; expelled from diocese and goes to Belgrade, 11

Vladislav (Mitrović), Bishop of Zahumlje–Hercegovina, 269

Vojvodina, the, 2, 4, 10; Orthodox Serbs and Montenegrins settled in, 2; Croat and Slovene Catholics in, 2; Protestant groups in, 2; killings of Serbs in, 13

Vovk, Auxiliary Bishop, later Bishop and Archbishop of Ljubljana; 71n, 85 & n, 86, 88 & n, 134, 139, 143, 238n; leads delegation to call on Kidrić, 85; second visit to authorities, 85ff; consecrated auxiliary bishop in 1946, bishop 1959, becomes archbishop 1961, 88 & n; character and actions, 88ff; accused of misusing confessional, 89; brutal attack on at Novo Mesto, 89f; fined for circular on religious instruction and two others, 90

Vučetić, the Rev. Stipe (NDH military vicar), 103, 116

Vujas, the Rev. L. (Orthodox), 251f

Vukmanović-Tempo, S. (Partisan leader), 53n, 143n; leads resistance in Macedonia, 182

Waugh, Evelyn, 28 & n, 29

Willebrands, Mgr (cardinal), 273, 274, 292

World Council of Churches (WCC) (*see also* Inter-Church Aid), 159, 198, 260, 262; visits Serbian Orthodox Church, 250

Yugoslav government, 143, 226, 292; prewar relations with Italy, Germany, Bulgaria, 7; signs Tripartite Pact, 7; Yugoslavia's foreign policy focussed on problem of Trieste, 81; attitude to Stepinac trial, 119; Stepinac trial determined nature of relations with Vatican, 120; complains to Vatican of unwarrantable interference, 140f; angry reaction to Stepinac's elevation to cardinal, 140; severs diplomatic relations with Vatican, 141; declares it is ready to negotiate directly with Vatican, 145; represented at solemn requiem in Belgrade, 153; contacts with Patriarch Gavrilo, 165f; advantages to in Patriarch Gavrilo's return, 165f; complains about Bishop Dionisije, 167; not prepared to accept Metro-

Yugoslav government (cont.)
politan Josif as patriarch, 195;
Pope John XXIII, initial attitude
towards, 228; bans Dum maerentes,
234; preliminaries to negotiations
with Vatican and attitude towards,
236; praises Serbian Orthodox
Church and the Moslems, 238;
attitude to appointment of apostolic administrators, 238; accepts
need to negotiate with Vatican,
242; negotiations with Vatican
begin, 245f; attitude to autonomous Macedonian Orthodox
Church, 265; attitude to unity of
Yugoslavia, 270; reasons for strengthening Macedonian loyalty to,
281; tightrope-walking between
power blocs, 290; relations with
Vatican improve, 292; welcomes
Marian Congress, 292; approves
friendship between Catholic and
Serbian Orthodox Churches, 292
Yugoslavia, 4, 136, 180, 226; generalisations about, 1; founded in 1919,
tension between Serbian and Croatian conceptions, 3; Hitler orders
attack on, 9; invasion by Axis
forces, 9 partitioned among Axis
powers, 9; Partisans direct appeal
to all Yugoslav peoples, 48; large
portions of liberated by 1944, 53;

young priests who believe in the
idea of Yugoslavia, 58; expulsion
from Cominform, 81, 83, 180;
Inter-Church Aid to, 159; as a
federation of equal nations, 173;
two opposing conceptions of, 178;
unity of and internal harmony in,
270; an unpredictable country, 292

ZAVNOH, 50; meeting in April 1945,
51; declares intended annexation
of prewar Italian territory, 53;
decree annulling forced conversions, 78, 154
Zečević, the Rev. Vlada ('Pop') (Ortho-
dix; Partisan; member, postwar
government), 49 & n; delegate to
1st AVNOJ, 50; baptises children,
50; appointed Commissioner for
Internal Affairs, 50; represents
government at installation of patriarch, 196
Zefirov-Popovski, the Rev. Vladimir
(Orthodox, Macedonian), 260
Ziherl, Boris (leading Slovene Partisan), opposes clericalism, 237
Živković, Professor Dr (Catholic, Slovene), 57n
Zoli, Corrado (member, Italian Geographical Society), 28
Žunić, Archdeacon Djordje (chef de
cabinet to Patriarch German), 256